Selected reviews from the Inland Waters Press website:

"Tranquility is beautiful! A brilliant story of life on the road less travelled. Poetic, funny, smart, and original – one of the best reads of 2015."

—Amy B.

"An amazing story about boats, love, misadventure, and growing up. I couldn't put it down. Just reading it made me a little more salty."

—Liam B.

"This book truly is a gift, and a pleasure to read. It's an educational adventurous love story. Looking forward to more from Billy Sparrow!"

—Lesa H.

"This memoir is a marvel. Billy Sparrow takes us on his incredible first voyage aboard his wooden boat a 29-foot sloop built in 1938. You will fall in love with the young Billy, and want to be his kindred spirit, and cry tears of joy when the boy in him, meets the man he is becoming. This story is rich with the sea, friendships, love, and grit that will make you glad to be alive! This book contains an accomplished writing style, and it will not be a surprise if it becomes a Northwest classic. It will sit on my bookshelf alongside *The Curve of Time*, Everett Ruess: *A Vagabond for Beauty*, *Living High*, and *West with the Night*."

—A.M.

"I picked up this book while in the middle of another. Suffice it to say, the other was put on hold as I joined the adventure with Mr. Sparrow. In this age of reality show adventure-lite, where YouTube videos supplant the need to actually experience life first hand, I thoroughly enjoyed this ride! I've always loved the classic explorer, survival and adventure stories. But, I've found few that come from our time and this place. Mr. Sparrow paints a wonderful and vivid picture of the Northwest and his perseverance, suffering, humility and success is an emotion-filled roller coaster ride that will leave the reader satisfied and a bit exhausted! Tranquility is poised to become a classic."

—Jeff B.

"What are we willing to risk in pursuit of our dreams? What do we truly need to find happiness? Vivid descriptions of experiences and raw emotions, along with much self-deprecating humor, are packed into this adventure story....a wonderfully written story that compels you to re-visit memories of your own adventures in life, how they have shaped who you've become and where you are headed. I couldn't put this book down, and lost much sleep staying up too late reading it."

—Tanya W.

"In his classic; *Once and Future King* T.H White tells us, "Experience is education and education is the key to self-reliance". If anyone proves the case it's our hero, Billy Sparrow. You'd better add arrogance, stubbornness, tenacity, incredible drive, and a lust for adventure. This is the story of a young guy with limited sea experience who decides to sail a small 29-foot wooden boat from Washington State to California. How hard can that be? Sparrow should have ended up run down, set adrift, drowned and sunk a hundred times as he learns sea craft in some of the hairiest waters of the west coast. Along the way he learns to repair, improve and sail his tiny craft. The charm of this tale is that a cocky, young buck like Billy is so willing to show us all his mistakes, bad decisions and numerous "educational experiences". The inspiration here is that by inventing, driving, thinking on his feet and sticking to his vision he pulls off his daring dream and flies in the face of less brave souls. In a world where so many young guys sit in front of computer games and the attitude seems to be, "Don't just do something, sit there.", Billy is a blast of cold sea air...a young guy who with courage, stamina and his eyes on the prize finds self-reliance, great skill, a little love, and the title captain."

—Tim S.

"Bridging a Twain-like self-deprecating first person tale and a cautionary, young person naive self-reliance, Billy Sparrow walks the walk. Or better, sails the boat. Fast paced, honest, almost too honest for comfort for any sailors, the story is a quick read. Actually a really good read for young people choosing a direction for their lives. Do they live in the fantasy adventure world of gaming or take real life by the throat. Spending some time with Billy channeling his real world Jack Sparrow may help at least a few of them choose reality over fantasy. Billy's misadventures, humor, and gritty persistence interspersed with his own freely shared developing philosophy makes a fan of the reader rooting for Tranquility and Billy both."

—Mark R.

"I've read dozens of books about heroes and crooks...Tis a bit unfair, I suppose, to borrow from one writer while reviewing another, but this book pulled me out of a reading slump much like Mr. Buffet's *A Pirate Looks at Fifty* did many years ago. Tranquility is a blend of mishap and adventure with deeply personal insights into the mind of a young sailor earning the title of "Captain". Any trip to sea is fraught with potential peril. Mr. Sparrow fills in a few of the blanks following the question "What could possibly go wrong?" And yet, the part that really grabbed me, was the author's unabashed foray into the inner chambers of his own psyche as his dream faded into an education-by-sufferance sort of affair."

—Koots

Read more reviews or submit your own: www.inlandwaterspress.com

From Marian
To
Papa

TRANQUILITY

A MEMOIR OF AN AMERICAN SAILOR

BILLY SPARROW

Inland Waters Press

PUBLISHED BY INLAND WATERS PRESS
2016
FIRST EDITION

ISBN9780692416044
LCCN 2015937412

Sparrow, William Stewart
Tranquility.

Maps and cover art were created by Hailey Elliot and Megan Stocklin.
Vessel layout, Laura Stocklin.
Flawless handling of important tasks too numerous to list, Stephanie Nouvel.
Tranquility was set in LTC Caslon.
Chapter and page numbers were set in **Windsor Regular**.

Printed in the United States of America

To purchase additional copies of this book, please contact IWP at one of the
addresses below.
Inland Waters Press P.O. Box 514
Olga, WA. 98279
WWW.INLANDWATERSPRESS.COM

In admiration of his character
and gratitude for his friendship
this book is inscribed
to
John Walters

While the events and individuals in this book are real, it was written more than fifteen years after the fact. Artistic license was taken with certain conversations too brief to remember in any detail. Unless otherwise noted, these instances are inconsequential. Names, locations on dry land and descriptions of certain vessels have been changed in order to ensure the privacy of those who may wish to remain anonymous. Any other omissions are inadvertent. Finally, it is an unfortunate and distracting convention of the English language that the individual is referred to as *he* –this book follows that rule for convenience, no disrespect is intended.

The Boat

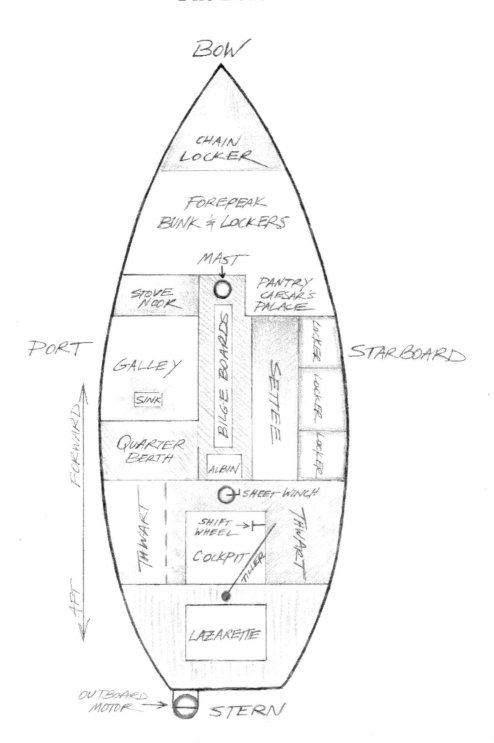

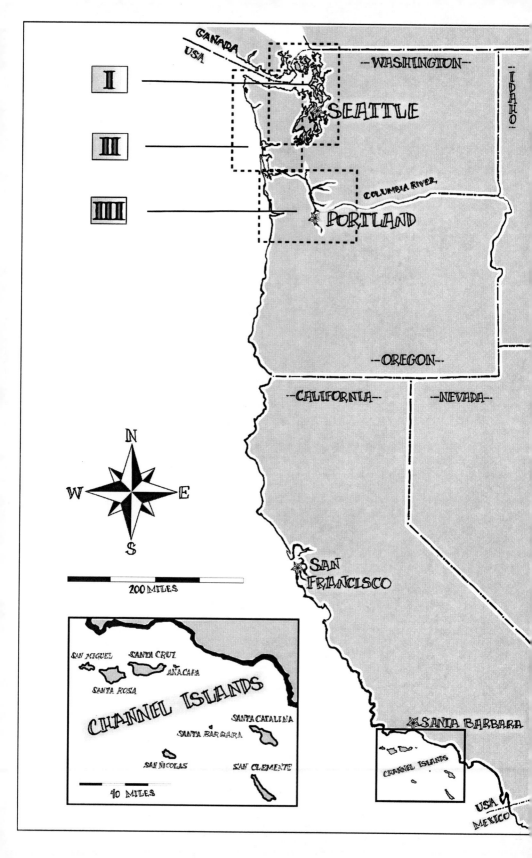

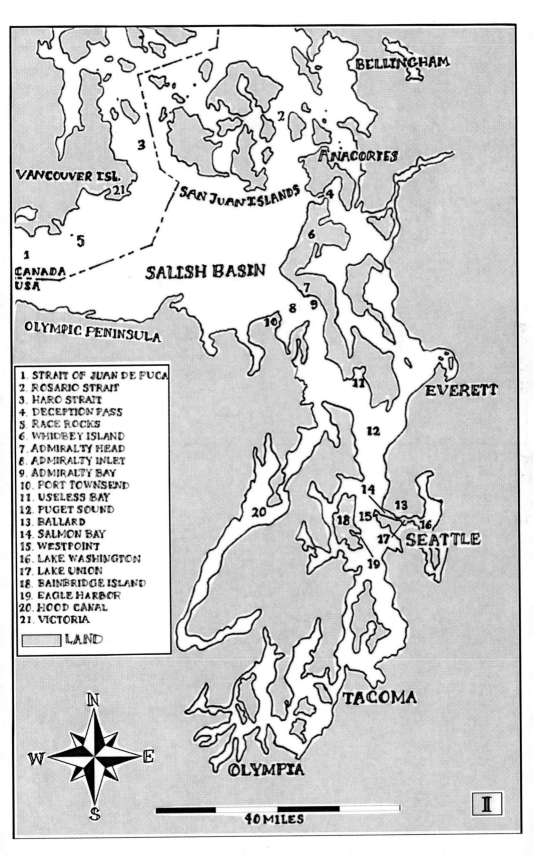

1. STRAIT OF JUAN DE FUCA
2. ROSARIO STRAIT
3. HARO STRAIT
4. DECEPTION PASS
5. RACE ROCKS
6. WHIDBEY ISLAND
7. ADMIRALTY HEAD
8. ADMIRALTY INLET
9. ADMIRALTY BAY
10. PORT TOWNSEND
11. USELESS BAY
12. PUGET SOUND
13. BALLARD
14. SALMON BAY
15. WESTPOINT
16. LAKE WASHINGTON
17. LAKE UNION
18. BAINBRIDGE ISLAND
19. EAGLE HARBOR
20. HOOD CANAL
21. VICTORIA

LAND

BELLINGHAM

ANACORTES

VANCOUVER ISL.

SAN JUAN ISLANDS

CANADA
USA

SALISH BASIN

OLYMPIC PENINSULA

EVERETT

SEATTLE

TACOMA

OLYMPIA

N
W E
S

40 MILES

I

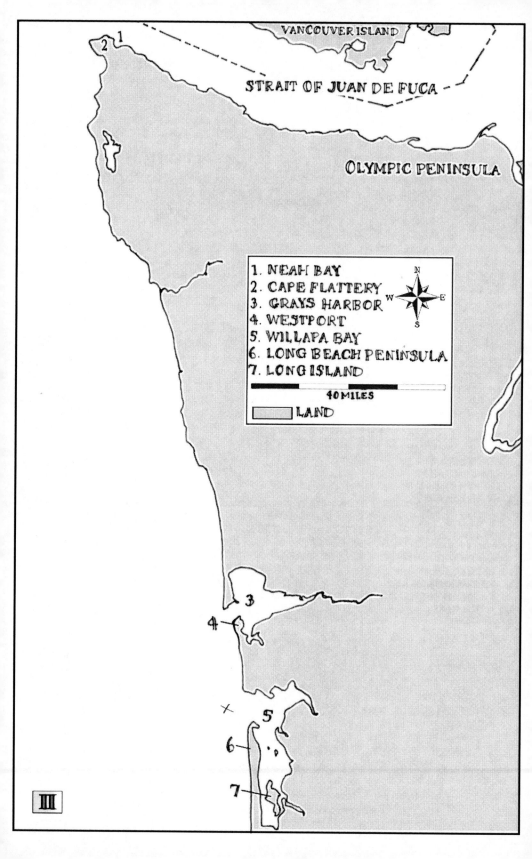

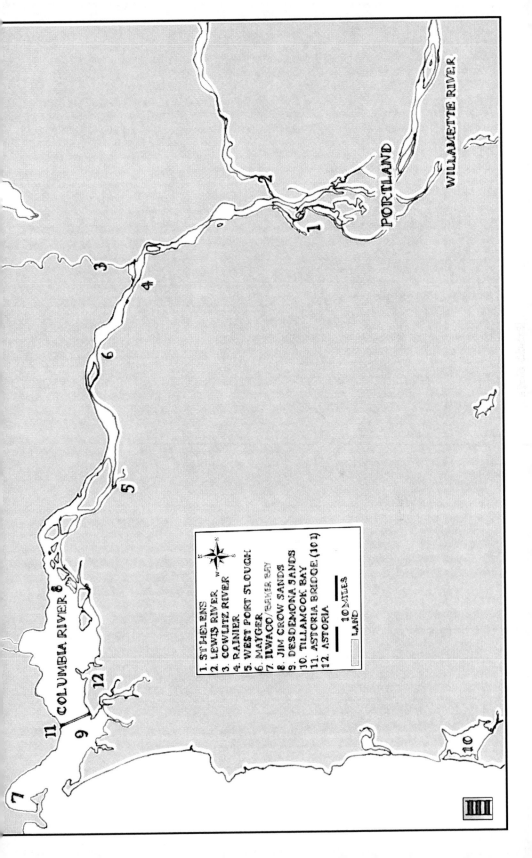

1

The warm weather inland that morning drew an ocean breeze onto the mainland while I slept. It sighed in and out along the misty California shore from north to south, bending around rocky points, filling into the broad bays and sheltered coves of the broken coastline, clearing them of fog. Translucent green waves cut by darting fish were following the wind. They silently rolled to shore and pitched and broke in the shallow undertow pulling south along the beach. Big clams and armored crabs were hiding in the wet sand, killdeer and plover flitted and snapped at lazy flies on the wing. A black boar trotted in the sea wrack, stooped to root, then continued on its way, smelling something in the air with an upturned snout. This isn't the horde coast, fenced-in and baking under the fiberglass skies to the south –there's no gray layer of smog visible from sixty miles out to sea. This is the coast where the cool northwest wind blows in from the ocean and northern fur seals come ashore to pup and lay in the sun. This is the coast where whales scrape themselves in coarse gravel at the bottoms of azure bays. This is the one where trigger fish and giant white sea bass hover in emerald kelp gardens just offshore, and tiny glimmering abalone shells wash up on the sand. There are no palm trees brought in on flatbeds and no hollow stucco Doric columns. There are no rusty dumpsters, no cinder pits, no lights shine on shore at night.

The first heat of the day was rising in the dry scrub oak valleys and lifting off the San Joaquin hardpan to the east, pulling the cool marine layer in. The sea wind leaned on tufts of shore grass, kicked up swirls of sand and curls of dry kelp and sent them scudding as it made its way down the beach. It blew into the bay where I was moored and spirited my little yacht away on her anchor chain. She paused at the end of her tether and tacked slowly, hunting into the wind. When she came around, her gentle yawing motion of the night before turned into a woozy lurch as she met the sea breeze and groundswell head on. The change in her movement woke me immediately, and when I opened my eyes, I lay still for a moment until I remembered what day it was. It was the last day, of the last leg, of a long and troublesome voyage I set sail on years before when I was an inexperienced young man. I began the cruise—a coastal passage of around a thousand nautical miles—on a foolhardy, ill-advised whim and it didn't help that I bought a tired and cranky old wooden sloop for the trip. I didn't know that at the time of course, but it's not like I gave it much thought. Before shoving off on my first sea voyage, I blithely assumed most of the difficulties I'd meet along the way would be minor: a torn sail, a lost anchor...boredom perhaps. And that any serious trouble, such as a storm, a shipwreck, or bodily injury of some kind would be enriching but quite unlikely. This proved to be a miscalculation which few words will ever do justice to. Although time has lent a certain swashbuckling appeal and a good deal of humor to my memory of the trip, and I now regard the whole thing as a colossal, but fortunate misadventure, it was a punishing ordeal to live through –so much so, that when I put pen to paper a decade later, the voyage was right where I left it.

When I shoved off on what I believed, and was told would be, a fair winds and following seas summer cruise from Seattle, Washington to Santa Barbara, California I supposed it would take me a few weeks to reach my destination. This might have been true, however, instead of finding smooth sailing, the voyage was chock-full of mundane and extravagant dangers from the get-go. As the setbacks and accidents and falling in love filled the pages of my log, my little summer cruise turned into an unbelievable, never-ending saga. To begin with, I made no headway for over a year. There was no wind to speak of, nothing worked the way it should or could have, and no matter what I knew or learned the hard way, it was never enough.

Do you wonder what the boat made of all this? Well, the boat went right along with every miscarriage of seamanship and questionable command of her captain—as if she knew no better—until I was forced by circumstance to abandon her for several months, leaving her to whatever fate had in store. I didn't know what I was doing, and when I finally thought I did, I wrecked my ship in a charming little rain-lashed corner of the North Pacific Ocean known as *The Graveyard of the Pacific.* I endured a hundred other misfortunes on the voyage and it's no exaggeration to say that I nearly got myself killed a few times along the way. I wasn't up to the task I set before myself and neither was the boat –it was as simple as that. But there was just something about the voyage that kept me coming back for more. I suppose that's what should happen when a young man meets an obstacle standing in the way of his dreams – he fights until he overcomes it, or until something terrible or wonderful happens to him. Unfortunately for me, the obstacle in my way was the sea. And the sea is terrible, and the sea is wonderful, and the sea never changes. So it did what it has always done to fools and dreamers –it made a man out of me.

The west wind was calling that morning, so I rolled from my bunk and made my way aft through the bouncing cabin. I slid the companionway hatch open, climbed the steps and looked out to sea. There in the haze, across a wide, wind-whipped channel, a rocky island lay low on the slope of the horizon. And that, dear reader, was a moment I waited a very long time for. It was a moment I endured an unbelievable amount of misery, toil and danger for. It was a moment I thought would never come. That speck of land was the beginning of a mostly uninhabited chain of beautiful islands and it was the first landfall of the summer voyage I dreamed up and set sail on five years before. At long last, I was there. All I had to do was sail across a twenty-mile-wide channel and drop anchor at the island. It was a formality by then, but it simply had to be done.

I ducked into the cabin and donned my foul-weather coat and pants. I pulled on my sea boots and watch cap, then dashed on deck and hoisted sail. I jumped to the anchor winch and got the hook up in a hurry. I ran back to the wheel and spun it hard-over. I trimmed the main and winched the headsail in flat as a panel, hurrying the boat around to the wind. She leaned to port under the force of it, keel and rudder bit, and she sailed off. Each one of those steps was just as I'd done them a thousand times and a thousand miles before, but I knew that day was going to be different. The boat sailed through the bay gingerly, heeling and picking up speed as the wind veered and unbent itself from the land. When she was well-underway, I headed her for open water on a starboard tack and steered for the distant island.

Out in the channel, away from the protection of the mainland, the westerly was building and the seas were rolling in long and low out of the fogbound Pacific Ocean to the northwest. The boat found her stride and began loping along nicely. She was an older vessel, built in 1967, but she was a good and seaworthy sailor and I'd taken my time setting everything straight with her. I'd gone over her hull and hatches, her sails and rigging, her rudder, ground tackle and engine. She was completely rebuilt, from stem to stern, from keel to masthead, and she was laden with new gear and fresh provisions –all of it meticulously stowed and perfectly balanced during months of sea trials and winter sailing from Puget Sound to San Francisco Bay.

The wind freshened offshore, and with the main, mizzen and genoa up, and flying along full-and-by, the lee rail dipped beneath the speeding waves and shipped a load of foaming seawater that sloshed back and forth along the lee deck as it drained overboard. Boats have individual personalities once you get to know them—no two are the same—and I'd learned by then that that was the temperament of my old Bermuda yawl *Isabel.* She was "tender" as they say, meaning she liked to heel over in fairly light winds. I knew she was just doing her thing –I knew it was okay. They say on the sea that constant vigilance is the price of safety. The ocean will not suffer a fool for very long, so when the wind began to gust, it crossed my mind to shorten sail and ease the strain on the rig, and I thought of ducking below to check for water in the bilge, but I sailed on instead, knowing that for once, I didn't need to do those things. Not on that boat, not in those waters and not on that auspicious day. Neptune must have agreed, because a moment later, I glanced overboard and saw a blue whale and her calf swimming behind the boat just beneath the surface. The larger and closer of the pair gave me a heavy-lidded wink as she drew amidships. They swam with me to windward for several minutes, diving and breaching so close to *Isabel,* I could have winged a sea biscuit clear over them. It was one of only a few good omens I'd seen since shoving off on that ill-fated voyage and I took it to mean something good was about to happen.

Out in mid-channel, a cross-sea was running before the wind, which was piping up into a yachtsman's gale (a landlubber's storm). I'd been in far worse conditions and reminded myself of that, but the sea is nothing to trifle with even on a calm day, so when I saw a coil of wet line hanging in the windward shrouds begin to lift in the breeze blowing across the slanting deck, I knew it was time to act. I eased the mainsail first, letting it spill some wind and I let the bow fall off a few degrees to port. This was a good thing to do. It put the boat back on an even keel, making her easier to steer and more comfortable in a seaway. It got her on a fairer course for the island and put her captain at ease. All was well.

Despite the unsettled sea, it turned into a lovely day when the marine layer burned off. The mainland hills and far-off islands took shape in the distance, their color changing from dull gray to deep, spring green as the fog lifted away from them. The breeze was building, and out on the open ocean, sky-scraping clouds were stacking up on the wild horizon and spooling off downwind, like they do in the South Seas. The gulls were swooping and calling in the kelpy air, the sun was shining overhead and the sky was turning stratospheric shades of blue. It was a good day to be on the ocean. It was a good day to be a sailor, and a good day to be alive.

The boat was sailing along marvelously, just past mid-channel, with the boom far out over the rushing water, when, without the slightest warning, *Isabel* plunged up and over a series of steep, haphazard seas before dropping into a deep trough. When she landed, she buried her bow beneath a small breaker which came rushing at her from out of nowhere. The wave hit her hard enough to drive her several points off course, and it boarded, pouring over the foredeck as she climbed to the crest of the next sea. It didn't clear fast enough, and her rearing motion sent a half barrel-full of whitewater charging aft along the deck. It surged up and over the cabin top, plugged the dorade vents and flowed like a stream into the cockpit. Before I knew it, I was standing in seawater –not a first for me on a boat, but a first on that boat. I dismissed the harrowing memory it called to mind, glanced up at the weathervane and down at the compass to check myself –all was well. *Isabel* hobby-horsed for a few seconds after the wave passed, the cockpit drained itself quickly and the sails snapped back into shape with a loud clap. She got on her feet again and we carried on. *Isabel* climbed to the top of the next hissing sea, picking up speed along the way, and punched through its crest with her knife-like bow. She was out of the water from sprit to keel for an instant, hanging over the next trough, almost bridging two short seas. I expected her to slam into the oncoming wave, but she dove down ahead of it instead. There wasn't a whitecap charging down the face of the wave to meet her, so when she came down, her bow drove a wedge of seawater out of her way a boat length wide, to port and starboard. The wind caught some of this and flung it up and over the cockpit where I stood braced at the helm. The spray pelted me from head to toe like a pail full of gravel. Seawater ran down my collar as it passed over me, the rest ricocheted like drum-roll shot off the mainsail. My yawl was a fairly dry boat –she just had a bone in her teeth that day was all. We charged up and over the next sea and the next and the next, the island drew near.

They say on the sea: *if you don't know you're okay...then you're not.* And they say: *if it can happen on a boat...it will.* But I knew by then that a well-found vessel wouldn't slam dangerously or take on water in those conditions. And although we were taking a fair beating, I knew we were going to be okay. Seaworthiness isn't something you can buy in a store, you don't slather it on with a chip brush over the weekend or stumble upon it in the classifieds at the back of a glossy sailing magazine. You must build it into a vessel and I'd built that one out myself, from a nearly bare hull, especially for those waters. I knew nothing bad was going to happen to us that day and nothing did –for once.

It blew half-a-gale the last few miles of the crossing and I certainly had too much sail up when I closed with the island, but the wind veered aft as expected, and with it almost behind me, I kept my trim little ship on a fair-enough course to enter the natural harbor on the island's eastern shore without tacking. A little while later, I dropped anchor and furled my sails in the head of a wide bay in the sweet smelling, arid little islands that I'd been bound to for so long. And that was that. One short daysail on the waters where I spent my childhood brought to a close what was, up to that point, the greatest adventure of my life.

However, it must be said, I set sail on that fateful voyage long before I knew the true meaning of the word *adventure* and long before I knew what a boat really was. It was before the wave knocked my ship down, before the fire and the shipwreck. It was before I bailed for my life in a sloop sinking in the surf on a dark and lonely coastline. It was before I heard the first unpleasant stir of mutiny in my crew, before I discovered the leak and before the knife went through my hand. It was before I furled stiff canvas in a frozen cloud burst, before the sheet ice cracked under my bows and snowflakes fell all around on the silent sea, melting into it like ghosts passing through walls. It was before the heartbreak, the desolation and the torment. It was before I ever fell in love with a siren in a seaside town. It was before the capricious sea cast its merman's spell on me and it was long before anyone would dream of calling me captain and mean it.

Now that time and distance have put the wicked difficulties and profound joys I experienced on my first sea voyage into the all-forgiving perspective of middle-age, I admire the youthful daring and single-minded persistence that got me through it in one piece –rather than being ashamed of it as I once was. When I think of everything that went wrong on that voyage, I honestly wonder how I ever survived it, and when I think of everything that went right, I wouldn't want it to have been any other way.

When you're young, you're carefree but foolish and you're plucky but unwise. When you're young, you don't have many reasons to *not* do something, so you don't think things through, even though you're sure you have. I now know this is what it means to be young and on your own in the world for the first time, but on those long-ago days, when everything was impossible, it seemed like I was the first person to ever think of going somewhere in a sailboat and I was convinced I'd own that witch of a yacht, and she me, for the rest of my life. She would never bend to my will and I would never stop trying to tame her. But any old salt will tell you, at the root of every one of my troubles, I'd only made the same mistake that all young men who dream of going to sea make when they've never set foot on a boat of their own. I set sail when the pleasures and perils of a sailor's life were still a fable to me. However: man buys boat; man sails off into sunset; man finds happiness, doesn't make for much of a sea story.

Instead of dying down as the sun dipped below the horizon that evening, the wind increased to gale force. The stronger gusts came spilling off the back of the island in big, sand-laden downdrafts which flattened-out the water around the boat and laid her over on her ear. That sort of wind is unusual in those waters, so I dropped a second anchor in case it was getting set to blow. Which it was, and did. When, you ask? In the middle of the night of course –we are on a boat after all. I didn't drag anchor, but I slept poorly thinking I would. It was so windy the next morning and the boat was slewing around so wildly, I couldn't launch the skiff to go ashore or weigh anchor to leave the place. So I spent that day, and the next two, weather-bound under the marginal protection of a steep sandy slope that rose high above the narrow white sand beach at the head of the bay. I knew there were far worse places than San Miguel Island to be stuck on a yacht and I was quite comfortable despite the conditions. A sailor travels with his home and I'd outfitted *Isabel* with scaled-down versions of everything that makes life on land pleasant: a well-stocked galley; a stove and kettle; a comfy bunk and sturdy table; the lamps, the photos of friends, the shelf full of books, even the little fireplace. Ducking out of the cold wind and fearsome sea into a warm, well-appointed cabin never gets old.

I cannot say I felt any *great* sense of relief upon my arrival in the Channel Islands. The gratification had been delayed for too long and I was an utterly different man on a completely different boat than the one who first set sail. At sea, as on land, there is *getting* there and *being* there. There is voyage and landfall –the two are very different. My arrival in Southern California that spring brought a difficult chapter of my life to a close and turned the first page on a new and carefree one. You can tinker with time though, so I pretended for a moment that five long years had only been three weeks and I fell for it. I was young and wild and free and I was soon spending that long-dreamed-of summer just as I'd always imagined.

When the gale blew itself out, I left the cold and inclement northwestern end of the chain behind me and sailed down to the sunnier and better protected islands in the southeast. In the deep blue bays and open roadsteads there, I moored my little yacht on luminous nearshore waters where she hovered obediently over her anchor for weeks at a time, casting the shadow of her elegant hull through turning sunbeams and silvery swirls of fish onto the rippled sand-flats beneath her keel. I could have been in a cabin in the woods, rather than on a boat some nights when the sea was so calm my ship barely stirred. I rolled from my bunk in the morning when the sun turned the seafoam green and the sky blue, or winked at me through a porthole glinting on the wooden cabin sides above my head. I spent my days like a castaway, earning my living spearing fish and foraging for scallops and lobster in the turquoise shallows and deep indigo bays that girded the isles of my childhood dreams.

With no firm plans and nowhere I needed to be for the foreseeable future, I hoisted sail when the wind blew in the direction I wanted to go and left my anchor on the bottom when it didn't. When the wind cooperated, which is often in those waters, I sailed in grand style with a full suit of canvas spread before it, steering my yawl over languid swells that carried her on her way beneath soaring cliffs, along broad desert beaches and into tiny jeweled coves, lit through-and-through by dreamy opaline sea light. That sort of living cultivates the latent human primitivism in a person, and whatever was left of that inside me was soon making subtle changes to my outlook that were impossible to undo later. Small urges normally overruled by mainland thinking took hold of me in the islands and I began living my life, not by the name of the month or by the hands on a clock, but by what I read in the prevailing weather, the phase of the moon and the altitude of the sun in the sky. My blood went saline and my nature turned heliotropic. I slept when I was tired and ate when I was hungry. I swam in the sea if it was pleasant and roamed the parched and brittle hinterlands when it was unsettled. I combed the stony beaches for useful things the high tide left behind and fetched my freshwater from steep canyon streams. I wandered through bright yellow coreopsis and sky blue ceanothus, I strung my hammock in stands of ironwood and giant live oak. I happened upon lush, aqueous fern canyons scented by warm sage and touched by mist where little cold frogs hid beneath stones and sweet-water pools shaded under big leaf maple. I lost myself in tiny glass vials of corymbs and berry bracts that weren't in any of the books. I warmed myself at night next to breezy driftwood beach fires and sat alone on shore for hours, gazing out to sea, transfixed by the changing light of the Pacific Ocean sunset as it shifted through a hundred hues of vermilion, pale rose and indigo. This is a very good way to live when you're young. It is true and right and lovely. You're pushing directly on life's mysterious spring and finding out that desire is ability.

I had nearly everything I needed to survive on the boat and I took little note of it when the coin of the realm reverted to uniform slips of colored paper sitting in a drawer. Money loses its meaning when there's nowhere to spend it and nothing defines the limits of your poverty or wealth as fast or as accurately. Rich or poor, it's all in your head. You never have enough, you never stop looking over your shoulder. That's the golden chain. You own things and they own you. As the days and weeks went by, the cloying abundance of the mainland and whatever was passing for reality there moved farther and farther away from me. I spent that summer lost in a marvelous merman trance, swimming through booming sea caves and trudging across sand dunes that ended in shimmering blurs on the shores of my own Socotra...diligently exploring every point of interest in the sprawling chain of enchanted islands that signified the end of the known world to me at one time.

There's a delicious sort of deprivation built into life on a small boat, though. There's only so much room for bottles of wine and tins of butter in the cool bilge. A sailor runs low on olive oil and coffee from time to time. So every month or two, I'd haul my anchor up and leave the islands behind. I'd sail north across the blustery main channel, steering for Larco's dip and the oil painting town reclining in lithe repose in the foothills of the Santa Ynez mountains. Beloved Santa Barbara, co-patron Saint of Sailors, whose streets are swept clean by the sighing sea winds and soothed by the shush of raffia fronds. Laid down in adobe and wrought iron, mission revival, red tile roofs and John Gamble green street lamps. It's sapphire Riviera, spilling bougainvillea and sunny ocean skies. It's warmer and has better art in the galleries than Carmel, but not Cannes. Surprisingly real for California (*hot oven*, roughly) with its vast oak understory, steep mountainsides and stony river beds; with its urchin divers, and lobstermen and ditzy JPL babes taking shots in the bars on Saturday night; with its fleet week, and swing dancing sailors in dress whites, with its fiesta, bad boy Italian chef (he knows who he is) and the one-to-five-star cuisine sustained on the lucre of the same clientele. There's big red wine in the hillsides and tamale parties at Christmas time, there's a hole in the wall vaquero saddle shop and a Sultan's Benz in the parking lot. The various enclaves and diasporas all do pretty well together there, and nobody really bothers the movie star in the busy harbor bar or the drunks camped out along the train tracks, just a few crucial degrees of separation away.

I didn't keep well on the mainland at that time in my life though. The sea would come calling when the goods were stowed and I'd set sail for the islands again. There's a healthy sameness to long stretches spent in uninhabited places, the days tend to run together making short work of a year and all of its well-meaning intention. Weak forces accumulate, small changes encourage others, and as I left my troubles behind, my long-delayed summer voyage stretched into another year, then two, then three. Before I knew it, my summer cruise spanned the better part of a decade.

The sea exerts a mystical pull on human beings that needs no introduction. And although I will not pretend to add anything new to the sea story genre, where everything that has to do with men, ships and the sea was already done and eloquently written about more than a century ago, I will say there's a sailor in everyone. Mention to people that you've been on a sea voyage, and fanciful images of royal blue oceans flecked with bright white sails, trimmed by good-looking people in billowy shirts and drab tan shorts spring to mind. The seafaring that goes on in daydreams is full of balmy winds, gleaming varnish, bare feet on wooden decks and dropping anchor in quaint little bays laved by the benevolent sea. The days are make-believe, the weather weightless and worry-free.

Tranquility

The boats practically sail themselves and the wind is always ready to carry them on their way somewhere new. Who in their right mind wouldn't want to do all of that? Or at least try?

I did. And that's where this story begins.

2

Seattle, Washington 1997

When the idea of buying a sailboat and going on a little summer voyage popped into my head on a cold and rainy Pacific Northwest morning, it arrived there intact and without warning. I was lying in bed, staring up at the dingy plaster ceiling in the small room I rented, wondering what I was going to do with the rest of my life, when for no apparent reason, I saw myself standing on the deck of a sailboat in the Channel Islands. I hadn't thought of returning to the waters where I spent my childhood for a long time, but in a moment, I knew I would do it. I was going to buy a boat and sail her from Washington to California. *And why not?* I mulled this question over for a moment or two— because that's what thinking is when you're in your early twenties—and I made up my mind. It was time for me to own a boat and time for me to see the sea again. How I went about it will be familiar to any fool or dreamer who happens to be reading this.

I was an impulsive person who fancied himself a man of means. I worked for myself and had nothing keeping me in Seattle, so I was free to go when and where I pleased. I wouldn't even have to go out of my way to finance the trip –because I was rich. I had my life savings, all $7500 of it, in a wad of large bills tucked into the front pocket of my blue jeans. They lay on the floor next to my mattress which, for comfort and convenience, was also on the floor. I knew some of my fortune would go to buying and outfitting a seaworthy vessel for the voyage, but the remainder, which I guessed would be around $2500, would be saved for what few expenses came up along the way. When the boat was ready to set sail, I would dispose of anything that didn't make sense to take on the voyage, then shove off for California. *Why not go sailing this summer? It will be fun!*

I imagined everything would be bright and bracing once I left the land behind. I pictured my cruise south unfolding as predictably and pleasantly as a 1930s Hollywood studio system script –an epistle to youth, a modern tale of derring-do and of course, *romance!* Once underway, I would immediately find clever ways to make a living with a boat, while leading the easy-going life of a charming young sailor. The wind would always convey me to my destination of choice, the dolphins would leap at the bow whenever I was on passage and the sun would shine down on my deck most days. I'd meet a pretty young woman who wanted to go sailing almost as bad as I did, everything would go smoothly there, and I'd earn a little extra cash by picking up day charters and small cargoes along the post-and-lintel piers jutting into the calm bays. You know, the calm bays I imagined were to be found a day's sail apart, all along the Pacific Coast of North America? No? At least I knew the problems, if there even were any, would be minor, or at worst, character building. A semester at sea, if you will.

It was early spring and I planned to arrive in the Channel Islands by early summer. *Summer! Summer! Summer!* This seemed like ideal timing to me, so I expected the itinerary to work out nicely. Once there, I'd spend a few months sailing from one idyllic island to the next, beach combing and spearfishing. I'd trade the leftovers of my catch among the other young sailors I met on my travels for any supplies I was running low on at the time. At a minimum, I would always find a way to get my hands on a sack of rice or a few gallons of fuel. And the rest of my needs? They would amount to mere details of course! In the unlikely event I ever got tired of living the sailorly life, I'd sell the boat, for a tidy profit, to another young man who was dreaming of the sea and I'd move on to something else. That was my plan and my plan seemed perfectly fine.

Besides, I already knew everything I needed to know about sailing! Thanks to a short stint in the Sea Scouts (picture Boy and Girl Scouts on boats) as a teenager, I could rig and sail a 30-foot fiberglass sloop and sort-of navigate. I hadn't tied a bowline or skippered anything larger than a dinghy in years, but that didn't seem like it would be much of a problem. To prove it, I didn't read one book or look closely at a single nautical chart to refresh my memory before shoving off. At that age, thinking things over meant assuming I was enough of a sailor to go on that sort of voyage. Once I papered over the gaps in my plan by telling myself I'd work everything else out along the way, I began looking for a boat. Actually, that's not as crazy as it sounds. I've since learned that buying a boat and sailing off into the sunset is a life-sized dream for a lot of people. It's on par with building a cabin in the country, opening a clever restaurant or buying a farmhouse on a little plot of land. It's starting over, it's spending one last summer at the beach, it's falling in love, it's writing the novel. There are just some things in life that are never going to happen if you think about them too much.

People do manage to set sail, but in the hustle-bustle of a modern man's sea voyage, the boat is frequently taken for granted and nothing about her is left to chance. Laden with brand new canvas and rigging, a fresh diesel engine, autopilot, radar, water-maker, life raft, satellite communication and a whole hell of a lot else, the vessel has been outfitted and provisioned close to home by a committee with a win at all cost attitude and the budget to match. Once at sea, the boat and her owners are backed by pre-positioned resources, the financial acumen of middle-age, modern marine communication and the luxury of turbine air travel –for rest stops at home of course. But for anyone who's young and daring or of limited means, how the boat was found, paid for and outfitted, i.e. the boat's personality and that of her owner, are an important part of the voyage –and because of that, those elements are usually included in a sea story. It's the small boats that go places—for the most part—and when a sailor of modest means gets into a jam, he must look only to himself and what he has aboard his vessel for rescue or relief. It was lucky for me that I was young and impatient when I made the decision to buy a boat and shove off in her. Youth is a brief moment, adulthood is full of fear and uncertainty, not bold confidence, and as the years go by, life decisions are more likely to be put off, forgotten, or unmade.

They say men go to sea because they must. And they must because they're unfit for life on land. Some go to sea because they suddenly find themselves on a narrow path which leads from their front door to a headstone on a hill somewhere. They go to sea because they chafe at the emasculation of the male mind and body, pay-as-you-go city living, franchise law enforcement and a government bought and paid for by corporations. They go to sea because they have an unusual fear of domestication and they resent the petty tyrants that keep the hands of the clock going around. They go to sea because they balk at the thousand hypocrisies and little injustices that landsmen must accept in order to live in the modern world. They go to sea because it is ungovernable and free and the little fat fingers of the paper push...err...–Pardon me. I didn't know any of that at the time. I was just going sailing for the summer. It was March and I figured I needed to be on my way by the first of June – so I got cracking.

No one *needs* a sailboat anymore, but for some reason there's a million of them out there. Most are well-kept, but you can find them abandoned on rickety docks and in boatyards, or propped up and long-forgotten in weedy back lots. That's probably the best place for a defunct vessel to stay, but once in a while, you come across a gem that just needs to be cleaned up and made seaworthy again. It never hurts to ask about a boat that looks like it's been sitting for a while. *But beware their owners.* They're often cranky, eccentric men of a certain age who can be surprisingly reluctant to part with a once-loved craft —no matter what state of disrepair she's fallen into. I found out later that it's a hell of a lot easier to buy a sailboat than it is to sell one, so keep that in mind if you go looking.

The first sailboat I was destined to own was listed in a buy-and-sell periodical known to cost-conscious shoppers all over the Pacific Northwest as *The Little Nickel.* I believe I was looking for something else that day, when my eyes were drawn to an ad with a catchy title:

-A LOT OF BOAT FOR A LITTLE MONEY-
-MAKE AN OFFER-

As I remember it, she was described as a classic wooden sloop (one mast) with a lot of life left in her despite having had her keel laid way back in 1938. The seller claimed that his vessel's 29-foot length, "workboat planking" and 5-ton displacement qualified her for "stout little ship" status. The boat came with several sails, a reliable two-cylinder gasoline inboard engine and lockers full of tools and spare parts. She could sleep four adults in her spacious cabin; there was a galley; a head (toilet); a coal burning cabin heater and a two-burner stove. She had all the usuals: electric lights; a pair of bilge pumps; depth sounder and a marine radio. If I remember correctly, the seller noted that he'd just taken her from Seattle to Alaska and back without incident. That's because the vessel sailed like a dream. There was no price listed for that much of a ship – *principals only.* There was a local phone number and a name though: Buddy.

I picked up the phone and dialed, and Buddy—bless his heart— answered on the first ring.

Buddy seemed extremely annoyed by any and all phone calls, and from the get-go, he was gruff and curt and kept interrupting me.

However, as soon as he figured out I was young, male and calling about the boat, his voice turned to velvet and he began telling little happy-go-lucky stories about her. She was built in Vancouver, British Columbia in the summer of 1938 and her design was one of a kind. Although she'd passed through several hands over the years, she'd spent her entire life "racing" and cruising Pacific Northwestern waters. Buddy told me photos of the boat from back in her competitive days still adorned the dining room walls of Seattle-area yacht clubs (he didn't say which ones) and to prove her fine pedigree, she had a first-place regatta plaque mounted on her bulkhead. Buddy said everywhere he went with the boat, old salts would pull him aside to comment on her pretty lines. Everybody else, including "young women" felt safe and at home in her. Why, in the seven problem-free years he'd owned the boat, she'd never run aground, never been towed, never been swamped. No one had even been seasick in her.

"That's a good old boat kid," Buddy said. "She was built back when they knew how to build boats and she can take you anywhere you want to go."

He put this to me in a breezy, I've-seen-it-all-and-done-it-all manner that was very persuasive. When I asked him how much he was looking to get for his boat, Buddy ducked the question and started telling me about some of the longer voyages he'd taken in her. He sailed her around Vancouver Island by himself one summer and he'd been in and out of every bay and port in southern Canada and Puget Sound. He'd lived aboard her through a snowy winter and spent entire summers cruising her on the northern inland waters of Washington State. Then, just as we were getting to his Alaska trip, Buddy broke off the narrative.

"Listen kid," he said flatly, "Alaska's really far away, it's really cold and there's no reason to go up there in a sailboat. I don't have a whole lot of time for stories today —this is a cash-on-the-barrel-head kind of deal."

Buddy told me to make my mind up about the boat quick, because her price was going up every day due to "all the calls" he was getting from "tire kickers" and the sorts of landlubbers and armchair sailors who spoke of "shipwrights and surveys" before buying a sixty-year-old wooden boat. He spat those words out in a tone of suspicious annoyance. Buddy told me in no uncertain terms that he didn't have time for *that* sort of nonsense. He let this important tidbit sink in for a few moments... and then he began talking me into a corner, trying to figure out when I could meet him down at the boat so we could "talk turkey." Buddy seemed a little scary over the phone and although I was intimidated, I reminded myself that feigning an abundance of interest in an item for sale was an old trick in *The Great Book of Men and the Disposal of Their Most Prized Possessions*. So I kept my cool and let him do the talking. He wanted to sell (I picked up on that) and I was pretty sure the "all the calls" part of Buddy's story was a white lie, I just wasn't sure if I could use it to my advantage.

As luck would have it, Buddy's boat was tied up in a marina on a lake close to where I was living. When Buddy realized he was speaking to someone who was five minutes away, he got a little ahead of himself and tipped a desperate hand. His voice slipped into an anxious tone as he tried to figure out what I was doing for the rest of the day. Then he completely blew his cover by suggesting we meet later. And that, dear reader, is when you let a guy sweat. It was a Monday afternoon and I was completely free for the rest of the day, but I told Buddy I couldn't meet him until the following Saturday. Buddy backpedaled from this delay with an airy assurance that he was free all day, every day, for the foreseeable future and next Saturday, or even the one after it, was as good a day as any for him. *Classic.*

When I hung up the phone that day, I was absolutely certain of two things: 1. Buddy wasn't someone to play around with 2. I had no idea how to handle a make-offer deal. Even though Buddy sounded desperate, I knew those two things put me at a disadvantage. So I decided my best strategy would be to hang back, let Buddy make the first move, and see where things went from there. It was already a done deal though, and I spent far more time that week thinking and daydreaming about owning an old wooden sailboat than anyone blessed with an average measure of common sense would have.

Buddy seemed like he might be the slippery type, so I arrived at the marina a little early the following Saturday to get the lay of the land and sniff out any funny business. It's a good idea to do a little recon when you're buying something *as is*. A guy might be busy sprucing up or making last minute repairs to damaged goods. Maybe he's warming up an engine so it starts at the touch of a key, perhaps he's brushing a little paint over a problem area. If he is, you want to know about it, so you can get the jump on him when it comes time to haggle.

The first thing I understood when I saw the boat was that men evidently measure their vessels the same way they measure other things. Buddy's "stout little ship" may have been a 29-footer—I never measured her myself—but I saw at a glance that her advertised length included everything about her –from the most recent coat of varnish on the tip of her bowsprit, to the curvature in the lens of her stern light. A vessel's length on the water, her wet length, is what's really important in a sailboat, and in this case, I was pretty sure I was looking at a 25-footer.

She was a pretty little boat though, with a forest green hull, light beige decks and spars. She had salty bronze ports in her cabin sides and oval panes of glass in her weatherboards. There was plenty of teak parquet and a pair of lattice thwarts (seats) in her cockpit. She seemed like a jaunty little craft and she looked like she was used to sailing. She was backed into her slip with her stubby bowsprit pointing toward open water and I took that for a good omen. Everything on deck and in the rigging was coiled down and ship-shape as it should be on a sailboat. She wasn't Bristol, but she had the usual touches found on a well-kept ship. There was a Turk's head on her tiller and other fancy rope work here and there. Her bottom was fairly clean and her paint and varnish were being kept up reasonably well. Her mooring lines were neat on the cleats and she had Flemish coils on the dock. The only thing I didn't like about her was her size. From a distance, she seemed well-proportioned and solidly built, but up-close, she was tiny and narrow, with decks no more than a foot or two above the water. I was trying to imagine how she would handle in a following sea with that low-slung stern of hers, when Buddy showed up.

He swept into the marina parking lot in a tough-guy, mid-eighties muscle car and performed a wide, tirey turn in the center of the lot where he hit the brakes with a little chirp. Then, steering in reverse with the palm of his hand, he gunned the car into a spot. *His* spot. The driver's door swung open, bounced back lightly off the hinges and Buddy–short, white and vigorous–leapt from the front seat, clearing the door with a little twist of his hips as it swung shut. He fast-walked to the gate, took to the ramp with a bouncy jog, and in a second, he was bearing down on me. Buddy had a successful, blue collar air about him, with the ruddy, oft-washed hands of someone who spent his days working with concrete rather than performing surgery. He looked to be in his late fifties, but moved like a much younger man. He sailed by me without a word and went straight from the dock to the lifelines. He vaulted them, landing in the cockpit with a little falling motion that he steadied with the hand that slid the companionway hatch open. It all happened really fast. I caught a whiff of cologne and salty wood –a good smell.

"Welcome aboard," Buddy said as he ducked below.

Her cabin had the usual layout of a small sloop built in the 1930s. Her interior was cozy with a lot of varnish and decorative wood. She was narrow and her roof was low. On the port side, there was a 6-foot quarter berth tucked underneath the cockpit and a large countertop with a sink and some lockers in it. Forward of that was a tiled nook where a cast iron cabin heater and a galley stove were bolted down. To starboard, there was an electrical panel, a long settee and a bank of lockers which doubled as the back rest. Forward of that, a bulkhead (wall) spanned nearly half the boat. The bulkhead afforded a bit of privacy for the porta-potty in the locker on the far side of it. The mast came through the cabin top a little forward of the bulkhead, the stove nook was opposite. Forward of the mast was a tight v-berth and chain locker. All in all, the cabin was much smaller than I imagined and the roof was definitely lower than I liked. An average man couldn't stand up in her without ducking his head, and if two people wanted to pass, one of them had to sit on the bunk or settee. The low roof was going to be a problem for John.

Buddy introduced me to the boat by showing me the quality of her construction. He went to a pair of thick oaken knees which hung down from the deck beams on either side of the mast like broad shoulder blades. "These keep the whole damn boat together," Buddy said, slapping and pushing on them (I rolled my eyes when he looked away). He pulled the cabin floorboards up and pointed out the stoutness of her ribs and the generous widths of her keelson and floor timbers. Buddy wrapped on the planking with his beefy knuckles and said: "This boat is work-boat planked with *genuine* Port Orchard cedar." I do offer my sincerest apologies to anyone I repeated those inane words to, and who may have looked on in wonder, silently pondering their meaning just as I did that day. Who knows what damage I've done to my reputation and to those of honest men all over the Pacific Northwest by carrying on about work-boat planking when, as far as I ever found out, it means next to nothing.

And while we're at it, a quick word on "Port Orchard" yellow cedar –just in case it ever comes up again. To clarify: Port Orchard is a large body of water in Puget Sound where there are a few small settlements. Port Orford on the other hand, is a port on the southern Oregon Coast where some of the finest old-growth yellow cedar in the region used to come from. Yellow cedar from almost anywhere is a prized boat-building wood. It's especially sought after for planking because it's easy to work and easy to bend in the shape of a boat. It smells like heaven when you saw it, it's forgiving and it holds a screw well; it's extremely rot-resistant and some even claim it's impervious to the dreaded shipworm *Teredo Navalis*...You don't say?

Around the Pacific Northwest, when a man tells you his otherwise average boat is planked with Port Orford yellow cedar, it's like a guy telling you his thrift store watch turned out to be a Rolex. That would be a very good thing indeed –if only it were true. But do you find a Rolex sitting on the shelf of any old junk shop? No, you don't. Has anyone ever thought their watch was a Rolex when it wasn't? Almost certainly. Can a fool tell you the difference? No, he can't. Whether it's told in a bar, on a dock or in a boatyard, the story of Port Orford yellow cedar always ends the same way in the Pacific Northwest: "You just can't get the stuff anymore," they tell you. And that's exactly what Buddy said with a meaningful nod in the bilge as he slid the floorboards back in place. These are the legends, passed down through the Y chromosome, that men *live* for. Now when a guy tells me his boat is planked with Port Orford yellow cedar, or that his engine block was cast in Windsor, Ontario I pretend like I've never heard of those places before. By the way, if you're ever down there, Port Orford is a pretty good small boat anchorage in northwesterly weather.

Buddy excused himself at that point and went up to the marina office, leaving me to poke around the boat on my own for a little while. I opened a locker and peered inside. The battery charger was humming away in there –it was hot and painted light blue. Its meter read thirty. I peeked under the lid of the engine compartment, reached in and put my hand on the block –it was cold and painted black. I pushed as hard as I could on the butt of the mast with both hands. It didn't budge.

Seems like a solid old boat, I thought to myself.

But what could I have possibly been looking for, when I knew next to nothing? What did I think I was going to find that day? A hole in the bottom of the boat spewing a geyser into the bilge? A family of rats gnawing a chicken bone in an out-of-the-way place? A fire smoldering behind the electrical panel? Maybe something along those lines would have caused me to look a bit closer at the boat I was thinking of buying instead of relying solely upon her seller for my survey. I did happen to notice a freshly photocopied article on the boat that afternoon: *The Art of Caulking a Boat*. This sheaf of paper was tucked into the top of a milk crate that held several small tins of paint, a few curled-up sheets of sandpaper and some stiff brushes. The cover page of the article featured a photo of an odd looking double-headed wooden mallet and a thick type of putty knife I'd never seen before. By the way, *The Art of Caulking a Boat* is not much fun to learn how to do on a hot summer day.

Buddy came bounding back aboard and picked up where he left off. He showed me how to work the galley sink, the cabin lights and the electronics. He talked me through porta-potty etiquette. He explained the three-bunks-sleeps-four situation: if there were four men aboard, someone, usually the smallest, had to sleep on the cabin floor. The walk-through ended that day with an energetic demonstration of how to operate the antique galley stove and the cabin heater. The cook-stove was a touchy, pressurized kerosene affair whose fuel tank had to be pumped up with one of those hateful thumb-operated mini-pumps everyone knows from the camping world. The pump plunger was situated in the most inconvenient place imaginable, in that you had to lean over the lit stovetop to work it –and one had to work it, constantly, in order to keep the thing going once it was lit. The stove was all brass and bronze, and soot and tin, and soldered copper tubes going this way and that. It wasn't hard to imagine a Roman soldier heating his dinner up on something just like it. Buddy began the demo by leaning far over the stove, bracing himself against the settee and ceiling. When he was firmly wedged in place, he worked the mini-pump with short, furious strokes until his face turned bright red. It took around a hundred just to get the thing ready to light. When Buddy caught his breath, he uncorked a small tin of alcohol and poured a shallow pool of clear fuel around both saucer-shaped burners. Then he stepped back, struck a match and held it to the closest one while keeping his body as far away from the stove as possible. When the match met the alcohol fumes, the first burner ignited with a blue *whoosh* that fanned out over the stovetop and touched off the second burner. "Easy-peasy," Buddy said, rubbing his hand on his pants to cool it. I smelled burning hair.

When the stove lit, a pair of foot-high blue flames began dancing around the burners and licking at the bent and dimpled kerosene tank which ran lengthwise along the back. From where I was standing, this tank looked like the log in a fake fireplace. However, according to Buddy, this was perfectly normal during the "pre-heat" phase of the operation. The flames began to subside after a minute or two, and that meant it was time to introduce the pressurized kerosene into the mix. To do this, Buddy crouched low to the floor, reached for the nearest temperature-control knob and rotated it with his fingertips about $1/128^{th}$ of a turn to the left. When he released the knob, a furious twenty-inch-high flame ignited in midair above the corresponding burner, the spitting tips licked at the ceiling timbers for a few seconds before dropping down into an unstable and hissing, bright blue rocket jet that clocked back and forth around the burner. I can't say that the cook-stove struck me as anything to be concerned about in a narrow wooden cave infused with half-a-century's worth of varnish and oil paint. I saw it as an interesting conversation piece, it was an antique –like the boat that carried it. Rather than being wary, I was looking forward to cooking on it.

"It's a two-burner," Buddy said as he turned the thing off.

Next up was the Tiny Tot. This was the little cast iron cabin heater that sat beside the stove. Tots were designed to burn coal, I think, and although I never found out how old it was or where it came from, it looked like it was built in England around 1800. There was even a Dickens-thin young girl cast into the fire-door to add a bit of cheer to its primitive design. Essentially, this type of heater is a vertical iron pipe 8 inches in diameter that's closed off at the bottom and fitted with a hinged fire-door and damper on its front. Jutting from the back of the Tot was a heavily-insulated stovepipe that went up and out through the cabin top. Buddy sat down on the settee across from the Tot and spread his legs wide. He placed two wads of newspaper and a 10-inch long stick of pitch-pine into the fire box and then lit the paper with a match. There was an instant draw through the open fire-door and tall, smudgy flames rose into the stovepipe. Buddy leaned back and eased the door most of the way closed with his foot. With the door cracked, the Tot started drawing in serious air, and a bright red hot spot began climbing up the back side of it. Pine smoke smells good in an old wooden boat, and I could feel the heat on my face from five feet away. If you left the door cracked, as I was planning to do, it would be like having a fire in your boat and I was already imagining a peaceful nightly ritual around my cozy little hearth.

"This thing will drive your ass out of here on a snowy winter night," Buddy warned me. "I mostly burn wood in there and I don't even think of adding coal unless it's below zero"–he meant below zero *inside* the boat–"Nope, no sir, you don't burn coal in there unless you see frost in here," he said, slapping the settee cushion. "FROST!...IN HERE!" he continued. "That's when you know it's safe to add one small piece of coal." He said this holding up a meaty fist to show me what size he meant. "One piece, no bigger than this, every three to four hours."

What is this guy's deal? I wondered.

It was fairly broiling in the cramped cabin by then, so Buddy suggested we move out to the cockpit so he could show me how to start the two-cylinder inboard engine. According to Buddy, the old Albin four-stroke was the one piece of equipment on the boat that could be relied upon without fail, one hundred percent of the time. With that said, he reached for the control panel, set the choke halfway and turned the ignition key. The motor fired right up and after a few seconds of idling, Buddy pushed the choke in with a little flourish. "This baby won't stall on you even when it's stone-cold," he said, revving the motor theatrically. On the starboard side of the cockpit, near the floor, was a small bronze wheel which rotated a full turn fore and aft. Buddy took hold of this wheel with both hands and turned it toward the bow, straining on it until the transmission shifted into forward with a thunk. "Shifter needs another lube," Buddy said under his breath as he shooed me out of the way. With her engine in gear, the little sailboat tugged at her dock lines and her tiller snapped to attention amidships as the prop wash flowed around the rudder. Roiling water gurgled under the transom and drove off astern, spreading out evenly along the sea wall behind us. The little Albin two-banger definitely had some torque.

"She can run like that day and night," Buddy said, giving me a little wink. "This boat can take a lot more than you can." Truer words were never spoken on the deck of a ship.

There was no doubt about it, that boat was itching to go somewhere and so was I. Buddy must have thought I was more than a tire kicker at that point, because he began laying the sailor talk on pretty thick, while saying and doing little things to make it seem like the boat was already mine and he was just showing me around –as men do when they're happy to be unloading something. Although the boat was a plain Jane sloop in every way, Buddy boasted of her easy handling and willingness to sail in any wind. He spoke of her obedience to her helmsman and of her preternatural sea-keeping abilities. Above all though, he spoke of her fidelity to her master: "If you take good care of her, she'll take good care of you." When Buddy strayed into overly specific nautical terms and minor points of interest in the rigging, I let my mind wander to the wide sandy beaches and secluded coves of the Channel Islands where I'd soon be anchored. I pictured the pretty little bays and natural harbors that stretch from Seattle to Santa Barbara –I was already on my way.

When Buddy lost steam with his carrick bends and jiffy-reefing grommets I looked him straight in the eye and asked him if he was ready to do a deal. Those were the first real words out of my mouth that day and they took us both by surprise. I think we knew I was going to end up with her, but neither of us knew how to make it happen so soon. Although my mind was pretty well made up, I told Buddy I was going to talk to a few people and make him an offer the following week.

"Just like that?" he asked, with a plain kind of disappointment in his voice.

"Yeah man, I'll call you Monday or Tuesday," I said, putting a leg over the lifelines. When I jumped to the dock, my index finger plucked one of the stainless steel wires (the backstay) that held the mast up. This disturbance sent a lazy wave up and down the wire from deck to masthead, jiggling the wooden spars and crosstrees (spreaders) more than I remembered from my Sea Scouting days. When Buddy saw what I was looking at, he said to me with another wink: "I like my boats like my women: a little loose." I suppose Buddy made the cocky working-class sailor thing work pretty well for him, but I promised myself, there and then, that I would never turn into such a foul-mouthed old sailor as he. As I was walking up the ramp, I heard Buddy mumble something about me making up my mind quickly because another young guy was coming to look at her later that same day. But I already knew I was the only real thing he had going and I pretended not to hear him.

I hurried home and called John.

3

Ring-Ring...Ring-Ring
John: "Hello?"
Me: "Dude..."
John: "Hey man."
Me: "*DUDE!*"
"Just tell me what's happening man..."
"Oh man...bro."
"What's going on man?"
"I'M BUYING A SAILBOAT!"
"So you're really gonna do it huh?"
"Yeah I totally am."
"What is it?"
"What's what?"
"What's the boat?"
"Some old dude's selling his boat, that's what."
"What else do you know about it?"
"It's an old wooden sailboat some dude has!"
"There's lots of different kinds of boats man...don't you need to like...find out more about it than that?"
"Like what?"

It was my dear friend John who dragged me down to a chandlery that catered specifically to wooden boat enthusiasts so I could ask the experts who worked there a few classic yacht questions and maybe pick up a couple of pointers before I plunked down a large part of my life's savings on a sixty-year-old sailboat. In this errand was a hint of the caution I should have had all along, but for some reason, the thought of doing it annoyed the crap out of me. I went along with John anyway, going through the motions and making a day of it. Unfortunately, I hated the place and everything in it the second we walked through the front door. I could tell at a glance that the place wasn't a chandlery at all. It was a silly boutique where retired professors went to buy plans for door-skin boats and cellophane packets of small brass wood screws for twelve dollars a pop. It was little more than a museum gift shop where doting wives went to buy their emasculated husbands spendy rigging knives and boatswain's pipe stocking-stuffers. I worked for an extremely shrewd businessman and sailor in a *real* chandlery when I was fourteen. I ate bean soup, slept on the floor before it opened for business, and, starting at eight o'clock in the morning, I spent the entire day lugging heavy sail bags around and sorting through crates filled to the brim with cold bronze winch parts, mooring tackle and heavy iron cleats. I hurt myself, in one way or another, every single day I worked there.

The real chandlery was packed from floor to ceiling with every marine contrivance known to mankind. There were foot-high piles of British Admiralty charts for faraway places sitting on timber galley tables. Ship's wheels leaned in a corner next to a stack of gilded escutcheons, kerosene dioptric sidelights, faded orange life-rings and fifty-fathom (300 foot) coils of line meant for rigging ships –not seaside restaurants. All of this pirate booty was rung up on an old-fashioned cash register tucked into a crowded nook in the middle of the store. I worked as hard as I could in the short time I was employed there, but due to a complicated transaction involving an amount of script I was owed and the ill-timed sale of a certain, green, 7.5-horsepower Scott Atwater outboard motor, I ended up owing the proprietor money. So one day, after I spent the entire afternoon slopping out the bilges of his fancy sailing yacht, *Sama----*, he unceremoniously fired me. That's a *real* chandlery. It was all my fault of course, and the man taught me a very good lesson. I tried to pay him what I owed him about twenty years later but he never got back to me. Maybe he didn't care anymore, maybe the letter never reached him. Either way, I never forgot the debt and I'm sure he'd be glad to know that.

The place where John and I went was run by an oaf of a man who'd evidently spent a fair bit of time drinking and blathering about boats. In his spare time, he'd done his little shop and himself up in the most affected maritime manner money could buy. These kinds of places are all cut from the same cloth, but as I remember it, the owner wore a sturdy, hunter green flannel, a wide belt with colorful signal flags on it, fresh carpenter's pants and the type of rugged work shoe only a lily-handed dandy could own. He was a mini-van with off-road truck tires. His clothes had never been dirty and the floor never had a wood shaving on it, but poking out of his shirt pocket was a sharp pencil and a small brass bevel gauge, as if he might duck out any minute and finish the breast hook in the 56-foot schooner he was building out back. Yeah...he was an old jack-tar alright. China-made half-models of famous sailing yachts lined the wall behind the register and five-hundred dollar brightwork bronze ports sat on pillows under glass in the countertop. It was obvious no real trade went on in that soulless place. It was a Pier 39 shop that was barely surviving on boat show trinkets and the last minute needs of urban kayakers.

"My friend here is buying a wooden boat," John said to the proprietor.

"Oh *is* he?" the man giggled, then snorted: "What kind?"

"It's a sloop," I said.

"Cutter?" he asked.

"*Sloop*," I said.

"Cutter *rigged*?" He pressed, giving an all-knowing wink to his audience who were sitting around the place on three low stools –losers and has-beens to a man. It seemed as if John and I stumbled upon a captain's gam! And we were the odd men out. It was officers versus greenhorns.

"She's a 29-foot sloop that was built up in Vancouver in 1938. She's work-boat planked with Port Orchard yellow cedar. That's pretty much all we know about her," I said.

"What's she got in her for power?" he asked.

"A two-cylinder Albin."

"Well...*that's* not a plus!" he said with a superior huff and another glance at his entourage who were stirring their canes at the prospect of fresh meat. "And just so you know," he continued, "she was probably built over in Port *Orchard* out of Port *Orford* yellow cedar. And if she was built in '38, she was most likely put together with iron screws, and in that case, you won't get very far in her without refastening the hull." The proprietor passed his final judgment on the boat with a little chuckle and sigh brought on by recollections of days of yore no doubt.

Well that clears things up! I thought to myself.

"I'm not ready to buy her anyway," I said, waving to John who was already heading for the door.

"Well then..." the proprietor said as we left the place.

I glanced through the front windows as we walked across the parking lot, and I saw them in there, four tubs of goo, having a salty old laugh at us. *Oh to be a fly on the wall when those retired sea captains spun their yarns in that old sail loft down by the docks! And to lay eyes—if only for a moment—on the South Sea Island Beauties that must have swooned at the unsheathing of their sabers!* I thought to myself derisively as we got into the car.

"Just go for it man," John said as we drove away. "But change her name *A*-sap."

"What happens, happens, dude," I said, buckling my seatbelt.

It was late March and I figured I had to step on it if I was going to set sail by June, so I decided to buy the first and only boat I looked at.

Around noon, a week after our first meeting, Buddy and I were sitting next to each other at the end of a long bar in an empty harbor restaurant not far from the boat. I remember the place being done up in the usual musty seaside manner: there was a brass port in the wooden front door; the dimly-lit dining room was cordoned off by low pilings strung with thick manila line; polished brass nautical lanterns sat on the tables and a painting of a ship in a storm hung under a weak lamp in the payphone nook –it was that sort of place. We'd met there to have a drink and talk turkey, but I still didn't have any idea how to buy a boat that was being sold without a price. I had the wad of cash in my front pocket and Buddy brought the title with him, but things had gotten off to a bumpy start. Buddy was on edge the moment he walked through the front door, and when I saw the unfriendly *go-for-the-throat* look in his eyes, I knew winging it wasn't going to work all that well with him. Instead of taking my time and waiting to see what happened that day, things began moving really, really fast. Buddy marched up to me on autopilot, I smelled whiskey on his breath and knew in a terrifying instant that I wasn't ready for him. Yes, over the past couple days I'd thought through various financial equations along the lines of: X to buy the boat; Y to fix her up; Z for food and fuel and charts and whatever else I might need to get to California –but I still didn't have any firm numbers to work with because I didn't have the faintest idea what Buddy wanted for his boat. The moment I saw him, I knew I'd made a huge mistake by coming there unprepared and it dawned on me that Buddy had the upper hand in the deal. It was too late to do anything about it, though. Buddy swooped in on me and tossed a Washington State vessel title and a pen on the bar.

"I don't have a whole lot of time for B.S. today, kid," he said, taking a seat on the stool next to me and snapping his fingers at the bartender –there was no one in the place but us.

"Double Jack neat," Buddy said.

"Make that a double," I said...regretting my choice of words as soon as I heard them.

An uncertain expression came into the bartender's face.

I felt Buddy fix his gaze on me.

"Make mine too," I said cheerily, before wincing. I thought I cleared up the misunderstanding with: "Make that two...I mean, make *two*, but make them both two doubles."

"*Oh...Jesus...Christ...*" Buddy said under his breath.

The bartender nodded –*he* got me.

I may have been totally unprepared to make an offer on the boat that day, but I wasn't *completely* green. I'd worked my way through the South Seas on a tramper; I'd done some exploring along the Mosquito Coast in Central America and I'd been through Alaska and British Columbia. I'd lived in Europe and Asia and I was proud to have paid my way through it all on the wages of a self-employed mechanic. I went into business for myself in my teens and I'd bought and sold plenty of cars and small machinery since then. However, I'd always known the worth of what I was buying. I'd always had a number to work with, usually the asking price, set by the seller. It doesn't even matter how unrealistic or fair the price is –it's just a safe and mutually agreed upon point of departure for a negotiation. It's the way the world works, and, up until then, I thought it was the only way. Now, for the first time in my life, I was facing a strictly "make-offer" deal. It was up to me to put the first number on the table, and that made me very uncomfortable. You can't just call up a wooden boat dealer and ask them what the old sailboat you're thinking of buying is worth. Buddy's boat wasn't mass produced –she was one of a kind, and because of that, she was only worth what someone was willing to pay for her. Unbeknownst to me, those people become fewer and farther between the older a boat gets. I actually had the upper hand that day and didn't even know it!

The drinks were poured and little-by-little the tense silence at our end of the bar gave way to even tenser chit-chat about the unusually sunny weather we were having that spring. Buddy was throwing off a seriously annoyed testosterone vibe and my double whiskey may as well have been a double espresso. I was so nervous, I was having trouble putting simple sentences together. I knew I had to say something about the boat, or ask her price, or make an offer on her, but my bottom lip started quivering whenever I tried to speak.

Buddy got the ball rolling for us with some Alaska talk: "I sailed her up to Ketchikan on the tail end of the spring southerlies a couple years back and I did a little fishing and cruising out Sitka way. There's a lot for a guy to do up there, and I thought of wintering over, but when the weather started to turn in late summer, I brought her back down to Seattle on the last of the northwesterlies. It was a nice little voyage," Buddy said with genuine feeling. "That there's a good old boat son. She won't let you down." Buddy wasn't the sort of sailor who owned a pair of topsiders or fancy foul-weather gear. He had big rubber boots and a rain slicker from the hardware store. He'd done a lot with his boat and didn't like to brag about it. I believed every word he said.

The Alaska story was followed by an uncomfortable break in the conversation that an experienced buyer would have immediately filled with follow-up questions or shallow banter and Buddy stared me down with a pained, imploring look during the silence. I knew I needed to say something quick and I was just about to, when an impossible number flashed like a bolt of lightning in my mind: $25,000. *That boat is probably worth TWENTY-FIVE GRAND!* I thought to myself. I was out of my league. I was wasting Buddy's time and he was going to get angry when he figured it out. It was a dreadful moment. Buddy was a fit, tightly wound man; he was staring at me over the bottles in the mirror and drumming his muscular fingers on the thick mahogany bar. He did not have kind eyes.

"Chsssh...!" Buddy exhaled, shaking his head, obviously totally miffed at me. There was no doubt about it, he was winding up for something.

"Double Jack neat," he said, hoisting a buff arm aloft which caused him to sway back on his stool. The bartender poured the drink, caught wind of the tension between us, and began tidying up close by so he could eavesdrop.

"How much do you want for the boat?" I heard myself say. My lips were trembling but I managed to get the words out.

"How much you *GOT?*" Buddy guffawed, leaning back to throw down a swig of whiskey. It was a strafe by an old pro. I was no match for him and we both knew it.

Fine, I thought to myself, *I don't even want the stupid boat anymore.*

And in that moment of clarity, the words came out all on their own: "I'll give you thirty-five hundred for the boat...today...in cash."

Buddy's eyes crossed a little when he heard this, his nose blew a big bubble in his drink, he inhaled some of it, coughed it out, and nearly fell off his stool. The bartender stopped polishing his glass mid-squeak. He looked to Buddy, then to me, then back to Buddy. Stunned silence filled our corner of the room. Buddy turned to me with a sad and shocked expression. He started to say something but thought twice about it and carefully set his drink down. The bartender leaned in slightly, and Buddy tilted toward me, steadying himself with both hands on the bar. His voice dropped into a threatening and eerily confidential register: "I won't take a dime less than five grand for that goddamned boat," he said, choking down something tight in his throat. "I'll sink her *myself* before I sell her for less than that," he continued, giving me an ominous, drunken wink.

"Done-deal!" I said putting my hand out for a shake.

Something must have dawned on him just then, because Buddy's expression became woeful yet relieved. It seemed to say: *I just got screwed here, but thank god I sold the boat!*

We never shook on it, but I did see a little tear welling up in his eye.

"I'm gonna miss that old boat," he said wistfully.

Buddy and I walked down to the marina and I counted out fifty crisp, one-hundred dollar bills onto the cockpit seat between us. Buddy didn't need no envelope. He scooped up the pile of bills with one hand, folded it in half and slipped it into his breast pocket, buttoning it. He did this slowly and without enthusiasm, so as not to arouse any suspicion on my part. We signed the papers a minute later, and she was mine. I wasn't really thinking about what I was doing that day, but it did occur to me that I'd just bought a sailboat without ever having sailed her. When I halfheartedly suggested to Buddy that he was going to owe me a daysail in order to show me the ropes, he laughed the idea off with a comment I shall never forget: "You sure want a lot for your five grand, kid."

I dodged that, and asked Buddy if it would be alright for me to call him if I had any questions only he could answer.

"I don't know where I'm gonna be pretty soon," he said.

I vaguely remembered Buddy mentioning that he was staying with a friend, so I asked him where he might be headed.

"I don't know...maybe back up to Alaska."

Before he left, Buddy asked me what my plans for the boat were. When I told him I would be taking her down to California that summer he asked me which trucking company I was going to use. When I said I was sailing her down there on her own bottom, Buddy's voice went a little stuttery and he started covering bases.

"H-h-hey kid," Buddy stammered, taking my collar and turning me toward him with a tipsy sway. "Listen up here...if-uh...if-you're-uh...gonna be sailing this boat on the ocean, you need to...well, you have to l-l-listen to me...*LISTEN* to me kid...If you're gonna be taking a trip like that in an old wooden boat, you have to go through her from stem to stern. You have to go through her with somebody who knows what they're doing.

"*Tranquility*..." Buddy said, "*Tranquility* is a lot of boat."

4

Even though I was fairly certain two months and twenty-five hundred dollars were more than enough time and money to get *Tranquility* ready for her voyage to California, I moved her to a less expensive marina across the bay (one that didn't require hull insurance as Buddy's marina did) and I immediately got down to business...such as it was to me in those days. Important note: The majority of boats kept on the waters surrounding the city of Seattle aren't moored on Puget Sound, but on freshwater lakes and canals. It's fairly confusing geography, even to some locals, but the principal waterways are Lake Washington, Lake Union and Salmon Bay. These bodies of water are lined with marinas, and the one I moved *Tranquility* to was typical of them. Bayside Marina was a warren of narrow, spider infested, covered wooden docks and open air slips spread out in the cool shallows along the south shore of Salmon Bay. The marina's covered docks were crammed with powerboats being kept out of the weather. There were Grand Banks, Dream Boats, Monks, Hatteras and a Blanchard or two. The open air docks were flanked by all sorts of sailboats: sloops; yawls and ketches; wood and fiberglass; well-kept and neglected; large and small; what-have-you. The ramps, docks and boathouses were connected to one another by walkways and unstable finger piers. All of it was held in place by creosote pilings ringed up and down with the dry whitish remnants of a hundred subtle differences in lake level.

I spent my very first morning aboard *Tranquility* in a way that would soon be familiar: I went through her completely, lazarette to forepeak, taking stock of her gear and supplies, cleaning and organizing as I worked. I took a few cartloads of old fenders, sour water hoses, sunblasted life vests and frayed dock lines up the ramp to the marina dumpster. I spent a couple hours going through a large coffee can full to the brim with old nuts and bolts. I cleaned each fastener with a stiff wire brush and sorted them into a large, divided plastic box which weighed around thirty pounds when full. It was heavy, so I put it down in the bilge. I came across an old pail of anthracite coal that was wedged in the bottom of a locker under the forward bunk. *You don't see that every day,* I said to myself as I hefted the bucket into a better spot. I tore up an ugly piece of burnt-orange carpet that some dim-wit had glued to the top of the beautifully varnished engine cover (this surface was part of the cabin stairs).

"Why would someone cover up such beautiful woodwork with this nasty old carpet?" I asked the man standing on the foredeck of the sailboat next to mine, when I heaved it onto the dock.

"It's so you don't go ass-over-tea-kettle when it gets wet down there," he responded kindly.

"Yeah...no kidding!" I said as if it had happened to me a hundred times. I did wonder for a moment or two how water might get in the cabin of my boat. I concluded that a really heavy rain would do it.

I went on the first of many supply runs later that day and I came back with a cheap car stereo and a can of adhesive remover to clean the carpet glue off the engine hatch. I hooked the stereo up to the main batteries, hung the speakers on cup hooks and got to work. The music sounded great and the upbeat tempo kept me going late into the evening. I stowed and re-stowed everything aboard the boat with ever increasing logic: tools here; engine spares there; books and charts up high; heavy things down low; emergency flares and binocular at the ready, and so on and so forth. The coal bucket eventually found its way back to the locker where it started. *Everything has a place on a boat!* I reminded myself, *and that's where it belongs!* It had been quite a while since I sailed, but a few things were starting to come back to me. Much of boating is innate really: keep the water out; keep out of the water; don't run aground; know your position. A child splashing around in a bathtub in the middle of a continent knows that much.

Before I knew it, it was two-thirty in the morning and I was exhausted and starving. The only food aboard was a heavy can of steak and potato stew that I found behind a panel in the galley —it had fallen back there years before, no doubt. I fished it out, dumped the gelatinous contents into a pan and, following Buddy's specific instructions, I lit the stove. It fired right up and burned hot. *Good ol' Buddy,* I thought to myself as I stirred the bubbling stew. The free meal made me giddy and I left the burner lit for warmth while I devoured it. I was just a man in his ship that night and there's nothing like a hard day's work on a boat to whet the appetite! When I finished eating, I turned the stove off and climbed into the forward berth. I pulled the working jib out of its bag, and, using it for a blanket, I bedded down for the night...nuzzled, as it were, to *Tranquility*'s bosom. The thought that I'd gone down to the docks one day and bought myself a sailboat sent a thrill through me that I hope I'll never forget. My feet did a few involuntary little kicks of joy under the scratchy sail cloth when I pictured it all over again. I gave notice on my rented room the next morning, pitched any possessions deemed unfit for life at sea by noon, and moved aboard. I couldn't believe it was as easy as that!

The weather was clear the next day, so I called John to invite him on a little sail. He wasn't home, so I decided to take her out single-handed. I would have liked some company, but it turned out to be a good thing I was by myself the first time I sailed *Tranquility*. The privacy allowed me to discover, and come up with clever ways to fix or hide, everything that was wrong with my new boat from nearly everyone who sailed in her –including myself. More on that later. Right now it's important to know that Salmon Bay, Lake Union and Lake Washington are linked to one another by way of narrow canals and to Puget Sound, and the Pacific Ocean beyond, by way of a pair of locks. The Ballard Locks. There's a lock for large vessels and one for smaller boats, respectively: the large and small locks. The locks are a busy bottleneck in boating season because all marine traffic: tugs in tow; tour boats; commercial fishing vessels; freighters and day-trippers wishing to transit from fresh to saltwater, or vice versa, must use the locks, and that's a hell of a lot easier said than done, my friend.

A skipper pilots his vessel into the locks per the direction of the lock master who's speaking to him through a bull horn mounted on a building that looks like an air traffic control tower. The lock I was directed to that day, the small lock, is a u-shaped, concrete chamber about a hundred-and-fifty feet long and thirty wide. It's filled with lake water and, more often than not, other boats in transit to Puget Sound. The lock chamber is controlled at either end by a set of massive iron doors. When you're going from the lake to Puget Sound (from east to west) the lake doors swing open, admit your vessel and then close behind you. When the doors close, most of the water in the chamber is drained into the sound by way of a large valve at the bottom of the lock. The boats in the chamber drop down with the water level until the valve is closed. When the saltwater doors open at the far end of the chamber, you find yourself at sea level and you're free to go on your merry way. This process is repeated in reverse order for vessels wishing to go from Puget Sound to the lakes.

You enter the lock at sea level, the saltwater doors close behind you and the chamber is filled with lake water until your vessel is floating at lake level. The lake doors open and you're free to head inland. These locks function with near flawless precision, and, for the most part, it is the mariners who use them that have made them famous for ending voyages prematurely or causing disaster on the final day, of the final leg, of a picture-perfect passage.

The very first problem I discovered with *Tranquility* had to do with her transmission. Unfortunately, I took note of it at an incredibly inopportune time. When the lake doors swing open to admit boats, a fair current runs from the lake into the lock as the water levels equalize. *Tranquility* got swept up in this current as I steered her into the lock, and, when I realized we were going too fast, I rolled the shifter wheel back, in order to put the boat in reverse and slow her down. But nothing happened when I turned it. She wouldn't go into reverse, only neutral or forward. A thrill of fear, the first of many to come, and one that will be familiar to any sea god or mortal who's ever passed through the Ballard Locks, shot through me from head to toe as *Tranquility* sped into the chamber and wedged herself between two waiting vessels. Luckily, the boats were securely tied along the sea wall and had plenty of fenders out, so there was no damage –just a warning from the lock attendant to take it slower. What can I say? It was my first time through!

By experimenting with the shifter wheel and the engine rpm as we dropped down to sea level, I learned that *Tranquility* would go into reverse only when an immense clockwise force was brought to bear on the shifter wheel. I assumed this was due to the linkage Buddy said needed a lube. I budgeted ten minutes for the repair, then put it far from my mind. After all, it was a big day for me! I was going sailing on my very own boat for the first time in my life! When the sea doors opened, I motored *Tranquility* out to Puget Sound, with my happy little heart squeezing in my chest and cold sea air filling my clean lungs.

Out on the sound, the sun was sort-of shining and a stout wind was blowing from the northwest at around twenty knots. A steep, two-foot wind swell was charging down the sound from north to south and serried ranks of waves stretched into the hazy distance as far as the eye could see. Leaving *Tranquility* to motor on her own for a minute, I dashed up to the mast and not remembering, or simply knowing no better, I hoisted every stitch of canvas on the boat, then ran back to the cockpit to trim the sails. When I had all of the lines as tight as they would go, *Tranquility* heeled over on her ear and lumbered off, motor-sailing under a full main and cruising genoa. When we had a good offing, I reached down and killed the engine. *Tranquility* was terrifically over-canvassed of course, but I didn't know that, so I steered her out of control for Bainbridge Island, which lay about five miles to the west. She covered the distance in a little over an hour (her top speed). It was a fair enough passage I suppose, and since the island was my very first landfall as a single-hand sailor, I took my vessel in close to shore for a look around. There wasn't much to see, just rocks and piles of beat-up driftwood strewn below an unstable cliff. When I noticed the depth sounder reading ten feet, I brought *Tranquility* about in a chaos of flailing sails and whipping lines and headed her back across the sound. *Tranquility* drew six feet of water, meaning she needed at least six feet of water to float. If you take six from ten, you'll have my idea of good seamanship at the time: last-second tacks in shoal water.

A short way back across the sound, I saw a fiberglass sloop motoring south with a lone man at her helm. He was dressed in a southwester hat, big orange gloves and a full suit of yellow rain gear. The sloop hove in close and I waved to her skipper, he looked old and pissed off about something –he didn't wave back. This became a frequent sight for me on Puget Sound: a sailboat motoring with her sail covers on, in fair winds and following seas with thick diesel exhaust blowing out in front of her as she plodded on her way. *Who cares about that guy! I just sailed my very own boat across Puget Sound!* I thought to myself with sudden cheer as the sloop and island receded in the distance. Indeed, it seemed huge to me at the time. I might as well have sailed around the world that day, for how good it all felt.

About a quarter of the way back to the mainland, I started hearing a consistent splashing sound next to the boat...*Dolphins?* Nope! When I glanced over my left shoulder, I saw a steady stream of water issuing from a through-hull fitting on the port side. *Must be a little rainwater in the boat* I thought to myself, remembering that *Tranquility*'s cockpit drained into the bilge, not overboard. The sound continued for half an hour or so, but I paid it no mind –until we passed mid-channel. That's when *Tranquility* started getting a little too hard to handle. It took two hands on the tiller just to keep her on course, and if I let her wander for a second, she would instantly round up into the wind and flog her sails. I was perplexed by her behavior, until, for some reason, I slid the companionway open and peered into the dim cabin.

Dear reader...what do you suppose I saw down there?

How about a foot-and-a-half of seawater sloshing back and forth between the bunks? The water was so deep, the floorboards were afloat. The *very* floorboards Buddy pulled up only days before, when he pointed out *Tranquility*'s stout construction! Instant all-hands-on-deck alarm, cliff-hanging-bad-dream terror, a generous helping of self-loathing dread –all are good expressions to use here. Honestly though, until you have seen that much water in a boat you just bought, or any boat for that matter, there really isn't a great way to describe the feeling it evokes.

I suddenly remembered I had no skiff!

I flew on deck, cast off the halyards and clawed the sails down, lashing them to the main boom and lifelines with quick-as-a-flash square knots. I jumped to the control panel, started the engine with shaking hands, and motored *Tranquility* full speed ahead for the mainland. With the boat back on an even keel, the second bilge pump kicked in, and by the time I made it into the shallows off West Point, the cabin was free of water. I figured I should still investigate though, so with *Tranquility* bobbing along a hundred feet from shore, I went below and took a look in the bilge. At that point, I expected to see water pouring into the boat through a sprung plank. Instead, I drifted downwind for an hour, watching an inch of seawater slosh back and forth over the keelson and ribs in time with the yawing of the boat. She didn't seem to be taking on any more water, so I chalked the whole thing up to a fluke and went back out sailing. *Tranquility* was a perfectly fine boat for the rest of the day.

She's probably just settling in.

I decided it would be wise to keep the whole thing to myself.

When I pulled up the floorboards the next morning at Bayside Marina, I found the same inch of water in the boat. I knew it was the same inch, because the tissue I tacked to the planking above the waterline in the bilge the night before was still dry. So there you have it. *Tranquility* had a "leak" but she wasn't *leaking* leaking...and after buying and installing a pair of the biggest automatic bilge pumps that would fit under the floor boards, I put the threat of sinking far from mind. Anyway, I had more important things to worry about that day: I had to fix the shift linkage in ten minutes.

How innocently did that repair begin? I remember it like it was yesterday: I grabbed a pot of grease and got a few hand tools together, I jumped on deck, and opened the hatch in the cockpit floor. This gave me access to the transmission and the propeller shaft. While observing the critical grease points on the linkage, I rotated the shift wheel through forward, neutral and reverse. I didn't have to do it a second time to find the problem. The hard shifting wasn't due to a lack of lubrication like Buddy thought –far from it. It was due to the fact that the entire engine and transmission were moving a couple of inches up and down on their mounting timbers, depending on what gear you were selecting. Hoping the motor mount bolts were merely loose from six decades of service, I slid into the cramped engine compartment, put a wrench on one of them and gave it a full turn to the right. As it was tightening down, a rust-colored paste oozed around the bolt as it bit and then spun in the nothingness of punky wood. Thinking this would be easily fixed with a much larger fastener, I loosened the bolt enough to get a pry bar under it. Then, working from side-to-side with the bar, I slowly extracted a rusty, needle-tipped, crooked witch's finger from the rotten engine bed. The other three bolts were in similar shape. When I removed the last of them, a trickle of water, evidently under some sort of pressure, began to issue from the hole. I wasn't sure where the water was coming from, so I jammed a piece of kitchen sponge down the hole with a screwdriver. That stopped it, so I forgot all about it.

It was pretty clear I was going to have to build a new engine bed before shoving off for California, so after lunch that day, I pulled the motor and transmission out of the boat using the main boom and a block-and-tackle. I hoisted the one-piece propulsion unit through the companionway, swung it over the port side and lowered it into a dock cart. I chiseled out the rotten engine timbers (the stringers) and pitched them in the marina dumpster. John—friend of the human race and ever willing to lend a hand—showed up the next day and helped me manhandle the motor into my car and down into the basement of the house I'd just moved out of (I planned to paint the block, rebuild the carburetor and adjust the valves while building the new engine bed). I didn't have anywhere else to work on it and my old landlord was kind enough to lend me the space. The man on the sailboat one slip over saw what I was up to, took a liking to me, and told me that a shipwright ran a shop close to the marina. On my neighbor's suggestion, I paid this man a visit the very next day. However, I didn't go there to hire him or to ask for any sort of guidance, as my neighbor advised. I went there for Honduran mahogany —about two-hundred-dollars' worth of it. *I've built a roof, a bedstead, a few theater sets...what's the difference?*

"Doing a little planking?" the shipwright asked as he rang up the rough, 4/4 boards on a carbon pad fished out from under a fragrant pile of wood shavings on his workbench.

"I need to build some motor mounts," I said, heading for the door with the first load of boards, which, incidentally, were entirely the wrong stock for the job I was about to do.

"Where do you keep your boat?" the shipwright asked. I gave him the name of the marina and then politely made it clear that I didn't have a whole lot of time for idle chit-chat that day.

A colossal mess was brewing back on the boat. Rotten bits of oil-soaked wood littered the cabin, the deck and the cockpit sole, leaving little dark stains on the teak parquet there. Much of the gear from the cockpit lockers, engine compartment and lazarette (stern locker) had been moved to the dock to make room. The boat was strewn with styrofoam food containers, tools and dirty rags. Some of the Bayside men would wander down to my end of the dock and stand by the bow or walk out on a finger pier to watch me work. Other than my neighbor and his wife, few had anything nice to say.

I went to work with a will, didn't know what I was doing, and quickly hit a snag: the old bed and the engine had been fastened to *Tranquility*'s hull in a way that wasn't quite clear. The mounting bolts appeared to have gone completely through the hull to the outside of the boat —as in, underwater. I pictured the pointy ends of four big lag bolts protruding from the hull at rakish angles and that seemed impossible...so I came up with a clever work-around. I decided to build the new engine bed directly on the keelson (the main timber running underfoot down the center line of a wooden boat). I designed the new bed so that its sides would rest partly on the ribs and planking for lateral support, while the main weight of the engine and transmission would be borne by the keelson. When I was satisfied my design would work, I spent a couple days building and installing it. The engine bed seemed pretty solid when

I was finished...that is, until I was tightening down the last bolt and heard a loud crack somewhere deep in the hull. I looked down and saw that the lowest mahogany plank, the very first one I installed, was broken cleanly in half. Fixing it required doing the job all over again, but since I was getting the hang of being a shipwright, the re-do only took me another day and a half.

The real shipwright showed up at the boat just as I was putting the finishing touches on the new, new engine bed. He was a big man, about fifty, dressed in a flannel shirt and work-worn overalls. He had a pencil stub over one ear, unkempt curly hair and a pair of dusty reading glasses tucked in his bib pocket. He stepped aboard *Tranquility* without asking, and peered into the engine compartment where I was making final adjustments. He took one look at me and my handiwork and said: "You might as well pull all of that crap out of there and start over with a little help from me." If you've ever been in a similar situation, and I'm sure you have, you'll know there's only two choices a guy can make at a moment like that: start over, or forge ahead. I silently pondered my options. The Albin was sitting in a dark basement, the boat was torn apart and I was running out of time and money. I stood up in the engine compartment and kicked the side of the bed a few times to demonstrate its stoutness to the shipwright, then I politely declined his help.

"She'll hold pretty well," I told him.

"Sure," he said.

Although I rushed through the engine work and the installation, it took twice as long to put the boat back together than it did to take it apart. There were a thousand little problems and unforeseen difficulties. A critical bed bolt was too long to go into the hole I drilled for it, and since the bolt couldn't be shortened and the bed was firmly fastened down, I had to buy a special angled drill motor to modify the hole. For some reason I no longer remember, I needed a huge pair of water pump pliers and a gigantic adjustable wrench, but Seattle Marine doesn't sell China Inc. tools so they were very expensive. One night, I dropped my last 5/8" socket into the bilge and it wound up where no magnet would reach. This happened at a key point in the job, and it was around midnight, so I drove twenty miles through empty Seattle streets to a 24-hour big-box store for a new one. Before I could finish what I was doing that night, the new socket fell in the bilge and joined the other one. From then on, I bought two of everything critical.

Try as I might, nothing in the engine compartment lined up on the first go-around. The exhaust hose was too long, the propeller shaft was too short and a fuel line was in the way of the flywheel –but who could say why? Pages of details, sketches and not-to-be-forgotten sundries were scribbled and crossed out on legal pads. A thick sheaf of industrial-strength receipts accumulated on the galley countertop – recording a hemorrhage of money the likes of which I'd never known. I had no phone at the time, so John was dropping by the boat for daily updates. On one of his visits, over a couple of unreasonably encouraging beers, we came up with a plan for a little overnight boating trip that will forever be remembered as *The Maiden Voyage. The Disastrous Maiden Voyage. The Infamous Maiden Voyage* –whichever sounds best to you.

John Walters was born and raised in Olympia, Washington. He's spent his entire life in the Pacific Northwest and it shows. For instance, take a walk down a Washington beach with him any time of year. There's a speck of a bird bobbing in the waves a few hundred yards from shore. You haven't seen it and never would have, but John is already pointing: "Why, it's a pied-billed grebe! The other one is a hooded merganser! And...oh! Look over there! A marbled murrelet! They nest in old-growth western red cedar!" Take a walk in the woods with him and you come upon a dead tree standing by itself. John reaches up and pulls a few white, lens-shaped mushrooms off the trunk and slips them into the bag he thought to bring along. "Oyster mushrooms...very tasty...they grow on dead alder...that's a dead alder...see the splotches on the trunk? –that's alder." Then he walks over to a low bush, plucks from it what look to you like the bright red poisonous berries from the warning signs in the trailhead parking lot, and pops them into his mouth one-by-one: "Thimbleberries...mmmm...so tasty!" And so on and so forth until you want to be his son or kid brother. John owned, among other carefully kept articles from his childhood, a pair of hiking boots and a small Swiss Army knife that he'd had for the past ten and fifteen years respectively. The knife was still sharp and the boots still fit. We made a Simon-and-Garfunkel-like pair –if the short one was an impulsive auto mechanic and the tall one was an easygoing naturalist with long blond hair.

John was living in Seattle at the time but he spent his summers on the Columbia River in Ilwaco, Washington where he worked for the state as a fisheries biologist. It was spring and he was getting ready to head off to work, so we agreed that I should hurry things up so we could take *Tranquility* on a proper voyage before he left town for the season. With a closer goal than Southern California suddenly in mind, I worked day and night to make it happen. But every evening I thought I was going to be done there was something else to do, and no time left to do it. This went on and on, and slowly but surely, things in the cramped engine compartment began to come together. On the last night of work, the eve of the maiden voyage (of course), I slid the propeller shaft, with its coupler, toward the transmission coupler and lined up the bolt holes. I put the four hardened-steel bolts through the couplers and began tightening them down, one-by-one. This action drew the propeller shaft toward the transmission by minute increments. However, as the two couplers came together it was clear they weren't going to line up *exactly*. The heights were fine, but the mating surfaces were off-center by an inch or two. I remedied this very slight misalignment by shoving the propeller shaft over with my boot while I finished tightening the bolts. I was a decent auto mechanic, not a marine engineer, not a shipwright. *What's the difference?*

5

I did not spend the Friday appointed for the maiden voyage in the way that a responsible captain would have. Instead of thoroughly preparing my vessel and testing the improvements I supposedly made to her, I spent most of the day driving around town with John, who was out shopping for a kayak. I didn't go with him just to keep him company, though. I had an important job to do: I was showing John how to pick out a good boat and he was buying me lunch to say thanks. As it turned out, John didn't buy a kayak that day, or ever after, and I'm pretty sure what went down on the maiden voyage had something to do with it. In fact, after our little weekend trip, John stopped talking about kayaking, and boats in general, for a long, long time, and there's no doubt in my mind that the experience laid the groundwork for one of his wisest and most enduring maritime insights: "It's much better to have a friend with a boat than to have a boat of your own," as he said at the time, and still likes to say, whenever a conversation turns toward anything at all to do with boats. I have no way of knowing if this insight was an original one or not. So let's just say it bears remembering now and at the end of this book, that the purest ironies are the least foreseen, and it wasn't long before his words came back to haunt him.

Around 4:00 pm that day, with an hour or so left until the high tide we were supposed to set sail on, I announced to John in my best captain-to-mate tone, that it was time for us to start thinking about our evening cruise. After a quick run-through of a short to-do list, we decided it would be best to split up, run a few errands on our own and meet at the boat by 5:00 pm. In the meantime, I was supposed to go down to the marina and get *Tranquility* ready to set sail. John was supposed to run home, pack his sea bag and grab some groceries for the weekend.

"No problemo cap-i-tan," John said to me with a little salute as we parted ways in the parking lot of Easy Rider Kayak Co.

When I arrived at the marina that afternoon, things were looking very good for a young Pacific Northwestern man with a boat. Fat salmon were splashing around under the docks, the skies over Puget Sound were clear and *Tranquility* was showing well. Everything was ship-shape and orderly on deck and in the cabin, so it only took me a few minutes to get her ready for our big night. Once I had the power cord coiled on the dock and the sail covers stripped off, there really wasn't anything left to do but sit in the cockpit and wait for John. Like most boat havens at that time of year, the marina was a ghost town packed with the idle vessels of absentee owners and 5:00 came and went without a stir on the dock, a peep from the parking lot or any sign of John. By 5:30 I was sitting at the tiller tapping my foot in irked silence, wishing we were on our way and wondering what the hell was taking him so long. Although I knew it wasn't at all necessary, I decided to pass the time by firing up the engine for a little test run. The old Albin roared to life at the touch of the key and, after a few rev-ups, I dropped the rpm down to a perfect, sewing machine idle, which it managed quite well even though it was stone-cold.

"Engine?...*Check!*" I said to myself. The shifter wheel in the cockpit rolled back and forth with greasy ease as I went through forward, neutral and reverse a couple of times. "Transmission?...*Check!*" Everything was as it should be down in the engine compartment, and it was pretty clear that *Tranquility* and I were not only ready for our maiden voyage, we were ready to set sail for California and I still had a month left! I killed the motor with a self-satisfied smirk and leaned back in the cockpit to wait for John.

A little after 6:00 he came sauntering down the ramp, tall and gangly, sporting a wide smile, wearing a knapsack, and cradling a small brown paper bag in the crook of his arm.

"Hey man!" he called out in his usual relaxed tone, throwing me a long-armed wave from the head of the dock.

"Hey six o'clock!" I hollered, tapping the back of my wrist and jumping onto the float to greet him. "Where's the grub?"

John flipped his long blond hair to one side as he approached and nodded down at the bag he was carrying. This bag was bigger than a kid's lunch sack but too small to hold a loaf of bread and I knew in an instant that John hadn't brought enough for us to eat. John passed me the grocery bag as he climbed aboard *Tranquility* and when I looked inside I saw the following items: one open and partially consumed ten-count bag of corn tortillas; a one-pound can of pre-cooked black beans; one carton of eggs. No more, no less. As far as I knew, there wasn't a single can of soup on the boat, not a sliver of chocolate, a tab of butter or a pinch of salt. I looked up at John in disbelief.

"Dude, are you serious? Is this all the food you brought us for two days on a boat?" I asked, following him into the cockpit, looking in the bag again.

"It's cool man," he replied, giving me a friendly pat on the shoulder as he slid past me on his way down the cabin stairs.

"DUDE!" I said, trying to be polite but authoritative. "This isn't enough food for two days on a boat!"

"Oh...it'll be enough man!" John assured me, in an unconcerned tone as he worked his way through the cabin stowing his gear. "You just want snack stuff," he said. "Besides, it's no fun when you have everything you *need* on an ADVENTURE!"

And so, with those fateful words hanging in the air, we stowed the rest of our gear, untied the dock lines and shoved *Tranquility* off for the Ballard Locks and the wide-open waters of Puget Sound. I'm sure there have been maiden voyages in the history of seafaring that were far more ill-conceived than ours. But dear reader, you must admit...we're off to a pretty good start.

In my view, it was more of an annoyance than a cause for alarm when *Tranquility*'s engine died three or four times as we chugged over to the locks. The old Albin fired right up after each stall, so I assumed there was just some air in the fuel line or a little water in the tank. John, who was up on the foredeck sorting out fenders and lock lines, didn't seem to notice, and, like any good captain, I didn't bother to mention it to him. Anyway, the problem fixed itself by the time we fell in with the other boats waiting to lock-through to Puget Sound that evening.

After a few minutes milling around the bay, we got the go-ahead from the lock master over the loud speaker and our group of boats began hurrying toward the entrance. On our way to the lock, I noticed the gear shifter was starting to get a little stiff again and it was becoming especially hard to shift into or out of reverse in a hurry. Unfortunately, by the time I realized I still had a problem with the shifter, it was too late to do anything about it. *Tranquility* was lined up on the chamber, and the current flowing into it from the lake, combined with our momentum, was carrying *Tranquility* toward the gargantuan entrance doors and the boats in front of them, at something over three knots.

In case you don't already know it, single engine boats, particularly sailboats, aren't all that easy to stop once they have some headway on. With fear flowing freely in my veins, I kept one eye on the vessels directly ahead of us and one on the tach as I rolled the shifter wheel from neutral to reverse, frantically trying to slow us down. Nothing happened. I tried rolling the shifter into forward, hoping to line up the reverse gear (it works in five-speed cars) and again, nothing happened. I yanked the shifter back and forth expecting a horrible accident. There were boats stopping and going wonky right in front of us, there were boats following close behind –but I couldn't slow down or speed up. There wasn't a whole lot I could do about it at the time, except keep the boat going as straight as possible as we drifted toward the entrance without brakes. Luckily, as we closed in on the boats ahead, a path opened up between them. So, pretending not to hear the commands being barked at us by the lock attendant jogging along the seawall 15 feet away, I carefully steered *Tranquility* around a waiting vessel—without acknowledging her skipper—and I slipped her through the lock doors.

My line cutting was met by an angry reprimand from the loud speaker:

"GREEN SAILBOAT! WAIT YOUR TURN!"
"GREEN SAILBOAT! WAIT YOUR TURN!"

But it was too late, and as we drifted toward the far end of the chamber, the reprimand became a plea:

"GREEN SAILBOAT! SLOW DOWN!"
"GREEN SAILBOAT! SLOW DOWN!"

John, who suspected nothing up until this point, was leaning far out over the water with one foot on the rail and a lock line in his outstretched hand. He shot me a wild look as I swung *Tranquility* hard-over for the starboard wall and we went breezing past the first and second tie-ups at an oblique angle. Knowing I missed my best chance to get a line on the wall, but hoping to avert the disaster waiting for us at the far end of the chamber, I rolled the shifter wheel back and forth as hard as I could, desperately trying to find reverse. While doing that, the transmission dropped into forward and bumped *Tranquility* ahead even faster. I instantly rolled the shifter back with all my might, put the tiller hard-over, laid on full throttle and hoped for the best. The old Albin two-banger let out a primal shriek and disgorged a huge plume of black smoke filled with sparkly filaments of asbestos insulation as it wound up to red-line. The transmission dropped into reverse at max rpm with a hull-jarring shudder. The propeller dug into the water, slowing the boat, but the prop over-spun itself a second later, grabbing at nothing in the boiling froth it stirred up. We'd been in the locking chamber about four seconds.

To save herself from a serious wreck, *Tranquility* needed to stop in a hurry and execute a course correction to starboard that would have been difficult in a twin-engine motorboat. Somehow she did it! Reverse gear held and she checked herself at the very last second, coming to a stop with a little uncertain wander just before her bowsprit would've rammed the sea doors. She sat there for a moment with her motor screaming and the propeller gnashing at the water, cavitating in a poisonous milkshake of oil, soot and foam. "Starboard," I said under my breath, "*starboard, old girl.*" The prop and rudder bit the water just then and *Tranquility* began to sidle to the right. She got herself close enough to the wall for John to get a line on a bollard and all of a sudden we were safe. The expectant hush of a barely averted disaster hung over the small locks for several seconds, until it was broken by a concerned word from somewhere along the seawall. This was answered by a couple of nervous chuckles from the boats tying up behind us and that was followed by the banter of relieved boatmen, on-lookers and lock attendants all around. We were *those* guys, we were yayhoos, pogies and soon to be much, much worse.

As we descended to sea level that evening, I revved the old Albin from idle to full throttle and back several times, setting off a series of concussive backfires which echoed off the damp dungeony walls of the locking chamber and set the eyes and silent curses of the other mariners dead against us for all time. I carelessly jammed the transmission from forward to neutral and reverse, over and over again, until I was satisfied that whatever was still wrong with the gear shifter, it wasn't serious enough to call off the maiden voyage. I did not do what I should have done that day, or for a long time afterward, because I wrongly concluded that *Tranquility* was just an old boat that needed a firm hand to guide her. By the time the lock doors opened onto the saltwater that evening, I'd convinced myself that the problem was her, not me. And on our maiden voyage, *Tranquility* went from being an inanimate object to a vessel with a mind of her own.

Puget Sound may not look like much when you see it from the deck of a ferry moving along at a twenty-knot clip, but it's a challenging and temperamental body of water to sail a small craft on. First and foremost, the skipper of a low-powered vessel like *Tranquility* must plan for the strong currents which go hand-in-hand with the fifteen-foot tides the region is known for. That's a lot of water moving around. When the wind blows hard in the opposite direction of the current—which can run up to seven knots—a foul type of confused sea is kicked up which can delay a voyage or put a small boat at risk. *Wind-against-tide* they call it. Puget Sound is nothing to play around with. It's a vast expanse of water, more inland sea than sound in places and the surrounding terrain is generally unforgiving. Shoals extend far from shore in many places, while in others the water is too deep for a vessel to anchor a safe distance from shore. The mainland and islands are heavily wooded, there's hundreds of bays and channels and inlets and passages that all look the same to the untrained eye, making it easy for a novice mariner to lose his bearings. To a beginner, Puget Sound waters can seem as listless or fearsome as the ocean. An anchorage that looks fine one day can turn into a dangerous blowhole the next, as the winds and weather move up and down the sound following the lay of the land. The forests come down to the shores of the sound, the hinterland rivers eat away at their banks, pick up dead trees and carry them to the sea, so there's logs and stumps adrift to watch out for year-round. Several busy ports are in the region, so there's a good deal of shipping traffic to steer clear of as well. You have storms in the fall and snows in the winter, gales in the spring and fogs in the summer. The pleasure-boating season is brief and uncertain, and, even in the middle of summer, the water is dangerously cold.

That is Puget Sound and a Puget Sound sailor is a very good sailor indeed.

And so, with nary a glance at the chart book and only a vague idea of what the tide was going to do to us, John and I motored *Tranquility* through the narrow sea lane, under the railroad bridge and headed her for the sublime and windless waters of Puget Sound. There were certainly no ill-omens to be read in the weather. It was shaping up to be a warm and lovely starlit evening. As soon as we were out of the shallows, we began steering a jolly old course that bent broad away from shore in a way that guaranteed we would be as far as possible, as fast as possible, from safety or assistance, for most of the night. We had no inkling of what was in store for us out there and, in a little while, we were much farther from shore than a minimum of caution would have allowed us to stray.

Tranquility

Tranquility was a fairly small vessel so John and I were seldom out of speaking range as we motored over the placid water that evening. A boat casts a fast-acting spell on landsmen and we were soon trying to outdo each other with witty, old-timey sounding sea-banter and jockeying for authority by pointing out lapses of seamanship that needed to be immediately corrected. We then gravely relieved the responsible party from his turn at the helm so he could go fix his mistakes. For instance, when the captain pointed out that a portion of someone's gear was improperly stowed, he took over the tiller with a meaningful nod while the other man put the tidy to his belongings. When the captain announced that he was going to switch off the emergency radio, due to an uninterrupted spell of heavy static, the other man greedily offered to steer while he attended to that important task. Perhaps someone just wanted a hat or sweater, a sip of water or a look through the binocular...? Well then, the other would steer, but also try to think of a reason to stay at the helm a little longer after the errand was run.

It has been said, and a daysail on busy waters will prove it, that when any two sailboats—no matter how unfairly matched—meet on the water, it's a yacht race. The sea is a legendarily difficult environment to survive in. Seafaring takes every worthy skill of man, and the deck of a sailboat, where nothing goes unnoticed, is the stage for an intricate way of life. If the competitive nature of seamanship can pit a square-sided Sacramento River hay scow against a fleet-footed Sausalito sloop in a sailing race...then what do you imagine it can do to two greenhorns cooped up on a tiny boat together? John and I were good friends, but we were young and out to prove ourselves, so time spent at the helm meant rank on board –regardless of who was supposedly in charge. It was all done with a laugh of course. But irreverence in the crew, when combined with incompetence in the captain, is a volatile mixture.

When we reached the middle of Puget Sound, we left our westerly heading and motored into the north with the sails up. However, we didn't know the true meaning of *north* or *west* yet and as the evening wore on, we began steering an ever-changing course for a dim and distant landmass which seemed to move and change shape before our very eyes. We learned later this was the southern end of Whidbey Island which lay about 13 nautical miles away. The newly turned ebb tide, which we also knew virtually nothing of, began doing its very best to take us there: bow first; stern first; when we thought we were sailing elsewhere; when we thought we were dead in the water, etc. At that point though, we had no idea there was anything unusual about our little evening cruise. I'm sure John and I thought we were doing exactly what any two mariners in the world would do on a maiden voyage. That impression proved to be short lived.

After a fairly aimless hour of motoring, John and I turned our attention to an enormous red and black freighter that appeared out of nowhere in the distance off our stern. She was coming up on us from out of the south and she was footing it fast. John, who was steering when we first saw her, was soon facing dead-aft watching her approach. We kept our eyes on the ship for a long time, transfixed by her steady progress, but it was impossible to say exactly where she was headed. One minute she seemed to be coming right for us and the next, she looked like she was going to pass far to the west. Yet all the while she drew nearer...or seemed to. It was pretty hard to tell, because the movements of the distant ship were soon influencing our own wandering course. When she veered a little to port, *Tranquility* veered a little to starboard to stay out of her way. And when she veered a little to starboard, *Tranquility* veered a little to port –all but guaranteeing a confrontation. As captain, I knew my job was to do nothing, act nonchalant at all times, and choose my words carefully. So it was John who spoke up first. He whistled through his teeth and said: "Just *look* at that thing! Do you think she even *sees* us?" Based on our relative speed and heading, I figured the freighter saw us and was going to pass a half-mile to the west and therefore posed absolutely no danger. I made up my mind that we were okay and I issued an authoritative, "Chill-out, bro" to John, who didn't seem put at ease by it. Then I hopped below deck, where, from a concealed location, I watched the approach of the ship through a porthole with growing apprehension. Ten uneasy minutes later, there was absolutely no doubt about it. The freighter was bearing down on us! And I had to do something quick...but what?

Hoping John wouldn't catch on, I casually drifted around the interior of the boat looking for landmarks through the portholes and, for the first time that evening, I took a close look at the chart book. Judging by the position of the freighter and the broad contours of the land around us, it was more than likely we were in the middle of one of the shipping lanes. I jogged back up the cabin stairs, sat in the companionway and informed John, in a matter-of-fact tone, that the freighter was probably "just some northbound traffic" that would stay in her sea lane until she reached the Pacific Ocean. I was the captain after all and I thought I should speak in easy tones when sharing my vast knowledge of ships and the sea with John, who was still learning the ropes. *No need to alarm the crew!* "Head a little more to starboard...if you want," I said, substituting picnic-boat ease for the alarm that was edging into my voice. John *seemed* like he wanted to head a little more to starboard, however, he pulled the tiller toward himself instead of pushing it away and *Tranquility* began a long, lumbering turn to port, and headed in the general direction of the freighter.

"BACK! BACK! BACK!" I hollered.

"I *am* back!" John said testily, leaning on the starboard lifelines with the tiller against his chest to show me how *back* he was.

"BACK!! BACK!! BACK!!" I yelled...but it was too late. *Tranquility* performed a broad yawing turn in the direction of the ship, settling onto a collision course with her for a few thrilling moments before carrying through with a three-sixty. Vital time was lost, and an almost imperceptible change in the freighter's heading meant that even if we steered at perfect right angles to her, she was going to pass by us very close. John brought us around into the east and did his best to keep out of her way with careful steering. Silent tension lingered on board until it was apparent that the ship had indeed "seen us" and had taken corrective action long before. Still, she drew near enough for us to feel the thrum of her engine and see the rust streaks on her hull and house. She came and went with the ponderous, rolling gait of a fully-laden ship. She was riding so low in the water that her anchors were splashing in her bow wave. She passed a safe distance to the west of us –but that wasn't the end of it.

"Get a load of those *waves*!" John said, marveling at the steep wake thrown up by the ship.

"Get a load of that *wake*," I curtly corrected him.

Wakes or waves, there was a rank of them gaining on our port quarter. They multiplied and steepened as they approached and anyone in their right mind would have wondered what they were going to do to tiny *Tranquility*, whose stern sat so low in the water. My blasé attitude toward our near miss with the freighter encouraged John to sarcasm and as the first of the waves approached our stern, he uttered a now infamous phrase: "*IT'S...AHHH...ROLL...ER!!!!*" he crowed, turning to me for a laugh. It's a multipurpose punch line that has stood the test of time, and we both cracked up.

When the first and largest wave in the set curled over John's head, he was sitting in the cockpit with his wrist dangling nonchalantly over the end of the tiller, smiling wryly at me —clearly satisfied with his remark and the hilarity it brought to the tense situation. But when he saw my eyes shift from his gaze to the crest of the wave looming over him, John turned around, and what he saw behind the boat gave him a start. Thinking the wave was about to break on deck, as I was, John abandoned his station in a single bound, leaving *Tranquility* to steer herself at full speed under power. He jumped out of the cockpit and into the companionway and we cowered there watching helplessly as *Tranquility* rose up the face of the wave, stern first.

"DUDE!! WHAT ARE YOU *DOING* DUDE!!??" I finally yelled, shoving him out of the way, falling into the cockpit as I reached for the tiller.

At the top of the wave, the boat yawed wildly and sheared off to port before dropping off the back of it and down into the trough with a bottomless, rearing lurch. The sound of crashing dishes and other items cast adrift in the tilting cabin hinted that all was not well down there. I was spilled in the cockpit, unable to see much, but I got hold of the tiller and pulled myself up by it. We were still motoring at full speed when the second wave lifted *Tranquility* up and shoved her ahead with an exhilarating Tahitian rush. She hit her stride and surfed down the face of the wave with a huge uncontrollable slew to starboard. Everything in the boat shifted in the opposite direction, and the Albin sang a high-note as the propeller lost its bite in the speeding sea. It was a moment of utter chaos and if you'd been standing on deck just then you would have been pitched overboard before you could think to hold on. I got to my feet as the third wave passed under us and I steered *Tranquility* off to starboard, idling the motor, gradually easing our motion as the last of the wake swooshed past.

When it was over, John turned to me shaking his head in wonder and let out a huge, very relieved sounding: "DUDE!!"

"DUDE! DUDE! *DU-UDE*!!!!" I said, in a grave indignant tone. "Don't ever leave the *helm* dude."

"Dude, take it easy! We're totally fine man!" John said, unconvincingly, trying to reassure both of us.

"Dude!!!!" I added.

"DUDE!" John exclaimed, obviously quite alarmed still.

We really couldn't manage much more than that for a few minutes. But oh-so-much-more was still to come!

We got our wits about us after a little while, dropped the slatting sails and resumed whatever course we thought we were steering that evening. We chugged along at a slow speed, taking turns driving and putting the cabin back in order. There were a couple of broken dishes on the floor and some silverware had hit the deck. The binocular, someone's clothes and a few books had gone flying, but other than that, there didn't seem to be any real damage. That is, until I brought *Tranquility* back up to full speed and felt a heavy vibration coming from somewhere deep inside her. A minute or two later, there was a distinct grinding sound underfoot and I noticed a wispy, foul-smelling gray smoke wafting around the cockpit lockers. Trouble was brewing down in the engine compartment.

I ducked into the cabin and opened the engine hatch. The motor seemed to be running fine in there, so I hopped back into the cockpit and lifted the floor hatch. When I did this, I noticed the brass pull-ring was much warmer than it had ever been. That part of the mystery was solved when I reached down and touched the top of the transmission. It was burning hot. A fresh dread came on in panicky waves. Without looking up, I reached for the ignition switch and shut off the motor. I had to use a folded up rag for a pot holder when I pulled the transmission dipstick out and what I read on it was sobering. It was bone dry and sporting the shiny blue-black shades of newly seared steel.

"Not good," I said under my breath.

"What?" John asked.

"We're a little low on oil bro," I mumbled as I maneuvered into the tight space between the burning transmission and the port side of the hull. I held a flashlight under my chin and, by squeezing and straining around hot iron flanges and snaking hoses, I managed to top up the transmission fluid. I didn't realize it until later, but as I poured in that first quart of bright red transmission fluid, an equal, although much darker amount, was trickling onto the new engine bed from somewhere underneath the motor. Anyway, the burned up transmission didn't matter as much as I thought it was going to.

After topping off the transmission, I closed the cockpit hatch, started the motor and slowly brought *Tranquility* back up to hull speed. The boat felt and sounded much better, and for several minutes, it looked like we were on our way again. I was almost beginning to relax when I happened to glance down at the engine gauges. The rpm, oil pressure and hour meter all seemed fine, but the needle for the temperature gauge was missing and I thought it had fallen off. Then I noticed the bright white wand tip. I hadn't seen it because it was leaning far to the right...it was resting on the little black peg just past the red zone. I *dove* for the key and killed the motor. I threw open the cockpit hatch with a vengeful bang and saw that the lever on the cooling water valve (the seacock) was shut. I must have leaned on it when I wedged myself into the engine compartment. The unrelieved suction in the cooling water hose, which lead from the seacock to the pump on the engine, had caused it to collapse along its entire length. John, who was in the cabin thumbing through the chart book of Puget Sound, came to the companionway when he heard the commotion.

"What's up, cappy?" he asked.

"Just checking some stuff out, bro," I said, reaching down to pull the lever of the seacock open. When I did this, a swoosh of ice-cold saltwater shot through the winding hose, popping it back into shape as it filled, and then percolated in, the overheated engine block.

There was even more trouble when I tried to restart the Albin. When I turned the key, I heard a loud click below deck and the cabin light over John's head flickered and went out. The lamp relit and glowed weakly when I switched to the spare battery bank, but when I tried to turn the engine over, nothing happened. Apparently all of the batteries on the boat were dead or dying —even though we'd been motoring all evening and were supposedly charging them. Not that that was terribly important either! One look at the creamy black-and-white meringue coating the engine dipstick told me that the old Albin had a blown head gasket...or a cracked block. Either way, it never ran again. By never, I mean for all eternity.

"What's the *deal*, man?" John asked, flipping the cabin light on and off a few times as the filament dimmed from yellow, to orange, to amber before going out for the rest of the voyage.

"The motor just blew up and the batteries are all dead, bro."

" *Yeah, right!* " John guffawed, "SURE MAN!" but when he saw the look in my eyes, he fell silent and turned his attention back to the chart book. Before I knew it, I was spitting out a parade of profanity that would've made a convict blush and I was slamming the flashlight on the cabin top.

"WHOA SKIPPER!" John hollered, poking his head out of the cabin again. "Take it easy before you break something else! We might need that flashlight pretty soon you know." It was probably a good thing Buddy was going to be out of town for a while, because, as John liked to say: "If Buddy ever finds out what you did to his boat...he's going to kill you."

When I calmed down enough to think clearly, I went up to the foredeck and hoisted the main and genoa. It was a fairly windless evening and the sails hung from the mast and forestay, gaunt, wrinkled and doing nothing for us. I went back to the cockpit and plopped myself down at the tiller –totally deflated and feeling very sorry for myself.

"What if you cook some grub for us while I try to sail?" I suggested to John after a little while.

"What do you want for dinner?" he asked.

I showed John how to use the antique galley stove as the sun went down that evening. I'd only used it once or twice myself, so I went over the steps with him three or four times and then quizzed him on its operation before handing him the matches and the tin of alcohol.

"I got it man," John said, rolling his eyes when he took them from me.

"Seriously?" I asked, holding on to the matchbook a little before letting it go.

"No problemo cap-i-tan."

From the cockpit, I watched John crank open the can of black beans and dump them in a small saucepan. He arranged four of our six corn tortillas in the bottom of a skillet and set it on the galley counter. A good captain learns to give his crew responsibilities that are balanced with privileges. He cannot do everything there is to do on a long voyage, so he must delegate whenever he can. Green crew members need to feel like they're taking part in things, it's good for morale. John was an experienced camper and knew his way around a pressurized stove, so I left him alone while he cooked dinner. Instead of micromanaging, I turned my attention to a zephyr that was spreading out on the water nearby, dimpling the surface of the sea as it wandered around *Tranquility*. It passed through her rigging, gently filling the mainsail, causing it to jibe slowly across the cabin top. When this happened, a bight of line hanging from the main boom caught the smoke stack of the Tiny Tot and pulled it off-kilter. I went on deck to free the line and straighten the stack. From there, I saw that one of the jib sheets, which had been dragging limply around the foredeck, was wrapped in a similar fashion around the anchor, so I went up to the bow and cast that line off as well.

Except for a cross-sound ferry lit up like a cruise ship, there wasn't another boat to be seen for miles. Dark blue inland waters stretched in all directions toward heavily-wooded headlands, rocky beaches and mysterious coves nestled in passages that led to who-knew-where. Except for the occasional cat's paw, the surface of the sea was perfectly flat and smooth. The lights on shore began to twinkle and shine in the distance. Deep blue skies reared overhead mixing little-by-little into obsidian as nightfall in the east crept up to the last of the sunset hanging over the purple, snowcapped Olympic Mountains to the west. A tight formation of red-footed sea ducks zoomed past the boat in a soundless black blur of papery wingbeats. They leaned into a steep bank just off the bow, broke apart as they hit the water, then dove out of sight with little squawks and splashes. Thin clouds, white on top and fiery on bottom, floated high overhead, tearing into gauzy tendrils that meandered and disappeared in the darkening sky. I drifted back to the cockpit and lay myself down on a thwart. The maiden voyage may not have been going very well, but I still had a boat and I was on my way somewhere in her that summer. And that, dear reader, is something for a young man to look forward to.

I heard the first *whoosh* move through the boat but ignored it. The second *whoosh* was followed by an *"A YEEE!"* from below deck. I sat up and peered into the dark cabin. John was perched on the forward bunk, straddling two columns of blue flame which leapt from stovetop to ceiling. He was stoking the fires with alcohol, poured from a small styrofoam cup and blowing on his fingers between flare-ups. He looked like a boilerman in the bowels of a steamship bound for Hades...step one didn't appear to be going all that well.

"Dude, are you sure you can handle that thing?" I asked.

"It's cool man, I'm still priming it," he assured me, tending fire, reaching between the flames to work the hand pump. I lay back down, stared up into the night sky and dozed off for a few minutes. The next thing I knew, a brilliant white light flashed somewhere out in space. Pots clanged, then crashed out of something's way...something that was moving really fast. When I opened my eyes, I saw a body rushing toward me, then over me, trailing a bright arc. John was in the cockpit –and he was on fire. A long blue flame was climbing up the left sleeve of his purple polar fleece. It reached into his armpit and curled over his shoulder. John windmilled his burning arm, fanning the flames as I danced around him screaming like an eight-year-old girl, patting them out with my bare hands. He stepped to the rail, put a leg up and started to jump overboard.

"NOOOOOH!!" I yelled in the half-light.

John looked into the black, ice-cold water, reconsidered, and began squirming out of the flaming sweater while shaking his arm up and down trying to put out the fire. His eyes were crazy, an abject expression of pain on his face. I smelled burning hair and knew John should have jumped overboard. Then, on one frantic up-swing of his arm, the flaming sleeve separated from the garment just above the elbow. It trailed gummy tendrils of melting purple plastic along his forearm as it sailed overboard and landed in the sea with a hiss. John dropped flat on deck in a single motion and plunged his arm into the frigid water.

"MAH...FAH...YAH!!!!" he moaned, writhing from side-to-side face-down on deck.

"MAH...FAH...YAH!!!!" he moaned as I smothered the low blue flames wafting on his back with a life preserver that was handy. The whole thing only took about five seconds from start to finish.

John was pallid, sweating and looking positively shocky. In a perfect world, I would have immediately administered first aid –but the boat was on fire and I had to deal with that. It was a scene from a maritime comedy of errors. I jumped down in the cabin, tore the fire extinguisher from its bracket, pulled the pin and let it rip. There were flames all around the stove nook and two tall rocket-jets were shooting out of it, they licked and spat at the cabin top, bubbling the paint overhead. The styrofoam cup John had been holding was a flaming blob of rank incense burning a divot into the cabin sole and, for some inexplicable reason, my sleeping bag was on fire in my bunk. The extinguisher on *Tranquility* was small, but it got the job done in a *jiffy*. When the fire was out, a chalky blizzard of retardant settled in the cabin and a little yellow cloud of it followed me around the boat and out to the cockpit when I brought the first-aid kit to John's side. The medical kit I assembled for *Tranquility* was bulky, well-stocked and expensive to put together. John had watched me work on it and made fun of it nearly every chance he got. When he saw it he'd often say: "Man...if you can't fix what's wrong with you with a roll of gauze and a piece of tape...you're a goner anyway!" He didn't crack any jokes when I slathered his arm with prescription-strength anesthetic: Xylocaine gel 2%, injectable –it's good to have around. I was happy I could do something to make John feel better –but what could anyone have done for me? Nearly run over; complete engine failure; no power; fire at sea and one man down. The maiden voyage was a catastrophe and it wasn't even half-over yet!

So there we were...drifting north into the night, without running lights, on an out-going tide, aboard a boat that looked like a torpedo hit it. We had a marine radio to call for help, but no power to run it. We didn't even know where we were! I was pretty shaken up and John lay in the cockpit moaning and sweating. I thought of shooting off a couple of the emergency flares, but there was no one around to see them. Besides, what were we going to say if someone came?

As time passed, the night began taking a serious toll on morale. John was completely out of commission and I was cold and starving. So I put a jacket on and tried to get something together for us to eat down in the pitch black cabin –but the stove wouldn't light (it never worked properly again) and my flashlight went out after a few minutes of trying. Hoping to shed some light on our ordeal, I took out the old kerosene lantern that came with the boat and tried to figure out how to work it. Unfortunately, as I was releasing the blackened globe to clean it, the lantern sprung from my grasp and bounced off the main traveler, ejecting the globe and spilling kerosene all over the aft deck. The globe wound up perched at the rail; when I reached for it in the dark, my fingers tipped it overboard and it fell into the sea with a liquidy plop.

"Was that the globe man?" John asked feebly.

"Yeah, dude."

"I smell kerosene," John said nervously.

"I know, some got spilled, but it's cool bro."

"Unghhh," John moaned in first-degree pain.

At that point, our best option was to continue drifting slowly but surely into the 1800s aboard an old wooden sloop on a night so still you could have lit a candle on deck, if only you had one.

A little while later the moon came up and it turned into a beautiful, sparkly clear night. John was feeling a bit better by then, so we ate our supper of cold beans and stiff tortillas in the cockpit, talking quietly and peering at the chart book in the moonlight. We'd taken a keen and anxious interest in our position since the fire and we were both keeping an eye out for helpful landmarks and a certain yellow buoy that we thought we'd seen just off the bow (in reality, we were miles from it). Nevertheless, after supper, while still drifting north at around half-a-knot, I thought I saw it again. I ran up to the foredeck to try to make it out, in the hope that it would give us some idea of our position. Going forward, I was relieved to see the buoy bobbing in the sea about a hundred feet up ahead. Although we were nearly dead in the water, it seemed to me like we were approaching it pretty quickly —*too* quickly perhaps, it was like it was moving toward us. Then, just as the buoy was almost close enough for me to get a good look at it, it sank.

"The BUOY just SANK! John!" I shrieked aft, believing anything was possible on a night like that.

"HOLY CRAP!" John croaked.

Then the buoy re-surfaced a moment later, clearly visible in the moonlight twenty feet away.

The buoy was a whale.

And the whale was checking us out.

"John! Get up here dude!" I yelled. Just as he joined me on the foredeck, the whale dove and swam underneath *Tranquility*, passing below her keel on the port side of the boat. We saw her go by together, trailing quicksilver bubbles and bright green phosphorescent pixie dust. She was plainly visible, snout-to-flukes, in the crystal clear moonlit water. John put his good hand on my shoulder, we turned and looked at each other in amazement. John has always maintained that this whale saved our maiden voyage —and I believe him. Nearly twenty years later, all either of us has to do to conjure up that mystical moment is say: *The Whale*. Indeed, after we saw the whale, our thoughts turned toward the positive in life and we began to talk of the adventures that were sure to come on my "solid old boat."

The whale definitely got us moving forward again. John dressed his burns and I consulted the chart book in the moonlight for fresh hints to the meaning of the landmasses we could barely make out. My best guess was that the headland the current was carrying us toward was Double Bluff on the western shore of Whidbey Island, and the cliffs that were darkening the sky low on the horizon could be none other than those surrounding a large bight in the island's southwestern shore known as Useless Bay (yes, it's actually called Useless Bay). It was the closest shelter for miles, so I decided we should try to make it there and drop anchor for the night.

Tranquility's purchase price did not include a skiff, so the first week I owned her, I bought a 10-foot inflatable boat and an old, but good running, Evinrude 18-horse outboard motor to power it with. We'd been towing this little boat behind us all evening and it occurred to me that we might be able to push *Tranquility* to Useless Bay by tying the skiff alongside her and running the motor. That's exactly what we did and we cheered ourselves when it actually worked! A couple of hours later, with great relief, we brought *Tranquility* into the bay and dropped anchor for the night. We did this in the usual manner of inexperienced and exhausted boatmen, that is to say, without making sure the hook was set, without knowing the water depth around us, our position, or how much anchor line we'd let out. Since we had no electricity and no lantern to speak of, we set no anchor light –perfect. I'm here to tell you, there's no better mix for a manifestly unsafe voyage than a starry-eyed fool, his best friend and an obstinate boat!

We cleaned up the cabin as best we could in the dark, made up our bunks and, after agreeing to head back to Seattle as soon as possible, we hit the sack like dead men. As I drifted into a fitful sleep that night, I had a vision of *Tranquility* resting on her beam ends (her side) high up on a sandy beach. That wasn't as troubling of an image to fall asleep to as it sounds. Rather, I told myself if the boat wound up wrecked the following morning –then so be it. In my mind, as long as nobody ended up dead, the whole thing had been worth it. *Forget California! I've had five grand worth of adventure in the last six hours!* It will surely come as no surprise to anyone who's ever seen, or heard, or read of the sea, to learn that it's no place for a pessimist. The utter indifference of the sea to every human endeavor is too easily mistaken by a pessimist for hostility toward him. However, an experienced sailor will know, it is the half-made plans of an optimist that the sea enjoys undoing the most.

We awoke early the next morning to an uncomfortable ride and the sound of rough water slapping the bow. When I went on deck to have a look around, I saw endless ranks of steep, closely-spaced waves topped by white caps charging up the sound. The waves were being driven into the north by a stiff, twenty-knot southerly wind. "Dude," I said to John, "we have to get the hell out of here," and there was certainly no arguing with *that*. It was Saturday morning and John was supposed to be on a Columbia River dock, inspecting salmon for the Washington Department of Fish and Wildlife first thing Monday morning. It was a fact he'd reminded me of every hour or so since the batteries went dead. But it had been a long night for both of us. We were still pretty beaten up by the first leg of our maiden voyage and neither of us was all that eager to begin round two. We were also starving, so, before doing anything else, I coaxed a wide, sooty flame from the stove and sort-of cooked our dozen eggs over it. We ate them, six each, in one go, out of the pan –gulping down the bland meal with a cold, paraffin-flavored tortilla and a cup of foul-tasting boat water.

"See dude?" John said half-seriously, "I told you we had enough food man."

Resigned to a long day without sustenance or comfort of any kind, we hoisted sail, hauled the anchor up and got under way.

Outside the minimal protection of Useless Bay, the wind was a bit stronger than I thought and *Tranquility* took off into the west making just under five knots. The wind was southerly of course, and that was a serious problem for us, because you can't sail a boat, much less a sixty-year-old one, directly into the wind –or even close to it. You must sail her at alternate angles to it, tacking back and forth. You reach your destination in a flanking manner if it's upwind of you, and if you happen to be headed in the *precise* direction from which the wind is blowing, as we were, that can be a long and arduous process. So we sailed west, because that was all we could do, and we went clear across the sound on our first tack, making pretty good time of it too. However, once we tacked back into the east, I noticed a slight problem with our progress. We were doing a lot of heavy-weather sailing, but we weren't going *south*. Halfway back to Whidbey Island, I realized we were slightly *north* of where we anchored the night before, meaning we were farther from Seattle than when we set sail. Leaving John at the tiller, I went below to confirm our position on the chart —but the water lapping at the edges of the floorboards drew my attention first. I casually slid the companionway hatch closed and quietly put a hundred strokes on the hand-operated bilge pump so John wouldn't know we were also sinking.

We left Useless Bay that morning at, or near, max ebb and the current and the wind were carrying us north faster than we could sail south against them. We were losing so much ground on our way back to Whidbey Island that we barely made it into the north end of Useless Bay. John, who had even less sailing experience than I did, was unaware of our plight.

"We're not going anywhere bro," I said when I went up on deck and took the tiller from him.

"What are you *talking* about man? We're jamming!" John said as he hoisted himself up to the high side of the cockpit and braced his feet against the opposite thwart. He was clearly enthused by the spectacle of the full main and genoa, which were pulling us along at hull speed over the heaving, wind-blown sea.

"Dude...no we're not! The current is *killing* us!" I hollered over the wind. John looked this way and that, trying to get his bearings. He began to speak, but crouched at the rail instead. He looked north and south and east and west, then into the frothing wake.

"We're going backwards man!" he yelled.

There was only one thing to do. We dropped the sails, brought the skiff alongside *Tranquility* and fired up the engine. It's pretty easy to move a small sailboat on a calm night with an 18-horse —even one mounted on an inflatable. But in the wind and chop that morning, the lightweight skiff began flying off the tops of the waves. Every so often, the propeller popped out of the water which made the engine over-rev dangerously. We needed some ballast in the skiff, so I asked John to ride in it —which he did. It took us forty-five minutes, running at wide-open throttle in separate boats, just to get back to where we spent the night.

We sure as hell couldn't stay *there*! So John and I motored along the shores of Useless Bay and headed for the south end of the island. We met with a favorable wind there and began sailing for land under the main and genoa. It seemed like we were making pretty good progress for a couple hours and our spirits began to lift with each passing mile. When the wind shifted against us in the early afternoon, I asked John to bring the skiff alongside so we could motor some more. He knew the drill pretty well by then and once he had the inflatable secure on the starboard side, he jumped into it and got the engine running. He stayed there for a minute, steadying it, as *Tranquility* got up to speed. The weather had improved as the day wore on and the skiff seemed under control, so John climbed back aboard and lay down in the cockpit for a nap. An hour or so later, as we neared the mainland, we ran into some heavy chop and the skiff began to plane and veer around. It was bucking and slamming into the hull so hard I thought it was going to upset.

"John," I said, shaking him awake and looking into his tired eyes, "we need some ballast in the skiff or she's gonna flip over man."

We both knew what had to be done, but instead of cheerfully complying with my order, John stayed curled up on the thwart and said: "Why don't you jump down in there yourself...*skipper*?"

I ignored John's insubordination and calmly explained a certain reality to him: "I can't do that right now, *dude*, I'm trying to sail this boat back to Seattle for us."

John thought this over for a moment or two before mumbling a cavalier and mutinous reply: "I can get this boat back to Seattle without your help...*man*." The next time I heard words to that effect uttered over the keel of one of my boats, I was offshore and the crewman who spoke them—a heavyset man I'd met that same day—was unfolding a big buck knife that his friend just handed him. I suppose even unflappable John had his limit. Be that as it may, *god and man have both decreed there can be but one captain to a ship* so I pointed into the skiff and looked straight ahead. Any questions? Of course not. What could he do at that point? Commandeer *Tranquility*? So in he went, trailing the wrinkled, sun-faded blue tarp he'd been using for a blanket. He was soon fast asleep in the bottom of the tossing skiff.

For my part, I took the first of many long, zoned-out watches that were yet to come that summer. Eventually the tide turned in our favor and the wind cooperated, so I shut off the engine, woke John up and we hoisted sail together. By-and-by we made our way south along the eastern shore of Puget Sound. I taught John how to sail that day and when we began to make out the white forest of masts that identify the outskirts of Ballard, he shot me a look of admiration, jumped to his feet with a smile and began vigorously patting me on the back.

"We're gonna make it!" he yelled.

"We ain't there yet, bro," I replied, trying to manage both of our expectations after that disastrous night.

By the time two o'clock rolled around, John hadn't mentioned anything about lunch, but I'd been having hunger pangs for the past couple hours. So, I gave him the tiller and went on a desperate search for grub down in the cabin. This yielded around eight ounces of stale honey-nut granola that I found in a bag tucked underneath a galley drawer. We devoured this greedily with no talk of an extra portion for the captain. We looked like two half-crazed castaways on a wooden raft by then! My hair was grime-filled and standing on end, my face was sunburned and salt crusted. John was bandaged, haggard-looking and wearing a sweater with one of the sleeves burned off. The rest of the day passed slowly, with many hoistings and dousings of sail and running the skiff alongside or trailing it astern. We didn't see a single boat that could lend us a hand or give us a morsel to eat. It was a long, hungry day with not so much as a teabag in the larder to take the edge off. We ran the outboard out of gas and had to siphon what little was left in *Tranquility*'s main tank. We blended this cloudy fuel with straight 30 weight motor oil to lubricate the outboard, which burned a special mix of gas and oil. We pressed on in that manner, hoping the engine wouldn't seize.

We didn't know we were going to pass right by a fuel dock so, by using our last *quart* of gas very, very sparingly and by exploiting every favorable eddy and breath of wind that came our way, we eventually locked into Salmon Bay and slowly motored *Tranquility* to her berth as the sun was setting. As we were coming into the marina, John emerged on deck with his sea bag and, the second *Tranquility* touched her slip, he stepped over the lifelines without a word and headed up the dock. He turned to me, walking backward and said: "Don't be surprised if I don't go sailing with you anytime soon."

He definitely had a point –John always has a point.

We'll catch up with him a little later.

6

The maiden voyage was a complete disaster and I awoke the next morning to a wreck of a ship. She was burned inside and smelled of hot machinery, melted plastic, kerosene and boiled battery acid. Everything in the boat was coated with a yellow patina of fire retardant. I took one look around the cabin and knew that all of the hard work and expense of the past month had come to nothing. Actually, it came to less than nothing, because with no engine, no batteries and no stove, *Tranquility* was significantly worse off than she was the day I bought her. I should have given up on the voyage there and then! That thought never crossed my mind of course. I was filled with the gamboling, can-do spirit of a young man, so I ignored the root cause of the setback, blamed the boat for everything and convinced myself that all *Tranquility* and I needed was a fresh start.

I went through the boat from stem to stern that day, cleaning and organizing. Everything aboard was mustered and sent out to the dock for a hardhearted review. Much of it wound up in the dumpster. I mended the charred shell of my sleeping bag and sanded the burn marks from the cabin floor and stove nook. I pulled all four of the heavy, lead-acid marine batteries out of the electrical box and slid them through the companionway and into the cockpit. Replacing them all at once would have emptied the ship's purse, so I planned to buy them one at a time: different brands; different terminals; different configurations—whatever was on sale—no mistakes spared there! As I put the boat back together that day and swept up the last of the extinguisher dust, I reminded myself that trying things before you're ready for them is part of what it means to be young. Although I had fresh evidence to the contrary, when I imagined what life was *really* going to be like once I set sail, I remained optimistic and dreamy: the effortless freedom and mile-making of a yacht running before the trade winds; the casual worldliness and vagabond confidence of sailors living by their wits in faraway places; the peace and serenity when man, ship and sea become *one*. Indeed, it seemed that paradise lay just over the horizon –all I had to do was set sail for it. When I compared the bold new direction I was about to take in life to the usual misadventures men are apt to go on in their early twenties, I knew I could do a whole lot worse than to buy a sailboat and go on a little summer voyage in her...no matter how it turned out!

There are some youthful indiscretions that no amount of luck or time will ever make light of however, and I still cringe when I remember I set sail that summer in a leaky old boat. I should have known better and I didn't. But why? I've tried to get back into the mind of that young man, to try to understand why I gave so little thought to all of the old tropes that rightly and wrongly describe owning a boat, and why I didn't even consider that there might be some truth to what everyone but me already seemed to know: *a boat is a hole in the water that you pour money into; boats, especially old wooden sailboats, are a lot of work; the two best days of a sailor's life are the day he buys his boat and the day he sells it* –and so on and so forth. I know there's no excuse for what I did. All I can say is this: I was young and stubborn and assumed nothing bad was ever going to happen to me. So, instead of reconsidering my cruising plans after my hair-raising maiden voyage, I committed myself wholeheartedly to them. Is there anything new in that?

When the first of May rolled around, I immediately got to work on an endless list of errands, repairs and upgrades that all had to be done before setting sail. I went back to work fixing cars, raised my prices to an obscene level and spent every minute of my spare time down at Bayside Marina, where I became a controversial figure. To begin with, I wrote off the Albin entirely and built an ungainly mahogany motor mount on *Tranquility*'s transom, where I hung the Evinrude 18 that saved our bacon on the maiden voyage. In my view, this clever work-around solved *Tranquility*'s propulsion problems for all time. However, the unsightly addition of a gigantic, space-race, 1968 short-shaft outboard to the stern of a classic yacht begged for, and received, the instantaneous and unanimous disapproval of the entire marina. The shipwright laughed out loud when he saw it and never spoke to me again. A dock wanderer pointed out that the propeller was too close to the surface of the water to push the boat in anything bigger than a one-foot swell. Another man warned me that the first cross-sea I got into would rip it off the boat and take *Tranquility*'s transom along with it. I ignored each and every one of these naysayers and dream smashers, because they weren't there when John and I were fighting for our lives off the iron-bound shores of

Whidbey Island. So what did they even know about it? They were probably just jealous!

By mid-May, everyone at Bayside Marina had heard about the know-it-all kid who was planning to sail the little green sloop down to California that summer, and almost everyone had something snarky to say about it. The only person who defended or encouraged me was the kindly man who owned the sailboat next to mine.

"Some people in this marina don't think you're ever getting out of here, but I believe in what you're doing kid," the man said to me one afternoon as he was hosing down the deck of his well-kept fiberglass cutter. "I have a little something I want to give you for your trip and the wife and I want to have you over for dinner before you set sail."

"Gee...thanks!" I replied, brimming with goodwill toward a fellow sailor.

Once I had the outboard squared away and the bungee cords pulled tight over the fuel tank I mounted in the cockpit, I sorted out the too-tall batteries, too-short cables and wrong-sized terminals in the electrical box. Then I turned my attention to the galley stove. I lugged that contraption to a local repair shop (it wasn't Sure Marine) and paid them $450.24 of my hard-earned cash to fix it. As I said before, it never worked again. So when I got it back and realized it had a whole new set of problems (fuel leaks...*really* bad ones) I pitched it in the Bayside dumpster without a second thought and bought a twenty-five-dollar propane crab pot cooker to replace it. This was a fairly dangerous device in its own right, and I was warned it was meant for outdoor use only, but it could boil a pot of water in about a minute and only had *one* moving part. Anyway, the crab pot cooker ended up being the only piece of equipment I ever installed on *Tranquility* that worked as expected every time I used it.

The one thing never far from my mind as I prepared to set sail that spring was *Tranquility's* intermittent leak. So, one morning, after devising a clever plan of action, I set out to find and fix it from *inside* the boat. How fondly do I remember that day? Beginning in the bilge at the base of the mast, I worked my way forward and aft with a package of brightly colored kitchen sponges. Tearing off little bits of them to use for plugs, I stopped-up the limber holes and waterways in the bilge, isolating the different areas of the boat. When the forepeak, cabin and engine compartment were all separated from one another by dams, I sucked all the water out of the boat with a shop-vac. When *Tranquility* was dry, I crawled back and forth over her floor timbers, peering into the bilge, looking and listening for spraying water or some other obvious sign of her leak. Before long, seeps of lake water started finding their way back into the boat, but they came from everywhere and nowhere. Dime-sized puddles began to collect down at the frame ends and they turned into pockets of standing water on either side of the keelson by the end of the day. That wasn't what I was looking for, nor was I bothered by it. Wooden boats of a certain age and pedigree are prone to leaks. It's a fact of life. Anyway, I didn't need to know whether *Tranquility* was a perfect boat or not, I needed to know why one minute she was completely fine, and the next, she was full of water.

When I checked the bilge the following morning, *Tranquility* had her usual inch of water in her and I was back to square one. I'd been living on the boat for several weeks by then and knew the automatic bilge pumps were only running for a few seconds every ten days or so, but just to be sure the pumps weren't covering up a *serious* problem, I vacuumed her out again and turned them off. No water lapped at the edges of the floorboards that day, or the next, and when I checked her a week later, there were only a couple more inches of water in the bilge than usual. *If Tranquility's leak is that slow, then what would account for a foot of water in her when she was under sail?* This did not seem like it was going to be an easy problem to solve by the first of June. Anyway, after my tests, I concluded that whatever was wrong with *Tranquility*, it wasn't serious enough to call off the voyage. Although a leak is an unfortunate thing to have in a boat, I was fairly certain the one in *Tranquility* could be kept in check with her new bilge pumps and batteries. I just had to keep an eye on her was all.

In case you don't know it, boats, especially old wooden sailboats, are a magnet for unsolicited advice and unwelcome visits from oddballs, cranks and misfits. As spring progressed and foot traffic on the docks picked up, a number of these strange folks came out of the woodwork and descended upon me. One afternoon, as I was minding my own business putting the final touches on a button-down tarp for the cockpit well—a clever solution of mine intended to keep boarding seas out of it—a man stopped by on his way down the dock and yelled at me: "Don't you know the first goddamned sea that hits this boat is going to rip that thing to shreds?!"

Another strange fellow dropped by *Tranquility* one day and invited me over to the locks to watch salmon come into the bay to spawn. He looked normal enough, but I was busy and politely declined his offer. Although I didn't know this guy from Adam, he grabbed my arm and tried to pull me down the dock with him, saying: "Come with me! I'm going to buy you lunch!" When I pulled away and stepped back to clobber him if need be, he hissed at me: "Come with me right now! –or I'll sink your boat!" It was pretty unsettling. Anyway, I'd been hoisting sails and cranking on winches and hauling things in and out of the boat for weeks by then and I was in fine shape. So when I made a fist and punched it into my hand a couple of times, he turned, ran up the dock and disappeared in the parking lot. I was on edge and didn't stray too far from *Tranquility* for a couple of days, but thankfully, I never saw him again.

Another man dropped in on me one evening while I was doing a little electrical wiring.

"Did you solder all of your connections kid?" he asked in a huffy tone without even saying hello. It was a question that apparently didn't need an answer, and before I could speak, he walked away, tucking a bottle of rum under his arm, shaking his head. By the way, if you're one of these know-it-all men, take it from me: try a little tact and someone who needs your help might actually listen to you.

The most memorable fellow I met that spring was a skinny man of about thirty with shaggy brown hair and a sun-worn, rat-like complexion. He walked up to the port side of the boat and struck up a conversation with me as I sat in the cockpit whipping lines. For the most part, these men have no real interest in you or your boat. They do not properly introduce themselves and they don't really care if you're busy or not. They're there for themselves; for catharsis; to live vicariously in what you're doing; to correct your mistakes or to satisfy themselves that you're actually a dim-wit who's about to get himself killed.

"I used to own an old wooden sailboat too," the man informed me, squinting up at *Tranquility*'s masthead and taking measure of her fore and aft. "That's how I got this," he said, cocking his head to the right, pulling back a shock of hair to reveal a nasty scar running diagonally across his forehead and down his left cheek. This was *his* thing, he probably walked the docks every spring to share his story and bother people.

"Yikes!" I said, leaning over the rail to check out the scar. "How'd you do that?"

"The boat did it to me...I was in a *terrible* storm"–I'm *so* sure– "and my mainsail *exploded!* They can do that at any time, you know?"

"Really?" I asked. I'd never heard of such a thing, but this man was living proof. A sail is under a fair bit of strain when it's full of wind, and if something were to go wrong...say, if the sail suddenly burst a seam or flogged itself to shreds, it made perfect sense that the pieces had to go somewhere –so why not through your face? I tried to picture it, but the scar seemed too deep and jagged to have been made by wind-whipped canvas.

"Yeah, it was pretty bad! I went on a helicopter ride that day," he said, "so I always wear a helmet whenever I go sailing."

"You wear a helmet when you go sailing?" I asked, wondering if I should add one to my list.

"Yes I do," he said. "You can never be too careful out there you know." I made a mental note of that.

And how they opined about the voyage to come! It was *shameless.* Everyone, whether they'd sailed down the west coast or not, had something pithy to say about the trip. On Friday, the consensus in Ballard was that I should stay close to shore in order to duck out of the weather at a moment's notice. By Monday, it was best for me to stay at least sixty miles offshore...because that's where the most reliable winds were to be found. A few days later, I needed to head out at least a hundred miles, in order to "get out past the continental shelf" because that's where the "calmest seas" were. And everyone—from circumnavigator to barstool captain—told me that all I would have to do when I reached the North Pacific Ocean that summer was "turn left" and put the winds and seas behind me. They claimed the northwesterly winds were the most reliable winds in the world and they blew down the west coast of North America without fail, all summer long, making the trip from Washington to California a "milk run" and a "two-week-long daysail" that was "all downhill." When is the best time of year to fall in with those fair winds and following seas? Some said any time after the first of June. Others advised me not to try it until mid-July. August was popular for a while that spring, but definitely not after the first of September –unless late August had been unusually pleasant, however, some people do like to do it in October...and so on and so forth, until I made up my mind to figure everything out on my own that summer.

An older gentleman that stopped by *Tranquility* for a chat one pleasant spring evening actually had something interesting to say: "I used to have a boat very similar to that one there," he said, nodding at *Tranquility*, striking up a friendly chat with me from the head of her slip. "It was back in the fifties...my father bought her for my brother and me when we were about twenty years old, I guess. We sailed her clear across the Pacific the first summer we had her too." This was the first *real* yarn I heard aboard *Tranquility*.

"Your dad bought you guys a sailboat out of the blue one day?" I asked, going forward, taking a seat on the hatch.

"Well..." he continued, "it was on the condition we sail her over to Hawaii by ourselves...my dad wanted us to earn that gift I think, and it ended up being quite an adventure."

In my mind, it was one thing to harbor-hop down a coast on your first big voyage and quite another to sail across an ocean. I'd spent some time thinking about safety since my trip to Useless Bay, and I was researching emergency equipment: radios; parachute flares; survival suits and satellite homing beacons that let the Coast Guard know you needed to be rescued at the flip of a switch. So, hoping to get a feel for what I might need on my own voyage, I asked this man about his.

"What sort of radio did you guys have on your boat?"

"Radio? Hmm...let me see...well, I don't think we had a radio, or even a battery, now that I think of it...our boat was pretty basic, like yours, only much older."

"Did she have any cabin or running lights?"

"We used kerosene lamps."

"What did you guys do when you wanted to get some rest at night?"

"Well, if the weather was nice we kept sailing, and if it was nasty out, we pulled the sails down and hit the sack."

"That's a pretty long trip," I said. "You guys steered all night long when the weather was good?"

"Well, you know...it was the *damnedest* thing, but that old boat could sail herself for days on end...if you had everything set just right with her, there were some nights we didn't even go up on deck."

"Whoa...that sounds great! So uh, what did you guys do for food in those days?"

"We fished and ate canned beans and peaches."

"Charts?" I asked.

"Maybe two or three."

"Wow! That's awesome! And you guys made it over to Hawaii all right?"

He thought about this for a moment before answering: "Sure we did! –*after* the knockdown. That wave damn near sank the boat. She filled up with water so fast!" He was evidently recalling aspects of the voyage for the first time in many years.

"So you learned a lot on that cruise?" I asked, weighing the prospects of my own voyage in the back of my mind.

"Well, yes and no," he said. "We had way more trouble on the waters between Seattle and San Francisco than we ever did going over to Hawaii."

"Really? You don't say?"

"There's a lot to learn out there, kid."

If you haven't earned your anchors yet, you might want to read that last line again. Because, of all the half-wit, third-rate advice I've been given in all my years of sailing since, that one did me the most good.

I may not have altered my cruising plans in any meaningful way after the maiden voyage, but the ordeal left me with a clearer, if somewhat incomplete, picture of the sorts of things that can go wrong on a boat. And like many novice mariners, I prepared for them by spending money. I shipped enough food and stores for six months at sea without touching land; I bought a spare genoa and a storm jib, solar desalinator, extra fuel and water jugs, axe, hammock, two brand new kerosene lanterns, skin diving gear, spear pole and fishing tackle. If my provisions ran out or spoilage set in, I had a razor sharp, 7-foot-long seal harpoon on the boat. I made it from an old oak oar, it had a break-away halibut head, a lanyard and float. I once had occasion to hurl it at a shark –she flew straight, men.

At some point that spring, I made the mistake of dropping by a franchise marine supply store. These places are all the same, so it's most likely the one you're thinking of: they sell overpriced anchor chain, pre-cut dock lines, fancy but affordable sailing attire and cheaply made plastic doodads to people who don't know any better. And they're very good at it. Although I was there for the least expensive marine-grade GPS money could buy, I ended up pushing a shopping cart out to my car that day. In it were some of the things that make modern boating so safe and enjoyable. On the advice of a scratchy-voiced, some-time seafarer who worked there for the discount, I bought, among other things, an autopilot capable of steering a 35-foot sailboat and an expensive SSB radio receiver. The radio was no larger than a paperback book and ran on AA batteries, but it was guaranteed by its maker to receive high seas weather reports anywhere, on any ocean, day or night. These seemed like good things to have along on the voyage and I planned to figure out how they worked as soon as I was underway.

They say on the sea that a boat is never finished and they say that a novice mariner is never ready for his first big voyage. He can prepare himself and the boat as much as he likes, but there will always be something more to do on a ship and something more to learn about the sea before shoving off. If a sailor tries to prepare himself at the dock for every need or mishap that he can dream up, an academic paralysis lodges in him that any serious sailor will instantly recognize. If a novice mariner is prone to morbid thinking or allows fear of the unknown to take hold of him –that is, if he lets a reasonable measure of caution become an obsession with safety and preparation, then no amount of radars, water-tight bulkheads, life rafts, charts, sails or money will ever be enough to let him set sail in confidence (I was a long way from knowing any of this). If a sailor ever wants to leave the stifling safety of the harbor behind him, he must learn to cross out unnecessary items from the endless lists of improvements that he and his vessel "need." He must do so, not just prior to the big voyage, but on the way as well.

No one *has* to go sailing of course, and there's a reason why goods and people don't travel by sail, for the most part, anymore. The whole thing is about hope now, not practicality. When someone sets sail these days, they're setting sail for adventure, novelty and a touch of the supernatural. Those are enticing but difficult things to fully prepare for. Anyway, when you think you're ready to shove off, the sea, and all its tricks and dangers, will be waiting for you just outside the harbor. The very first wave that slaps the side of your boat will tell you whether you're ready to be out there or not. I was certainly no one to emulate, and there were many more things I should have done before shoving off that spring, but I did everything I reasonably could at the time to prepare for my voyage. This took longer than expected, as always, and it was mid-June before I was ready to set sail. Before leaving Seattle though, I took my neighbor up on his dinner offer.

The man and his wife, who were in their late forties, lived in a modern condo close to the marina. When I rang their bell the night before I was planning to shove off, they welcomed me into their home with hugs and cheerful well-wishes. While the man cooked dinner, the wife took a motherly approach to me, asking how I was doing, how the boat was coming along, the state of my finances and what my itinerary was.

She turned to me at one point during our conversation and said, in quiet confidence, gesturing to her husband with a little nod: "You know he really wants to go with you."

I was touched by this and it set the tone for the rest of the evening. We ate heartily and threw back the whiskey. My voyage was deemed a success—there and then—due to the simple fact I was actually setting sail the next day and not just talking about it like a desk-jockey would. All sorts of positive predictions were made about the cruise –among them, that I'd meet a young blond along the way who would sail down to California with me. The husband and wife were both experienced mariners, and they told funny sailing stories over dinner that ended with little lessons I would be wise to keep in mind on my voyage: *don't make landfall at night; know your position at all times in coastal waters; shorten sail when you first think of it; double check your navigation.* This was the right sort of talk to have before shoving off on my first sea voyage and I really listened to them. As the evening wound down, we drifted into the living room and sat around the coffee table for a last cup of cheer and some final words of wisdom. All in all, it was the perfect send-off, and as I was thanking them and getting ready to head for the door, the husband snapped out of a yawn, jumped up from the couch and went into the next room. He returned a moment later, carrying a heavy sheaf of papers.

"I have a little something for you," he said, as he set the thick bundle down on the coffee table. When I opened it, I saw that it was a full set of nautical charts covering all of the water between Seattle and the Channel Islands –principal rivers, anchorages and harbor charts included. It was an unbelievable gift that left me speechless.

"I've always wanted to do that trip, kid," he said, smiling at his wife, who reached out and put a hand on his knee. "But I got married instead." It was a real moment...and it was the first time I'd seen a complete set of charts for the waters I was bound for. There were around thirty of them and I realized it was a hell of a lot farther from Seattle to Santa Barbara than I thought. There were also long, unbroken stretches of shoreline in Oregon and California without a single sheltered bay or a settlement of any kind. In some places, the nearest roads were several miles inland. That was real ocean and that was a lonely, inhospitable coast.

7

When Ballard saw me last, I was driving into a strong northerly wind, hunkered down in *Tranquility*'s cockpit, wearing a blue river rafting helmet and a nylon safety harness around my waist, because I couldn't figure out how the shoulder straps went. I reached Puget Sound later than planned that day and instead of free-wheeling California sailing, I found myself pounding into a cold headwind and a newly turned flood tide. *Tranquility* was making the best of our ill-timed departure, gamely plodding along in her signature fashion, losing a little ground on each tack as the wind and current carried her south faster than she could sail north. Still, it was the proudest day of my young life. Of course there had been setbacks and unforeseen difficulties that spring—none of which were *my* fault—and it took me longer and cost me more to get the boat ready than I expected. But I reminded myself that it had only been three months since I first dreamed up the voyage. In that short time, I'd bought a boat, fixed her up and was on my way somewhere in her. That was a *sensation* to me at the time.

There's nothing in the life of a sailor quite like the outbound leg of his first real sea voyage. There's no pride like the pride he feels when he sees his vessel down on the docks with her sails neatly furled, and he knows he's about to embark on a great adventure in her. It's a king-crowning moment the first time you muster enough courage to leave the safety of the land behind you, the first time you watch your home port disappear over the horizon without fear. The first night at sea, the first dead calm, the first big blow and the first mesmerizing landfall –there's just something about your first voyage that stays with you forever. And if somewhere along the way you happen to leave a little blood in the sea, or the sea gets into your blood, there's a part of you that never comes home.

Although I wouldn't have traded places with anyone that day, I wasn't leaving Seattle quite as cleanly as I thought I was going to. In early-June, the Bayside scuttlebutt had it that the shipwright said if I ever managed to set sail for California, *Tranquility* and I would never be heard from again. Then I found out he bet someone I wouldn't even make it as far as Neah Bay that summer. Those are fighting words to a Pacific Northwest sailor and I knew I had to prove him wrong in a big way –and

I did. But we'll get to that part of the voyage later. First, in order to understand why an experienced mariner like the shipwright would wager that a novice sailor with a marginal boat might perish or give up on his voyage long before reaching Neah Bay, one needs to know what lies between the relatively protected waters of Puget Sound and the North Pacific Ocean. Like the St. Lawrence River on the east coast, this part of North America is little known outside the region.

Although its actual dimensions may be quibbled about, taken as a whole, Puget Sound is a vast inland bay that runs north and south through western Washington for about ninety nautical miles. Depending on where you choose to measure from, it's one, five or thirty-five nautical miles wide. Most of the sound is broken up by peninsulas, islands, inlets and canals. It's bound on the west by the Olympic Peninsula and on the south and east by mainland North America. The majority of vessels entering or leaving the sound do so by way of Admiralty Inlet, a north and west facing channel near its northern end. The Pacific Ocean lies about eighty nautical miles to the northwest of Admiralty Inlet and those eighty miles are not usually, but should be, divided into two very different bodies of water –both of which must be crossed in order to reach the open sea. Moving from east to west, the first of these is a large, complex inland bay and the second is a long, inclement ocean strait that serves as the far western border between Canada and the United States. These two bodies of water are incorrectly referred to as a contiguous strait. I have no idea why this is, because an eighth grader can tell you the difference.

The large inland bay, bound on the south by the Olympic Peninsula, and on the east and north by Whidbey Island and an extensive archipelago, is a few hundred square miles of water bristling with marine-grade dangers. Offshore rocks, strong tidal rips, sandbanks, low-lying islands, reefs and shoals are found in all but one or two of the main routes that lead into or out of the bay. The areas that are free from obstructions are busy shipping lanes and convergence zones used by pleasure boats, freighters, fishing vessels, ferries and other marine traffic bound for the Pacific Ocean, Puget Sound, British Columbia and Alaska. The winds and seas and fogs that sweep into the bay from the Strait of Juan de Fuca have come from the open ocean and present a formidable obstacle to small, low-powered vessels heading west. As strange as it may seem, this inland bay bears no specific name on most nautical charts of the region, so for the rest of this story, I'll refer to it as the Salish Basin, because it most certainly isn't a strait.

If you make it to the western edge of the Salish Basin in one piece, the narrow, unwelcoming waters of the Strait of Juan de Fuca await you. The straits, as the Strait of Juan de Fuca is locally known, connect the Salish Basin (see how nice that sounds?) to the North Pacific Ocean. The straits run in a northwest to southeast direction for about fifty miles and vary from eight to twelve miles in width. They're bound on the north by the bluff, broken shores of Vancouver Island and on the south by the jagged off-lying rocks and stony beaches of the Olympic Peninsula. The straits are known for heavy shipping traffic, big westerly winds, fast moving fog and steep, crowding seas. Strong currents run through the strait and the long stretches of mostly uninhabited coastline that border it to the north and south offer meager protection from the prevailing conditions. Westbound vessels traversing the straits must take the winds and seas directly on the bow, eastbound vessels take them on the stern.

Neah Bay, for its part, is a wind-blown, fog-bound port of refuge at the far western end of the straits. It's about five miles east of Cape Flattery, the headland at the northwestern tip of the Olympic Peninsula. Neah Bay is the principal settlement of the Makah Nation, whose members have occupied the region since time immemorial. In strictly nautical terms, however, Neah Bay's doorstep-of-the-sea location makes it a popular last stop for pleasure craft on their way to the Pacific Ocean, as well as a first port of call for vessels heading inland from the open sea. If you know anything at all about the waters of the Pacific Northwest, you know that no one in their right mind would go anywhere near Neah Bay in an unseaworthy boat. Neah Bay is the sort of last-chance harbor where sailboats limp in after big blows and are abandoned or immediately put up for sale by their terrified owners (the port sells these boats for past-due moorage from time to time) and any novice sailor who wants to live long enough to earn his anchors would be wise to steer clear of the area until he gets his sea legs –preferably, by sailing elsewhere.

But the shipwright's words burned in me as I prepared to set sail that June, and I decided to prove his predictions wrong by sailing every inch of the way from Ballard to Neah Bay. Not only that, I vowed to sail the entire way to California as well. Lying in my bunk at night before shoving off, I thought of ways to let the shipwright know a thing or two about my epic voyage. I settled on mailing him a photo of *Tranquility* anchored in Neah Bay and another of her alongside the dock at St. Francis Yacht Club in San Francisco. No note, no nothing, just two pictures of the boat, featuring the outboard motor. To me, sailing all the way to Neah Bay meant that I could only use the wind to get there, and I planned to hold myself to that rule with the following exceptions: I could motor a short distance (only at right angles to my course) in order to enter or leave port, and I could motor to avoid imminent danger, say, if a ship were about to run me down. But I forbid myself to motor in the direction of Neah Bay *or* California, just for the sake of mile-making.

To that end, I carried on sailing back and forth off Ballard on my first day of the voyage, and the wind and current drove *Tranquility* farther and farther in the opposite direction of the Pacific Ocean. I was very happy to be on my way despite the conditions, and a couple of miles south of Ballard, I tied the tiller amidships and dashed below to grab a bite to eat and a hot cup of tea. *Tranquility* kept herself on a straight-enough course while I did this, and I ate my first meal of the cruise on the high side of the boat, making little course corrections with my foot on the tiller. Other than the contrary wind and current, it seemed like I was off to a fair start.

After lunch, I passed by an older fiberglass sloop that was bucking into a steep wind chop just north of Eagle Harbor on Bainbridge Island. She had her sail covers on and her fenders dragging along in the water. When her skipper—who was done-up like an arctic explorer in a bright orange exposure suit and snow goggles—noticed my helmet, he gave me an enthusiastic thumbs-up. I was dropping a brand new salmon lure over the side just then and pretended not to see him. *Why don't you try sailing, poser?* I said to myself under my breath as I let my tackle out behind the boat on two hundred feet of braided line meant for albacore tuna fishing. And so, I spent most of the first day trolling for salmon and sailing back and forth across Puget Sound between Eagle Harbor, Elliot Bay and West Point.

It was a long afternoon slogging against the tide, and by the time the current turned in my favor, I was exhausted and the wind was turning light and variable. *Tranquility* was almost stalling in her tacks and I should have anchored somewhere for the night, but I felt I had to make it a few miles north of Ballard on my outbound leg. So I sailed on, ghosting my way north, inch-by-inch, short-tacking under a full main and genoa.

Tranquility

A sudden rush of adrenalin shot through me just south of Ballard, when I noticed my troll-line veering and dipping behind the boat. I threw the lashing back on the tiller, jumped to the aft deck and gave the tuna cord a cruel yank. The line went wild. "FISH ON!" I yelled at the top of my lungs, pulling the line in hand-over-hand as a nice-looking salmon sheared and jumped and dove behind the boat. The action was a big boost to morale and, as *Tranquility* sort-of sailed herself abreast of West Point, I hoisted a bloody, flailing fish into the cockpit. With that, I became a sea gypsy, making do on nothing other than Neptune's bounty and my cagey wit.

Since I was making northerly progress for the first time that day, I left the lashing on the tiller, pulled out my brand new serrated fish knife, and began cleaning my catch under sail. As I was slicing the belly of the salmon open, I heard some splashing in the water and looked up just in time to see *Tranquility* glide past a large log floating just below the surface a few feet from her port side. It trailed a beard of moss, was pockmarked with propeller dings and streaked with red and blue bottom paint –attesting to a long career ruining voyages. Such logs are a constant and completely unpredictable threat to small vessels plying the waters of the Pacific Northwest. Unless they're floating vertically, with most of their length below the surface (called a deadhead, and dangerous in its own way), drifting logs have the tendency to align themselves parallel to the wave train, which makes them nearly invisible from the low decks of a small boat. The log I passed that day was minimally buoyant and impossible to see until you were right on top of it. Even when you're maintaining a proper watch, a drifting log can sneak up on you out of nowhere. One good way to spot them is to look for an orderly line of bright white seagulls perched side by side on the water. Seabirds alight on floating logs from time to time and the behavior is a tip-off.

I barely felt it when the knife sliced through the top of my left hand –just a faint burning sensation when the salmon did a death heave. But when the razor-sharp serrated edge went bumping over the first knuckle of my ring finger, I almost puked. I pulled my hands out of the fish without looking at the wound and washed them over the side. As I sat in the cockpit with the sails flapping, applying direct pressure to the cut, a wave of panic shot through me from head to toe. This was followed by a long, dark spell of nauseous tunnel vision. When I noticed blood dripping onto the toe of my boot I knew I was probably going to need some help. This was a woeful and complicated proposition. I pictured going for a short trip in a Coast Guard boat and wondered if a thousand-dollar ambulance ride would also be involved. Either way, I'd be spending the evening getting stitches in a Seattle-area hospital. *What to do with the boat in the meantime?* An ominous series of turns began playing out in my mind, each leading to a new problem or delay. This morbid thinking went on until I remembered the anesthesia and suture trays in the first-aid kit. I'd stitched myself up before, but something about doing it on the first day of my voyage gave me pause. Accidents never happen until they do, and the sea isn't for sissies, so what needed to be done needed to be done. After a few minutes of deep breathing, I took a peek at the damage. It was a clean cut, right down to the fat and white bone –about an inch long. The knuckle was out and it was bleeding big-time.

I brought the first-aid kit out to the cockpit and worked fast. I irrigated the gaping wound with saline, flooded it with iodine and daubed it dry with sterile gauze. I rinsed the surrounding skin with a damp compress and, after applying a stinging coat of tincture of benzoin to help them stick, I drew the gash closed with a few butterfly strips. I dressed the hand with polysporin, gauze and waterproof medical tape. After a short rest and another cup of tea, I looked in the chart book for somewhere other than Ballard to spend the night. There weren't many options, so I set my sights on a small cove about five miles north, on the eastern shore of Bainbridge Island. I spent the rest of the evening sailing there and dropped my hook just before dark. The cut probably looked worse than it was...but still!

I set sail the next morning on a northerly wind with an outgoing tide and as soon as I hit open water, I knew it was the *Bon Voyage* I missed out on the day before. It was a brilliantly sunny day, although not as warm as it looked. Air isn't warmed directly by the sun; it takes on the temperature of whatever it's blowing over. To the north of Puget Sound there's little more than fjords and glaciers, snow-packs and icy straits. So the wind was cold and heavy –like usual on Pacific Northwest waters. It didn't help that I was bundled up in blue jeans, a painter's cap, a poly-cotton sweater and thin rubber boots. *Tranquility* didn't seem to mind the cold; she leaned into the stiff breeze under a full main and genoa and took off sailing like a boat half her age. The Puget Sound was navy blue and glistening, the clouds were driving and the wake was swishing, the hinterlands and islands turned malachite green, the snowy mountains to the east and west hovered over it all in the silent, crisp spring air. There was no steep wind chop, no white caps, no countercurrent to lag us, and not another sail to be seen on the water. I sailed into the north, tack after glorious tack, and with the current helping me for the very first time, the sound was mine to master. I even got a horn blast from the captain of a ferry, and a crowd of passengers bunched up at the weather rail to snap pictures and wave at us with the arms of their infants in the blustery wind. Landmarks, headlands and a lighthouse hove into view, drew abreast and dropped astern in a timely manner. I was beginning to find out that *Tranquility* was an unusually difficult boat to steer in any sort of wind, but she took pity on her injured captain that day. She handled well-enough and kept her bilges dry. California didn't seem all that far away.

The tide must have turned against me at some point, but I never noticed because the wind held strong into the late afternoon. The north sound is nice and wide which makes for easy sailing, and there isn't a whole lot that can stop a young man on a day like that. So, instead of looking for an anchorage as the sun went down that evening, I switched on the running lights and cooked up a big pot of potato-salmon stew under heavy sail. The wind came down after dinner but I kept on past sunset with no particular destination in mind. By 11:00 pm, *Tranquility* was ghosting on faint airs into a dark, starry night with her red and green sidelights shining on the damp genoa. Sometime after midnight, when I was too tired to keep my eyes open, I hopped into the cabin and consulted the chart book under a lamp. As luck would have it, I was less than a mile from Admiralty Bay. This is a large bight on the west coast of Whidbey Island that offers excellent protection from northerly winds. It was the best anchorage for miles around, so I motored into it—guided by what I thought was the lighthouse on Admiralty Head—and dropped anchor in shallow water.

That night I dreamed *Tranquility* was laying on her side in a rain puddle in the middle of a shopping center parking lot. I'd sailed her up a roadside ditch to get in there, but I couldn't get out for some reason. Just as I was putting my shoulder against her hull to push her toward the ditch, the shopping center turned into a small boatyard. The shipwright was there and we were working on an old wooden ketch together. When he told me it was going to cost ten thousand dollars to fix the boat, I remember thinking that that wasn't as much money as it sounds like to a landsman.

I awoke in the weak light of dawn to the sound of water rushing all around the boat. *Tranquility* was yawing from side to side and there was a heavy vibration coming from somewhere up forward. I was yawning and dozing in a half-conscious state when something big struck the bow and thumped its way down the starboard side. I jumped out of my bunk, hit my head on the oaken knee next to the mast and ran to the companionway to see what was the matter. Out on deck, *Tranquility* was shrouded in pea-soup fog with only a dull blur hanging in the misty haze above her bow pulpit to indicate where the sun was rising. The sound of rushing water was coming from a long line of low breakers crashing onto themselves a boat length from the stern. I was trying to make sense of this, when another loud bang at the bow sent me flying to the foredeck where I watched a big log, with the root-ball still attached, scrape its way down the port side of the boat. The anchor line was stretched bar-tight and nearly horizontal over the surface of the water. When I put my foot on it, I learned where the vibration was coming from. I also noticed the anchor roller had carried away from the starboard side of the bowsprit at some point. All that was left of it was a jagged bronze footing and a few bent wood screws turned pink and chalky with age.

I didn't have the *faintest* idea what was going on. *Am I too close to shore?* I asked myself, descending into the cabin to turn on the depth sounder. When I flipped the switch, the machine whirred to life and I stood before it trying to decipher the twenty or thirty flashing orange depth returns that were reading anywhere from zero to eighty feet of water under the keel. I looked out at the tumbling line of breakers and searched my groggy mind for an explanation. There was no swell and very little wind that morning, so how could there be breakers? *Did I drift out to the Pacific Coast last night?* I wondered, thumbing through the chart book to see if that was a possibility –it wasn't. Visibility was down to about thirty feet in the fog, and since I hadn't figured out how to use the GPS yet, I decided the mystery would have to go unsolved until the sun broke through. This seemed like the safest, most prudent course of action, so I double checked the cleat hitch on the anchor line and went back to bed.

Sometime later, I awoke to dramatic, gunwale-to-gunwale yawing, accompanied by the sound of water raging like a river all around the boat. I lay there for a few minutes, rolling bonelessly back and forth on my bunk, pondering the deteriorating situation. "What in the hell is going on out there?!" I finally yelled, throwing the covers off and striding angrily on deck in my flip-flops and underwear. There was a long line of standing waves breaking ten feet from the stern and the dinghy was planing and frolicking around in them like it was being towed up a river behind a jet-boat. Rafts of freshly uprooted bull kelp sailed past the boat in a stew-like mix of dock parts, crab pot buoys, stumps and other flotsam. A small tree drifted by, collecting bits of driftwood in the green leaves still on its branches. I was just starting to wonder how a live tree could make its way out to sea, when I caught a split-second glimpse of a lighthouse through the shifting fog. The tower seemed like it was a little too close to me, as in, directly-overhead-too-close to me. I went below for another look at the chart book, and a little rudimentary geometry solved the puzzle. I was anchored directly off Admiralty Head instead of deep within Admiralty Bay. A second glimpse of the lighthouse through the companionway allowed me to fix *Tranquility*'s position somewhere along an arc of words that girded the headland on the chart: "TIDE RIPS" they read. That explained *a lot* but there still wasn't anything I could *do* about it. The current was streaming by and *Tranquility* didn't have an anchor winch. I knew there was no point in trying to heave it in with one hand and I certainly wasn't going to cut my main anchor loose. So...I went back to bed.

Brilliant sunlight shining through the portholes woke me up around eleven. The boat was listing fifteen degrees to starboard for some reason, but she was perfectly still. The vibration in the hull and the sound of rushing water had ceased. When I slid the companionway open and poked my head outside, the standing waves were gone, the fog had lifted and the skies over Admiralty Inlet were perfectly clear. I was anchored in a rather scenic spot too, so close to the sea cliffs and the pretty lighthouse. A small ferry was passing in the distance, looking like a green and white antique toy. I liked it there, but sensed it was time to get going, so I dressed and went on deck.

When I got up to the bow, I found the anchor line hanging straight down in the water and under so much strain it was digging into the gunwale, pulling the bow down and to the right. There was no current, so I had no idea why that was, but it was obvious I'd never see my anchor again, so I went to the cockpit for the fish knife intending to cut myself free. But just as I was about to saw through the line, something stopped me. It was caution –the very first of the voyage. For some reason, I thought I should lash the knife to the end of the boat hook and saw through it from a safe distance. I'm so glad I did that! There wasn't any sawing really. When I set the blade against the strand, the whole thing exploded in a whipping unravel that sent the boat hook flying to the rail. The bitter ends of the anchor line shot across the deck from starboard to port, trailing hot tufts of downy nylon. My face would have been in the way of that if I'd cut it by hand. *Good call*, I said to myself, striding back to the cockpit.

I didn't know any of this at the time, but a minimally equipped cruising sailboat will have at least three anchors aboard. Because conditions on the seafloor vary widely, these anchors should be of different designs to accommodate sand, rock, kelp, etc. At least two of the three anchors should be married (attached) to separate rodes (chain, line or cable) and those rodes should be connected to strong points on the boat at all times. Except when at sea, one of the anchors should be instantly deployable for obvious reasons. When it comes to ground tackle, it is better to have and not need than to need and not have. However, anchors and the act of anchoring, are probably the most contentious subjects in the maritime world, so we'll leave it there. Suffice it to say that *Tranquility* had come to me with only two anchors and the loss of the main one that morning left me with nothing but a small lunch hook on a hundred feet of line with minimal chain. I needed ground tackle pronto, so I set sail for a small settlement six miles to the southwest, spread out along the northern shore of a large bay on the Olympic Peninsula. I learned from the chart that it was Port Townsend. I'd seen the lights of the town shining in the distance the night before. I'd never been there, never heard of it and didn't know the first thing about it, but I was pretty sure I was sharp enough to find an anchor somewhere over there.

If you happen to know some seacraft, and you're still pretending to find the patience and time you'll need to get through the rest of this book, thank you. I'd also like to offer you my *sincerest* apologies for any offense I may have caused. Furthermore, I ask that you at least *try* to forgive me for my youthful ignorance and bear in mind that a fully-rigged sailboat is *The Foremost Human Article* – its use governed by a million-and-one arcane rules, each with a long list of exceptions. No one comes into this world knowing the rules, and an experienced and fair-minded skipper will be the first to recall a hundred ways in which the sea tricked him long after he thought he did. The sea can be unforgiving, to say the very least, and some of the best sailors in the world have lost their boats and their lives due to far less serious mistakes than I was making. Like them, I believed in my voyage enough to put myself at risk for it, and I refused to let the blunders of my first year at sea keep me from it. I survived the voyage to California and I went on to spend most of the next fifteen years cruising various sailboats far and wide. I suppose I turned out to be a halfway decent coastal sailor in the bargain. But this isn't a story *about* sailing. So, fair warning dear reader, if you find yourself wondering how much more of this you can take: A. Imagine if you were me; B. There's far better and far worse things to come before this voyage is over.

8

The old heart of Port Townsend is a quaint waterfront settlement of nineteenth-century brick commercial buildings and fine Cape Cod homes spread out on pretty hillsides with a view of northern Puget Sound and the Salish Basin. The place is one-part traditional Victorian seaport, steeped in Pacific Northwest maritime culture, and one-part stagecraft. Someone just happening through today might mistake it for any number of tourist towns you find along the coasts of North America. However, you will come across significant human history there, as you will almost anywhere in the Pacific Northwest. As recently as a hundred years ago, S'Klallam canoes lined the beaches of the bay now known as Port Townsend. The region teemed with permanent and seasonal native settlements, large and small, long before and long after Captain George Vancouver gave the bay its English name after the Marquess Townshend in 1792, while he was mapping the northwest coast aboard HMS *Discovery* for the British Crown. In its heyday as a commercial maritime hub, Port Townsend was the sort of rough and tumble Pacific Coast shipping town where you could get Shanghaied in the back room of a boarding house if you weren't careful. There were saloons and brothels, sawmills and muddy roads –the forest was a *nuisance* to these newcomers, for the most part, *not* something to be revered and cared for. Looking at the place now, it's easy to forget that long before we were an agrarian nation, long before we were an industrial nation, in fact, long before we were a nation, North America was the domain of mariners. The northwest coast was frequented by seafaring First Peoples and, to a lesser extent, by European sailing ships, long before what we think of as the white man, arrived by land. What follows are a few of the broad contours of modern Pacific Northwest settlement history.

The Europeans, primarily the Spanish, Russians, British and Americans (overlapping but essentially in that order) did not sail to the northwest coast for the reasons you may first imagine. This is because the typical plunder in those days (timber, arable land, fish, gold and slaves) were readily available without setting sail on an epic and expensive voyage: from Western Europe, south through the Atlantic, around treacherous Cape Horn, to a coast equally inhospitable and more unknown than Patagonia was at the time. Vitus Bering, the renowned Russian explorer, roamed his namesake Strait and Sea as well as the North Pacific Ocean, in 1728 & 1741 respectively, by way of the Kamchatka Peninsula and the Aleutian Islands rather than the Atlantic.

The Spanish got a jump on the Russians in the early 1700s however, when they sailed to the northwest coast primarily to survey and plant a flag in the terrains "given" to them by the Pope in the 1494 Treaty of Tordesillas. This document "settled" a contentious dispute brewing between the Spanish and the Portuguese over North and South America. As usual, the natives already living there were not consulted in the matter –then *or* now. In the treaty granted by the benevolent Pope, the Spanish were "given" everything west of Florida and the Portuguese, all that lay to the east –hence the *colonial* languages of Mesoamerica and Brazil. Every so-called private land right on both continents can be traced, over several ill-defined gaps, fraudulent paperwork and saber rattlings, directly to this or some other equally-questionable fiat treaty. Think about *that* the next time you drive through the one-square mile Quileute Indian Reservation out on the west coast of the Olympic Peninsula or when you see a *No Trespassing* sign staked out on a Puget Sound beach house lawn.

The Spaniards, for their part, visited the northwest coast from time to time in the 1700s on a desultory search for the fabled Northwest Passage (they wrecked near present day Nehalem, Oregon in 1707) and to see for themselves a vast and virtually uncharted coast which they never had more than a tenuous grip on north of the Presidio in San Francisco Bay. That outpost was established in 1776, a date that will be familiar to many Americans. Other than that, there was no good reason for Europeans to visit, much less occupy, such a remote and inclement region.

In the late 1700s, that all changed for the British who were exploring the eastern Pacific for their own ends. As the story goes, Captain James Cook sent native-tanned sea otter pelts on a trading ship bound from Nootka Sound, on what is now the west coast of Vancouver Island, to mainland China. Sea otters were abundant in the Pacific Northwest in the 1700s and they were and are notable for their thick luxurious fur. If you're judging by hair count, an adult sea otter has around one *million* hairs per square inch of hide; no other easily-exploitable sea mammal even comes close.

It's important to note that at the time, and ever after, the British and other Europeans were enamored with Chinese trade goods: silk, porcelain, lacquer work décor and teas among them. The same cannot be said for China's astute opinion of what the British had to offer them in return –other than sterling silver, which was hemorrhaging into British trade ships bound for the Orient at the time (the Russians and Spanish were already trading Pacific Northwest otter furs with China). A Chinese official once quipped that he and his compatriots simply had no need for "clever" European "contrivances". That was true, apart from otter pelts, which once sampled, wealthy Chinese could not get enough of. It's been said that a single sea otter pelt could fetch a value in silver equal to a British seaman's wages for a year. Suddenly voyages to, and small settlements along, the Pacific Northwest coast looked profitable. The Brits, seeing an opportunity to balance their burgeoning trade deficit with China, negotiated a condominium rule of the Pacific Northwest with the Spanish. But as the population of sea otter passed *peak fur*, their numbers dwindled and the Brits went looking for other trade goods. There wasn't much to choose from in the region.

So they settled on something that was little known to the world at the time and virtually unheard of in China. It was an easily-transportable, stable compound that when smoked was almost as irresistible as otter fur: *opium* from the Asian sub-continent, Bengali opium, to be precise. One might be forgiven if they see a template for the existing international illicit drug trade in what followed. As always with easy-money schemes, the opium-fueled magic carpet ride didn't last as long as the Brits would have liked. When the Chinese Emperor's minions started returning to the Forbidden City from Canton with reports of rampant drug addiction and all of its attendant ills, he outlawed the import and smoking of opium. Of course, the Brits, being merciless colonizers of those they considered sub-human, ignored this decree, and, after a shipment of their state-sponsored opium was seized and destroyed by Chinese customs officials, they fought a series of increasingly hypocritical and violent drug wars with the sovereign nation of China in order to protect its grip on the highly lucrative—let's go-ahead and call it what it was— heroin trade.

At the time, China was a nation with around 5000 years of recorded history. Entire schools of art, thought and philosophy had developed, flourished, died out and been rediscovered by other scholars.

They were the first culture to issue paper money. They experimented with earthquake seismographs, invented gun powder, the umbrella, the magnetic compass, the stern-hung rudder, the concept of water-tight bulkheads (having taken a cue from the air-tight segments in bamboo) and a whole hell of a lot else that I can't think of right this minute. While we're on the ever-uplifting subject of European hegemony, it's worth mentioning that modern humans settled North America, in part aboard vessels, long before they made it into Western Europe overland –now put *that* in your pipe and smoke it.

For better or for worse, to step aboard a boat nowadays, especially an old wooden sailboat, is to take a trip in a time machine with its dial stuck on the past. A voyage under sail is a participant-observer lesson in world history writ large. And because the United States is first-and-foremost a seafaring nation, it's a lesson in American history as well. The commercial center of our country, Manhattan Island, was settled in 1624 by the Dutch West India Company because of the fine natural harbor that surrounds it (arguably one of the best on the Atlantic). The greatest public works project in the early development of the United States was the Erie Canal, which opened in 1825 and links New York City to the Great Lakes and beyond. It was not surpassed in scale or impact until the passage of the Interstate Highway Act in 1956. There were towns along the Mississippi River and elsewhere that could only be reached by boat even in those relatively modern times. In the mid-thirties, not long before *Tranquility* was built, Puget Sound was still being visited by schooners like *Maid of Orleans*, a fur and copra trader, former blackbirder and Aleutian Islands freighter. The three-masted lumber schooner, *Clarence A Thayer* was working up and down the west coast of Washington as late as 1950. After a brief visit to Seattle in 1956 for temporary repairs, she made her final voyage from Puget Sound to San Francisco Bay where she was rebuilt and put on display at the Maritime Park. You don't save a ship like that by slapping a mocked-up bowsprit on her and lag bolting a few planks to her starboard bow! It takes real leadership *and* a checkbook to do something like that.

We may go boating now for the leisurely pleasure of doing so, and modern craft may be built and marketed to the general public as toys or gaudy floating palaces for moneyed one-upmanship, but no other endeavor has shaped human history and culture as much as seafaring. You need look no further than our language for proof of that. Take *cybernetics, blog* and *skyscraper* –familiar, modern terms to be sure. Yet all three derive directly from vessel nomenclature. Cybernetics, from the Greek *kybernetes*, meaning to govern or steer a ship; *skyscraper*, a sail spread high above the deck of a windjammer or other sailing ship; *blog*, from *web* and *log*. What's a *log*? It's the written record of the movements and business of a ship. The first standardized automotive engines in the United States were modified marine engines. The rules of conduct and procedure aboard the International Space Station are, at their root, naval law. These are the first examples that come to mind, but the list goes on and on. Hoist a sail or learn to tie a bowline on the deck of an old wooden boat in this country and you're really doing something special.

The wooden boat building Port Townsend is famous for these days is an imported, revival industry that took off there in the 1970s. Before that, relatively few vessels had their keels laid there. Since the disco era, the town has become a nationally renowned center for the practice and teaching of traditional boat building methods, repair and restoration. Every sort of marine specialist can be found at work in Port Townsend today. There's hundreds of sail makers, riggers, painters, electricians, caulkers, fiberglass men, shipwrights and mechanics, just to name a few. The town is a bastion of maritime knowledge, history and old school seamanship –all of it taken seriously by its stewards. But this is a weighty and bickersome subject, so I won't delve into it any more than is needed to give you some idea of the place I was setting sail for on day three of my great sea voyage. For my part, I had some of the cussing and drinking down, I had the boat, the disheveled look and the bandaged hand, now all I needed to do was learn how to sail without going down to Davy Jones' locker and I'd fit right in!......No?

I left Admiralty Head in my wake and made my way across the inlet to Port Townsend, where I tossed my hook over the side a safe distance from Union Wharf. By the time I had everything sorted out on deck and swallowed a bite of food, I felt like I'd been at sea for weeks and I was eager to go ashore, so I changed my clothes in a hurry and rowed the skiff to the dock. You see a very different side of town when you arrive by boat. There's a backstage element to it, like peeking at an audience from the wings or entering a theater through the exit. The sea is a kind of one-way mirror and the innumerable species of vessels and sailors that ply it are a mystery to landsmen in a way that roads and cars and drivers will never be to a mariner. The piers and slipways of a waterfront convey the strange people and business of boats directly onto land. Comings and goings in that part of town are mostly anonymous, sudden and final. This makes frontage roads and seaside alleyways a good place for the fulfillment of immediate needs, the abandonment and reassignment of property and, of course, lingerers on furtive missions. It's the same story in any port in the world.

At the first corner I came to I noticed a rough-and-ready looking fellow standing in the doorway of a bar trying to light the stub-end of a smashed cigarette with another just like it. He looked the part, so I asked him if he knew where a guy could buy an anchor.

"Right this way," he said, turning on his heels, flicking the smoldering butt into the middle of Water Street. I tagged along right behind him, imagining my sea gypsy luck, until he turned a corner and slipped into the driver's seat of a tiny, rundown motor home.

"Hop in," he said, leaning over a pile of dirty clothing to push the passenger door open for me.

Well, I thought to myself, *he's either going to rob me or take me to an anchor.* Everybody knows nothing bad can happen to you when you're young! So I hopped in his rank-smelling jalopy and we puttered away from the curb. I remember driving a long way from the wharf that day, and after several twists and turns up steep streets, we arrived at an old, two-story house in a hillside neighborhood overlooking the sound.

"Follow me," he said with a quick glance up and down the street before getting out.

We walked along the side of the house to a mossy shed in a brambly backyard with a view of Port Townsend Bay. The man took hold of the wooden door to the shed with both hands and forced it open, kicking tufts of grass and clods of dirt out of the way.

"In here," he said, waving a hand through cobwebs, stepping into the dark.

Robbed or anchored...? I inadvertently placed my hand over the wad of bills in my front pocket. It was a toss-up at that point. I needed an anchor by nightfall so I stepped through the doorway half-expecting to be jumped.

"Do you live here?" I asked in a happy tone, pretending like the idea was a nice one.

"You could say that," he replied cautiously. When the man got his bearings in the shed, he hefted a large wooden crate from the dirt floor to the top of a workbench. He crouched down in the dusty, slatted sunlight coming through the wall and peered at the old house jacks and yesteryear homeowner clutter piled underneath the bench. "I don't think I have an anchor anymore," he said in a used-to-bad-luck tone of voice. But something dawned on him just then and he dropped to his knees and began clawing at the ground in front of me with his bare hands: "I do have some chain though."

The treasure was buried in the floor apparently, and he proceeded to dig up a few very rusty lengths of half-inch chain with big hooks on either end. He shook the caked dirt from the links as he yanked them out of the ground and when he laid them end-to-end, they came to around twenty feet.

"What do you get for something like that?" I asked, not really wanting them.

"How about one-fifty?"

"How about twenty-five?" I countered.

"Deal!" he said, clapping his hands together and hiking his pants up hip-by-hip. He hauled the chains to the front yard before I could change my mind.

When the money changed hands, the man kindly offered me a ride back to the waterfront and I accepted. We returned to the wharf the way we came, but he drove differently, killing the engine to coast down long hills and whenever we sat at a stoplight. He pulled over with a leaning swoop just as we turned onto Water Street. He flipped his sun visor down and sat way back in his seat while a black sedan with tinted windows passed through the intersection ahead of us. For some reason, the whole thing reminded me of my very first day in Seattle when I was twenty-two. I'd hitchhiked there from Anchorage, Alaska to meet a friend, and as soon as I hit Pioneer Square, a man walked up to me holding a small wooden box and asked if I wanted my shoes shined. I said yes for some reason when I knew I should have said no, but it was too late. The smelly man fell upon my left wingtip and began rubbing it with a greasy black rag. After a few seconds of "shining" I realized my left shoe was being destroyed by whatever was on the man's tattered rag and I pulled my foot away. I'd already given him my last dollar, and just as I started to say something about my shoe, the man grabbed his things, bolted down the street and ducked into an alleyway.

Why did I get my shoes shined?

Why did I just buy twenty-five-dollar's worth of rusty chain?

When the RV guy dropped me off at Union Wharf that day, he made a great show of unloading my chain for me and then asked for a little gas money. It was one of those shoe shine deals, so I offered him a five-dollar bill and he snatched it out of my hand. *Never gonna end up like that*, I thought to myself as I flaked the chain out in the bottom of the skiff for safekeeping. Then I hit the town: young, callow, on an adventure and pretty much as green as can be.

It didn't take me very long that day to find my way to the shipyard and harbor at the west end of town. The port was your typical Puget Sound pleasure craft marina. It was a large area of nearshore shallows, hemmed in by rock jetties and filled with docks and slippery wooden finger piers. The gangways are steep and treacherous at low tide, the slips and side-ties are all held in place by old creosote pilings sprouting grasses and small plants from the rotten cavities in their tops. The shipyard was a fenced-in gravel lot full of tall metal buildings and hauled-out ships –no more, no less. I walked the docks for a couple of hours, admiring the well-kept yachts and asking around for an anchor. I gathered from the few people I spoke to that most of the trade in used marine gear was being handled at a nearby chandlery. I couldn't figure out where the place was, so I decided to head back to the boat for the evening. On my way up the ramp, I noticed a dozen or so healthy-looking red rock crabs fighting and skittering in the shallows along the marina embankment. I grew up spearfishing and knew they weren't going to be there when I returned, but I ran back to the skiff and fetched my mask and spear pole off the boat anyway. Thinking someone would care, so pretending to do something else (what, I don't know), I spent the rest of the evening rowing around, pronging crab into the dinghy on the sly. I managed to get four of them, but red rocks are mostly claw, so I ate my entire catch for dinner, back on board *Tranquility* that night. *What would THIS dinner run you in a fancy restaurant?* I asked myself as I sucked the tough, salty meat from the steaming red pincers.

My second day in Port Townsend got off to a bumpy start down at the chandlery, where I was not well-received by its proprietor. The business was located in a ramshackle building standing by itself in the middle of the marina parking lot. The place was surrounded by old mooring buoys and big coils of line, rusty ship anchors and other heavy-duty marine gear that looked like it just fell off the back of a truck. I don't remember having seen a sign out front and I wandered around it once before I found the entrance. I walked through the narrow front door toting a 7-foot oar I spotted in a pile of junk behind a restaurant that morning. This oar had a hole drilled through the center of its blade, it was noticeably bent because it must have been mounted on a wall at some point, but I figured it might come in handy, so I grabbed it. It was dim and musty inside the chandlery, with the tangy smell of mahogany, manila and varnish from long-ago voyages hanging in the air. The place was full of folding tables and metal racks piled high with older marine equipment. There were lifeboat compasses and taffrail logs, mechanical gauges and antique bronze ports turned green with verdigris. Mismatched fenders and life rings hung in random spots. There was a shelf of radios and an old ship's wheel or two. Plastic milk crates full of tools and blocks and tackle were crammed underneath the tables. The floor and walls were uneven, there were no lights on and the back rooms were cold and shadowy. Those elements lent the establishment an 1850s frontier trading post feel, and that impression was amplified by its owner. He was a big man and he fixed me with an unrelenting, accusatory stare the moment I walked through the door. I *remember* him with a bushy beard and an eye patch (scout's honor) and he was wearing layered clothing from a time period I couldn't place. I believe he had an overcoat or duster on, and he stood behind a glass case that may have held hunting knives or pistols or both. Green and yellow cartridge boxes lined the shelves directly behind him and I got the feeling there was some gunsmithing or gold work going on at a little desk in a busy corner behind him. The proprietor never moved from his station at the glass counter though, and his watchful demeanor seemed to be saying either: "I am armed" or "I might help you," but I couldn't decide which. He made me uneasy and I figured he had a dirk or a Derringer on him.

I was too nervous to ask if he had any anchors for sale and didn't see any laying around, so I drifted around the place perusing the inventory. Some of the gear I'd never seen before and didn't know the use of, so I nodded to myself with pretend understanding of things I had no business touching and kept my eyes out for an inexpensive hook. I felt his eye drilling into me as I browsed. I knew he was hating me, hating my bent oar and hating every move I made. He was despising my youth, begrudging me of it and vetoing everything I considered purchasing due to price or purpose. I thought to myself: *Aren't we in the United States of America anymore? Isn't this a public establishment? Don't I have the same right as anyone to be in here this morning?* But one split-second look into his hard eye told me that we were not, it was not, and I did not. Who could blame him for that?

I made my way over to a pegboard crowded with old bronze snap shackles and high-quality blocks (pulleys to a landlubber). This board stood a little out of the proprietor's line of sight and when he shifted ever-so-slightly in its direction a very clear telepathy crossed the room from him to me: *Don't even try it kid.* I poked around for another minute or two to see if I could provoke him into speaking, but he didn't utter a word and I grew bored with his surly attitude.

"You got any anchors in here?" I finally asked.

"What size boat," he intoned flatly, stripping all the question from his words.

"Thirty-foot sloop." *That's right...*

"Hooks are over there," he said, pointing to the far wall with his left hand. His right hand hovered at his hip when he spoke and he adjusted his gaze, dividing the distance between me and the anchors as if he were waiting for a clay pigeon to be lobbed across the room from an unknown location. I figured I needed to shop fast. A Northill anchor like the one I lost off Admiralty Head was going for the breathtaking sum of $275. *Holy moly!* I thought to myself, setting it back down. Other anchors, either too big or too small for *Tranquility* were also out of my price range. However, the man knew his business, so there was a rusty Danforth style welded anchor, pieced together from round stock and half-inch steel plate, going for $35. I carried it to the front counter, taking care not to bump into anything along the way.

"Look here," I said to the man, leaning my oar, blade-up, against the glass countertop. "I like the price but I wonder if this will rust through on me." I was pointing to a half-inch shackle hole drilled through the thick, flat bar shank, fully one inch from the nearest edge.

"Not in your lifetime," he croaked, clearing his throat. "Need any chain with that?"

For some reason, probably fear, I didn't get why he was asking me if I needed chain. I was there for an anchor and had barely managed that.

"Cha...like chain, chain?" I stammered.

"YES!! *CHAIN!!*IT'S WHAT MAKES AN ANCHOR WORK! –OR DON'T YOU KNOW THAT YET??!!" Those words tumbled out of him all at once, as if they'd been pent up for years. They were words like water, water that had risen drop-by-drop behind a dam of patience every time he had to deal with a young fool fresh off a boat.

"Ohhhh...*anchor* chain!" I said, finally catching his drift. "Ha Ha Ha!" I guffawed, losing control of my voice. "NOPE! I'm okay in *that* department. I found a really good deal on some when I got here yesterday!"

I poured all of this out to him in a jarring, cheery tone that made him wince as if I'd yelled it right in his ear. Without moving his head, the proprietor shifted his gaze from the hole in my anchor, to the hole in my oar, to my sternum. He placed both his hands palm down on the countertop and shifted his weight onto them, leaning toward me menacingly –I could smell him and I thought he could hear my heart pounding, so I laid my money on the counter, grabbed my stuff and got the hell out of there. I remember him simply and affectionately, as *The Pirate*.

On my way back to the wharf, I saw an enormous, fine-looking wooden sailboat propped up in the middle of the shipyard. I'd never seen a vessel like that out of the water before, so I cut through the marina parking lot and went over to the fence to have a look at her. She was a grand old cruising sloop from the 1930s –flush deck, full-keeled and massively built. She was a blue water leviathan, about 50' on deck, and you could tell she'd been around the world more than once in her day. She was well-kept but undergoing major hull repair. There were clean tarps staked out on the ground all around her and her starboard side was flanked by scaffolding. Her stern and transom were laid open from keel to deck and several planks were missing above and below her waterline. A huge pile of thick anchor chain sat on the ground beneath her bows. Somebody was going whole hog on that boat. The yard gate was wide-open and there were several people milling around the other hauled-out vessels, so I thought it would be okay if I went in for a closer look. A portly, east-coast-tough shipwright of about forty was standing on a ladder under her stern. He was straining deep into her, tracing a door-skin jig (thin plywood used to make patterns) with a yellow pencil. When I took up a position a respectful distance from the edge of the tarp, the shipwright stopped what he was doing and glared at my feet for a moment before turning back to his work. I could see up into the boat from where I was standing. She had a parlor-sized cabin with kerosene lanterns and red velvet on her bulkheads. She was a real ocean-going yacht with big chrome winches, a spoke wheel and heavy bronze turnbuckles. She had her masts out of her. The shipwright came down the ladder holding the jig between two fingers and walked over to his workbench without looking at me. He carefully traced the card onto a block of hardwood and then ran a power-planer over one edge of it, carefully trimming it to the outline of the jig. He returned to the ladder and started to climb, but thought of something else and paused with one foot on the bottom rung. He took a deep breath, let out a huge sigh and turned to me. I took two steps back.

"Can I help you with something today?" he asked in an edgy tone.

"Oh no...I'm fine...I was just...well, that's about the most amazing boat I've ever seen in my whole darn life," I said.

To this friendly comment he replied: "So why are you telling *me* about it? Is it because no one else will listen?"

I can't say Port Townsend was growing on me at that point, or vice versa, but the idea that I could stay anchored in the bay for as long as I wanted, definitely was. It's a sailor's birthright to drop his hook when and where, and for how long he pleases; if he's not endangering or impeding the safe navigation of any other vessel, there's absolutely no harm in it. I was used to paying moorage by then and the thought that I could anchor somewhere for free while my hand healed was very appealing, so I decided to hang around town for a few more days and see what happened.

I learned the importance of proper anchoring one windy evening when I saw a 50-foot wooden ketch drifting through the anchorage perpendicular to the wind. She had no sails up, no lights lit and no one on deck. She was dragging anchor toward the deep water and busy shipping lanes of Admiralty Inlet and I was the first one to see her go. I threw on some clothes, wrestled the outboard onto the stern of the skiff and went speeding after her. There were half-a-dozen other boats in the anchorage and another skiff, driven by a lone man, set out for her as well. I arrived at her side first, jumped on deck and pounded on her cabin top hollering for her owner, but there was no answer and the companionway was locked. The other skiff arrived the next moment and the man and I ran up to the foredeck to see if we could stop her by letting out some anchor chain. It was a good idea, but we soon realized the weight of her ground tackle, which was hanging straight down in the water, was jamming the chain brake. She was a big boat and had an electric windlass, so we tried the controls on the foredeck and in the cockpit, but the breaker was switched off somewhere below deck and nothing happened when we pressed the UP / DOWN buttons. It was too windy to tow her with our skiffs and no one else came to her aid –it was all on us.

Luckily, there was a gigantic second anchor on the bow (a 50kg Bruce, on 1/2" BBB –for those who care) and it was shackled to a length of brand new galvanized chain that led aft and down through the foredeck by way of a chrome pipe with a cap on it. We jumped to this anchor, but not knowing the boat, it took us a couple of minutes to get the stops pulled out. When the anchor was ready to drop, I put my foot on the shank and exchanged a serious look with the man. We didn't know how deep the water was, or how much chain was in the boat, but we were drifting offshore and it was all we could do to save her. So, when the man nodded, I shoved the anchor out of the roller with my foot. It tipped over the bow and crashed down into the water, trailing a blur of chain which came flying out of the hawse pipe and went pouring over the bow like water over a fall. When the anchor touched bottom, the boat slowed some and began to turn into the wind. But just when we thought we were home free, the unattached end of the chain came flying out of the pipe! It sailed over the bow and disappeared into the sea without a sound (about $2398.32 all told). The man and I shared a woeful glance. I'll have you know, nothing goes south as quickly as it goes south on a boat. So there we were, drifting downwind, into a seaman's bad dream.

Sailors are obliged to help one another out of a jam however, even if the sailor in need is nowhere in sight, so we fell upon the jammed anchor winch with everything we had –it wasn't much. I will admit that it was I who saved the day (*finally!*) when I wedged the blunt tip of a dive knife—found in a cockpit locker—underneath the chain brake serving the main anchor and was able to pry it up. There were around 350 feet of chain still in the bow and we dumped every inch of it. A minute or two later, the vessel fetched up on her ground tackle, turned into the wind and set her hook. I found out later that she'd just been launched in

Ketchikan, Alaska after a 10-year owner build. She was just two weeks into her maiden voyage when she arrived in Port Townsend.

How tenuous of a presence is a wooden boat?

I decided to buy another anchor while I was in town.

Word of the close call got around the harbor pretty quick and the next morning, the owner of a big English Channel cutter, that was anchored next to me, rowed over to *Tranquility* to hear the story firsthand.

"That's a stout looking boat you have there," I said to the man as he came alongside. "What's she built of?"

"Guess!" the man responded cheerily.

"Wood?"

"No way! Too many problems with rot and shipworms in wooden boats!" he said with an intense look in his eyes.

"Is she fiberglass?" I asked, sort-of playing along, but really just wanting him to tell me.

"Fiberglass boats need *upkeep!*" he said with a little too much gusto for such a dull game.

I took another look at her. She appeared to be massively built and she sat very low in the water. She had a thickness in her bow that I'd never seen in a sailboat before and she barely stirred when the Port Townsend ferry went by. Every other boat in the anchorage faced east into the flood current or west into the ebb. But her bow pointed north day and night, a lodestone in the sea flowing around her.

"She's steel!" I said conclusively.

"STEEL? *STEEL?* Ha ha ha ha ha," the man chuckled. "Don't make me laugh, steel on its own isn't *strong* enough for a boat. *Rain Dancer* is ferro-cement! Ever heard of that?" he asked, letting go of an oar and offering up his hand for a shake. "I'm Jacques, I'm an engineer." I didn't shake his hand.

"Your boat is made out of...cement? Like, *sidewalk* cement?" I asked, pretending to have never heard of such a thing.

"Yes sir!" he enthused letting an odd Mediterranean accent slip. "She was built with the finest mixture of concrete known to mankind. I bought her for next to nothing, she's solid as a rock and *very* low maintenance. A lot of people still don't know that concrete is the best thing there is to make a sailboat out of." He was one of the true believers.

"How...er...how do you get wet cement to stay in the shape of a boat?" I asked, leading him on.

"That's where the ferro comes in!" he said giddily. "You take rebar and chicken wire and weld it all together in the shape of a hull...it's like a really strong wicker basket if you do it right. When you get the rebar into the shape of the boat you want, you spread freshly mixed concrete all over it and wait for it to dry. It is like the Maasai Mara home, only better. She doesn't leak a drop, she sails like a dream and you wanna talk about *nimble*? Just *look* over there!" Jacques jabbed his left pinky at *Rain Dancer.*

I looked at the boat again and noticed that her wind speed and direction instruments were mounted on the tip of her bowsprit, instead of at the top of her mast. I took another look at Jacques too. He was a small, wiry man in his mid-fifties with a very dark tan. He was wearing a loose-fitting tank top and a pair of un-elastic, sun-bleached girl shorts. He was very tan underneath those as well, small and skinny, like a tan, plucked chicken. Jacques looked like he spent his twenties and thirties having a good time on Ibiza rather than working on a PhD in materials science. I instantly dismissed him as a quack. Anyway, I had an important project to do on the boat that day, so we didn't talk long. Unfortunately, that wasn't the last I saw of him.

In the vast and mutable vernacular of the sea, there are what are known as "wet" boats and "dry" boats. A dry boat is one with a deck and cockpit that waves and salt spray do not board while sailing in normal weather conditions. A dry boat can be driven at hull speed on a fairly inclement day without her crew and helmsman getting soaked to the bone. A wet boat, on the other hand, seems to beckon waves on deck and spray into her cockpit even in mild weather. *Tranquility* was such a boat —and not just because of her low-slung lines. The turn of her hull at the stern had the unlovable tendency to vault wave-tops into the cockpit whenever the wind rose above fifteen knots. She did this at odd times though and only on certain points of sail, which made it all the more aggravating. People who own wet boats keep spray out of their cockpit by lashing weather cloths (strong curtains) to the lifelines that surround it. I'd been wondering if weather cloths would work on *Tranquility,* so when I came across an old genoa sitting next to a dumpster at the marina, I decided to cut a pair out of it and see for myself.

The sail was large and ungainly, I had limited marlinspike skills at the time and after wrestling it out of the skiff and into the cockpit, I spent an hour pulling it this way and that over *Tranquility*'s deck, trying to figure out the best way to cut it up. It was a sail for a really big boat and had a thick stainless steel cable running through its luff that I had no way of easily removing or cutting. So, instead of making a normal set of weather cloths, I folded the entire sail over the rail and wrapped it around the aft end of the boat, on both sides, from mast to stern and back. This made a weather cloth that ran almost halfway around the vessel. The edges met at the hull quite nicely though, and before I knew it, I was stitching it to the lifelines and slicing the overages off as I worked my way around the gunwale. The job took three days.

Jacques rowed by on day two.

"What's all this?" he asked, dipping an oar and turning the stern of his skiff around until he was face-to-face with me.

"I'm making a weather cloth," I said, running a big sail needle back and forth under the top lifeline with a palm (a large thimble worn on your hand) and a pair of needle-nose pliers.

"Don't you think that sail is going to scoop up some water when the boat heels over?" he asked, reaching out and pulling the fabric into the shape of a scoop just ahead of where I was stitching.

"I'm not done with it yet," I said, pulling the sail cloth away from him, "and it's only going to be on here until I get to California."

"You're sailing down the west coast in THIS boat?!" Jacques exclaimed with genuine alarm in his voice.

"What are you *talking* about guy?" I said. "This boat is awesome! I bet she could ride out a hurricane!"

"OH MY GOD! Let me knock on wood for you, kid," Jacques said, rapping his knuckles three times on the teak thwart between his legs.

A guy with a boat built out of pulverized rock and chicken wire is giving me a hard time now? What the hell is going on here? At least wood floats!

Jacques began rowing away, but he shipped his oars and drifted for moment. "Good luck on your voyage," he said, turning to look over the side of his skiff. "But just remember, no matter how far offshore you sail, the nearest land is always a lot closer than you think."

What are you even saying dude? I thought to myself as I waved him off. It took me a couple hours to realize the land he was talking about is at the bottom of the ocean. However, I dismissed the entire warning and all of the underlying concerns with the following reflection: *You don't even faze me bro!*

On the third day of work, I was hanging over the starboard rail running some final stitches through the sail cloth girding the aft end of the boat, when I heard a series of light, rhythmic knocks move slowly past the port side from stern to bow. When I looked up, I saw the top of someone's head go by the weather cloth. I couldn't see the person's face and thought little of it, until a few minutes later, when the knocks returned and I saw a yellow kayak heading for *Tranquility's* starboard side. It was being paddled by a young woman who looked like she just stepped out of an Ingmar Bergman film. She had long blond hair, pretty bright blue eyes and a perfect, sparkling smile. This lovely creature asked me two questions as she glided by: "Do you happen to know what time it is?" and "What did you do to your hand?"

Her name was Lisa and I invited her aboard for a cup of tea. She was happy and chatty; I liked standing beside her, I liked the sound of her voice and we took to each other immediately. We talked for almost an hour, and when she had to say goodbye, I invited her out for a daysail. To my surprise, she accepted.

No one who minds being disappointed very much will make pleasure boating plans more than a day or two in advance in the coastal regions of the Pacific Northwest. The weather there is too changeable to depend on for long, and while Puget Sound summers have been known to go on and on forever, they can just as easily last for two or three weeks. There are some sorry years when it never seems to come at all. The day appointed for my sail with Lisa dawned cold and dreary, and as I worked my way around the boat sprucing her up, I expected the trip to be canceled at any moment. But the Angel of the Waters said that we must go, and by the time I fetched Lisa from Union Wharf that afternoon, the skies were clearing, the winds were coming up and the sailboats of Port Townsend were heading out on the bay as they do on fine summer days. Sloops and schooners, yawls and ketches, antique and traditionally rigged, began sailing back and forth along shore or they jibed and ran across the bay, cruising in and out of the sunbeams shining down on the glistening water from behind the driving clouds. That's an average summer day in Port Townsend, but it was all new to me, so I hoisted the main and genoa in a hurry and we fell in with the stately procession.

When *Tranquility* found the wind, she took off sailing down the red brick waterfront and post-and-lintel piers of the town, following a long line of boats heading out to the point. *Tranquility* was a little out of control with too much sail up, but the day was too marvelous to care. We were cracking along, flanked by a bevy of classic yachts with the bell buoy clanging out a mariner's song in the yachtsman's gale blowing through Admiralty Inlet. Lisa's corn-silk hair was flying high around the cockpit, catching on my beard and fingertips. She never pulled it away, never moved her knee back when it touched mine, never took her eyes off me and she never let her pretty little smile wane. Suddenly it was all worth it: the mysterious leak; the nightmarish maiden voyage; the foolhardy departure; the injury; the blatant ridicule —all of it was reset when I looked into Lisa's lovely blue eyes. She was the closest thing to a mermaid a sailor can hope to find in all of Neptune's Seven Seas, and she was spending the day with me.

When we sailed into the wide crescent bay northeast of town, I jibed *Tranquility* and ran her broad off the wind with her skirts up, yawing big and easy over the gentle swells until we were far out in Port Townsend Bay. With the wind dead aft and the boat moving at speed, the air became weightless and warm. When we turned to look at the scene behind us, sunlight and atmosphere had melded into a single, luminous medium. Across Admiralty Inlet, columnar clouds towered over the eastern horizon. They broke into billowing airships that soared up and over the green foothills trailing long, transparent shadows into the dappled countryside. The windy sea flecked with slanting sails, the lighthouse, the old-fashioned port town and the sky were all rendered in the sublime hues and fetching brushwork of the most optimistic maritime art. It might as well have been 1897 rather than 1997 by the looks of it. But what's time on a day like that?

I brought *Tranquility* about near the far shore of the bay, and steered her close on the wind for the open waters of Admiralty Inlet to the northwest of Point Wilson. This was a long passage and we sailed in silence, falling under the spell of pitch and yaw, letting the troubled world fall far away from us. When *Tranquility* met the countercurrent swirling around the point she sheered wide to starboard and I could tell it wasn't a good day for open water. So I tacked her and ran in close to the beach, steering for the anchorage. Then we did it all over again.

Lisa was born in a seaside town and grew up on boats with her father. Although she knew far more about sailing than I did, and could have corrected me a dozen times that day, she was gracious and pretended not to notice any of my mistakes. However, everything you need to know about a voyage can be read in the face of the captain, so she registered my occasional worry with a faint nod to let me know it. When she took a trick at the helm herself, I jumped below and fetched her little interesting things to look at and bites to eat. While I was down there, I committed an innocent deception: I pumped the bilge when she looked away, but there was no water in the boat.

Summer days run long at those latitudes and we were the last boat back to the anchorage that evening. I dropped the hook a good distance from the wharf and set it under sail with the chain rattling out of the hawse pipe as we came in. *Tranquility* fetched up on her ground tackle all at once, with a wide, fluttering turn into the wind. I leapt to the mast, threw off the halyards, and dropped the sails on deck just as she came around to the breeze. It was a regatta finish and my first anchor under sail, but I pretended like it was old hat and Lisa went along with it.

When we had *Tranquility* put away, it was a little too early to say goodnight, and getting to be a little too late to be on the boat with any propriety on a first date, so I rowed Lisa to the wharf and took her out for a sunset dinner. She was even more beautiful on land than she was at sea. I was utterly taken with her and I believed she was thoroughly impressed with me. There was a glass of wine, words of compliment and self-deprecation, and little-by-little the evening turned tender and intimate. An unspoken promise was made by the time our plates were taken away and I knew with a thrill, which words cannot possibly describe, that I could stay in Port Townsend for as long as Lisa would have me. *Does it really matter?* I thought to myself as I gazed at the angel sitting across from me, limned in amber candlelight, *whether I sail for a day, or a month, or a year, before I find something like this?* That was only the first hint of an insight which would grow into the central revelation of the voyage. Unfortunately for us, that was more than a year away, and I hardly knew what to do with it even when it came.

I stayed in Port Townsend courting Lisa for weeks, when I could have been out sailing the North Pacific Ocean. But there was no voyage and no such thing as time when I was loving her. There was just holding hands and summer sea fields and long beaches piled high with stones the sea rolled round and sorted. There were only doorways in the clouds and listless summer nights under star-strewn skies reflected in a sea so calm we really couldn't say whether the heavens were above or below. There were only Winslow Homer days, when the red and green sea buoys keeled deep in the flood and ebb currents sent coursing over the contours of the seabed by the sun and moon. There were only crackling beach fires and warm flannel blankets; wine corks and seashells in my pockets and long looks of love. The first time I touched her, we lay in the forepeak entwined in each other's arms, kissing and kissing and kissing until we wore out our smiles and the sun came up and we laughed at ourselves for forgetting to sleep. She was a good girl with a contempt of danger and an indomitable spirit. I tried my very hardest to win her heart, but she was too innocent to hold anything back, so we lost ourselves in the tall grass of summer together, letting it happen, letting it be what our bodies wanted it to be. I said, "I love loving you," and she said, "I do too...I do too."

I suppose it was when it only could have been. It was that precious moment of youth when the bonds of friendship and love are easily made, broken and mended. It was when we looked for ourselves in each other and liked what we found. It was before we knew what the world was and our place in it. It was when we could still laugh at death and believe it was only a chore for brooding mortals; it was when we knew nothing of time, our cold affluent outlaster. It was before our bones moved uneasily in our skin and long before every injury was one. So we carried on without thinking—serenely unaware that anything in our little world would ever change—for as long as life would let us. We spent those weeks rediscovering the sun together, and sailing my sloop on the sound, and knowing each other's lips and breath and noses from endless sidelong kisses.

Lisa did not look for a problem where there was none and could not be convinced to find fault in anything. She couldn't even be persuaded to speak badly of someone who'd possibly done her an unforgivable harm. She somehow loved willingly, and allowed herself to be loved, and I took her beauty, wisdom and diffident manner for granted, blithely unaware it would be in such short supply elsewhere. But I was young and didn't know enough about love to know that I could have stayed with her and lived the sort of normal life I would come to envy so soon. I spent our time together foolishly until the last of it was gone. Is there any truer sign of the artless coin of innocence and love than that?

No there isn't. So, if one day you find yourself somewhere like that, please do not do what I did next.

I was in love with Lisa and I believed she was in love with me, but the summer was sliding by and my impatient youth came calling. So one morning, when her golden hair was falling all over my pillow, I asked her to sail away with me and she said yes. I did my best to describe the wonders in store for us in the Channel Islands and I minimized the risks involved in getting there. We were young and thrilled by the thought of setting sail together.

But her father was a consummate seaman, shipwright and wood carver. He was known for fetching up on log-strewn northwest beaches with nothing but hand tools, and, after a few weeks or months, he would leave those beaches in the boats he built there. He'd recently lost a ship in a hurricane somewhere off Mexico. When he got wind of our plans, he took one look at me and one look at *Tranquility* and put an end to them with a word.

I was privately outraged that he forbid her to go on a voyage that she would have survived, but scarcely would have enjoyed. I was unsure of myself and the boat, and I must have known it was for the best, because, to her face, I accepted the decision like a gentleman. You can think that I conceded too easily in the matter, and you can think that I should have fought for her, but what could I have done? Abandon the voyage? Kidnap her? Swallow the anchor? I suppose I could have done a lot of things differently that summer, but this was before I knew what real regret was. So, believing our parting was fated, I set a departure date and held myself to it. The separation would mean far more to me later than I allowed it to at the time. I'm not ashamed to admit that I looked for her on the streets of Port Townsend, every time I was there, for the rest of my life.

And that, dear reader, is what it's like when a sailor leaves a woman he loves.

9

I left Port Townsend on a windy summer evening in early August, and despite the raw longing and thoughts of turning back, it was a real thrill to be on my way to California again. Even though I'd begun to see that certain aspects of the voyage were more complicated than I first imagined, it seemed to me like my life as a sailor was coming together quite nicely: I had a girl who cared for me in a pretty seaside town; I had a boat that was capable of taking me places; I'd fed myself on the bounty of the sea to some extent and I'd even made a couple hundred dollars from a day charter I picked up on Water Street. There had been no serious mishaps since I anchored in the tide rips off Admiralty Head and *Tranquility* was in fine trim after a month of day sailing and tinkering with her rigging. She seemed ready to be on her way again, and as soon as she met the west wind, she took off reaching out of town with steep decks under a full main and working jib. It was a heartening scene for a young man making his way in the world for the first time and the evening began to feel more like an exhilarating arrival than a sorrowful departure.

Love can do a lot but it can't keep the sun from rising. Still, I missed her.

I do yet.

At the crescent bay just outside of town, I put *Tranquility* hard on the wind and steered her for the open waters of Admiralty Inlet. Once she settled into her rhythm, she began to leap at the three-foot seas sweeping in from the Pacific Ocean eighty miles away. We crossed over to Whidbey Island in no time, I came about north of Admiralty Head, and short-tacked into the Salish Basin. This was big water to me at the time and it looked as vast as a sea on the chart.

It was a windy evening, the salt spray was flying and *Tranquility* was making good time, so I kept sailing west until I reached the lee of a long sandspit on the north shore of the Olympic Peninsula. This spit was several miles from Admiralty Inlet and it would have made perfect sense to anchor under its protection for the night and get a fresh start the next morning, but the tide was with me and the wind was strong and favorable, so I put *Tranquility* on a port tack, and headed her north into the Salish Basin and the fast approaching night. When I had a good offing, I lashed the tiller, made a careful scan in the fading light for boats and logs, then jumped below to fix myself a cup of tea.

Whenever I let *Tranquility* sail herself in the weeks prior, she always needed a certain amount of tending to stay on course. However, that evening, the combination of wind and tide and shortened sail kept her true while the kettle boiled, and for a long time afterward. Instead of steering, I sat in the companionway, perched half in the cabin and half out, sipping my tea and keeping watch. This is a good moment in the life of a sailor –the boat taking care of you like that. I believe I chastised *Tranquility* for her bad manners the first few weeks I owned her and I remember being very satisfied with myself for having prevailed in man-versus-boat. What else could I make of things? I was on my way to the Pacific and *Tranquility* was steering herself as I'd been told a sea-kindly vessel would, once everything was set "just right" with her. The outboard may not have looked like much, but it was doing the job. The wiring I installed way back in Ballard was working fine and the weather cloth had yet to scoop up a single drop of water. All was well!

An hour later, *Tranquility* was still on course and I was dozing off, leaning on the companionway hatch with my head rolling from side to side on my forearms. The evening was a tempestuous but clear one, with miles of visibility. There were no other boats on the water and I hadn't touched the tiller since before my tea, so I let myself rest. There had been a last minute frenzy of activity in the days before I set sail and my final parting with Lisa was sad and difficult. I thought of these things as the evening wore on, and little-by-little the thrill of departure faded as *Tranquility* made her way northwest. *The boat is sailing well and the settee is right there, so why not steal down for a little nap? Yes, I'll just set the alarm for fifteen minutes and take a load off,* I thought to myself, yawning on the companionway hatch as *Tranquility* heaved and rolled over the sea. Single-hand sailors all over the world pass entire nights sleeping in short stints broken up by quick glances at the radar—if they have one—and careful looks around the horizon for ships. Before I knew it, I was standing in the cabin fluffing up a pillow and winding the clock. I set the alarm and lay down on the settee with my boots on.

Seventeen minutes after closing my eyes, I was standing on the cabin top with my arms around the swaying mast, scanning the sea for running lights. *Tranquility* was driving into the night and there was nothing to be seen on the water except winking lighthouses and the orange glow of Victoria, British Columbia on the northern horizon. I went below, reset the alarm and lay down. I closed my eyes. *So this is how it's going to be until I get to California*, I thought to myself as I drifted off to sleep. A few minutes later, *Tranquility* dropped off the back of a wave and the sails lost their wind. However, just as I was getting up to correct her, she got back on her feet and continued on her way. I could tell by the movement of the boat and the sound of the wind in the rigging that we were still on course, so I kicked off my boots, rolled over, and went out like a light. About an hour later, the weak clanking of an unwound alarm hammer woke me from a sound sleep. I stood on the engine hatch, sliding around in my socks, scanning the horizon from the warmth and safety of the companionway. It had grown cold and overcast and *Tranquility* was sailing herself into a dark and windy night. She was throwing off red and green spray at her bows and dipping her rail into the sea now and then – *Tranquility* had a bone in her teeth! I went below and double checked the chart. There was nothing up ahead but open water and four or five empty shipping lanes. I set the alarm a third time, got undressed and climbed into my sleeping bag.

When I woke up the next morning, I found *Tranquility* ghosting along in sunshine and light air a few hundred yards north of a group of islets and reefs known as Race Rocks. This is an area of foul grounds beset by heavy tide rips, and scene of numerous shipwrecks, located just off the jagged southeastern shores of Vancouver Island. Everything seemed fine with the boat and our heading that morning, so I let her sail on while I made myself a cup of coffee. Then I sat in the cockpit and watched the pretty scene drift by. There were ten or fifteen aluminum skiffs, crewed by pairs of old men in denim and flannel trolling for salmon around the rocks. I waved to some of them, but they didn't wave back. *What's up with the Canadians?* I wondered as I sipped my coffee.

Race Rocks is perched at the eastern entrance of the Strait of Juan de Fuca and the view from there is full of the majesty and grandeur of Southeast Alaska. On the southern shore of the straits, ten miles away, snowcapped mountains and timber-filled valleys stretch east and west along the Olympic Peninsula, almost as far as the eye can see. To the north and west lay the steep and heavily-wooded shores of Vancouver Island. To the northeast, the San Juan and Gulf Islands spread out for miles. Blue waters driven into the straits from the North Pacific Ocean by wind and tide, stretch in all directions. The curvature of the earth makes everything seem endless out there.

The Strait of Juan de Fuca is a starkly beautiful but fearsome body of water for a novice mariner to gaze upon —its dangers are evident on the chart and in real life in a hundred ways: few and widely-spaced anchorages; sea winds and ocean swells driving the length of it unopposed by any prominent headland; loads of shipping traffic; sea fog and strong currents that flow east and west through it four times daily (two floods, two ebbs). It's the sort of place where you'll want to look before you leap, or you'll wish you had. It's a mistake, though, to assume that once you're clear of the strait you're any better off on the shores of the North Pacific Ocean. A small, low-powered vessel will find herself *utterly* exposed to the whims of the wind and sea anywhere within about fifty or sixty miles of the west coast. Heading south, virtually every all-weather harbor between the Strait of Juan de Fuca and Point Conception is entered by way of a shoaling tidal estuary or, more commonly, a treacherous river mouth. Ocean winds and swells drive into those rivers, which are made shallow at their coastal termini by sandy deltas (bars). Breakers meeting a west-flowing river, and river meeting tumultuous sea, can stir up the water for miles offshore. Add to that, four times daily (two highs, two lows), the unfathomable energy of the rising and falling ocean tides.

The gravitational pull on the earth from sun and moon not only affect the depth of the seas. There's a tide in a lake and in a teacup. There's even one on dry land. The *rock* in the middle of the North American continent bulges skyward up to three feet in places due to the pull of those celestial bodies. These *solid-earth tides* contribute to the breakdown of bedrock in the North American tectonic plate.

Back out on the west coast, the high tide is so powerful it reverses the flow of rivers when the flood pushes inland, and the low tide increases their normal westbound flow when it ebbs. Because of that, entering or leaving a west coast river is a terrifying experience at night or in unsettled weather and the stress of timing a safe transit over a bar is never far from a novice mariner's mind, even on a calm day. The river entrances of the Pacific Northwest are well-suited to a seaman's final moments and the place names along the Washington Coast generally reflect this: Dead

Man's Cove; Destruction Island; Cape Disappointment; Devil's Fat Nut Sack –just to name a few. They don't call the waters of western Washington *The Graveyard of the Pacific* for nothing! If you wind up earning your anchors there, you can sail more than half the Seven Seas in confidence.

On my first day in the straits, a light westerly was blowing in from the sea, so I struck the working jib and hoisted the big genoa in its place and set out for the Olympic Peninsula at a snail's pace. I figured I was only a couple of days from Neah Bay and, at most, a couple of weeks from California. *I'll be anchored in the Channel Islands by the first of September*, I told myself as I steered over the long, low swells moving in from the west that morning. You may have guessed that *Tranquility* was not a particularly fleet-footed yacht, and she wasn't. She usually didn't reach five knots in anything other than the most favorable tailwind and she was an *especially* poor sailor when heading into light airs like the ones blowing that day, so we made painfully slow progress. I was still intent on sailing every inch of the way to Neah Bay, so I spent most of the day tacking in circles going from one fluky zephyr to the next.

A fiberglass sloop about the size of *Tranquility* hove in sight around noon...or shall I say, the bare mast of a sloop hove in sight around noon. She came up out of the east under motor with her sail covers on and she continued west, lurching over the swells. A man stood at her helm decked out in bright red America's Cup gear and a woman was braced spread-eagle against the cockpit coaming. Her sun hat was pulled down tight. Wide, wrap-around old-lady sunglasses hid her features; she did not look like she was having a good time. *Anybody can motor bro*, I said under my breath as they chugged by.

Tranquility got caught up in the afternoon flood heading east and I passed the remaining daylight hours and most of the evening short-tacking into the west, neither gaining nor losing ground. Around midnight, I found myself drifting in a dead calm about a mile from a broad headland on the south shore of the strait. I was midway between two anchorages so I was faced with the prospect of motoring east to one or west to the other. I motored east according to my rule and spent my first night in the straits rolling in a little bay on the peninsula –just about due south of Race Rocks. And so, after an entire day of sailing, I'd made no headway to speak of. I was used to that sort of progress though.

The next day I hit the ebb perfectly and made my way west slogging against half-a-gale which stirred the sea into an ecstasy of wind-against-tide confusion. I spent a long, queasy afternoon sailing back and forth across the straits, making the most of nearshore calms and cursing the flood when it came. Although I'd covered at least forty miles over the bottom by the end of the day, I was crestfallen that night when I found myself in another rolly bay just fifteen miles northwest of where I'd spent the night before. This is the meaning of amateur sailing on the northern inland waters of the Pacific Northwest. It's a lot of sound and fury signifying nothing until you figure it out. Even intrepid Captain Vancouver's log mentions aggravating days spent stuck at headlands as contrary winds and currents pulled his ship one way, then pushed her back. Vancouver didn't have a motor to move *Discovery* with —men in rowboats towed her. In that manner he somehow managed to map most of the intricate passes, fjords and scattered islands of the northwest coast in a few years.

The following day dawned clear and bright, with a low swell and a good-natured west wind blowing in the straits. *Tranquility* took to the conditions nicely under the main and genoa and we made out for Vancouver Island, catching a helpful ebb along the way. This turned out to be one of the longest and most memorable days of the voyage, and I crossed the straits twice, making up all the westing I lost over the past two. Sailing those waters is like sailing through mountain passes —it's as if a navigable channel has been cut through a national park. I'm used to such seascapes now and wouldn't be particularly inclined to repeat the passage, but I was stunned by the raw, natural beauty at the time. Twenty or more rivers and creeks empty into the straits on both sides of the border; hoary firs and winsome red cedars abut the stony beaches. Fry teem in the shallow bays; seals and sea lions haul out on the rocks; orca and gray whale roam east and west following salmon, Dall's porpoise and krill. Bickering gulls dive on anchovy and herring balls, while small sharks thrash at the schools from below, touching off huge bait fish boils that spread out on the surface of the water as they scatter from the onslaught. Deer and black bear forage along the shores, pandion hawks perch in snags glassing you with cold contempt, big ravens hop along the beaches pecking in tide pools and the sugary eyes of dead sea mammals. Murres and auks, surf scoters and oyster catchers, squabble and whistle and call. Some fly by with tiny silver fish hanging from their beaks. Sea-going tugs churn along towing barges. Fully-laden ships emerge on the horizon and steam into view —making their way, sublimely indifferent to the prevailing conditions. I never dreamed such scenery lay in wait just around the corner from crowded Seattle.

I raised the lighthouse on Waadah Island around 10:00 pm that night. This is a small, heavily-timbered islet which guards the entrance to Neah Bay. The steady winds of the day had long since eased to an intermittent breeze, and by the time I was in sight of the Neah Bay entrance buoy, its bell was silent and *Tranquility*'s sails were lilting and dewy. I absolutely refused to motor the last hundred yards though, so I spent two grueling hours sailing in the faintest nighttime airs, working against countercurrents and tacking on cat's paws until I dropped the buoy astern. Then I fired up the outboard and motored deep into the bay where I dropped anchor for the night, secure in the knowledge that I'd proved the shipwright wrong. **DEAD WRONG.** I did not stay secure in that knowledge for very long.

I awoke early the next morning to the sound of hollering and banging on my deck. When I popped my head through the forward hatch, I saw a fully-crewed Coast Guard boat idling alongside *Tranquility*. "Your boat is about to go on the rocks skipper!" the captain yelled to me from the open bridge of the boat. When I looked aft, I saw *Tranquility*'s stern bobbing twenty feet from the rocky eastern shore of the bay. I was certain I'd dropped my anchor in deep water the night before but there was no time to figure out what went wrong. I jumped on deck in my underwear and bare feet, fired up the motor and pushed *Tranquility* into deeper water. As she moved away from the rocks, the skiff, which I'd been towing since Port Townsend, began to move toward *Tranquility* as if self-propelled. Its bowline had become tangled in the propeller, and the propeller was reeling it in. Before I could process any of that, the skiff rammed into the stern and the motor stalled with a violent jerk.

And... *Tranquility* began drifting back to the rocks! I ran to the bow and pulled the slack out of the anchor line, trying to stop her, but it totally wasn't working. I flew to the cockpit, jumped into the skiff and untangled the shredded line from the propeller. As soon as it was free, I realized the shear pin in the prop shaft was broken and had to be replaced. Bad times! Changing the pin from the bow of the bouncing skiff was a hair-raising five-minute fire drill, but I got it all sorted out before *Tranquility* went on the rocks. I found out why she was drifting when I pulled the anchor up and it came to the surface in a ball of chain-wrapped kelp. Taking no more chances with anchoring, then, or ever again, I dropped my hook and every inch of rode in the middle of the bay —equidistant from all dangers.

I spent a couple of days in Neah Bay fueling and watering the boat, fetching last minute supplies and picking up local knowledge from the inhabitants. What I learned of the surrounding waters did not make me enthusiastic to return to them. An old man at the Big Salmon fuel dock had this to say about the northwest coast of Washington: "Ohhh yes! Neah Bay is *lovely...just lovely* this time of year...why, August and September are probably the *best* time for this place...of course there's the fog to contend with out in the straits...and we often have a *TERRRRIBLE* storm sometime in September."

A Makah fisherman standing nearby added: "There isn't any time of year around here I consider safe, weather-wise. One minute it's Disneyland out there and the next it's rollin' *big*-time."

I heard stories of women screaming incoherent maydays into the radio when their husbands were washed overboard or fell deathly ill with seasickness. There were harrowing tales of disabled boats being driven onto rocky shores by gale force winds. Abandoned sailboats (and they were all sailboats) sat forlornly in the small marina, corroborating what I'd heard from the locals. It was a familiar tale in Neah Bay by then: young man or cute couple from Seattle buy a sailboat hoping to commune with nature, they stop in the bay for fuel on their way to Mexi...You can imagine how fast that chapter can end. I wasn't going to let other people's sob stories stop me though, I'd come too far to give up.

The night before I set sail for the Pacific, I sat in the cabin programming realistic waypoints into my GPS. I knew that a sailboat of *Tranquility*'s design could make around a hundred miles a day without trying very hard, so I punched in waypoints that were sixty miles apart and went to bed. *What's sixty miles a day when you're sailing on open water? That's like three knots an hour*, I thought giddily as I drifted off to sleep. At sixty-odd miles a day, the Channel Islands were about two weeks away. It's really not all that far when the boat is sailing well.

10

I suppose my first day on the North Pacific Ocean began auspiciously enough. The fog that hung in the straits and draped the rugged outlines of Waadah Island all night long started to lift as the sun came up, and a tangy, guano-scented twenty-knot northwesterly began blowing through the bay soon thereafter. Out in the straits, a smooth swell was rolling in from the open ocean, and by 9:00 am, the sun was shining in a crystalline blue sky. It was unusually warm that morning, and when I listened to the marine weather forecast over the radio, it called for three-to-five-foot seas and winds of ten to fifteen knots –both for that day, and most of the coming week. This seemed like a good weather window to set sail for California in, so with a mix of fear and anticipation, I pulled up my anchor and motored out of the bay. When I neared the entrance buoy, I could hear its bell clanging around halfheartedly in the moderate breeze. I expected conditions to pick up offshore though, so I hoisted a reefed main (made smaller in area by tying the lower half of it to the boom) and the small working jib as a precaution. Neah Bay is five, very long and nerve-wracking slow-boat miles from Cape Flattery. The cape is the most northwesterly point of land on the Olympic Peninsula, and in the continental United States. Like many headlands on the west coast, Cape Flattery is a magnet for thick weather and vessels navigating close to shore in search of a landfall. Over the years, several ships have wrecked on and around it or had their last-known position recorded there; it's an area that commands the respect of mariners the world over. In order to pass this fearsome cape and its off-lying rocks at a safe distance, I planned to sail halfway to Vancouver Island before tacking west into the open ocean. This was an overabundance of caution but those waters require it.

When *Tranquility* met the full force of the wind blowing in from the Pacific that morning, she leaned to starboard and took off sailing north on a port tack, pitching and rolling over the swells. As I sailed farther and farther out into the strait, the wind began to back (to change direction counterclockwise); this allowed me to steer a more ambitious and time-saving course that bent well to the northwest of Vancouver Island. Eventually the wind shifted enough to let me head *Tranquility* for the open sea –sooner than expected and without tacking. The strait is an unpredictable body of water though, and as I neared the mid-channel buoy at its seaward entrance, *Tranquility* sailed into a wide area of westbound current where she began hobby-horsing and tossing spray high over her bow like buckets full of cold diamonds flung into the air. A wind-against-tide situation makes for very uncomfortable running in a small boat. She will sail or motor through the rough patches if you make her, but she plunges and rears and the current drags at her and shears her off course the entire time. The seas there can be as confused as a washing machine and are jarringly out of phase with a vessel's natural movement. The boat never seems to get on her feet or break free of the charging waves –it's stopping and starting, herky-jerky boating at its worst. *Tranquility* muddled through this stomach-churning troubled water for an hour or so, and when it looked like I finally had enough sea room to clear the cape, I put the helm hard-over and tacked her into the southwest. At the time, I believed this was the most important course change of the voyage: this, at long last, was the left turn of Ballard lore.

I held my breath as the boat passed through the eye of the wind, waiting to see where it would blow when *Tranquility*'s bowsprit pointed south. As the boat turned left, the breeze circled the foredeck to the right. When it blew over the beam, it sent the tell-tales in the rigging aflutter. *Tranquility* eased over onto her new tack and her sails crossed the deck to the port side. When I let the weather sheets go, they filled with a satisfying, fulsome bang. The wind continued shifting to the right, it passed over the cockpit, and when it tickled the back of my neck, I knew without looking that it was blowing over the stern –just like everyone said it would. *Hurrah! Hurrah! Hurrah!* With *Tranquility* headed southwest instead of northwest, the swells which she'd been struggling through a moment before began to lift her gently from behind and push her on her way. *Hurrah! Hurrah! Hurrah!* This is what's meant by the expression *fair winds and following seas.* Life's a pleasant downhill run instead of a struggle when the elements are behind you!

A couple of hours later, Cape Flattery and tiny, off-lying Tatoosh Island (where the cape's 165-foot lighthouse is located), were well in my wake and I was sailing south along the Pacific Coast at last! There is nothing in the world like setting sail for the unknown on a voyage of your own making. Everything is new again, every door has been flung open, anything is possible. On that day, I knew what it meant to be rich and successful and I knew what it meant to strike out in the world entirely on my own. Although there have been many ups and downs since, that feeling has never left me.

When *Tranquility* settled into her new course, I picked up the GPS and watched my progress to the first waypoint for a minute or two. According to the little LCD screen, everything was going as planned on day one. The boat was heading for the first of a series of arrows I programmed along a north-south axis that stretched from Cape Flattery to Point Conception in California. The arrows were overlaid onto an otherwise featureless grayscale sea and, as a record of my advance so far, a short, squiggly black line backtracked up the coast and turned east, indicating the straits. I calculated my ETA to the first arrow based on my present speed, and figured that I'd be sailing over it and deleting it from memory early the next morning. Seeing my voyage spelled out so clearly was very comforting. All I had to do was sail south, and if you can sail south for one day, then you can sail south for two or three days, and so on and so forth, until you reach your destination. In my view, the only problem that day was we were only going three knots. No *real* sailor can sit idly by when his boat is under-performing! So I went to the foredeck, pulled down the small jib and hoisted the big cruising genoa. Then I shook the reef out of the main and brisked it to the top of the mast. The extra sail area didn't increase *Tranquility*'s speed for some reason –but so what? I was finally on my way south! I was really doing it! I wasn't *motoring* to California, I was *sailing* there –and that was the whole darn point!

The northwesterly eased considerably by mid-afternoon, and little-by-little, *Tranquility* began losing speed. When she fell below two knots, I tacked toward the coast and went searching for the wind in that direction –assuming I'd merely sailed out of it. There wasn't any breeze to be found in the southeast however, and an hour later I was ghosting toward shore about seven miles south of Cape Flattery. By late afternoon *Tranquility* was dead in the water, silently rising and falling in place on the low glassy swells passing under her from out of the northwest. I sat at the tiller for several minutes expecting the wind to pick up again, but it had gone elsewhere and didn't seem like it was on its way back any time soon.

Inexperienced sailors make a common and understandable mistake when planning for their first sea voyage. They spend all of their time preparing themselves and the boat for the worst imaginable conditions. When they encounter the light airs and dead calms that are far more likely—and far more demoralizing—on a long voyage, they don't know what to do. I'd sailed some before and despite my early enthusiasm, I knew the wind wasn't always ready to convey a boat to her destination just because her captain was ready to set sail for it. I knew the doldrum drill, so I took out a book I'd been meaning to read, leaned back in the cockpit and was soon flipping the pages. This was all for show of course —my mind was on the wind. The most consistent wind in the world. According to Ballard lore. As it was passed down to me. By people who knew way more sailing stuff than I did.

Tranquility's light pitching motion turned into a roll in the perfectly still evening that followed. The sails began to pop and slat back and forth, batting the still air in time with the yawing of the boat. This is a grating sound when you aren't going anywhere and it's hard on the cloth as well, so I went to the mast, cast off the halyards and dropped the sails on deck in two rumpled piles. They say on the sea that the best way to get the wind blowing is to take the sails down or start the engine, and sure enough, two minutes later, the wind picked up to ten knots. TEN KNOTS! I tossed my book on the thwart, leapt to the deck and skipped along the cabin top to the mast. I yanked the main and genoa up, dashed back to the cockpit and tore the mainsheet in hand-over-hand. I cranked on the sheet winch and trimmed up the genoa. The rigging shivered as the sails snapped and billowed into shape, then we were on our way again! I brought *Tranquility* around to the southwest and steered her offshore, singing to myself, tapping my foot in the cockpit and palming out a little conga number on the tiller.

"YES! YES! YES!" I said as the boat began making easy headway over the gently heaving sea. As soon as we were moving along, I grabbed the GPS and recalculated my ETA to the first arrow based on my current speed. If the wind held like it was supposed to, I'd be sailing over my first waypoint early the following afternoon. At that rate I'd be to California in about thirteen days, maybe even a little less with any luck. It all seemed so easy at that moment. Unfortunately, the wind I was basing the estimate on turned out to be a zephyr and *Tranquility* was ghosting along five minutes later. "NO! NO! NO!" I said as the sails sagged and the boat slowed to a lolling wander.

Tranquility

But what could possibly get me down? It was only my first day on the North Pacific Ocean! Sure, I'd have rather been sailing, but there's plenty of other things you can do to pass the time on a boat. So I pulled my brand new fishing rod out of the forepeak and went to the stern to mooch for salmon. After a few minutes of jigging a bright chrome spoon in twenty feet of water, I started getting little hits on the line. Half-a-dozen silvery fish were sculling and rolling around the flashing lure – they were some fine looking salmon, but none of them took the hook and I lost interest. When the sun went down that evening, I sat on deck and read by candlelight for a couple of hours. It was utterly windless and the candle's flame was as still and unperturbed as if it were burning in a bedroom closet. It was the calmest night on the ocean I'd ever seen. Nothing moved on the water. No birds, no ships, no bull kelp – just the slow flash of the lighthouse on Tatoosh Island and the sound of the sea lapping under *Tranquility's* stern. So peaceful, so gentle, so lovely and serene.

I sat at the tiller for several hours that night, peering up at the stars, waiting for the wind, willing it to come, expecting it, calling to it, begging Neptune to send me on my way south. I doubled up watch caps, put on gloves and a sweater. I donned my foul-weather gear and boots for extra warmth. I sat vigil for the wind that night, but no wind came and no wind would come; it might as well have been a wake. About 3:00 am, the sound of water exploding behind the boat startled me out of a doze at the helm. I spun around in terror, expecting to see the bow of a ship running me down, but it was only another gray whale, stopping to check me out. There still wasn't a breath of wind, so I dropped the sails, trudged into the cabin and crawled into my bunk. This is no way to begin a voyage, my friend. But I didn't know that yet, so I really couldn't have been happier as I drifted off to sleep.

The good ship Tranquility found her way into another roadside ditch that night. I could see where it led to the sea, but the way through was blocked by low-hanging tree limbs. I consulted the chart several times, but the chart maker must have forgotten something, because there was no other way in or out of the ditch. I managed to turn Tranquility around, but she ended up in a narrows and wedged herself there. No going ahead, no going astern. I jumped from the deck to the muddy bank and tried to push her somewhere else, but the channel closed in around her until she was landlocked. Up on the road, cars sped by full of passengers with their faces pressed up against the windows –looks of consternation and woe blurring past.

I awoke the next morning to the sound of voices and the gurgling exhaust notes of a small marine diesel idling close by. I rolled out of my bunk half-asleep and bumped my way through the cabin. I slid the hatch open and climbed the stairs. Squinting through the brilliant sunlight, I saw a man standing in the cockpit of a large sailboat bobbing in the sea no more than eight feet from *Tranquility*'s port side. I looked at this man and his boat twice before I realized it was Jacques, the safety-officer-engineer-guy with the ferro-cement tub from Port Townsend. He and his wife were on their way to Mexico and they pulled up alongside *Tranquility* to say *hi* on their way offshore. Or so I thought.

"So!" Jacques said, folding his arms atop the steering wheel before him and speaking to me in the subtly condescending tone of a father who's caught his son playing in a park on a school day. "What on earth are you *doing* out here?"

"I'm sailing to California," I said with a yawn aimed in his general direction; I knew what was coming next.

"No! You're NOT!!" he yelled, banging both his palms on the wheel, trying to make me understand something only he could see. "You're going to get yourself KILLED out here pal! No life raft? No radar? In THIS boat? Come ON man!!" Jacques was fuming. Purple veins bulged from his skinny tan neck –he was about to lose it. Luckily his wife, who was built like a dorm room refrigerator, was just emerging from the cabin. She clipped her safety line to the one going to Jacques and began caressing his forearm. She whispered something soothing to him that must have been along the lines of: "You tried Jacques, he isn't your responsibility."

It was a sunny, perfectly calm morning on the water, yet Jacques and his wife were decked out like clowns in heavy-duty sea boots, foul-weather coats and bibs. They both wore urban adventurer sun hats cinched down over their ears. They had on matching pairs of sailing gloves and inflatable life vest/safety harnesses clipped to short tethers that ran to a strong point bolted to the cockpit coaming. These tethers caught under their feet when they moved about. Each had an identical smear of green zinc paste covering their nose and cheekbones. They looked like they just arrived on a boat from Antarctica and it didn't seem like they enjoyed themselves along the way. They were dorks and I hated them, but they hated me more. I wonder though, how people make it to that age without knowing that life is one-part learning, one-part résumé reality and the rest, spellbinding delusion? Anyway, there wasn't a whole lot anyone could do or say at that point, so after asking me a few more questions they already knew the answers to, they motored into the shimmering distance, trailing a gray cloud of diesel exhaust and I never saw them again.

When I got my bearings that morning, it was pretty clear the current was carrying *Tranquility* offshore and into the southwest. I could still see mountains and land to the east, but the coastline had disappeared over the horizon. Peering through the binocular, I could just make out the top of the lighthouse on Tatoosh Island. The perfectly windless sea stretched away in smooth undulations as far as the eye could see and *Tranquility* barely stirred on it. When I say it was windless that morning, I'm not exaggerating. It was so still on deck that a flock of pillow-down fell at my feet when I flicked it from my shirt collar. I hoisted the main and genoa anyway, and they hung from the mast doing nothing while I made an elaborate breakfast of eggs, fried potatoes, kielbasa, toast and coffee. After my meal, I read and dozed in the cockpit for a few hours. I told myself I was taking it easy after my big push into the open ocean, but I was waiting for the wind. The most consistent wind in the world.

Day two was a silent, languid, Ancient Mariner kind of day –the only movement on the water was an ocean sunfish (mola mola) that paddled by the boat around noon. At some point, I realized I felt freer than I'd felt in a very long time. No one knew where I was and no one could have possibly come looking for me. I knew I could be out there for months, sailing where the wind blew. Before shoving off that spring, I had no idea you could go to sea in the old-timey way and be out there with no one bothering you for as long as you wanted. This was a real discovery at the time. Beware though, that sort of free living will turn you into a sovereign state, and that will complicate your life back on land, where almost nothing is free and clever little laws have criminalized the meaning of life wherever a fee has yet to be enacted.

I awoke from a nap later that day, to the raspy sound of a thin, nylon sail filling and collapsing in extremely light air. I thought I was imagining this, until I heard a woman's voice. When I sat up and looked around the boat, I saw a modern, 40-foot fiberglass sloop slowly coming up on me from out of the north. She was sailing along at less than a knot under an immense light air spinnaker that was barely held aloft by some breath of northwesterly wind too weak to even shift *Tranquility*'s genoa from where it hung over the foredeck. As the sloop drew near, I saw that she was being driven by a good-looking couple in their early thirties. The man steered and the woman stood at the port shrouds on look-out. I waved to them but they didn't wave back. I tried to make eye contact with the helmsman, in case he didn't see me sitting behind the weather cloth in the cockpit of the sailboat a hundred feet away, but he kept his eyes fixed on the compass as they ghosted by. My own gaze went from their boat to mine as I tried to figure out why *Tranquility* was dead in the water and they were sailing south. It hardly mattered though, because even if I *was* sailing south at a knot, it would have taken two more days of nonstop running to reach my first waypoint. Four days to sail just sixty miles, and there were nine more waypoints to go after that! The math wasn't working very well with my plan for the rest of the summer. Still, I went on deck and pushed the main boom out over the water and I held the clew of the genoa to the rail trying to get it to billow in whatever faint wind might be blowing out of the north. *Tranquility* wouldn't budge though, and when the main began slatting a little later, I dropped both sails on deck.

Compared to what was to come, day two wasn't all that bad really. I got a lot of reading done and made a huge pot of stew with a whole canned chicken (yes my dears, an entire plucked chicken, bones, giblets and all, stuffed into a quart-sized tin can that's cooked alongside a thousand others in a mid-western autoclave—mmmm—feel the magic of *that* for a moment), black olives, tomatoes and plenty of Parmesan cheese islands floating on top. Around sunset, the wind picked up to ten knots. "TEN KNOTS!" I hollered as I ran to the mast and hoisted sail for what seemed like the millionth time of the voyage. Then I hopped into the cockpit and pulled the mainsail in and cranked on the sheet winch to trim the genoa. When the sails billowed into shape, I brought *Tranquility* around and steered her south, making around three knots with the wind dead-aft. I calculated my ETA to the first waypoint based on my current speed and heading and figured I'd be sailing over it early the next afternoon. Unfortunately, the wind I was basing this estimate on turned out to be another zephyr and *Tranquility* was ghosting along five minutes later. Then she was dead in the water. I sat at the tiller waiting for the wind until midnight; when it didn't come, I dropped the sails and crawled into my bunk. I'd done very little sailing in the last 24 hours, but I couldn't have been happier. I was on my very own boat in the middle of the North Pacific Ocean after all! I was on the voyage of a lifetime! It's the sort of thing people dream about, yet there I was! What did I expect? It was only day two!

Ah, the elation of *Day Two*. How immediate, how genuine and how very short lived! I now remember the following week as a long, slow-motion montage set on a tiny sailboat affixed to an utterly windless sea. It begins when I am leaning over the rail for hours trying to snag a salmon. I've tied a sinker and large treble hook to the end of the tuna cord and I'm yanking it up and down through a school of fat fish. There's concentration-drool spooling into the sea from my lower lip and I see my haggard, sunburned face and wild hygroscopic hair reflected in the water alongside the hull. I do not care, I do not blink and I do not catch one – they're too fast for me. I spend catatonic afternoons staring up at the cloudless blue sky, daydreaming or watching transparent atoms and squiggly filaments drift across my eyeballs; I blink to restart them when the show is over. There are crisp early mornings sitting in the warmth of the companionway with hot cups of coffee, I'm watching the sun rise over the mountains of the Olympic Peninsula. I understand there is quiet majesty to spare in the world and I wonder where all of the other young sailors are that summer.

I'm below deck, deep into the charts, planning, plotting, estimating and hypothesizing over the whys and wherefores the winds of the world blow or do not blow. I conclude I will be in the Channel Islands no later than October 15th –even if I have to motor the entire way there. I decide to sail though, and I commit myself to the voyage all over again— as originally conceived—no matter how long it takes. I allow for years, but I'm confident I will be in California in a few weeks' time. All the while, I'm drifting farther and farther offshore, but there isn't any wind I can sail on. To spite it, I refuse to motor when I so easily can. I have forty-six gallons of fresh gasoline aboard –I never touch it. I've turned into a sailor by then and I tell myself it has to be the wind or nothing.

I'm sitting down in the lantern-lit cabin, sanding one of *Tranquility*'s spare double-blocks to baby skin smooth perfection with 700 grit paper. Then I begin varnishing it to a flawless gleam with a crafter's paintbrush –ten transfixing coats in all, at a hundred strokes each. I convince myself it will be worth money someday...*big* money. I lay in my bunk in the deepest, darkest hours of the night with the SSB radio on my chest as I slowly roll the station dial through 29,999 frequency digits. One pass takes over an hour. I never find a station to listen to but I'm unable to stop trying. I tune in to mysterious plucking noises and modulating twangs and ponder their escalating and collapsing scales for minutes at a time. Static from the lonesome universe or the tell-tale noise of secret doings –I wonder which. I read and then re-read the radio pamphlet and I walk around the cabin in my socks with the thin wire antenna, trying to position it better. This doesn't help and I decide my new radio is broken. I carefully put it away. It cost me $400 and I want to return it someday.

I live under the tyranny of the zephyr all the while. Each time it blows, day or night, I hoist for it, and each time it goes on its wandering way in ten or fifteen minutes. It blows for an hour just once, but it's all the same to me by then. I'm on a pilgrimage, so I hoist the sails and steer the boat for a few hundred or a few thousand feet when I have hundreds of miles to go. I know it doesn't make sense to hoist sail for a few minutes, but it's an involuntary action for a sailor. I will do it a thousand times, on a hundred different passages to come.

I end up drifting past the first waypoint of my epic sailing voyage. I am twenty or thirty miles to the west of it though, and with that much error in my course, I don't even bother to delete it. My eyes must be getting funny too, because the boat seems bigger and I seem smaller every day –then all of a sudden, I'm a giant and *Tranquility* is a dinghy. At some point, my eyes are so worn out I can no longer read, so I begin talking to Billy instead. This goes on until I'm reciting lines from high school plays and cracking myself up with jokes I can't remember. I box the compass over and over again, reciting its cardinal and inter-cardinal points aloud: north; north by west; north-northwest; northwest by north; northwest and so on and so forth until I'm through south and back around to north. I have serious conversations with friends and family, with the boat and myself. There are no ships, no flotsam, no birds and no wind; not a single light on the sea or aircraft in the sky. The ocean is completely empty except for the occasional mola mola and I wonder why I'm seeing so many of them so far north. I don't know it yet, but there's a strong El Niño that summer and a windless high pressure system is parked over the eastern Pacific. The water is so warm along the west coast of Washington that people are catching tuna twenty miles from shore and spotting mola mola in the mouth of the Columbia River –someone even catches a billfish there.

While rummaging through the boat one morning, I'm shocked and deeply saddened to find that the fastener container I meticulously organized my first day on the boat filled up with saltwater at some point –most likely when *Tranquility* flooded off Bainbridge Island the first time I sailed her. Every nut and bolt in the box is ruined by rust, so I dump its muddy reddish contents over the side and think back on how much I've learned since those first days. I remember the maiden voyage and smile to myself. I wonder how John's summer is going on the Columbia River. This reminds me of Lisa for some reason and I am sad for the rest of the day.

Around noon on day nine, I fixed my position and found that I was forty or fifty miles northwest of Grays Harbor on the southern Washington Coast. I was more surprised to learn that I was almost ninety miles south of Cape Flattery. I couldn't believe the northwesterlies didn't blow and I resolved to motor south if they hadn't picked up by the following morning. That pact turned out to be a poorly timed one.

The skies slowly clouded over as the sun set that evening, and around 10:00 pm *Tranquility* began to buck uncomfortably and the wind started to blow for real. I was already in my bunk but I bundled up and went on deck. Standing in the cockpit, I realized it was twenty-five knots of warm wind and I was suddenly invigorated, so I tromped to the mast and hoisted the main and the small jib. When they filled, I brought *Tranquility* around into the south and she took off with the wind at her stern. I sailed into the southeast for almost an hour, making a little over four knots. I was wide awake by then and singing made-up sea shanties to myself. The wind was holding, and I was thrilled to finally be on my way. I planned to sail all night long.

When I remembered to turn on the running lights, the compass blinked to life and its red lamp shed light on a serious problem: I was sailing south but the compass was pointing northwest. I looked at it several times before I leaned over and tapped its dome. It was a new instrument and I was hoping the card was stuck, but I saw it swinging freely when the boat slewed around. Something else was wrong, but I couldn't figure it out. *Tranquility* was running as fast as she could but her handling was abnormal. I looked up at the mainsail: it was pressed against the spreaders and the boom was far out over the water. According to the weathervane at the top of the mast, the wind was nearly dead-aft. I glanced at the compass again and it was still pointing northwest –yet I was certain I was sailing south. The seas were all wrong too, and I assumed a big storm was on its way. I was sailing up and over a long swell with a steep wind chop running behind the boat. *This is impossible! The long swell and the wind chop should both be behin...*and then I realized the wind was coming from the south and I was sailing northwest. This was a dismal moment and I slowly brought *Tranquility* around for the reckoning. When she came about, the wind was strong and right on the nose. This meant I could sail for Canada, Alaska, Hawaii or the Washington Coast, but California was entirely out of the question. I chose Washington and sailed east. Apparently no one who offered me advice in Ballard that spring had any idea I could expect southerly winds off the Washington Coast in summer. It's fairly common but it's the last thing *I* ever expected. This was a ruinous development and I was angry and frustrated but there was no help for it, so I bottled it up along with everything else that had gone wrong on the voyage and I sailed where the wind would let me. Imagine you are me just then! After everything I'd been through on my way to the North Pacific Ocean, after waiting *nine days* for a northwesterly to send me on my way, and when the wind finally blows, it's a southerly?!

It was a rough night at sea for an unhappy man on a tiny sailboat. *Tranquility* slogged east for hours through a steep three-foot wind chop that was crossing the groundswell rolling out of the northwest. This made for a topsy-turvy ride. *Tranquility* was yawing rail to rail, plunging up and over triangular seas, driving straight through whitecaps. She dropped into troughs that knocked the wind out of her and there was *plenty* of sea spray flying over the weather cloth, striking me in the face and running down my collar. *Tranquility* was working pretty hard and she began pumping a continuous stream of crystal clear seawater from her hull –the first I'd seen in a long time.

As the uneasy night wore on, I fought the tiller and my exhaustion to keep the boat heading east. At some point, I began steering for a cluster of lights that appeared on the distant shore. I was delirious by then and expected to spend the rest of the night in a marina –if I could just hold on long enough. But I was at least twenty-five miles from the coast, and the lights I was sailing for were mounted on the masts of three trawlers. I do wonder from time to time what those fishermen made of me when I sailed between their boats. As I drew near the lights, I thought I was heading for a harbor dock with fishing boats tied up to it. In reality, the vessels were positioned in a broad semicircle far out to sea where they were working a net. I came up on them at hull speed and sailed right through the yellow circles cast on the sea by their sodium lamps. Those fishermen must have thought *Tranquility* was a ghost ship –god only knows what they made of her pilot. I caught a brief, incredulous look that passed between two of the men in bright orange slickers leaning over the rail of the nearest vessel. This is where yarns come from I suppose –the trues ones at least.

By sun up, I was smacking myself in the face, trying to stay awake until I reached the coast. I'd sat at the tiller all night long and wanted to be on dry land more than anything in the world, but it turned out to be a long and unsatisfying morning. The wind eased little-by-little as I neared shore—which drove me *absolutely* bonkers—and every mile that may have held some promise of a clean ending to the ordeal began taking longer and longer to cover. Then, with just a handful left to go, the wind died on me completely. I was wrecked by fatigue at that point and could go no further under motor or sail, so I dropped the main and jib and fell into my bunk, leaving the boat to drift on her own. When I closed my eyes, a confused midnight sea and a glowing red compass card appeared before me and began revolving around each other in concentric circles. I'd reached that point of zero-gravity exhaustion where I was weirdly aware I was sleeping for several hours. It wasn't very restful and I awoke later that afternoon in a foul, rummy old mood.

When I fixed my position, I learned that I was approximately five miles due west of Grays Harbor. This was a lucky break considering my confusion with the compass the night before and the fact that I was still getting the hang of navigating with a GPS. I hadn't even followed a proper course to get where I was –it had been too rough, so I just steered east as best I could, knowing only that the coastline would appear before me at some point. That strategy seemed to have worked pretty well, but I was in no shape to dwell on my good fortune. After ten days at sea, I should have been in Northern California, not Washington and the thought of that made me desperate to get off the boat.

So, without double checking my navigation, I quickly plotted a course for the entrance to Grays Harbor and began motoring toward it at full speed. As I made my way east, a bewitching siren's song began playing over and over in my head: *call Lisa; hot shower; greasy hamburger; long night's sleep; call Lisa; hot shower; greasy hamburger; long night's sleep; call Lisa...*I reached back to make sure the engine was running at full throttle. It was.

Although I'd never been into Grays Harbor before, something didn't seem right with the lay of the land as I neared its entrance. I can't explain this other than to say it was a nervous feeling that couldn't be ignored. I brought the chart up to the cockpit and tried to reconcile its drawn features with what little of the shoreline was visible through the binocular. To the south of me lay a low, sparsely wooded sandy peninsula, and to the north, a broad green point receded in the distance. There were a couple of aids to navigation off both of these prominences and they appeared to mark a channel which led to a wide inland bay. *Yes*, I thought to myself with hazy certainty looking back and forth between the chart and the entrance, *I'm definitely headed for port.* The only real discrepancy I found between the chart and what lay ahead was that on the chart the entrance to Grays Harbor looked like it was protected on its north and south sides by rock jetties. I hadn't seen those jetties yet, so I pressed on at full speed, expecting the confusion to clear itself up before I made landfall –which of course it did.

There's an art to crossing a river bar in the Pacific Northwest. They are the vigia of the region and a whole host of magnificent treacheries await inexperienced mariners there. One doesn't just drive his vessel toward a river entrance at full throttle like I did that day. A sailor who lacks local knowledge of the bar he wishes to cross must prepare in advance of his transit –not try to figure it out as he goes along. That being said, no amount of reading or tip-gathering from locals can prepare him for anything other than the most mild summertime crossing. Experience is little guarantee of perfect safety on Pacific Northwestern waters and mariners who've spent their entire lives crossing bars there have ended up meeting their end on one. They don't call those waters *The Graveyard of the Pacific* for nothing! The seafloor and shores surrounding Pacific Northwest river mouths are strewn with the bones of ships and men who thought they were going to make it into or out of port in one piece –god rest their weary souls.

On a chart, a river entrance won't look like much to a fool or a greenhorn. For the most part, it will appear to be a channel that's protected by a pair of jetties. This channel will look like it leads from the sea to an inland bay like any other. When a bar is seen from upriver or from a little ways out to sea, it may appear calm. However, a river bar is the chaotic meeting place of the primordial, hydraulic forces of nature and conditions on them change quickly. River and sea collide in opposition on a bar and since neither can yield very much, their energies are combined and converted into a terrifying sea state that can stack up and stretch for miles offshore. Add to this tumult any additional weather phenomena such as springtime runoff, storm surf, rain, fog or wind and you have the makings of a mariner's worst nightmare. There really are no words for it and by the time you realize you're in trouble on a river bar, it's usually too late to do anything about it.

There's even more going on below the surface. A river deposits an endless load of silt onto its bar, and these accumulations dam up the river and drive its navigable channel hither and yon, shifting the safest route through it day-in and day-out as the river finds the path of least resistance to the sea. These deposits eventually form deltas that become so heavy they down-warp the continental shelf underneath them. However, to get a more practical idea of the quantity of silt discharged by west coast rivers, take a look at the sand beneath your feet on any ocean beach in Washington, Oregon or California, and remember that nearly every grain of it was brought there from the mountains by a river.

There's a long list of considerations when crossing a bar and any serious mariner will do his own research before heading for one. Broadly speaking though, high tide, or just before it, is generally considered the safest time to cross, because the increase in water depth has a calming effect on breaking seas. Rising tides are also favored by low-powered vessels due to the slack or east flowing currents found in river mouths around high water. Of course there's much more to crossing a west coast river bar than that, so you'll want to plan ahead.

I reconsidered my wait-and-see approach a mile or so from the entrance to Grays Harbor when I caught a glimpse of what looked like the back of a breaker rolling toward shore. I didn't know how far away I was from the wave, so it was difficult to judge how big it was –or whether it was a wave at all. If it was close by, what I saw could have been a little whitewater stirred up by the current. But if it was far away, it could have been the back of a roller. It was impossible to tell, so I came about, put the engine in neutral and radioed the Coast Guard for a bar report.

The Coast Guard has done an effective job of letting the boating public know they're there for them at west coast river entrances. The USCG maintains a station at Grays Harbor, which is a busy timber and fishing port, as well as the outlet of the Chehalis and Elk rivers. There's a lot of vessel traffic in and out of there year-round, and the Coast Guard will happily radio a mariner a fresh bar report. They'll even come out in a boat and escort him across it. The same goes for all of the principal river entrances on the west coast of the United States.

My first call to the Coast Guard that day went a little like this:

"Vessel *Tranquility* hailing Coast Guard, come in, over."

"This is Coast Guard station Grays Harbor, go ahead *Tranquility*."

"I'm wondering how the bar is today."

"It's all clear, skipper –come on over."

"Umm...just like that?...it's like...all fine and everything?"

"Roger that skipper, been calm and clear for days and our surf boat was just out there for the afternoon report –it's looking really good right now."

"Roger, I'm inbound."

"Coast Guard standing by on VHF channels 16 and 22."

It sounded like a pleasant summer day on the Grays Harbor bar, and it was. I put the boat in gear and headed for the entrance even though the features I was seeing on shore weren't lining up very well with what was on the chart. I was tired and couldn't put my finger on any outright deal-breakers, so I continued on at full throttle. I suppose I was getting used to things looking different in real life than they did on my charts, and I was getting used to there being no wind when people said there would be, and I was getting used to radios and compasses not working like they were supposed to, and...I was getting used to things not being quite right on my voyage. *Dude...that's totally Grays Harbor*, I said to myself, even though I hadn't seen the jetties yet.

I doubt I'll ever forget the heart-stopping exhilaration that exploded in my chest and shot out through the soles of my feet when that wave curled up behind *Tranquility*. She caught it just before it broke on her stern and it carried her up its face like a bathtub toy. I fell out of the cockpit when the boat lurched over and I flew into the port rail, snapping it off at its base. Only the tight-fitting weather cloth kept me and the GPS and the chart from flying overboard. The motor screamed for a brief instant when the prop came out of the water, then it stalled. Everything in the boat that wasn't bolted down crashed around in drawers and lockers. The fuel tank threw off its bungee cords and smashed into my right foot. I did not let go of the tiller when I fell, and that turned *Tranquility* broadside on top of the wave. This probably saved her from pitchpoling (flipping end-over-end) but she did go over the falls, landing on her port side with the wave as it crashed all around her.

So there I was, banged up and cowering in *Tranquility*'s cockpit. She was drifting in a wide area of shoals, surrounded by low breakers. By some miracle, no other wave broke on her just then –it would have been the end of us. I dove for the engine and plugged its fuel line back in, realizing why it died and what saved it from throwing a rod when it over-revved. I yanked the pull cord, it fired right up and I laid on full throttle. I ran north along shore, dodging whitewater and the green crests of see-through waves. When a route opened up between the breakers, I swung the bow into the west and headed for open water as fast as the boat would go. *Tranquility* climbed to the top of the first wave she met, it was much taller and steeper than it looked and she balanced on its vertical lip for a terrifying instant before dropping off the back of it with a bottomless plunge. I had to endure several more frightening moments teetering between life and death before *Tranquility* was out of immediate danger. It was bell-clanging mayhem even then. I grabbed the radio mic and called in a frantic mayday. It was an *actual* mayday:

"MAYDAY! MAYDAY! MAYDAY! THIS IS THE VESSEL *TRANQUILITY*. I ALMOST GOT CAPSIZED BY A WAVE OUT HERE!!"

"Vessel hailing mayday. This is the United States Coast Guard, what is your position, over?" (It was the same coast guardsman I spoke to earlier).

"I'M OFF THE ENTRANCE TO GRAYS HARBOR AND I NEARLY GOT CAPSIZED ON A WAVE OUT HERE!!"

"Roger sir, how many persons are on board your vessel including yourself? Over."

"IT'S JUST ME!"

"Roger skipper, Coast Guard resources are being deployed to your position right now, are you wearing a life vest at this time?" I grabbed a life vest from the cockpit clutter and held it to my chest.

"YES I AM!!"

"Roger sir, do you know the water depth where you are?" I jumped into the cabin and flipped on the depth sounder.

"I'M IN TEN FATHOMS!" I yelled into the mic.

"Roger, sir...can you anchor right now?"

"YES! STANDBY!"

I went forward with the boat still in gear and she began a wide u-turn and headed for the surf line. After a desperate struggle with multiple lashings, I pitched the anchor over the bow and made its line fast just as *Tranquility* caught up on her hook and executed an abrupt, deeply carving, and most un-tranquil 180-degree turn toward open water. I flew back to the cockpit sidestepping over the rotating deck.

"DONE!" I yelled into the mic as the boat continued doing circles around her hook.

"Vessel *Tranquility*, stand by."

I went to the stern to kill the engine and when I got back to the radio, I overheard part of the conversation going on between the lifeboat sent to rescue me and the dispatcher on shore.

"Roger, motor lifeboat 3859, good copy, you say you don't see a sailboat out there?"

"Roger, we came out and made our turn, it's flat calm and there's no vessel on or near the bar at this time, over."

"Roger, good copy 3859...standby...*break-break*...Vessel hailing mayday, this is the United States Coast Guard, do you copy sir?"

"Roger."

"Skipper do you have any way of determining your *exact* position?"

"Roger..." I picked up the GPS and read the coordinates into the mic.

"Roger sir, good copy, standby."

A dreadful feeling came over me as I sat there with the mic half-an-inch from my lips. I glanced back and forth between the shoreline, the GPS and the rumpled chart before me. Maybe I *was* going to get myself killed. The radio crackled to life a minute later.

"Motor lifeboat 3859, this is Coast Guard station Grays Harbor: come in, over."

"This is 3859, go ahead."

"3859...uh...he's uh...about ten miles south of you...he's off Willapa Bay."

"Roger that...good copy...does he want to rendezvous for an escort into Grays Harbor?"

He wanted to rendezvous.

If you don't know it, Willapa Bay is a vast tidal estuary on the southern Washington Coast. It's the outlet of the Naselle and Willapa rivers and its entrance is to Grays Harbor what an unimproved logging road is to a four-lane highway. The seaward approaches to Willapa Bay are surrounded by sandbars, shallows and breakers; there are no jetties there. The Willapa bar is essentially the same undeveloped, undredged, ocean-river interface you would have found when the west was first explored. The entrance is confusing to a stranger because there's more than one marked channel and those channels are shallow, winding and subject to frequent change. Mariners are strongly advised to avoid the ocean entrance to Willapa Bay if they lack extensive local knowledge of the area.

I agreed to an escort into Grays Harbor that evening, but it took several hours to meet up with lifeboat 3859. What happened was I decided to motor north in order to save some time, but I went right past them and they me in the half-light of sunset. After an unbelievably long radio and coordinate saga, I finally fell in behind 3859. Once I was following them they radioed me several times to ask for my position and compass heading. *They must know I'm right behind them!* I thought to myself each time they called. Alas, much of the confusion of the past 24 hours was cleared up when I had a brief and embarrassing radio conversation with the Captain of the lifeboat as we made our way north:

"*Tranquility* this is Coast Guard vessel 3859. Do you copy, sir?"

"Roger 3859, go ahead."

"Captain, we've been plotting your course and...well, are you aware that your compass has approximately 25 degrees of error in it?"

"Negative."

"You'll want to look into that, skipper."

"Roger that."

I followed lifeboat 3859 across the Grays Harbor bar and pulled into a slip at the Westport Marina around 2:00 am. The Captain of 3859 had a few reassuring words for me and then his men carried out a vessel safety inspection which *Tranquility* somehow passed. When they left, I cleaned up the cabin as best I could and crawled into my bunk. I was badly shaken, humiliated and disgusted with myself. In this low, low state, I swore the first of many oaths to come on that voyage.

I'm done sailing. And I meant it too.

11

I spent a couple of fairly depressing days in port, lying in my bunk with the Willapa Bay incident playing over and over on the deck timbers above my head. There were no two ways about it: I was lucky to be alive and lucky to still have a boat. I began to wonder if I should continue the cruise or put *Tranquility* up for sale while she and I were still in one piece. There were sober arguments for and against, but neither option seemed like it would lead to a prompt or untroubled conclusion to my little summer voyage. On the one hand, I'd thrown my lot in with *Tranquility* for good or ill when I shoved off for California in her. Everything I owned was aboard and without her, I'd be homeless. On the other hand, the certainty of spring was long gone, summer was coming to an end, and for the first time, I was truly afraid of the sea and what it could do to me. When I searched inside myself for some of the carefree spirit that got me as far as Westport, and might be drawn on to continue the voyage, it remained as elusive as the northwesterly wind.

After some soul-searching, I realized that continuing on was just as fraught as giving up would be. And let's be honest: you get hit by the bus no matter how cautious you are in this life. So I decided to keep going, but I vowed to be a little more careful along the way. When I was able to file the Willapa Bay incident alongside the mysterious leak and the engine blowing up and the fire and the slice in my hand and the raging current and the mockery and the lack of wind, I figured I needed a little break from the voyage. I judged it wise to stay in port until the northwesterlies began to blow for real.

My decision to carry on gave me the courage to get out of bed. I ventured up the ramp on my third day in port and headed into the small, but formidable, seaside town of Westport, Washington –and lo-and-behold! Here at last were the young sailors of the Pacific Northwest I'd been looking for! Only in real life, they were the sixty-something RV crowd, ensconced in self-propelled floating condominiums and giant fiberglass sailboats which were, virtually without exception, motored everywhere they went. Alas, so much more drinking about sailing goes on in this world than actual sailing! At the uptown end of the port, I'm surprised to find row upon row of well-heeled pleasure craft securely tied to the docks. Their owners are spread out on the floats in lawn chairs, sipping cocktails or zipping around the marina in brand new inflatable boats outfitted with 50-horsepower engines and beer coozies. This sort of mariner has a folding bike, a monogrammed dock cart, a moped and a small car with him. They're fussing with expensive-looking crab pots and satellite dishes and water toys and generators that won't run the microwave, cabin heater and blender all at the same time. Oh! –and they're just waiting for one last spare part to come in the express mail. The dumpsters are overflowing with tall kitchen trash bags stuffed like giant white sausages. This is what so much of pleasure boating has become, dear reader.

It's been a long, hot, Washington summer by the looks of it, and the wives and grandkids are all seasick and sunburned and out of sorts in their scratchy life vests and sandy day-glow water shoes. The new son-in-law has on the board-stiff flannel, but he can't tie a salmon leader or fillet a rockfish to save his life –much less steer the goddamned boat. There's tipsy barbecues on aft decks, plastic pirate garb, China-made Old Glorys and plenty of freckled, once-buxom cleavage on display. The abruptly shifting, ethereal blue light cast by onboard entertainment centers illuminate the marina at night like a casino aquarium. Instead of fish behind the tempered glass, extended families sit on comfy cabin sofas in front of blockbusters unreeling on silent big screens. The soothing, plaintive stylings of Kenny G, Yanni and gaudy arias kick off the unsteady mornings and waft over the harbor all day long. *My god* I didn't fit in with them. I was at least twenty years younger than the sailors I met that summer. What an outcast I was! Scruffy, poor, inexperienced and oh-so-stubborn. With such a marginal boat, I couldn't have paid one of those people to go sailing with me! That wasn't the sort of seafaring I wanted to do anyway.

The enchantment of the sea is still there though, and once in a while you'll see them hanging around the American ports: the palmy, golden-skinned older men. Some handsome and smiling faintly, some grim-faced, distant-eyed and tired. They make unlikely crews of long-acquainted mariners and rabble-rousers: the subtle and soft-spoken class men strolling down the docks alongside kindhearted preppy wives and one-time dabblers in blue women and the picaresque. You see them sitting around the lantern-lit cabins of swept-window mahogany sport fishers, slack anchored on still isthmus waters. They're men who have grown up around boats and they've been places and done things and they know how to make a thing pay. They're at ease in their shirtsleeves and faded, long-bill caps and brightly colored canvas sneakers from eastern seaboard resorts you've no cause to have ever heard of. They're up late on summer nights, tapping the glass, sipping coffee and short drinks, yarning for real. The lines are all coiled down on the cleats and the deck head above the galley table is ship-shape and bristling with out of date charts and fishing rods served with blue and gold filigree, all deeply lacquered and kept like new.

They're getting few and far between though, as are the faded photos of South Seas atolls pinned up on their bulkheads –snapped as an afterthought on long-ago days from the spoked wheel of a blue water ketch cruising the trade wind route. Their collections of sun-bleached specimens from tropical wrack zones and the vasty Minoan deep have been boxed up and left in someone's attic...or worse. Those dried out curiosities, minutely-whorled shells and fossils from a briefly glimpsed world told the secrets of the seas and brought home tales of adventure through sunlit coral spheres, crowded with fish veering and backing in blue-green lagoons. They recounted devilfish lore of Melanesian frogmen, Mussulman sponge divers and weather-bound tropical fish collectors gone blowsy and half-native. All of it fetched from afar and in no need of embellishment.

The surface of those waters are barely scratched anymore, life is on land now and there's simply no time for it. It's all still there despite what they tell you, and our desire to experience it never goes away. It's been kept alive in blue-bound books full of stories of the sea and barnacled curios leaning up in front yards and through innumerable mysterious objects procured on watercolor days and set out for others to marvel at. They're talismans, precious treasures and experiences briefly captured by the mind, improved upon only slightly over the course of a lifetime, then passed on to children who don't know how costly they will be to keep. The old want to remember the bright nacreous days gone by and they want to pass them on to others, so they've been bequeathed again and again by parents who take their children and their children's children down to the sea. This is its own kind of seafaring, it's in our blood and it'll never leave us.

The town of Westport was a thriving bazaar of wholesome Pacific Northwest summer fun and that didn't help my mood one bit. There were salmon bakes and fish and chip shacks and ice cream stands galore. The bars were full every night and there were whale watching excursions and crowded bottom fishing charters –hawked alongside every other offering I had to give a wide berth to. I couldn't afford an outlay of more than a few dollars that week, due to the middle-of-summer mooring fees I was supposed to be paying the harbor master, so I browsed in a used bookstore and kept to myself. I settled on a fifty-cent paperback and steered clear of the happy times on my way back to the boat. It was going to be a lonely week and I was so unsettled by what happened on the Willapa bar that it never occurred to me to anchor outside the marina where I could recuperate for free and in peace. A quick accounting and onboard inventory that night revealed that my money *and* my provisions were running out faster than expected. So I began surreptitiously crabbing off the dock to supplement my dinners of reconstituted black bean flakes, tinned kippered snacks and industrial-strength instant mashed potatoes, seasoned with cheap Mexican hot sauce. Fall and winter were right around the corner and I reminded myself I would want to eat then, too.

On my Westport wanderings, I came upon an unkempt, crowded industrial supply store that served as an unofficial tool rental and pawn shop to cash-strapped fishermen and other down-on-their-luck seafaring types. This slowly-going concern was housed in a spacious beige metal building on a sandy side street. There was no sign out front and no need for one; if you lived or worked in the area, you had dealings with its proprietor, and if you were a visitor in need of something, you would be steered there sooner or later. It was one of those places, it was of a kind, and it was full to the brim with men's things. Hydraulic pumps, bronze salmon gurdies and beat-up metal boxes full of rusty boat tools sat on the floor. There was an old Lincoln arc welder and an antique oxy-acetylene torch cart left out. There were conduit benders and peavies leaning in the corner. There was a pipe lathe, a drill press and bandsaw for sale, general use, or both. Traces of a distant, more orderly past were still visible down certain aisles: the paint section was straightish and the abrasives shelf was laid out in a reasonably logical order. Chaos had prevailed though, and there was no sign of an impending counterattack. Twenty-year-old displays at the aisle-ends held new-old stocks of dusty industrial blocks, beefy marine-grade hose clamps and expensive American tap and die sets. One wall was devoted to every length and width of fan belt known to mankind –another to cork gaskets. The overloaded front counter was a sight for men to behold: within its dense strata of unopened envelopes, yellow invoices and hastily-penned sketches was a record of the business adventures of the proprietor and the fortunes of Westport fishermen and tinkerers. The requisite holed pistons, broken chain links and twisted pump shafts were set out by the jalopy register as object lessons to last minute corner-cutters, young men on the make and ne'er-do-wells. Expired displays of marine epoxy had hardened samples in front of them that held coins and bolts and copper pipes in their impossible grips. There were long, illuminated banks of foot-thick plumbing catalogs and auto part inventories, opened up in their reclining cradles like scholarly texts. Then, in the way-back, I caught a glimpse of something truly unexpected: The taillights of a DeLorean buried under cardboard boxes. On the store side of the counter stood a pair of well-worn swivel-top shop stools –naturally.

After a browse through this wondrous establishment and a long preamble of my freshest woes pitched as humorous chit-chat to the proprietor, I sold him my only power tools. This kindly man took pity on me and gave me a good price—sight-unseen—for my sad items (a cheap scroll saw, drill motor and circular saw) when he could have had them for almost nothing, or not at all. I thanked him with feeling, but he waved me off. "Bring 'em by tomorrow afternoon," was all he said.

When I added the money I made to what little I still had, I was able to pay my harbor fees for the rest of the week and make a pair of expensive phone calls. One was to Lisa, but there was no satisfaction in it. Her mother answered on the first ring and curtly informed me that she was in Tofino, Canada with her father and couldn't be reached by phone. And—this took a little longer to sink in—Lisa's mother didn't seem to know who I was. The second call was to John, who I knew would still be walking the docks of Ilwaco, Washington measuring Columbia River salmon for the state. He wasn't in his office when I rang, but I left him an upbeat message asking if I should pay him a visit on my way down to California. I left out all of the urgency and drama. Good times follow John everywhere he goes and I wanted to be part of it without being a drag. He isn't one to say *no* to a friend.

I spent a long day on the dock rehabilitating *Tranquility*. I fixed her broken rail and completely reorganized her cabin and cockpit lockers. I threw away half-a-dock-cart of ruined rice, pasta and sea biscuits that soaked up saltwater at some point or another. Anything close to the bilge, or that could possibly be reached by the water in it, was moved elsewhere. I adjusted the rigging, repaired a couple of torn batten pockets in the mainsail and reeved a new genoa halyard. I got the propane tank and the gas cans topped off and I watered the boat. Then, just before my moorage ran out, I received an uplifting voicemail from John through my pager service:

"Hey man! You should *definitely* stop by on your way down the coast! The fishing has been epic and Dalty"–Dalton, looong story there–"has been railing it in the woods and ponds for weeks! Anyway, if you're coming, when you get into the Columbia River, just stick to the north bank and then hang your first left. You follow that side channel into Ilwaco Harbor. It's a little confusing up there, but you'll figure it out when you see it. Oh, and be super-duper careful on the bar, man. And stay away from the south jetty! A couple of geezers got nailed out there big-time last week! I think one dude drowned or something. Ha! Ha! Ha! Hope to see you soon!"

The Columbia is the largest river on the west coast of North America. Its infamous entrance is feared by mariners because of its insatiable appetite for boats and men. The currents that run in the lower Columbia are strong, the bar you must cross to enter it is shallow, the navigable channels are narrow, winding and crowded by sandbanks. On top of that, the region is famous for sudden, extended bouts of extreme weather. The entrance to the Columbia River is about thirty-five nautical miles south of Grays Harbor and that on its own is a pretty long run to make down an unforgiving coastline in a somewhat-less-than-five-knot boat. Ever since my call to John, I'd been nervous about the trip to Ilwaco, and to prepare for it, I'd been reading up on the Columbia bar and listening to weather forecasts. They always called for the same thing: light and variable winds and a low, westerly ground swell. The written advice I came across for mariners headed to the Columbia bar for the first time can be summed up as follows: cross only in settled weather, at or near high water and get a bar report. *Pretty basic*, I figured as I psyched myself up and got *Tranquility* ready to go.

Tranquility

I left Westport on a hot and airless late-August day, and after a long look through the binocular, and a final call to the Coast Guard, I motored *Tranquility* across the Grays Harbor bar without incident. It felt good to be on my way south again, but I was on a tight schedule and tense because of it. I had a long way to go that day and not a whole lot of time to do it; this lent the passage an apprehensive, business-like feel. In order to reach Ilwaco before dark, I would need to cross the Columbia bar about two hours before high water that evening, then motor upriver to the Ilwaco channel at full speed. This itinerary didn't leave much time for sight-seeing along the way, but I planned the trip well and was confident I'd get to the bar on time.

Because I was under the impression that the lack of wind the last few weeks was an anomaly that would soon pass, I held out hope of doing a little sailing that summer. So, expecting the northwesterlies to magically pick up just outside the harbor, I hoisted the main and genoa and motored down the perfectly still coastline, keeping an eye out for wind. Two listless hours later it was more than clear I wouldn't be doing any sailing that day. Instead, I faced a long, unhappy trick at the helm with nothing to do but watch the compass, listen to the incessant drone of the engine and breathe in the oily exhaust drafting over the transom. This fact ate at me until I remembered I was the proud owner of a brand new autopilot. *What better day to break it out than this?* I asked myself. It was more than pleasant on the water, the batteries were fully charged and I'd steered by hand all summer long –I'd earned myself a little break. *Go ahead and let a machine do the work for you today.* Then I reconsidered: *Perhaps it's best to leave the autopilot for a less important day. I'm on a tight schedule after all, what if something goes wrong?... But what can possibly go wrong? The autopilot is new and guaranteed to work and I will sit here and read while it does its job.* Still, I decided to leave it for another day. But a few moments later, I was chiding myself: *Why did I buy an autopilot if not for a day like this? I could be reading right now or relaxing on the foredeck. Instead, I'm sitting here in the broiling cockpit, motoring. Why not let the autopilot do the work today?* I decided to go for it.

The type of autopilot I bought for the trip was a one-piece unit. It was an ergonomic rectangular plastic box, a little bigger than a deck of cards in cross-section and about two feet long. Housed within this box (the control unit) was a horizontally oriented, telescopic, metal control rod that you attached to a pin screwed into the top of the tiller. The opposite end of the control unit had a pin protruding from its base which allowed it to sit securely in a deck socket. An internal compass kept track of the boat's heading and the device used a small electric motor to extend and retract the control rod, which in turn moved the tiller back and forth to keep the boat on course. I read and re-read the operating instructions before I even brought the autopilot up on deck. It was pretty straight forward:

Place control unit pin into deck socket and attach control rod to tiller pin.
1. Plug unit in.
2. Turn unit ON.
3. Steer desired course by tiller.
4. Momentarily press and release ENABLE button to set and maintain desired course.
5. Press and hold GAIN button to adjust for the prevailing sea state.

Not too shabby!

I grabbed the autopilot and set it in the deck socket. I attached the control rod to the tiller pin. I plugged the unit in and turned it ON. I steered the desired southerly course (minus the 25-degree error in *Tranquility*'s compass) and pressed ENABLE. It was a perfectly calm day on the water, the low silky seas were serene and untroubled everywhere you looked. When I released the ENABLE button, the autopilot started humming and the control rod began making little jerky in-and-out movements and the boat stayed on course. *That's so rad!* I said to myself as I jumped into the cabin to grab a book. When I returned to the cockpit a few moments later, *Tranquility* was motoring east instead of south. She was headed straight for shore. The control rod was still going in-and-out of the control unit with earnest little movements as if it were weaving the boat through a hundred buoys. I was instantly annoyed and frustrated. A retarded monkey could have kept the boat on course that day! It was as flat as glass! I pulled the control rod off the tiller, corrected the boat, reset the unit, and pressed the GAIN button for a couple of seconds. As I did this, the jerky movements of the control rod transitioned to slow extensions and retractions that caused the boat to swing broad to port, then starboard, on a wide hunt for the desired course. I pressed the GAIN button for a couple more seconds, and with the control rod fully extending and retracting, the boat began making 180-

degree course changes. I pressed and held the GAIN button until the control rod was making its quick, feverish adjustments again. The boat stayed on course for a couple of minutes, then she slowly turned to starboard and headed offshore. I removed the autopilot, carefully placed it back in its box and grabbed the owner's manual to see if I'd missed anything. I held the instruction page six inches from my eyes and looked at every letter of every word printed there: *unit, pin, plug, on, enable, gain.* It was all spelled out in plain English! I started all over again. When I hit the ENABLE button on the third go-around, *Tranquility* stayed on course for about thirty seconds before drifting off to port and heading for shore –the autopilot didn't seem to notice.

I spent a couple of hours stopping and starting the boat, adjusting her speed and heading, and setting and resetting the gain, but I was finally forced to admit the autopilot wouldn't steer a skiff. I threw my hands up in disgust, stepped away from the tiller and cocked my right leg back wanting to kick the entire goddamned thing overboard, but not being able to afford it. *Almost a thousand dollars for a useless radio and an autopilot that can't steer a small sailboat on a perfectly calm day?! When I'm selling my tools for gas money and port fees?! And there's NO WIND?! What else can go wrong on this GODDAMNED TRIP??!!* I asked myself with throat-constricting frustration.

"WHAT IS GOING ON WITH THIS GODDAMNED VOYAGE??!!" I screamed over the perfectly silent, placid blue sea.

I tinkered with the autopilot longer than I should have *and* I completely misjudged the time it would take to reach the Columbia River that evening (or should I say night?) because it was dark by the time I arrived at the north jetty. Instead of crossing the bar two hours before high water, in order to take advantage of the last of the high tide's push upriver, I arrived a little after high water, which meant I'd be fighting an ebb current for at least some of the way up to Ilwaco. I'd seen this coming when I was still five miles away, though, and since it was dead calm, I cut in toward shore to speed things up. The mouth of the Columbia River is about three miles wide and in order to cross the bar while steering a safe, mid-channel course between the jetties, I had planned to approach it from the open water to the west. But by dusk, I realized there wasn't enough time for all of that, so I made some adjustments to my course and ended up cutting in so close to shore that I approached the river mouth from the north and slipped around the tip of the jetty with only twenty feet of water between *Tranquility* and the toothsome jumble of rocks there. That was me trying to be more careful I suppose. I'm sure my instant death at the muzzle of the mighty, mighty Columbia wouldn't have been wondered over for very long –if the wreckage were ever found. *What's the big deal anyway?* I thought to myself as I made my way around the end of the jetty and headed upriver, standing in the cockpit with the tiller between my knees, steering by leaning side to side with my hands in my pockets, as you do when you cross a dangerous river bar at night.

An echoing horn blast and a brilliant spotlight beam shining down on the cockpit from the bow of a freighter-sized Army Corps of Engineers dredge startled me from a sleepy daze as I neared the Ilwaco channel. The ship was the hard-working *Essayons*, whose crew removes, and dumps out to sea, eight million cubic yards of silt from the mouth of the Columbia River every year. If this were a single block of sand, it would have the footprint of a football field and stand somewhere around three-quarters of a mile high. The dredge was right behind me and apparently needed to stay on course, so after giving her bowman a big salute, I swung a left between the pair of wooden breakwaters that protect the Ilwaco channel from the river, and I headed inland.

It was a moonless night, I was tired, and the Ilwaco channel is winding and unlit. Baker Bay, the small body of water it wends its way through, is shallow and undeveloped –not that I'd ever looked at my chart of it. I was expecting to get there before dark, so I was steering only by the sailing directions John left on my voicemail. The breakwaters were well-marked, though, and as soon as I passed between them, I saw what could only have been the lights of the Port of Ilwaco twinkling in the black distance a couple of miles to the north. I flipped on the depth sounder, pulled out my spotlight, and began heading for the first channel marker I saw. This was a red, numbered reflector, nailed to a crooked piling on my right. *Right-red-returning*, I mumbled to myself as I slowly motored past it and began steering for a well-lit dock that appeared a few hundred yards away on the opposite side of the channel. I shined the spotlight up ahead of the boat as I made my way inland. The channel was much wider than I expected, and the beam crossed the darkness a few times before picking out the second piling; I carefully lined *Tranquility* up on it. A few minutes later, I glanced at the depth sounder in the cabin and noted that its whirring dial was flashing a zero, or pretty close to it. *Great!* I thought to myself, *now the depth sounder's broken too!*

I slowly motored abreast of the lighted docks to port and headed up the channel for about a half hour. For some reason though, the lights of Ilwaco never seemed to get any closer. I figured I was fighting a current, so I reached back and wound the engine up to full throttle. After another half hour, the harbor lights still seemed as far away as ever. I wasn't positive though, so I stood on the thwart and shined the spotlight aft. I could just make out the second piling in the distance but the lighted docks to port hadn't dropped very far astern. This was perplexing, so I left the boat running at full throttle and went up to the bow for a look around. Open water and a small island lay up ahead, behind the boat, roiling prop wash trailed astern, but we didn't seem to be going anywhere. Then I noticed that the little bits of leaves and sticks floating beside the boat were strangely inert and there was no wake spreading away from the bow. *What sort of channel is this?* I wondered, tromping back to the cockpit. I glanced in the cabin at the depth sounder and it still read zero but I knew that couldn't be right...

Then it dawned on me: I'd run *Tranquility* aground. One probe over the side with the boat hook confirmed it! I jumped to the motor, put it in reverse and gunned it over and over again, but *Tranquility* was stuck fast and had been for almost an hour –no problem though. *At least the tide's on its way back in!* I thought to myself cheerily, as I chucked the anchor overboard and paid out thirty feet of line. *Don't want to drift away on the high tide!* With that, I went below and climbed into my bunk, believing I'd be back afloat in no time.

I woke at a deep and dark hour, when a sudden lurch to port rolled me over in my bunk. I lay there with my back up against the mast for a few seconds trying to make sense of the strange new disturbance. *Hmm... Tranquility shouldn't be leaning over if the tide's coming in*, I thought to myself, completely befuddled and on the verge of drifting back to sleep (this is why you don't make landfall in unfamiliar places at night). I pulled my pillow to my chest and hugged it close, pretending it was Lisa cuddling next to me. I clamped my eyes shut and slowly put the pieces of the previous day back together. Eventually it occurred to me that I'd crossed the bar a little after high water, which meant the tide was on its way *out* when I entered Ilwaco channel, not coming *in*. Somehow I mixed this up. Anyway, *Tranquility* wouldn't be afloat until the next high tide. What would become of her in the meantime was entirely unclear to me because I'd never run aground before. I sensed what was coming wasn't going to be all that much fun. I sat up on the edge of my bunk, lay my head in my hands and let out a long groan. Some sort of new doom was on its way and I grabbed two fistfuls of hair and squeezed until the strands began to pop and break. When it started to really hurt, I asked myself a simple question: *Say there Billy...does the tide come in or go out after a flood?...or don't you know that yet?*

I got dressed, flipped on some lights in the tilting cabin and went up on deck. *Tranquility* was leaning hard to port as if she were sailing in a strong breeze. I sat in the dark on the high side of the cockpit and watched her inch into the river little-by-little as the tide fell around her. Seeing *Tranquility* stranded like that and knowing she would be stuck there until sometime the following day brought on a special kind of misery with Ilwaco so close by. I honestly didn't think things could get any worse until, for some unknown reason, *Tranquility* started to submerge. Not that she was sinking *per se*, she was just leaning so far over that the river began lapping at the edge of her deck. *What's this?* I wondered as the river crept aboard my boat. In an hour, *Tranquility's* port side was awash and the river was licking at the bottoms of the glass ports in her cabin side. When the glasses were half submerged, I glanced at *Tranquility's* low-slung stern and her deep cockpit—which drained directly into the bilge—and I wondered how far she might lean and what I was going to do if she didn't stop. When the seals in the ports began to leak (they could be opened for ventilation) I jumped below and tightened the thumbscrews on them with an adjustable wrench. A tingling rush of extreme dread shot through me when the glass in one cracked as I tightened it. Expecting *Tranquility* to begin flooding at any moment, I rushed around the boat, shutting the seacocks for the galley sink and the defunct inboard engine. When that was done, I jumped on deck, threw a bucket into the cabin just in case I had to bail at some point and I stuffed a sponge into the cockpit drain –not that that would have made much difference, because there weren't any seals on the cockpit locker doors. Still, it seemed like a good idea to me at the time.

About three hours after running aground, *Tranquility's* low side was completely underwater with her ports submerged, looking like eerie Captain Nemo aquariums with the cabin lights shining through them just below the surface of the greenish river. Two panes of glass, one of which was cracked all the way across, were all that stood between *Tranquility* and total destruction that night. She kept leaning and leaning, until the top of the cockpit coaming was only an inch or two from the river. If water began spilling into the cockpit, I knew no electric bilge pump or frantic one-man bucket brigade in the world would be enough to save her. That was a hairy couple of hours watching poor *Tranquility* lay over on her side! Her hull eventually touched bottom though, and the tide went out without flooding her.

When I was able to descend to land that night, I had my very first look at *Tranquility*'s undersides. She was nothing special below the waterline, except she was much bigger than I expected. Her poor-handling was explained by her stubby bows, slab-sided bilges and three-quarter cutaway keel upon which hung a too-small rudder. A wobbly, beat-up, two-blade propeller protruded from her stern timber. I pushed on her thick slimy sides: she was heavy and didn't budge. I made a fist and punched her on the bow for all the trouble she'd given me. Except for the pool she lay in, she was on dry land. It occurred to me that she was in my natural element for once. She couldn't just shy away from me like she did when I tried to exert my will on her from a skiff. One doesn't have to work very hard at assigning human traits to a boat, by the way – spend enough time around them and you'll learn that each has a particular personality and temperament.

So there we were, stranded in a shallow puddle, in the dark, no going ahead and no going astern, just like in the dream. There really wasn't a whole lot I could do about the situation until the next high tide, so I climbed back aboard and tried to get some rest. *That's it...I'm done sailing*, I said to myself as I drifted off to sleep on the settee cushions that I laid out on the galley cabinets. This short span of cupboards was the only thing close to a horizontal surface in the boat that night.

The roar of a speedway for semi-trucks woke me early the next morning. When I crawled into the tilted cockpit, I saw an endless procession of fishing boats—big and small, private and charter—heading for the Columbia River. I was taken aback by my new surroundings to say the least. The broad channel I entered the night before had been reduced by the falling tide to little more than a muddy, cut bank ditch which *Tranquility* lay far to starboard of. Most of what had been Baker Bay was a vast expanse of hummocky sand. *Tranquility* was perched high and dry near the top of the tallest hummock of them all. This rise had some bushes on it and was perched at the far southwest corner of the dunes. *Tranquility*'s keel was a couple hundred feet from the nearest water and Ilwaco Harbor lay a mile or so to the north. A narrow beach backed by crumbling cliffs topped by forest, lay to the northwest. To the south and east was the wide Columbia River. Oddly enough, directly to the west, on the opposite side of the channel, were the low buildings, safety orange helicopter and docks of a large Coast Guard station. These were the lights I passed by the night before. Seeing a Coast Guard base so close to my wrecked sailboat gave me a feeling that's difficult to put into words.

I spent the early part of the morning fetching pails of river water and scrubbing sea growth from *Tranquility*'s hull with a stiff deck brush. I pulled the anchor and rode out of the bow, walked it down the slope to the edge of the channel and stuck it in the sand. I led the bitter end of the anchor line up and over the stern and wrapped it around *Tranquility*'s sheet winch in preparation for pulling her off the beach at high water (an anchor so set is referred to as a kedge, using one to move a vessel, is known as kedging). I threw the rolled-up inflatable off the foredeck and pumped it up on the sand, just in case I needed to abandon ship.

The tide started coming in slowly around 9:00 am. It crept up the sand menacingly, washed over *Tranquility*'s keel and began climbing up her sides, probing here and there, looking for a way in. The river rose up to her cabin top again and *Tranquility* began gently bouncing her side on the sand. When she was almost upright, a large inflatable boat with an inboard engine zipped over from the Coast Guard station and a few corn-fed lads and lasses in work blues offered to give me a hand. I thanked them and welcomed their help.

When *Tranquility*'s keel began bumping on the sand, we cranked on the sheet winch together and tugged at her from behind with the big inflatable. We ran back and forth across the main deck trying to rock *Tranquility* loose. We called charter boats on the radio and asked them to strafe us with wakes as they went by, hoping the wave action would free her. Three big boats ran past us, but she wouldn't budge an inch. Desperation set in just before high water, and with no clearly designated leader, the operation descended into chaos with plenty of hollering and ill-considered, but well-meant, strategy changes. The anchor broke out and for a little while, we thought we were winching *Tranquility* off the sand. Then the chain came up to the stern and we knew that was a bust. We struggled with her for an hour after high water before giving up.

"The only problem," said a young coast guardswoman, "is that last night's high tide was the highest of the period, so the highs to come are going to be lower and lower until it turns around again...so you might actually be stuck out here for a couple of weeks." With that dismal prospect settling in my mind, the coasties jumped in their inflatable and sped back to their base. The United States Coast Guard is in the life-saving business, not the property-rescue business. They did offer to take me to shore and I thanked them, but declined.

This wasn't the low-point of the voyage one would imagine. I was really worried about *Tranquility* but I didn't have a whole lot of time to sit around and ponder what two weeks stuck on a sandbank was going to do to the boat or my chances of reaching California that summer –or ever. If the next high tide was going to be lower than the last two, I needed to do something quick—I hadn't the faintest idea what—but I was pretty sure I was going to need John Walters for it. So, with everything in my world freshly in doubt and absolutely no idea how *Tranquility* would fare on the outgoing tide, I sprang into action. I heaved the outboard onto the skiff, threw a few things in it, bolted some food and made a beeline for Ilwaco Harbor. An 18-horse pushes a 10-foot inflatable along at a pretty good clip and I made it across Baker Bay in just a few minutes.

The Port of Ilwaco is a much smaller and far more quaint version of Westport. It has the day-trippers and summer moorage guests and the fishing charters and a few shops selling the usual coastal kitsch. It's all centered around the sort of working harbor you find on the east coast, with its small fishing fleet and weathered docks, the clapboard ice-house and fish buyer's warehouse on the end of the pier. With its old families, hardscrabble work boats and mismatched color schemes, it has an American folk art tone without any pretension. The moment I set foot on the dock, I saw John walking toward me in his forest green vest and Department of Fish and Wildlife hat. He was putting his long knife back in its sheath and tucking a clipboard of salmon stats under his arm. He must have seen something in my eyes as we approached each other, because as soon as he looked up, an expression of instant recognition and understanding crossed his face. He burst out laughing at me from twenty feet away.

"Wher...? Ha! Ha! Ha!...Wher...? Where's *Tranquility* man? I heard some guy crashed his sailboat out there! But I never thought it was *YOU!* Ha! Ha! Ha! What are you gonna do now? What about California?" John asked, putting his hand on my shoulder, giving me a friendly jostle. Word travels fast in a small town. I've heard it said that the only problem with living in them is that people know what's going on with you before *you* know what's going on with you.

"Well," I said sheepishly, "I was hoping you'd give me a hand out there at high tide tonight. *Tranquility*'s in pretty bad shape right now dude."

"Oh, don't worry man! We'll get her off of there somehow!"

"Sven! Sven" John hollered to a guy our age walking down an adjacent dock. When Sven looked over, John pointed to me. "This is my friend who's taking us salmon fishing! This is the guy I was telling you about! That's his green sailboat out there!" Sven raised his arm high overhead and gave us a thumb's up.

"Sweeeet boat! Call me!" he yelled, holding his hand up to his ear like a phone.

I poked around the harbor for half the day and when John got off work that afternoon we drove out to the small farmhouse he and Dalty spent summers in, so John could attend to a few pressing matters of his own. I sat on a beat-up living room couch while John sorted through some mail Dalton left for him on the little formica kitchen table. He looked over a credit card bill for several minutes trying to figure something out. When he put it down, he picked up the new Campmore catalog, leaned back in his chair and began thumbing through it, lingering in the outdoor apparel section, sipping thoughtfully at an ice-cold bottle of apple juice he pulled from the fridge.

"Polar fleece prices have sure come down in the last few years," John said between sips.

"Oh have they?" I asked, drumming my fingers on my knees and working my foot on the floor like it was running the treadle of a sewing machine. "Um...John...I don-"

John spoke up just then: "So...uh...you say the keel's stuck down in the sand pretty far man?"

"Yeah dude, it really is."

"And the next high tide is late tonight...but it's going to be *lower* than last night's?"

"Um...yeah bro, I'm pretty sure about that."

"How *much* lower is the real question man," John said, putting down the catalog and reaching for his tide book.

"Who even knows," I said miserably.

"So...the river's getting *shallower* every day...but she's sitting on *sand* right?" John continued, thumbing through the pages of tide predictions, looking at the heights and times and thinking it through. "Sand's soft, man!" he suddenly exclaimed. "So why don't we just take some shovels out there and dig a big-ass trench behind the boat and pull her out through *that* when the tide comes in?"

I sat up.

We looked at each other for a moment.

It was just crazy enough to work!

John and I raided the tool shed behind the house for anything that might come in handy during the excavation. We made a pile of shovels and buckets and pry bars, boots, gloves and chest waders. Imagining *Tranquility* propped up at some point, I started dragging four large timbers to the door.

"Not gonna need those. No ways. *Tranquility*'s coming off *tonight* man," John said, vetoing the posts as soon as he saw them. When I heard that, I knew who was in charge of phase two of *Tranquility*'s salvage. The Columbia River was John's territory, and at that moment, I put *Tranquility*'s fate entirely in his hands. When we had everything ready, we loaded up John's Volkswagen van with the gear, but before we left for the harbor, John went back in the house for fifteen long minutes. When he returned, I saw that he'd changed his shoes and socks.

"Dude!" he said, climbing into the driver's seat. "I've been walking around *all day* and my feet are totally killing me man."

"Sucks to be you!" I said, turning to him for a laugh. John and I both knew *Tranquility* was in serious trouble and we knew we had a long night ahead of us.

As we were transferring our gear from the back of the van to the skiff, an old man approached us in the harbor parking lot and struck up the sort of totally unhelpful conversation smart-ass men like to have with dim-wits whenever they get the chance.

"Stuck on Little Sand Island are ya?"

"Yep that's me," I said, dropping a dock cart next to John at the back of the van.

"That's real bad timing you know? Last night's high tide was the highest that's gonna come for *several* weeks now."

"Yeah, we know about that already!" I said giving off a harried, unwelcoming vibe.

"Many, many years ago another sailboat got stuck right where you are...took 'em two years to get her off the sand too...only she sunk the same day she was re-floated! Heh-Heh. That old boat was a *toooooo-tal loss*, too much strain on her timbers I s'pose. I guess you know about that too, do ya?"

"Not really," I said, but I was pretty sure it wasn't applicable to my situation. I hoped to god it wasn't.

"Yessir...you can read all about that one at the maritime museum over in Astoria...if'n you care to. Course, sometimes the sand just sucks a boat right under and they don't get no chances to save her. So you boys is real lucky I guess –that river's a mighty mean one."

"Okay pops, maybe we'll see you later?" I said, stepping between him and John and turning my back.

"May indeed be," he said walking away. "May indeed be."

John twanged out the dueling banjos from *Deliverance* on his lower lip when the man was out of earshot.

My stress level ratcheted up a few more notches when the outboard began misfiring and died on our way out to Little Sand Island. It took us almost an hour to row to the boat and John made a plan for us as we went.

"Okay man, here's the deal: when we get out there you're gonna see if you can fix the engine and I'm gonna start digging the trench. Cool?"

"Cool."

"When you're done, you help me dig until the tide comes in, got it?"

"Got it."

"Then you're gonna cook up a little chow for us and after we eat, I'm gonna get some shut-eye. Don't wake me up until she's standing, okay?"

"Okay."

Tranquility

Over the years I've learned to listen to John. He's super-duper smart.

We hit the sand without a word that evening and began running the shovels and other gear up to *Tranquility*. We dragged the empty skiff around to the low side of the boat so I could get the engine aboard and John began opening up a wide trench along *Tranquility*'s keel, digging with the methodical, automatic shovel work of a pro. I heaved the engine into the cockpit and transferred it to the motor mount. We did these things without talking, each knowing what needed to be done and doing it, one anticipating the needs of the other and setting things within his reach or moving them out of his way. I hoped the engine only had fouled spark plugs due to the long motor from Grays Harbor and the exertions of the afternoon salvage attempt. As soon as I had a new set installed, it fired right up.

"Propulsion!!" I yelled to John.

"Roger, come dig!!"

"Anchor!!" I said.

"You better do it quick!!" John hollered over his shoulder.

I leapt off the boat, jogged the anchor out to the edge of the channel and buried it in a deep hole. When that was done, I ran around to the high side of the boat and jumped in the trench next to John. His eyes were set and there was sweat dripping from the tip of his nose. He'd dug a two-foot-deep ditch alongside and underneath the keel and I began extending his yeoman's work aft toward the main channel. When the keel was completely excavated, John joined me on the beach behind *Tranquility*. I don't know how much time we had before the tide came in, all I know is it was a do-or-die situation and we dug in silence, breathing deep in the warm, sweet-smelling summer air. We dug without pause as the sun set and the silently rising tide overflowed the main channel; we dug as the stars came out and the river crept up the sand, turning it black in the still twilight; we dug with our boots underwater; we dug with the icy river numbing our groins and we kept on digging until it topped our waders and our shovels brought up thin, liquidy sand.

"This is such a trip!" John said as we sloshed back to *Tranquility* in the dark. "I didn't know you could do this with a boat!"

"Yeah, but you're not supposed to," I said. We threw the shovels in the skiff, hoisted ourselves into the cockpit, changed our clothes and I fixed us some chow.

As John slept, I tried to imagine what two weeks stuck on Little Sand Island was going to be like. I supposed I could make a decent life out there. Town wasn't far and I figured I'd have some visitors. I could paint the bottom of the boat and maybe even find a way to prop her up between tides.

Running aground became an area of interest of mine the first year I owned *Tranquility* and I learned many of the ways to re-float a boat that's been stranded. The first strategy is avoidance, of course. Study your charts; know your position; know the water depth and bottom characteristics around you; know where you're going and know what the tide is doing. If you do run aground, try to back her or tow her off immediately. If you're by yourself, row an anchor out to deep water and try to kedge her off stern first. If it's a sailboat, tie the boom out over the water and use the end of it to hoist the skiff –this can tilt the keel off the bottom enough to allow her to escape. If the skiff isn't heavy enough to heel the vessel over, swamp it. If it's windy and you're sailing when you run aground, pull the sails in tight to lean the boat over. Small boats can sometimes be towed off by their halyards because the leverage where the lines come out of the top of the mast is enough to tilt a light-weight keel off the bottom. If it's a really bad grounding, you'll need to jettison as much weight as possible. Fuel and water are very heavy, so are anchors and chain. Each case is different though, and it's best to keep a boat away from land. There's an old saying about running around: *There are those that have and those that are going to.* It's worth remembering.

I woke John when *Tranquility* was upright and he came on deck without a word and started cranking on the sheet winch with an eye overboard like he grew up on a Thames River barge. When the anchor line was as tight as it would go, I started the engine and gunned it in reverse. We kept at it for an hour but she didn't stir. When high tide arrived, *Tranquility* was definitely on her feet, but she stayed put for some reason. I wound the engine up to full throttle and let it surge while John cranked on the winch until the deck began to click and pop. I went up to the bow and shoved on the sand with the whisker pole but *Tranquility* just tilted to starboard with a high-centered wobble. The keel didn't bounce on the bottom like it did that afternoon. I wondered if we'd dug deep enough and a sinking feeling began to nibble at me, but I ignored it. I ran back and forth across the deck like we did earlier, but *Tranquility* wasn't swaying much. We threw everything we had at her, but when the high tide in John's book came and went, we were still on Little Sand Island. John wound the winch up to the next gear-straining level and I floored the motor without caution, but still she stuck.

Fifteen minutes after high water, John went and sat in the cabin and I killed the engine and plopped down at the tiller. This was the low point of the voyage you may imagine and our talk turned from salvage to *Tranquility*'s chances for survival. However, just when it seemed failure was certain, something odd happened: the anchor line went slack. I leaned over and gave the winch a few halfhearted turns. The line tightened and then went slack again. I cranked in another foot and then a few inches, thinking the anchor lost its bite. There was nothing for a minute and then I felt the keel thump the sand.

"SHE'S MOVING!" I screamed. John flew out of the cabin like he was on fire all over again and cranked on the winch with jerky stops and starts.

"ENGINE! ENGINE! ENGINE!" he hollered. I jumped to the motor, fired it up and dropped it in-and-out of reverse, gunning it like it was a brand new dirt bike and not a thirty-year-old barn find. *Tranquility* surged aft a few feet then stopped with a sticky nudge. I revved the engine and slewed it to port and starboard trying to walk *Tranquility* off the sand. She didn't seem to be moving and then the line drooped into the cockpit all at once. When John saw it he yelled, "GO! GO! GO!" and turned to the winch, cranking on it with both hands like a madman. *Tranquility* made halting progress through our ditch for about fifty feet and then she just slid off the back of Little Sand Island. She was afloat!

"SHE'S OFF! SHE'S OFF! SHE'S OFF!" we shouted, giving each other stinging high fives. We shouted some more when we circled around to the main channel and we shouted again as we wound our way past the Coast Guard station.

When we calmed down, John turned to me and said, "Dude," in a serious tone. "DUDE! You HAVE to stay *between* the pilings man! They mark the channel and they're numbered from like one to twenty or whatever. See that green one over there? It's fifteen and the red one over there is sixteen. They go *up* in number the closer you get to a port." I nodded enthusiastically. I'm not sure if I knew the number part.

"You should come out to the farm tonight," John said. "I think you and *Tranquility* need a little alone time man."

"Thanks dude," I said. "I love you, you know?"

12

John and Dalty lived in a small caretaker's cottage on the Paradise Cranberry Farm. The farm, which was owned and operated by the family of one of John's closest friends, was situated in a dense stand of old-growth forest in the middle of the Long Beach peninsula. The Long Beach peninsula is what its name implies: it's a twenty-mile-long, two-mile-wide sandspit that runs north and south adjacent to the Washington Coast. It begins just north of the Columbia River mouth and ends about ten miles south of Grays Harbor. There's farms and small settlements, trailer parks and wide-open pasture surrounded by fertile sandy lowlands broken up by woods, salt chucks, lakes and tidal sloughs. Long Beach is the largest town on the peninsula. Along its main drag you'll find all of the usual Pacific Coast diners and small shops, with the exception of Marsh's, a storefront curiosity museum that's been in business since 1935. The place is full of wild taxidermy, old logging and cranberry implements, shrunken heads, antique games of chance and wooden peep-show booths. There's bins of saltwater taffy, arrowheads, tropical seashells and reprints of old Washington postcards and photographs. It's the stuff kids' summer dreams are made of.

To the west of the peninsula is the North Pacific Ocean, to the east are the broad, shallow waters of Willapa Bay. This body of water is one of the healthiest estuaries in the United States, its marshy shores and winding channels teem with fish and wildlife: white-tailed deer; water fowl; raptors; mollusks; crab and salmon just to name a few. Willapa Bay is home to mysterious, uninhabited Long Island, where herds of elk roam old-growth red cedar and hemlock forests. The island has the highest concentration of bears in the state, and if you're ever there on a full moon, you'll get some idea of what the Pacific Northwest looked like a thousand years ago.

Regular hours weren't kept at the cottage, so when John and I arrived around 2:00 am, the front yard was lit up like a fairground. Dalton was home, and as usual, he had every light in the house on. The front door and screen were standing wide open. The bare bulb on the front porch was being mobbed by a hundred species of moth and other critters which flew in and out of the house, buzzing and banging on the single-pane living room windows. When we stepped inside, Dalty was pulling a cookie sheet of puff pastries out of the oven. "Dig in," Dalty said, tilting the battle-worn pan toward us, pushing his sweaty eyeglasses onto the bridge of his nose with a flour-dusted finger. Each delicate bun was topped with a sizzling dollop of white cheddar and a sliver of blackened yellowtail fillet.

But how best to describe energetic little Dalty? I mean, without immediately getting into his inappropriate jokes about mentally disabled quadriplegic children in rocket-propelled wheelchairs or creepy old men named Bob, who go on inner-city bus rides dressed as nuns looking for anonymous love on Halloween night? You know you shouldn't laugh at these jokes because your mama raised you right, but the humor is too earnest and the delivery too perfect and you just can't help yourself.

Dalty, Dalty, Dalty Wilkes: he was a gifted chef with all of the know-how and hard living that went hand-in-hand with the many years of restaurant life he had under his belt. He was also a talented woodsman and probably one of the finest fisherman the world has ever known. No, you do not know what I'm talking about yet. And you do not know someone just like him. Sorry, we're not talking about your brother or uncle here, we're talking about Dalty Wilkes. When I say he was a good hook, I'm referring to the pure soul of the little native fisher-child wearing the loincloth, who paddles you over to a stream bank in a dugout canoe, where you're taught to pick nameless wriggling baits from the underside of a tangled mass of water weeds. I'm talking about the primitive sagacity that warns you not to eat before you go fishing, so your hunger is there to give you edge. I'm talking about the tropical island son who can tell the difference between the dorsal fin of a blacktip reef shark and the wing of a ray skirting the surface of an atoll lagoon, from a hundred feet away. I'm talking about the guy who moves the bucket of catfish behind the log because he knows if it gets kicked over in the dark, those spiny, amphibian-like fish are going to slither back into the water, injuring and slipping out of hands on the way. I mean that you can stand next to Dalty Wilkes on the bank of a pond with two identical rods, reels, tackles and lures between you, and he'll pull in fish after fish and you'll catch one, or more likely, none at all. When you switch rods with him on a gentleman's bet, he does it all over again, while dragging on a cigarette and talking incessantly. One reason he's catching more than you: he's fishing closer to the little rill that feeds the pond and that's where things are happening. This isn't a fish story; he often did it, and not just to me. John can tell you sometime, and he'll have to, because even though Dalty Wilkes was one of the few North American anglers to have ever worn out a hook file, he wasn't one to boast, so someone's going to have to speak for him.

Dalty had a preternatural understanding of the behavior and desires of fish gleaned from a lifetime spent in pursuit of them. His formative years went to digging up rare baits, and examining the stomach contents of the species he stalked, and in learning their habits and life cycles from proximity and observation. Oh, and he'd read *all* the books, but don't talk to me of books! You can't put something in a book that you haven't done. That was Dalty *exactly*. He would already be where you were headed. He would know the strikes were going to come on the beat-up lures, the ones missing paint and barbs and the stepped-on ones with the asymmetrical wobbles in their tow. He would know the bite could start when the boat was turned around at the end of a long drag through a hot spot and not necessarily while you were on it. Dalty's eyes were always on the rod tips and he would be the first to set the hook, the first to flip the bail and let the line run free. Dalty was full of sayings and adages, many of which were NC-17. The only general audience one worth remembering was: "You can't catch a fish unless your hook is in the water."

If a dude on one of our many salmon fishing trips thought he was dropping some serious knowledge on the guys by mentioning that Columbia River old-timers have been known to spray WD-40 on their hoochies to attract the fish, Dalty might carefully steer the conversation toward the range of troll wire voltages preferred by Cross Sound salmon fishermen, or how they keep sperm whales from stealing the fish they're reeling in. Dalty wasn't competitive, but he could have been. I've fished with guys who keep track of whose fish is whose, and who caught the biggest, and how many, and that sort of insecure male nonsense. But for Dalty, it was strictly between him and the fish —whatever was going on there. He took angling seriously and it certainly got personal, but it didn't go any further than the fish he was after. Besides, he could out-catch anyone and everyone and I'm not just talking numbers here —I'm talking *zeal*.

"Just one more cast," he'd say as the rods were being broken down at the end of a long day. "Just one more cast," he'd say when the latches on the tackle boxes were snapping down and the beer cans were getting stomped. "Just one more cast," he'd say when the men were taking to the trail or weighing anchor. "Just one more cast," he'd say when they began to row away or disappear around the bend. *Okay Dalty, Just One More Cast.* It'll be your epitaph, though.

Dalty Wilkes didn't see the outdoors from behind the windshield of a fancy Subaru wagon. He wasn't separated from the elements by high-tech gear too fashionable to scratch up. He saw his world in person, on foot and in his everyday clothing: crawling on hands and knees through underbrush and blackberry to the forgotten lakes and overgrown ponds he and John found on old black and white survey photos at the library; casting slider rigs into the murk of golf course lagoons for catfish at midnight; spending short winter days in an icy tent pitched on the surface of a frozen pond with a cheap sleeping bag wrapped around his legs, trying to catch six-inch trout out of a hole he hacked in the ice with a kindling axe. Dalty lived in a world that was different from yours and mine and he looked on fences the way a bumblebee or a rabbit might. Don't bother trying to keep up with him in the bush either. He goes through nettle and over uneven ground like a Sitka buck. He's moving fast because he's using a stick to knock the stinging plants out of his way. You can keep your fancy rifles with the engraved receivers in their velvet-padded gun racks over the fireplace, because Dalty could do it for you with a .22 or a hardware store shotgun with slugs in it.

His cars were whatever came his way and they were always full of bits and pieces of plants, fungi and animals, be they endangered or invasive, edible or poisonous, there were desiccated turds and skins and smelly old bones waiting on the dashboard for analysis and/or positive identification. The trunk was an unclean abattoir and the macabre final resting place of (according to John) entire populations of Washington fish. Cut out one of the men in the old photos of duck hunters, where on the fence behind them fifteen mallard drakes hang by their scrawny necks, and you will have an idea of the kind of man Dalty Wilkes was. Not PC enough for a generation of know-nothings raised by other know-nothings? Then go back to your video games and television sets.

And Dalty's fishing rods and tackle boxes? What would *Field and Stream* make of those? How would they fit into the glossy catalogs put out by the cubiclejacks over at Huntco every quarter? Not very well I think. The rods were usually discount store and garage sale cast-offs missing eyes and tips and grips, the reels were in similar sad shape. The old metal tackle boxes he owned looked like rusty rat's nests inside: almost nothing store-bought or organized or new. He began rigging by pulling out a ball of tangled up fishing line full of split-shot sinkers, hooks and swivels. He'd snip off what he needed with nail clippers. Snicker if you like, but I assure you, for every varnished Hollywood fish trophy sitting on a sometime-sportsman's mantle, Dalty had a hundred or more to his name and a much better story to go with them. Dalty wasn't after trophies though. He was a consistent producer in fresh and saltwater. Dalty didn't just *catch* fish...he was *of* them.

Here's a specific instance, we went for a drive together around the peninsula one day that summer. We were out looking for crawdad ponds, I think, when Dalty stopped at what was no more than a roadside ditch (it was less than a foot deep and you could see the bottom). On a hunch, Dalton swung onto the shoulder and jumped out of the car. A fishing pole appeared in his hand as he walked to the ditch, and on his first cast, he pulled an eleven-inch wild cutthroat trout out of it. He took the fish off the hook, snapped its neck without even really looking at it, and slipped it into his jacket pocket. Dalty kept a rod tucked under the roof rack of his beat-up station wagon and it was ready to go at all times. I didn't even have a chance to get mine out of the back seat.

Wiry and tough as an Oregon logger, without a trace of gristle on him, Dalton Wilkes was a man to have with you when the going got tough outdoors. He was a man to put at the top of your desert island short-list (or if *Red Dawn* ever really went down). He was an artist of course, a painter, and a gifted storyteller, joker, tinkerer and schemer. He wasn't frivolous; he was complicated. Dalty was an unpredictable mix of ribald irreverence and straight-laced compunction so you never knew what tack he might take in a given situation, say, when a question of household propriety, or holiday etiquette arose. With his eyeglasses, lady troubles, wild living, button-down shirts, and that unquenchable interest in the piscine, Dalty Wilkes cut a fairly scumbled Bukowski–Ricketts silhouette.

What of our friend John Walters? Well, if you boiled down the fair American bones of every Eagle Scout and bicycle-riding country doctor that's ever lived, and inserted their DNA into the Fourth of July offspring of Abraham Lincoln and Betsy Ross, you'd get a decent copy of him. Raised by the school teacher daughter of a Washington hay broker and the land-surveyor son of a woman who came west swaddled on a buckboard and lived long enough to fly on a Boeing jet, John's upbringing was classic American. It was one part Norman Rockwell commemorative calendar, one-part *Stand by Me* and one-part heavy metal. Dalton and his twin brother Daryl (there were two of them for god's sakes and it's been hard on the world) who grew up next door to John, were responsible for the soundtrack and some of the other eyebrow raisers.

Who on earth except John Walters can say they're visited by wild ducks? Who can claim migratory birds as close friends? They know where John *lives,* or lived rather, and they still stop by his childhood home every year to visit his parents as they make their way from wetland to wetland up and down the Pacific Flyway. Why? Because young John raised wood ducks for years in a kiddie pool in his backyard and the spot was picked up by the larger avian culture. That's a class of animals with extremely good eyesight and a very, very long memory. See his photo? The one where he's nine or ten and standing in his mother's kitchen cuddling the downy duck chick to his bare chest? How precious is that? If you unraveled John's entire ball of string, I'm pretty sure you'd find that moment at his core.

I ask you, what grown man has paper-route anxiety dreams? And money from that first job still earning interest in his hometown bank? John reads the voter education pamphlets that come in the mail, and in the fall, he gets up early to meet with his children's teachers about the lesson plan for the coming year. He takes parenthood and careful driving and visiting his folks and riding his bike to work and every other civic duty seriously, even though his country was sold to the highest bidder right before his eyes! *How sad is that?* Still, he votes responsibly, does everything else he should do, and somehow finds time to victory garden. His flowers and peas spill all over themselves in the spring. The salad greens come up in thickets, are snipped at for months, then left to go to seed. In late summer, the ground under his tomato plants are splattered red with fruit too heavy to hang on the vine any longer. The old neighbor ladies slink in and out of his front yard in the evening, stealing vegetables from him. They can't seem to stop themselves, but John just waves to them and laughs. He's the most mild-mannered, clear-headed person I've ever known. And he's blessed with the good looks and sensibilities of a male mind forged in small town America a century ago. John is curious, intelligent and gregarious, perhaps, to a fault. He's good with women and children, of course, but men who don't really understand what females find attractive won't notice him in a crowd. The ladies flock to him just like his pet ducks did.

John and I took a seat at the kitchen table, Dalty brought us two cold Rainiers from the fridge and a puff pastry each. After a sufficiently embellished rundown of *Tranquility*'s escape from Little Sand Island, the conversation immediately turned to fishing: the day's catch, the word on the docks, who, where, what boat, species, size, the regs, relative edibility, bait used, time of day, how it all happened and who was thinking what and when and why. It went a little like this:

Dalty: "The skipper on the *West Wind* told me the coho mooch has been going crazy outside"–he meant across the bar–"said the whole boat limited in about an hour this morning."

John: "Yeah man, I was there when they came in at *9:30*!"–that's a *quick* trip for a charter boat full of pogies–"They had a couple hogs with them too...Ricky on *Sandy J* told me they've been slaying big Chinook on the low slacks up at north bridge." John let this valuable tidbit float on the air of the kitchen, shooting me a knowing look and a wink while he waited to see what Dalty would do with it.

"*What the...?* That's just weird."

"I know man...*I know.*"

"Two Beer Tommy told me there's a killer sturgeon bite happening on the lower Naselle right now."

"On what...like those ghost shrimp that guy Randy has been getting?"

"You got it..."

"I checked a private boat today that had a cooler full of legal lingcod...said they got 'em with frozen squid on drop rigs, just inside the tip of the south jetty."

"Yeah, but the south jetty?...*inside?*" Dalty's eyes were cautious, untrusting.

"It's been pretty calm out there the past two days...nobody's talking about breakers."

"I wouldn't risk it."

"Still...those were some big-ass lings."

"OH! I almost forgot! I caught a bucket full of dungies"–he meant dungeness crab–"on my lunch break and they're still out in the car!" Dalty said.

"I hope they're not funk, bro! Say, Dalty...what's for dinner anyway?...there's that sour cherry reduction and the rest of those baguettes and the asparagus."

"Are you thinking what I'm thinking?" Dalty asked.

"What, like dungeness cocktail and then sear those albacore steaks with the cherry glaze and serve it with the asparagus on the side?"

When Dalty went to get the crab, John turned to me and asked in a hushed tone: "Dude, how many people you think we can fish from your boat?"

When I crossed the Columbia bar, I intended to stay in Long Beach about a week before continuing on to California. But running aground and almost losing *Tranquility* in such an excruciating manner, right on the heels of the Willapa Bay incident, really took a toll on my confidence and morale. I didn't think about it like this at the time, but I needed to feel safe again before heading back out to sea. So, it turned into a *Boy's Life* summer except with gourmet food, cars, women, beer and cigarettes. Thanks to the liberal return policies of businesses that deal with wealthy people, I was able to arrange a complicated refund-by-mail scheme for the autopilot and the SSB. This would put almost $900 in my pocket and John fronted me a few hundred of it while I waited for the check. I ended up signing most of it over to him for our lifestyle.

The Paradise Cranberry Farm was a wide expanse of shallow, loamy bogs surrounded by thick forest, ponds and lush fields. It was the fertile sort of place where a green fence post could sprout new growth when pounded into the ground. The rhododendrons grow three stories high there, flocks of geese fly overhead and barred owls hoot their eerie hoots in the deep woodsy nights. You can hear bears crashing through the underbrush from a quarter-mile away and the elk are everywhere.

The caretaker cottage wasn't much, but it was enough. The house was a small, single-story, clapboard-like structure with a low front porch and a backdoor off the kitchen that led through a woodshed into an un-fenced side-yard. The plot was surrounded by big Doug fir, fragrant red cedar and alder. When you walked through the front door, there was a cozy living room on your left and on your right, a 1940s kitchen, a small bathroom and John's bedroom. John found the house and spent the first summer there, so he had dibs on the room. There wasn't much in it, just a small dresser, a bookshelf packed with well-thumbed field guides and a cardboard salmon-mobile slowly wheeling on the ceiling in the corner above his bed: Chinook, coho, chum, pink and sockeye all casting a spell over him as he slept. Dalty and I crashed across from each other on a tired pair of comfy living room couches. It was a cowboy pad but a Morris Graves sculpture sat on the coffee table between us, and a good print of *The Blue Boat* and some of Dalty's fish paintings adorned the dingy plaster-and-lath living room walls. The only thing the place lacked was privacy.

A cranberry farm needs a lot of water, but it's not used on the berry plants: it's used to flood the bogs at harvest time. Cranberries are extremely buoyant and water is pumped into a ripe bog to allow a self-propelled beating machine—similar to a highway sweeper that floats—to run back and forth over the berries, freeing them from the plants by agitation. Once that's done, they're skimmed like millions of bright red fishing corks into a corner of the bog where they're removed with a deep metal tub called a cranberry scoop. The water on a cranberry farm is an agricultural tool that's kept on the property in ponds. Long ago, some thinking person stocked the ones on Paradise Cranberry Farm with perch, crappie, bass and catfish and they've run amok ever since. There are ponds in the area that haven't had a lure cast in them for years and I've pulled fish out of peninsula ponds that weren't even hooked. They were just tangled up in the line after hitting the bait so many times. The sporting, foraging and bushwhacking in those parts is world class.

It was good living on the farm. You'd come home after a long day of exploring and find a paper grocery bag full of chanterelle mushrooms on the kitchen table, or a 16-quart stockpot full of chunky gumbo bubbling on the stove. People were always coming and going with wild food and drink and there was the usual brisk exchange of goods and services that you find in a small rural town. Our freezer was a fish cop's nightmare: heavy albacore tuna fillets and headless salmon were stacked like cord wood at the back and little plastic containers held what looked like congealed blood and caviar. Freshwater fish from long gone summer days grew ice crystals in the door cubbies, one degree of separation from dungie bait. There were vac-pac bricks of white sturgeon hush money and frozen tubs of picked crab meat that may or may not have come from an illicit trotline or a restaurant cooler. Don't ask me what was in the refrigerator or cupboards, or how it all got there, all I ever saw were delicate, piping-hot buttery rolls, prime cuts of beef and coffee cakes, fish tacos and skillet breakfasts that Dalty seemed to pull out of thin air.

I doubt it will come as any surprise to learn that Dalty cooked on the same caliber of equipment he fished with. He was a great believer in the toaster oven, and what melted cheese wonders and sizzling, dripping fish steaks he and John pulled from that long-suffering machine! With its missing buttons and murderous splatters on the glass door, it looked like it spent its formative years in the breakroom of an Alaskan oil rig. Dalty was also a fan of heat-and-eat beginnings for beautifully rendered meals. I once saw him prepare a dish of frozen prawns poached to supple, yielding perfection in heavy whipping cream and amaretto. He set the piping hot plate of shrimp in front of a proper and bookish PhD candidate —who'd survived as long as she had by imposing one delayal of gratification after another on herself. She ate each one of Dalty's prawns slowly, in a careful, dainty silence. When they were gone, she stared at the empty plate for a few forlorn moments. Then she picked up the dish and said to the room of red-blooded young men watching her eat: "I'm sorry, I just have to do this," and she lapped up every last drop of sauce on it.

Dalty served me the most satisfying meal I ever ate. It was a surf and turf plate, made up just for me, with a big T-bone steak, a swordfish fillet, tangy chanterelle salad and a jelly jar of big pinot. I finished it off with a hot slab of homemade, wild blackberry cobbler, vanilla ice cream and good coffee with thick cream. It didn't stand out as anything special at the time; that was just how we ate on the farm. If Dalty were a woman I'm sure he could have raised a half-dozen children on his own.

And the platter of blackened, Cajun fried, wild catfish? With the lime-garlic-cilantro-crème fraiche dipping sauce that the three friends washed down with a half-rack of ice-cold Rainier at one in the morning? Dalty swore the dish could only be prepared on a white-hot skillet. If a tab of butter instantly caught fire when it was dropped in the pan, you knew it was ready for action. Unless you were needed in the kitchen, it was best to stay outdoors before dinner on Cajun night. The smoke inside the house was too thick, the humidity too high and the hot kitchen air too laden with lung-searing red pepper gas for anyone but Dalty. When John saw a freaked-out mosquito trying to escape the house by squeezing through the weave of the screen door, he decided there could be no more Cajun blackening. This order caused a mini revolt on the farm, and to put it down, John bought Dalty a little camp stove to cook on in the woodshed on Cajun night.

Dinner was usually served at 11:00 pm or later and epic dish duty always followed. As low man on the totem pole, KP and cutting board labor were the only help I could offer. What could I have brought to our household from the stores sitting on *Tranquility*? A two-pound jar of marinated artichoke hearts? Cans of 99¢ chili? A stale bag of dehydrated black bean flakes? Other than a five-pound bag of French roast and a whole canned chicken (which Dalton drank out of a greasy plastic bag while we were on an evening hike through the middle of Willapa Island bear country), I didn't have much to contribute in the way of supplies.

With the struggles and disappointments of the voyage at a safe distance, I spent what was left of the fine summer weather as an understudy to John and Dalton in the kitchen, in the woods and on the front thwarts of canoes. We fished *Tranquility* up and down the river that September and took her back and forth across the Columbia bar several times. We towed plug-cut herring for miles in the brackish river and cast rubber grubs and old standby lures into the ponds until our arms wore out. I caught my first big bass and catfish on the farm, though none were as nice as what Dalty would reel in while half-trying. When John released his biggest fish, Dalton—who never got used to the spectacle— was quietly inconsolable. But I liked that about John. He was a biologist who knew how to have fun and I learned the name of a bird or two from him, plucked pasty berries from the low bushes he pointed out, and even had occasion to crack one or two of his field guides. Meanwhile, Dalton was doing spore tests on mushrooms he wanted to eat and counting the tricuspids in the jaw fragments he found in the woods. John, who had two wildlife degrees, would adjudicate questions of safety and edibility by reading key identifying phrases aloud from the pages of detailed notes he'd taken in his 400-level marine invertebrate and forestry classes. Dalty could be reckless, and I knew nothing, so it was up to John to keep us from dying. A typical bush-whacking exchange:

A bird of prey, unseen, screeches somewhere overhead.

Dalton: "Sweet red-tailed hawk!"

John, after a moment of reflection: "I'd go peregrine falcon on that one, Dalty."

Me: I'm just realizing the sound wasn't a car alarm.

While exploring on my own one day, I came across an overgrown culvert hidden in the tall weeds along a dirt road that ran behind the farm. After hopping a wooden fence, I followed an old footpath across an embankment to a little tree-shaded cove at the back of a big pond on an adjoining property. It was cool and quiet in there. A pair of bottle-blue dragonflies were buzzing in low over the water, snatching little white-winged flies from the edges of busy swarms. One dragonfly veered under a tree chasing bigger prey, it swooped low on the water and vanished in the turbid roil of a large mouth bass. Before I mentioned the cove at the cottage, I snuck back to it with a canoe and caught two big bass there, one right after the other –just like they do in the beer commercials. I brought John there for a little fly fishing the next day and when he caught a prize winning crappie on his first cast, he declared it the new hot spot. We brought Dalty the following night and caught six or eight fat catfish in a couple hours. It was my first big discovery and I was proud to show it to them. I'd done good and I knew it. But really, what was all new to me was just another Washington summer for John and Dalty. I grew up on the edge of a paved-over city and I'll be forever grateful to them for including me. It was the time and place for that sort of living and I hope to do it again someday. If I never do, I'll be more than happy to kick the bucket with one of those farm days in mind.

We built a hillbilly hot tub out of an old cranberry scoop that John and Dalty pulled from the weeds behind the workshop one afternoon. We set hay bales in it for seats and lined them with blue plastic tarps for comfort. We dropped one of *Tranquility*'s bilge pumps into the scoop for a circulator and ran the pump hose to an automotive radiator left roasting on a propane crab pot cooker, running wide-open in a cinder block crucible we built for it. The water flowing back to the tub from the radiator wasn't hot enough to *scald* you, but the heating system was unregulated and tended to run away –which made the scoop as hot as a pot of Dalty's gumbo from time to time. Let's not get into how we got the bilge pump to run on household current –all you need to know is we got it working surprisingly well after a few tweaks, and its inauguration was occasioned by a raucous party that was well-attended by the opposite sex. Even though this usually amounted to John's marine biology girlfriends dropping by to gaze at him and listen to his hilarious stories of growing up next door to the Wilkes twins, I'll have you know that less magnetic, but equally earnest, young men managed to earn themselves quite a reputation that summer.

The crab pot cooker was accidentally left on after one memorable late-night party and the loud hiss of hillbilly-hot-tub-China-Syndrome woke John early the next morning. When he opened his eyes, he saw shadows of yellow flames dancing on the walls above his head. When he looked out his bedroom window, where the hot tub's burner had been placed for ease of operation (and convenient shut down if the action suddenly moved to the bed), he saw the gas line on the propane tank whipping back and forth in the cool morning air, spewing flames from its melting tip like a North Dakota oil well flare. John dove out the window in his birthday suit and shut it off before we were blown to smithereens. There wasn't any serious damage to the tub or the house and the accident led to a breakthrough in the design's safety and efficiency. We went to a double radiator configuration and submerged them in a large vat of water, which was kept at a low simmer, and we added a stove regulator, which cut down on our fuel costs *considerably*. Our hot tub proved to be an inexpensive and popular one –there's been at least two others and no one has died that I know of.

Something was always happening on the farm. Dalton came home all scratched up one evening, saying he'd been chased away from an abandoned apple tree by a big black bear. He survived the encounter by vaulting a fence and diving head-first into a blackberry bramble on the far side of it. He looked pretty shaken up and he was lucky the bear wasn't nimble or angry enough to follow him.

"Dalty's *always* getting chased by bears!" John said when I brought it up to him later, thinking it was something really special.

A major disaster was narrowly averted when Dalty's potato gun malfunctioned one night while we were launching a sprouted bag of Yukon Golds one-by-one into the forest on the far side of the bogs. The gun was a type of cannon made from big PVC pipe, and it could lob a half-pound potato around a thousand feet when the air/fuel mixture was just right. It really went *KA-BOOM!* The accident happened when the hairspray propellant suddenly misfired while John was testing the ignitor. The breech was open when he struck the spark and the backflash caught his eyebrows and hair on fire. John rolled away from the explosion, landed at my feet and I quickly patted him out –it was the usual. John: flash fires,

Dalty: angry bears. John had a succinct rule for surviving life with the twins: *Just duck.*

I don't know if the northwesterlies blew while I was at the farm. It never seemed like it when I was on the river or at the beach, but I didn't listen to the weather except when we were planning a fishing trip on *Tranquility*. I kept the urgency of the voyage at bay by telling myself I could get going again by early October. But a big blow kicked up in late September and John and I went up to the lighthouse to check it out. One look at the Columbia told me that the pleasure boating season was coming to an abrupt end. Wild water stretched up and down the mouth of the river as ranks of fifteen-foot shore breakers crashed between the jetties at max ebb. Confused water stretched up and down the coast and far out to sea. The wind was almost strong enough to hold you up when you leaned into it. It was a southerly of course and it wasn't even a bad one.

As the fall approached I started thinking about wintering upriver in Portland, Oregon. I figured I would find an inexpensive place to tie the boat up and go about my usual off-season work as a freelance auto mechanic: it paid well-enough and was easy to get established. All I ever had to do to drum up steady work was put up fliers on university bulletin boards and get a pager with a local number. College students are always looking for an off-the-books deal when they're footing the bill. They like the illusion of sticking it to the man, too. Anyway, I figured I would be on my way to California again the following spring.

There were some end-of-season parties and the weather stayed nice enough to do a little surf fishing. Dalton got ahold of an aluminum skiff, we threw the big 18 on it and the three of us explored Willapa Bay and spent a night at Long Island. But autumnal weather came along much sooner than I wanted and I tried for as long as possible to ignore the sensation that the earth was tilting away from the sun a little more each day. When the unmistakable fall came, it erased the long Pacific Northwest summer days with a single hesitation of a Rorschach cloud scudding before the sun. I watched it linger there, weakening the heat and light, casting its hiver spell on the land. Only when the writing of winter was on hill and field, and elliptical shadows of leafless trees were stenciled on the roads and farm buildings, did I realize how quickly it could come. The mornings and afternoons were particularly sun-bereft and the land grew lonesome for a bit of its warmth. Plein air days succumbed to moody ones. Dismal night fogs settled on the pastures and hung in the bogs, generalizing familiar shapes; it would lift a few feet by mid-morning and return after sunset. New water appeared on the land and a humid, inclement wind would pick up and blow into the northeast. In a lull between barometric pressure changes, strange waterfowl showed up on the pewter ponds, bringing with them clear evidence of the end of the pleasant season and the arrival of a more permanent and mature time of year.

The inhabitants of Paradise Cranberry Farm watched the seasonal leave-taking of fair-weather people with quiet displeasure, as they were drawn onto the roads and highways like leaves drifting from a brook to a stream. The urban orientation of the women we were loving and the men whose backs we were slapping came to the surface and led them away from smallsville to more populous and livable winter climes. John was heading to Costa Rica in a month, Dalty spent his winters in Puyallup and I had nowhere to go but *Tranquility*.

The season ended well-enough, I suppose. When the day for loading the cars and saying the goodbyes arrived, it was short and sweet with crimson afternoon light falling on the cottage and front yard, turning everything rosy. Dalty wasn't much for farewells, so he hopped in his wagon and left the farm doing an intentional fishtail on the gravel apron. John and I didn't say much on the ride down to the harbor; we just watched the incandescent sunset flashing in the treetops. It was filtered through the atmosphere just enough to let you look directly at the sun. When we reached the south end of the peninsula, I saw a large herd of elk running north across the verdant land in the last of the golden light. It was a good and memorable send-off and I kept it to myself. We rolled through downtown Ilwaco slowly and pulled into the empty harbor parking lot. I unloaded my gear at the top of the ramp, wished John good luck on his trip and just like that, I spent the evening by myself aboard *Tranquility*–the first in a long time.

A big southerly kicked up later that evening and raindrops began to fall on *Tranquility*'s deck like pebbles. So much water drained into the boat from the cockpit, the bilge pumps came on. Between that and the cold, cramped interior, being in the cabin was like being underwater. A late night wind-shift brought the gusts pushing upriver, right through the harbor. They leaned on *Tranquility* where she sat at the dock, blowing her down and out to the ends of her mooring lines. In the lulls, she rebounded and worked up against the timbers, churning her fenders into the untreated dock until they rubbed up a thick, splintery paste. The wind blew so hard I thought the float was going to carry away at one point, so after rigging a safety line to pull myself back to *Tranquility*, I set off in the skiff with the spare anchor and dropped it out in the middle of the harbor in case the pilings let go. I went on deck several times that night to reposition fenders and secure the flailing skiff and yank on lines that were whipping against the mast so hard they shook me in my bunk. *Tranquility* bucked and slammed more than conditions seemed to warrant and after my last trip on deck, I was so cold and wet, I threw a couple of lumps of coal into the Tiny Tot and lit them with a big ball of newspaper soaked in kerosene. I did this without thinking.

When the coals lit and the stove began to draw, I opened the damper and let it rage for a little while. This instantly cheered things up below deck. In ten minutes, the stove and the air around it were hot as a forge. I backed away and sat on the engine hatch to see if the heat was more bearable over there, and it was, until I started to feel the vacuum rushing in the boat and the cold air being drawn through the gaps in the companionway hatch. The Tot began huffing and puffing, making intermittent *whooshing* sounds, accompanied by flaming backfires that leapt through the fire door. The deck head above the Tot was getting too hot to touch. "Holy crap Buddy!" I said, turning the damper closed. This had no effect —except to make it suck harder on the air around it. The back of the Tot turned bright red and it began whistling to itself. I glanced at the fire extinguisher and noted the reading on its gauge: full. After a minute of fire safety planning, I snatched up the stainless steel tongs from the galley and went over to the Tot. Wiping the sweat from my brow with a bicep, I reached out with the tongs and shut the flue. When I did this, the little coil of spring steel that served as its handle snapped off and I threw it and the tongs in the sink and ran water over my burning hand. *Jiminy Cricket!*

I came up with a new plan and after wrapping my hand in a shirt, I went at it. I slid the companionway hatch back, then went to the fire door and swung it open. I reached the tongs into the inferno and carefully removed the largest lump of coal. I walked backwards to the companionway, and not really wanting to climb the stairs with a crimson rock, I heaved the lump of coal through the hatch and let the wind carry it over the side. I did the same with the second lump. The boat was uncomfortably warm for a couple of hours, then it was quite cozy until dawn.

The next morning was clear and bright, and when I went on deck, I learned the reason for *Tranquility*'s rough ride the night before. A key fender had popped at some point, which allowed her to rub up against the dock. A two-square-foot section of her hull planking had been pulped, taking the paint and wood down about an eighth of an inch. The change in her ride drew a hard-laid dock line across her gunwale which ripped up a couple feet of varnish. This was the paint and varnish I'd spent the last few days of fine weather slathering on. *This much trouble tied to a dock? What's winter going to be like?*

13

If you're going to do some rambling in this world you have to learn a little bit about yourself along the way. Otherwise, you roam aimlessly from place to place, wondering what you're all about and where you really belong. This happens to people who move around a lot, they fit in everywhere but nowhere and that's a lonely sort of life to lead. If you learn to listen to your body while you're knocking around, and not just your mind, it will tell you when it's time to stay or time to go, and it will tell you whether something is right or wrong for you. When I cast off my dock lines and made my way through the winding Ilwaco channel for the last time, my mind wanted to stay, but my body knew winter was coming and it told me to head inland. I'd just turned twenty-five, I believed my future was waiting for me around the next bend, so for better or for worse, I went looking for it there.

I smiled to myself as I motored past Little Sand Island and when I reached the Columbia, I steered into mid-channel and had a look at the bar, just in case a northwesterly was blowing and the sun was shining and the dolphins were leaping down the coast showing me the way to the Channel Islands. It was not, they were not and what I saw out there gave me the willies instead. The last of the storm waves were crashing in terrific slow motion onto what looked like a sandbar that had formed just outside the north jetty. Inside the south jetty, colossal white combers peeled along the gray rocks and broke on top of each other, throwing sea mist high into the air. In the roar, you could hear the ocean saying *no.* So I pushed the tiller away from me and headed *Tranquility* east. *Next summer*, I said to myself as I motored under the pale-green truss bridge that spans the Columbia River at Astoria, Oregon, ten miles upstream from Ilwaco.

I got a late start that day and the tide was about to turn against me, so I tossed my hook over the side in Astoria for the night. This was the largest town I'd been to since I left Seattle, and it was a great pleasure to sit down in a diner for a piece of pie and a cup of coffee. It was a little taste of the security and normalcy I was heading for, but I got carried away: I picked up a newspaper. I set it right back down. I wasn't ready for *that* sort of security and normalcy yet. I was sailing in the general direction of Portland, but it had been so beautiful on the river that afternoon, I began having fanciful notions of anchoring in a small town and chopping firewood or doing other odd jobs to get through the winter. I thought if I put my mind to it, I could make the coming months just as enriching as the summer had been, and although I knew they would be colder and wetter, I was expecting them to be much safer.

I caught an early afternoon flood tide with a little sea breeze behind it the next day, and I sailed *Tranquility* wing-and-wing upriver, jibing between the channel markers, slowly making my way east. The lower Columbia is broad as a sea for several miles as you head inland from the bar. The navigable channel, which accounts for only a small portion of the three-mile-wide river you see at high tide, runs along the Washington bank until Baker Bay before abruptly crossing to the Oregon side. Big cargo ships run up and down the Astoria waterfront. A few miles east of town, the channel crosses back to the Washington side where it narrows and fills in with shoals and low-lying sand islands. When I sailed into this well-marked area, there was a wind-shift so I began making short reaches back and forth across the channel with the gentle sea breeze quartering the stern. Of course, I was an expert riverman by then, and the idea of sailing all the way up to Idaho—if only for the sake of putting the feather in my cap—crossed my mind as I hove abreast of some shallows in an area known as Jim Crow Sands. Then, just as I was leaving those shoals in my wake, and while still well-inside the channel markers on the right bank, I felt a heavy lurch through the soles of my feet and *Tranquility* stopped dead in her tracks.

She was aground –but how could she be?

"NOOOOOOOOOOOO!!" I yelled as I dove for the engine, started it and dropped it in reverse, laying on the throttle. *Tranquility* wobbled a little as the propeller bit in, but she stayed put. Adrenaline dumped into my veins, I fell upon the mainsheet and jib winch and flattened the sails, praying the light wind would tilt the keel off the bottom enough to free her –but still she stuck! I killed the engine and flew up to the foredeck quick as a flash, pulling the skiff along *Tranquility*'s port side by its bowline. I skipped over the deck cleats and winches and whipped the end of the line around the outside of the stays, catching it in my free hand as I danced by the rigging. Up at the bow, I pitched *Tranquility*'s main anchor and rode into the skiff, then I jumped into it from the tip of the bowsprit, landing on the thwart facing aft with my hands at the oars. I rowed away for mid-channel with perfectly timed, catch-pull-feather-recover strokes, kicking coils of anchor line over the transom with my left foot. I rowed as far into the channel as length of line would allow, tossed the hook over the stern, then rowed like mad back to *Tranquility*, fighting the current inch-for-inch, all the way to her side. The whole thing took me less than five minutes and it was probably my finest moment as a boatman up to that point.

As soon as I jumped on deck, I began pulling the slack out of the anchor line. When it was taut, I whipped three turns of it around the sheet winch and cranked until the deck timbers creaked, trying to kedge her off. When that didn't work, I started the engine, dropped it in reverse, and wound it up to full throttle, then I ran up to the main deck and jogged back and forth across the boat, throwing my weight far out over the water by hanging on to the stays, trying to work her off the sandbar. On my thirtieth or fortieth trip across deck, *Tranquility* slid back and the anchor line went slack. *Yes! Yes! Yes!* I thrilled to myself, clapping my hands together and hiking my pants up hip-by-hip as I jumped into the cockpit and cranked on the winch in a dizzy rotation. But the line started coming in a little too easy. *Tranquility* wasn't moving! The anchor was dragging across the bottom of the river! I hauled the hook up to the rail, threw it back in the skiff and went through the operation all over again –just as fast and with the same maddening results.

"CAN'T ANYTHING EVER GO RIGHT ON THIS GODDAMNED BOAT??!!" I screamed as loud as I could, flexing every muscle in my body and flopping onto my back in the cockpit. I lay there motionless until *Tranquility* was leaning well to port with her vulnerable cockpit facing the run of the river. *This must surely be the end of Tranquility*, I thought to myself as an eddy, topped by a beige bun of foam and bits of sticks, swirled up to her port side and spun off downstream past that low-slung stern of hers. *So be it! So be it! I don't even care anymore!*

And then I got angry. Really, really angry. Instead of resetting the anchor, dropping the sails or preparing to abandon ship, I took out the GPS and fixed my *exact* position on the chart. This confirmed what I knew by looking at the river: my keel had touched bottom well-inside of an imaginary line drawn between the two closest channel markers to starboard. I was at least thirty feet in the channel, following the rules and doing everything right when I ran aground, but rivers don't play by rules!

It's what you *don't* know that ends up mattering in life. The feeling of disgust and frustration with myself and the boat were overwhelming, mind bending really, but there was no outlet for it, so I pushed it away and sat in the cockpit while *Tranquility* shifted drunkenly on the sand, digging her keel deeper and deeper into it. There was no shovel aboard and no one to call upon for help. This one was going to be all on me.

A little while later, a fully-laden ship appeared in the west and steamed up the channel toward *Tranquility*. She altered course just-so as she neared Jim Crow Sands and then continued on her way upriver. A man dressed in a white officer's uniform with a gold braid cap stepped smartly from the wheelhouse and waved to me from the starboard wing deck as the ship–which must have needed around thirty feet of water for safe running–swept by doing at least ten knots, a hundred feet from *Tranquility*'s stern. That gentleman must have seen my slanting decks and full sails and thought I was having a *dandy* little sail upriver that day. *I really suck if I can't keep this teacup in a channel big enough for that ship*, I sighed to myself as I went to the mast, cast off the halyards and dropped the sails on deck. There wasn't much I could do at that point, so after resetting the kedge anchor, I sat in the cockpit and watched poor *Tranquility* lean into the river.

It was an exquisite mental torture to know that I'd run aground on my first solo outing since my wreck on Little Sand Island (of course I was in the *goddamned* channel!!). Of all the self-inflicted wounds of the voyage, this was the only genuine accident and the ironic timing of it plucked at me over and over again. Every mishap on a boat must be laid at the feet of her captain though –no matter what the circumstances are. This will seem unfair to a landlubber who's used to seeing his role models quietly settle while admitting no wrongdoing. There's no such dodging of blame on a ship. The law of the sea doesn't allow for it, and even if it did, seafarers hold themselves to a much higher standard than landsmen. Sorry, but it's true. Of course there are lucky ships and unlucky ships – you don't have to take my word for it. Seamen have written about and spoken of this truth for centuries. There's just something about a boat that goes far beyond her captain and those who sail in her. It is her, it is what she is, and it's no accident that a vessel is a she –even though no one can say why. Don't bother looking to boats for an explanation of this, look to human nature. I don't have the faintest idea what women see and admire in most men, but I guarantee you it's not one-tenth of what men see and admire in the plainest woman. Who does the pursuing after all? Who gets tongue tied? Who squanders their treasure? It's the same with boats I tell you. Who does the building, maintaining and sailing –for the *most* part? Anyway, the question is not whether a boat is like a woman, it's whether a *woman* is a *vessel*, and we all know the answer to that, because we've all been carried in one. By the way—if you're wondering if I'm a closet misogynist—the two most accomplished mariners I personally know are women: Sarah Stevens and Nancy Griffith. The former is a Mate in the United States Merchant Marine, the latter is a South Pacific seafaring legend and Captain of the *Avatapu*, a break-bulk freighter out of Rarotonga, Cook Islands -I've had the pleasure of sailing under both.

It was still light out when I began to see the sandbar underneath the boat. When her port deck dipped below the surface of the river, I knew *Tranquility*'s position was going to be a serious problem. As the tide fell, an enormous sandy island emerged from the river south of my position. It was the rest of Jim Crow Sands. To the north and east were off-lying river rocks, five-hundred-foot cliffs and a narrow cut bank with a few scraggly trees clinging to it. These weren't the still waters of Baker Bay on a midnight ebb tide, this was a mushy sandbank in the middle of the mighty, mighty Columbia River. When *Tranquility* leaned into the water up to her cabin sides and ports, the river began to nudge her this way and that until it was flowing around her bow and stern with equal force. A roil of water started to curl up along the port side of the boat, spilling back on itself in a continuous, gurgling loop. Fortunately, the crest of this small standing wave was half-a-foot from the top of the cockpit coaming. Unfortunately, *Tranquility* didn't *stay* in that position. The water flowing around her began to undermine the keel the way the undertow on a wave-swept beach pulls the sand out from under your feet. *Tranquility* shifted around and sank in the sand until the river was flowing by, no more than an inch from the top of her coaming. I expected her to founder at any moment, so I gathered up the ship's papers, my belongings and the emergency flares. I threw them in a waterproof bag and prepared to abandon ship. Dear reader, I must say, the idea was definitely starting to grow on me -how about you? If you want, I can drop you off at the next port.

Tranquility eased down and down until she came to rest on her side at the edge of a steep bank. Her cockpit and companionway faced the river the entire time, but for some reason it didn't spill into her. However, when the tide came in later that night, another cold and dark one to be sure, her hull began leaking badly. When I saw water swirling under the edge of the galley cabinets, I jumped into the cabin and checked the seacocks in the engine compartment and galley. That wasn't where the water was coming from, but there wasn't any time to make sense of it. *Tranquility* was filling up fast and high water was hours away. The only way to save her was to bail. For how long was anybody's guess. I suited up in full battle gear out in the cockpit. I stripped off my blue jeans and polyester cable knit and stepped into a heavy pair of corduroy pants which I tucked into the high tops of my new, steel-toe rubber boots. I changed into a scratchy, all-wool flannel shirt and a thick lambswool sweater and cap. That became my costume for the next few years –no other outfit was sturdy enough for life aboard *Tranquility.* You can pretend to be a wooden boat sailor, but you can't pretend to dress like one.

I jumped into the cabin with a 5-gallon plastic bucket, took up the floorboards and bailed for hours under a dim cabin lamp. Because *Tranquility*'s cockpit drained into her bilge, I only had two options for dumping the bucket: I could walk it aft, climb the cabin stairs, cross the tilting deck and empty it over the side; or I could open the main hatch aft of the mast, hoist the pail high overhead, and dump it onto the cabin top and let it run overboard from there. After trying both awkward maneuvers a few times, I chose the main hatch. This, and everything else there is to do on a sailboat, is the reason why there's no "in shape" like a sailor is in shape.

If you're not perfectly clear on what was happening with the river that night, it's because the subject of tides, estuaries and channels; high and low water; flood, ebb and slack currents are a confusing one. In the Columbia, the flood tide moves west to east upriver, and the ebb tide moves east to west downriver. High tide (high water) at Astoria comes earlier in the day than it does twenty miles inland. And low tide (low water) comes earlier in the day twenty miles inland than it does at Astoria. These differences must be accounted for when navigating. Adding to the confusion, the flood and ebb *currents* which accompany high and low water don't necessarily follow the state of the tide closely. Generally speaking, max flood current occurs at a given location before high water and max ebb current occurs before low water. How much before depends on where you are. The high slacks and low slacks are the short periods of time between tides when little or no current is running. Because there are two high tides and two low tides in most 24 hour periods on the Pacific Coast, there are two flood currents and two ebb currents and two high slacks and two low slacks. Where the Columbia is broad, the slacks are longer and the flood and ebb currents are weaker than where it's narrow. Don't forget about storm surge and daylight savings time! Or that one of the high tides is higher than the other and one of the lows is lower...and so on, and so forth, until you have no idea what the hell is going on.

Suffice it to say that on the flood that night, the mighty Columbia reversed its course through the narrows and flowed inland, rippling around the high side of the boat. Big, unfriendly eddies swirled upstream in the dark and slewed *Tranquility* around on the sandbar. She leaked the entire time the tide rose, and I bailed myself into an out-of-body experience trying to save her. I fell behind the rising water at one point and it topped my boots. That was the most water I'd ever seen in *Tranquility,* but it wasn't the most water I was ever to see in her. The cold river felt good in my hot boots and I stripped off my sweater and flannel and kept up the bailing as *Tranquility* slowly got back on her feet.

Have you ever wondered why a boat floats in the first place? I sure as hell have, and I found out that surprisingly few people know the correct answer to the question. The lid of a styrofoam cooler floats quite nicely when it blows overboard on a windy day. Is that because of the air trapped in its styrene cells? A cookie sheet will float if it lands on the water just right, and there's certainly no air trapped in sheet metal. So why do both float? *Tranquility* was built of wood and she floated, but so did Jacques' concrete tub. Everyone knows a piece of wood will float when it's pitched into the sea, but a chunk of concrete? Did Jacques' vessel float because it happened to be in the shape of a boat? Did *Tranquility* float simply because she was wood? Yes and no. If Jacques' boat were built of lead it wouldn't float and neither would *Tranquility.* The reason something floats has to do with its weight compared to the weight of the water around it. When you stick your finger into a full glass of water, the amount that spills over the rim is equal to the volume of your finger. The *weight* of the quantity of water your finger forces out of the glass is your finger's *displacement.* Whenever an object is put in water, it displaces water. An object will float, no matter what material it's made of, or shape it's in, as long as its total weight is less than the total weight of the water it has displaced. Once an object weighs even one gram more than the water it displaces—whether due to the material it's made from, a hole that lets water in, or any other extra weight—it sinks. It sinks because the force displacing the water is greater than the force of the water pushing back against it. The flavor of the water a boat is in makes a difference too. A boat will float higher during winter on the North Atlantic Ocean than it will on a freshwater river in the tropics. Temperature and salinity affect a vessel's displacement.

That's all fine and dandy, but in the grand scheme of things, the natural rest position of every vessel afloat is, sadly, at the bottom. Every boat in the world takes on water, either through a leak in her hull, precipitation or the condensation borne by the air. The sea is hostile and the dipolarity of naturally occurring water (its simultaneous positive and negative charge) causes it to degrade every substance it comes in contact with. Water is the universal solvent, it is the body attacking itself. Fiberglass delaminates, wood rots, steel rusts, aluminum corrodes. It is in the entropic nature of a boat to go down someday. It can't be stopped, and a vessel only remains afloat due to your constant intervention. This is what it means to own a boat; this is what you're up against.

Who knows what time it was, but at some point that night, *Tranquility* was almost on an even keel. I was at a new and unknown state of exhaustion, rigid from working wedged at the mast with my legs braced against the bunk and stove nook. I'd bailed and lifted and bailed and lifted hundreds of buckets of water by then. You don't feel it when you're doing it. There's long spells of inattention blindness and full-body zone-outs when everything's on the line and you know you can't stop your work for more than a few seconds. Eventually *Tranquility* was upright and her keel began to bump on the sandbar. When she was off the bottom more than she was on it, I climbed on deck and gave the sheet winch fifty cranks. *Tranquility* slid off Jim Crow Sands, veered daintily into the river and fetched up facing east with her stern over her anchor – as if she'd been there all along.

I hauled the hook aboard with reserves of energy I didn't know I had, and I motored inland, carefully feeling my way through the channel in the misty night for two more tense and cruel hours. I was completely shattered, but I managed to reach the wide water up at Mayger's dock on the Oregon side of the river. After consulting the chart for any sign of trouble above or below the surface, I dropped the hook and tumbled into my bunk. I was still in a fit when my head hit the pillow. I writhed around in an agony of relief and trembling self-loathing. For the first time, I allowed that the shipwright in Ballard may have been right all along. Then I remembered I was in the channel when I ran aground and that made it much, much worse. The ordeal looped round and round in my mind, keeping me awake as I relived the grounding, the flooding and my narrow escape in minute detail. When the part came where I was *still in the channel* when the lurch moved through the boat, I felt a sharp twinge in my side. This went on and on until there was light in the eastern sky, I knew I was safe and I was able to fall asleep.

The grounding on Jim Crow Sands was the first psychological test of the voyage. The others, although frightening or stressful, were mostly physical challenges. These demand a certain kind of strength and make a certain kind of man out of you: sailing a boat single-handed; going without sleep; hauling up an anchor; enduring constant weather changes; pulling a boat off a beach. But the grounding on Jim Crow Sands was different. It was a physical test to be sure, but it was so unexpected, so mundanely threatening and so poorly timed that I knew it was only a mistake of luck that *Tranquility* wasn't lost there and then. I realized I needed her more than she needed me and that began to weigh on my psyche. If something happened to her what would I do? I was nearly broke, down on my luck; where could I turn? She was all I had and I nearly lost her while I was doing everything right. This was crushing, but not as crushing as what was to come.

The next morning I awoke to a deep rumble, a clanging bell and a ponderous, rhythmic *clop-clop-clop-clop-clop-clop* that had me up on deck in my skivvies before I was even awake. There was a train lumbering along the starboard riverbank, just a muscular, black engine pulling a caboose downstream on rails laid right at the water's edge. I saw the man running it and ringing the bell. He was dressed in a blue shirt and a blue cap with his elbow resting on the windowsill of the cab. It was a glorious and crisp October morning, sunny with the leaves turning. There was a dog barking in the distance and, here and there, wood smoke rising into the cold, ceramic blue sky –it drifted away and hung low over the Oregon hinterland. It was a pretty fall day on a North American river. *Who gets to see this sort of thing anymore?*

I stayed anchored off Mayger for a couple days, drying out and pulling myself back together. I rowed to shore and paid the men in the wooden boathouse next to the dock a visit. We had a cup of coffee and looked at pictures of the five-foot sturgeon they'd been catching. They showed me the town's old and perfectly running International firetruck and I told them a little bit about my voyage, but I knew playtime was over. Winter was right around the corner and I wasn't in the mood for any more mishaps or setbacks. I realized that chance had gotten me into a sailor's life, but it was going to take design and hard work to get out of it. I decided to sail to Portland as soon as possible, find some work, move ashore and plan my next move from the safety of dry land. With a little luck, I figured I could do all of it in a month. It was good to have a new plan and as soon as I got my wits about me, I left Mayger. After an uneventful and surprisingly pleasant daysail, I came alongside the town wharf in Rainier, Oregon.

As I was tying *Tranquility* up to the float, I noticed a well-dressed, middle-aged man eyeing me from the road. He had a cosmopolitan air about him and he eventually walked down the dock and struck up a friendly conversation with me.

"Where you out of son?" he asked, doing little double-takes at me and the boat. I had to think about the question for a moment.

"Let's see...I suppose I left Seattle in June."

"You've come all the way from Seattle, Washington in this old sailboat? What an adventure!" These were the first unsolicited words of encouragement I'd heard since shoving off.

"Only took me *four months*!" I said, with a laugh at myself.

"Who cares how long you took doing it? You're on a life adventure that most people only dream of! Good for you, kid! You'll remember this for the rest of your life!" This guy was really cheering me up. "So what are you doing in Rainier?"

"Fetching some gas," I said, lifting an empty jerry can out of the cockpit.

"You stay right here!" he said, taking the can from me. "I'm going to buy your gas for you! It would be my pleasure!"

You get these guys from time to time. They're the ones who've already done what you're doing. Maybe they did it right where you're doing it and they've come down there for another look. These are the men who watch you without telling you what to do or how to do it. They're the ones who spy on you from the pierhead when you're rowing out to your boat. They're the men who leave handy things in your cockpit when you're away. Seeing you on the water brings it all back to them.

Sometimes they have a chat with you, but they pretend like they've never set foot on the deck of a boat themselves or they just reminisce from a polite distance and go on their way. I probably had about $200 at the time, and six gallons of gas represented a good chunk of my working capital, so when the kind man returned with the fuel and a paper bag with a deli sandwich, soda and chips in it, I thanked him sincerely. He wouldn't hear of it though, and after a long chat he wished me luck on my voyage and went on his way.

There was no wind when I left Rainier the following morning and as I motored upriver, I reviewed my travel times and positions on the chart to get an idea of my average speed and fuel consumption. A careful calculation of my daily runs since leaving Ilwaco put me just two days from Portland. If all went well, I would reach the city before sunset the following evening with a couple gallons of fuel to spare. With a day and time of arrival in mind, I began picturing a clean and uncomplicated end to the first leg of my little summer voyage. I was really looking forward to the predictability and comfort of city life: in Portland there would be safety for myself and the boat; there would be new people to meet; work to do; warmth and distraction. I dreamed up an affectionate girlfriend to thrill with tales from my summer of derring-do. I convinced myself that Portland would be the end of my troubles and I couldn't wait to get there. I couldn't wait to be off the boat.

Much of the Columbia River below Portland is green and bucolic. There's open pastureland, wooded islands and little sloughs that run parallel to the main channel or head inland to small burgs and settlements. Several small rivers and creeks empty into the lower Columbia, and place names reflect the changing history of the region: the Cowlitz, Kalama and Lewis rivers; Coal Creek slough, Ditch Number 10, German Creek. There's rolling hills and farms and small river towns. The Washington side is more developed but I think the Oregon side is prettier. I'd never been on a real river before. There was a steady flow of commercial vessel traffic: ships and tugs towing barges steamed by, trailing gnashing roils of murky prop wash; rivermen in bright orange caps and heavy duck jackets sped to and fro in camouflage jon boats filled with reddish wet firewood and young hunting dogs. The Columbia is a hard-working river and *Tranquility* was the only sailboat on it that time of year. I wondered if she'd ever been up there before –it seemed like she had.

I was motoring at full speed when I began to see the outskirts of St. Helens, Oregon in the distance. This small town was my designated halfway point between Rainier and Portland and I planned to spend the night there. Because the twists and turns in a river are longer in real life than they look on a chart, and the current is variable, but always against you when heading inland, the day took longer than expected. When I fixed my position and checked my actual speed I realized it was going to take me a couple hours longer to reach St. Helens than I thought. This delay made me incredibly antsy and it also meant I was burning extra fuel, which *really* started to tick me off. It was another unforeseen wrinkle in a well-made plan. It meant another stop for gas and oil, another expense, another string attached, another delay after so many.

When I was about two miles from the docks and landings of St. Helens, a wind came up from astern and began tickling the hair on the back of my neck. It picked up to a nice, ten-knot breeze, a breeze blowing straight to St. Helens. I figured it would probably push me along at about three knots, which was only slightly slower than I was going by burning the last of my fuel. *Hoist some sail dude*, I said to myself. But I wasn't in the mood for a fickle wind, so I played it safe and let it blow for several minutes. *I should sail!* I said to myself after a little while, but I couldn't commit. St. Helens was just up ahead, it was right there! *I will freak out if something happens like it did the other day*, I warned myself. A few minutes later, a chipper, commercial voice piped up in my head and began advising me: *Why not sail? It's far more enjoyable than motoring! It's healthy for you and the environment, it's quiet, it saves fuel and it's a whole lot of fun!* Then I remembered the autopilot: *Nope...no ways bro...I'm sticking with the sure thing for once.*

Motoring seemed like the most prudent plan at the time, given my iffy emotional state. After all, how many times had I hoisted for a wind that died as soon as the sails were up? It had happened to me more times than I could count. *Not sailing. Nope. No ways bro. I'm just gonna motor. Town is right there!* Another voice chimed in: *DUDE! Don't be such a wuss! Go up and hoist the main at least! Use this wind! That's what this boat's for —it's a sailboat. Besides, you're wasting fuel and you're low on money.* There was absolutely no good reason to sail the last couple of miles to St. Helens. I would have been there in half-an-hour had I kept motoring, so I can't honestly say why I unfurled the sails. I suppose it's what a sailor does. Even if the wind has died on him a hundred times the instant he's hoisted for it, he still hoists for it when it blows again. If I wanted to be reasonable, I would have taken a bus to Portland or never left Seattle in the first place.

When I had the main and genoa halyards shackled to their sails and the sheets laid out to run free through the blocks, I returned to the cockpit, killed the engine, swung the boat downstream and headed her into the wind. I went up to the mast and hoisted the main and genoa. It was good to have the sails up and once they were trimmed, *Tranquility* took off sailing downstream. When she was up to speed, I put the tiller over to bring her about and head upriver. *Tranquility* didn't have quite enough momentum to come all the way around though, and just as she turned toward the right bank she lost way and began to fall off downstream. I wasn't going fast enough to tack. *Ha Ha –silly me.* That's easily fixed and I put the tiller back over. *Tranquility* slowly fell away from the current and continued sailing in the opposite direction of St. Helens. After a minute or two, I saw some wind stirring the water along an island off to starboard, so I steered for it. *Tranquility* heeled over nicely when the gust hit her and she really started to move downriver. When I sailed past the spot where I first noticed the wind, I put the helm over a second time. *Let's go honey*, I said as she turned for the right bank and started to come about in the current...but I must have misjudged her speed again, because she still wouldn't come all the way around.

"Okay!! BRO!!!!" I hollered, as I headed *Tranquility* downstream again. When I was absolutely certain she was up to hull speed, I shoved the tiller hard-over against the starboard coaming and held it there. But she still wouldn't come about! I sat there stunned as *Tranquility* fell off and gathered speed downstream. In my mind, this was a violation of the physical laws that make a sailboat a sailboat. I may not have been the best navigator or voyage planner or captain in the world, but I definitely knew how to *sail*. Yet *Tranquility* refused to answer her helm!

My hands still tingle, there's a catch in my breath and murder in my heart when I recall that day.

"This boat doesn't even sail! It can't even turn!!" I screamed, suddenly kicking the tiller hard-over and ramming it into the cockpit coaming, where it left a dent that became a permanent reminder of that terrible moment. I throttled the tiller with my boot again, and again, and again, like I was stomping the neck of someone sent to kill me. "Look at

THIS!" I yelled at the river and sky, as the current carried *Tranquility* farther and farther downstream. In fact, due to the wind and current, I couldn't keep her *from* sailing IN THE OPPOSITE DIRECTION. This was too much for me to take. After everything—and there had been a lot to choose from—*this* is what broke me.

Men's tears do not fall often or easily, and the couple tears I shed that afternoon were the most silent and bitter I've ever known. They signified the futility of that god-awful moment and a million others which didn't warrant mention until now. There was the time we were fishing *Tranquility* on the Columbia with five people aboard, and Dalty asked me if it was okay that a blue line was hanging over the stern. I said *yes*, knowing he was referring to the six-inch blue line that had been dangling from the bottom of the weather cloth since I left Port Townsend. It wasn't *that* blue line of course, it was *another* one, and when it made its way into the propeller a few moments later, the outboard jerked to a halt just as we were falling in with twenty other fishing boats making a turn at the end of a busy drag around buoy 10. And the time I was griping to John about the tendency of things I dropped to magically find their way into the bilge, no matter where they were dropped from. We were standing in the cockpit and I was removing the cap from a tube of super glue. The cap slipped from my fingers and landed on the 1" cockpit drain. It swirled around the rim and disappeared into the bilge...forever. We just looked at each other. And the special tools I dropped overboard? And the foot-long gash in the inflatable that took two entire days to repair because the glue refused to stick? And the locker doors that swelled up at random times and wouldn't open or close? And the epoxy that wouldn't set? *All* of it—back to the first time I put a wrench on the Albin in Ballard—was just under the surface. It wasn't filed as far away as I thought.

The boat wouldn't come around because the current was stronger than the wind that day. I didn't realize this, so I tried to come about one more time. When *Tranquility* was up to speed, I put the helm hard-over, desperately trying to bring that accursed ship back on course. But she simply wouldn't mind her helm! *I don't know how much more of this I can take*, I mumbled to myself, genuinely worried about my sanity for the first time in my life. As soon as those words left my lips, I went completely mad and my frustration turned into a lucid, unchecked rage.

I threw open the starboard cockpit locker and grabbed the handle of the axe –the one I'd been told to keep on hand for some emergency or other. It seemed like the right time to break it out. I envisioned taking full swings at the mast with that sharp, single-bit Connecticut, until the spar fell over the side, taking the rigging, the mainsail and genoa right along with it. The sheath, or perhaps the blade, caught on something in the back of the locker and I couldn't get it out no matter how hard I yanked or twisted. If the whale saved John and I on the maiden voyage, then whatever kept that axe in the locker is what saved *Tranquility*. Had the axe come out, I would have chopped the mast down there and then. That's no idle boast. *I'm sorry it didn't!* If it had, it would have saved me all the trouble still to come.

I had no axe, so I sought my revenge in other ways. I kicked the weatherboards right through the companionway scuttle, sending them flying into the cabin, smashing their little antique oval panes and splitting the wood of the companionway from deck to cabin top. I used the toe of my right boot to kick out each of the glasses in the old engine gauges and I karate-kicked the companionway hatch open so hard the stops broke. The hatch flew off the tracks and crashed into the back of the mast, snapping its rain lip off. I put the heel of my boot through both cockpit locker doors, breaking them in two, and I didn't even care that I did it! It felt so good and so right that I went back for the axe, bent on killing *Tranquility* on the spot. It came right out.

I was unsnapping the leather sheath when I heard four or five *thundering* horn blasts echo down the riverbank. When I looked upstream, I knew they were meant just for me. A stories-high, blue and white car carrier was bearing down on *Tranquility*. The vessel was shaped like a Soviet apartment block turned on its side. She had the current behind her and was restricted to her course by her draft. *Tranquility* was drifting through a narrow section of river just then, and the ship couldn't steer clear of her without running aground. It was a move it or lose it moment. It was the tonnage rule and several others. I wanted to kill *Tranquility* really, *really*, badly just then but I did not want to kill myself, so I dropped the axe and fired up the motor, slamming it into forward. As soon as I wound it up to full throttle, the skiff snapped to attention and charged toward *Tranquility*'s stern. It slammed into the back of the engine before I realized what was happening and the motor jerked to a familiar halt. The skiff's bowline had tangled in the propeller while I was trying to come about in the swirling river. And, of course, the wind had died while I was flipping out. So there we were, dead in the water and about to be run down. As far as I could tell, going nowhere with tremendous effort and at great expense was the only thing *Tranquility* liked doing more than surfing or laying in the sand. I took one look at where the ship was, one look at where I was, and did the math. I glanced at the oars in the skiff and made a brief, psychotic little speech to *Tranquility*: "Well, this is finally it! Are you happy now? You should be! This is what you've wanted all along...isn't it? WELL??!!...ISN'T IT??!!" *Good riddance!* I dropped the tiller in disgust. I hopped below, grabbed a knife and the bag with my wallet and the ship's papers in it. I climbed on deck and began to cut the skiff free with hatred in my heart and a look of death on my face which I saw reflected in the river and will never forget. I was going to row away and watch *Tranquility* be run down, or driven ashore and smashed up by the ship's wake; or she would last be seen floating down the mighty, mighty Columbia River to whatever end fate had in store for her. It was a crime of passion and I didn't really care how she met her end. I was *done* with her.

I was sawing through the bowline when something stayed my hand. I can't say if it was greed or mercy, but I flew into the cabin and grabbed the toolbox. I crunched my way back to the companionway, purposely stomping on the glass and wood covering the cabin sole like a kid jumping through a puddle. I gained the deck, heaved myself into the skiff and, knowing the drill from so many times before, I unwound the shredded line from the prop, spun off the hub nut, and replaced the shear pin in a few deft motions. When it was done, I dove into the cockpit, fired up the engine and motored *Tranquility* out of harm's way, with no more than a few minutes to spare before the ship steamed down the narrow channel.

So there I was, twice as far from St. Helens than when I set sail. I dropped the sagging main and genoa and motored upriver slowly, using nearshore eddies and mink trails to make up the ground I lost. What a lovely way to reach a port of call! What a splendid voyage! In St. Helens, I spotted a marina with several unoccupied slips and I drove *Tranquility* into the first one, without even bothering to reverse. She stopped when her bow rode up on the walkway. When I jumped onto the dock with the stern line in hand, my feet went right out from under me on the slick planks and I crashed down on my tailbone. The impact knocked the wind out of me and touched off skyrockets before my eyes. The dock was coated with a green slime Pacific Northwestern boatmen will be very familiar with. I lay there, staring into the clear blue sky, in renewed breathless insanity. I wasn't done with the boat yet. I was going to have the last laugh, even if I had to trade jabs with her for the rest of my life. She was going to feel some pain. Lucky for me, there was a stack of four-by-fours sitting up at the head of the slip (the slips were empty because the marina was under repair). As soon as I could stand, and before I even tied her up, I hurled a few of those three-foot-long timbers at *Tranquility*, taking my time, launching them butt-first, carefully, and as hard as I could at her cabin sides, deck, mast and cockpit –it didn't help and I don't recommend it.

It must have been quite a scene though, the two of us celebrating our arrival like that. When I was finished, I made my lines fast and went out for a bite to eat in a surprisingly upbeat mood. While I sipped my beer and munched my fries, I asked myself a couple of questions that any fair-minded person would have asked themselves by now:

1. What did Buddy know about *Tranquility* and when did he know it?

2. Why continue?

You can judge for yourself what the answer to the first question is. But the second one is a bit more complicated, and cuts a little deeper. It's a question everyone must ask themselves at some point or another over the course of a lifetime. My answer to Question Two had been in the back of my mind since the first time I sailed *Tranquility* and discovered her leak: I continued the voyage because I feared a life of regret more than I feared the consequences of carrying on. Even though it seemed unreal to me at the time, I knew I would be old and tired one day, and I wanted to know that I'd lived my life to the fullest while I was young and spry enough to do so. I continued the voyage because it was the right time in my life for that sort of thing and I was healthy enough in mind and body to recover if *everything* went wrong.

Dear reader...will it surprise you to learn that that's *exactly* what was waiting for me around the next bend?

Tranquility the day after I bought her

Deck and cockpit layout

Port Townsend on a fine summer day

My first time in the Salish Basin, with Race Rocks just off the bow

The public dock in Portland, Oregon

Dark times in Portland. The torn dollar bill can be seen to the right of the porthole.

14

When I reached the confluence of the Columbia and Willamette rivers, the brown paper leaves of fall were all over the water and the air was colder and damper than it had been in Astoria. Broad farmland lines the banks of the Columbia downstream of the mouth of the Willamette, but just above it, the transition to urban sprawl is abrupt and noisy. A railroad trestle and busy interstate span the Columbia there, its banks are crowded with shipping terminals, commercial buildings and an international airport. Most of the well-kept city of Portland, however, lies to the south along the heavily built up banks of the Willamette River. Its lower reaches, between the Columbia and the first of the Portland bridges, are an industrial waterway full of ships, chemical plants and railway yards. A mariner coming into Portland for the first time by way of the lower Willamette will be surprised to find such a pretty river town waiting for him upstream.

Despite careful planning and an early morning start, the trip from St. Helens was long and frustrating. The current in the Columbia pulled at *Tranquility* all day, making the short passage endless. Heading upriver in a low-powered vessel is like driving on a road that moves toward you while your destination remains fixed; it is climbing the down escalator or pedaling into a headwind. There were ships to avoid, buoys to round and broad river bends to negotiate. None of it was dropping astern fast enough to satisfy my need for a clean end to the voyage. I fell behind schedule and it was almost dark when I entered the Willamette.

Downtown Portland is only a ten-mile-run from the confluence, but the strong current that evening, and my dwindling fuel supply, kept the tension level sky-high until the very end of the trip. It was long after dark when the tall buildings of Portland came into view, and the glimpses of city life I caught in their glow made me incredibly anxious to get off the water. As usual, the water wasn't cooperating and by coming into an unfamiliar place at night I was breaking a rule I knew better than to break. There was no help for it, and that was extremely disheartening to me. How many nights had I spent crouched at the tiller waiting to get into port? It always took hours, sometimes even days longer than I expected. I rarely arrived somewhere the way I imagined! No matter how carefully I planned, there was always an unforeseen difficulty, a tortuous delay or accident that ruined the pleasure of fetching up somewhere new.

Knowing that night wasn't going to be any different added a dose of gall to my anxiety.

As I motored up the Willamette past dry docks meant for oceangoing ships with propellers as wide as *Tranquility* was long, her stature was reduced to dunnage in comparison and I laughed to think I ever sailed her on the open ocean with her low-slung stern and leaky hull. *I'm so done with this voyage!* I thought to myself with a huge sigh as *Tranquility* inched her way upriver at walking speed. The run to town took me twice as long as expected that night and I do not remember being relieved when I dropped my anchor in a bay between the sodium shadow of the Hawthorne Bridge and a small riverside park in the middle of Portland.

For the first few days, it looked like things were going my way in the big city. I received a modest boost to my finances when I sold a few small winches I scavenged from a wrecked sailboat I came across while exploring the Washington Coast that summer. I set myself up for mechanic work the same way I'd always done it before: I bought a pager and put up fliers at local colleges offering discount auto repair to students. This small business had never failed me when I needed quick cash in Seattle and I expected it to work just as well in Portland.

After a couple of days at anchor in the bay, I noticed a small powerboat coming and going from a long, L-shaped pier that touched land at the south end of the park. This dock jutted into the river and acted as a breakwater for a private marina tucked between it and shore. In the evenings the dock was used by joggers, fishermen and people out for a stroll along the riverbank. When I rowed by for a closer look, I learned that the entire thing was a courtesy pier provided by the city to boaters who wanted to sight-see or run errands in town. There was a time limit posted on one of the pilings –eight hours, I think. I'd learned by then that public tie-ups were rarely monitored and only blatant abuse of them invited consequences. So the next day, instead of rowing the skiff over to the park as I'd been doing, I brought *Tranquility* to the dock and left her there while I went into town to put up fliers. When I returned that evening, all was well with the boat. I'd left her for almost ten hours but there were no tickets on her or any other sign of trouble; there were just some elderly Chinese fishermen using her hull for a windbreak and her foredeck for a coffee table. I suggested we all go fishing sometime but they pretended not to hear me as they picked up their cups and pushed breadcrumbs around the deck with balled-up free napkins.

That was my first Saturday in Portland, and I was desperate for an evening on land, so I changed into my best clothes and went into town like any young swashbuckler on shore leave. I strode up the gangplank confident my young vitality and the change of scene would immediately put the difficulties of the voyage into a lighthearted, cocktail-party perspective. I'd meet some people, have a drink and a few laughs, then get on with my life. I knew from past ups and downs that you have to act normal before you can be normal, and since losing it off St. Helens, I really wanted some of my boring old life back. After a short walk along the waterfront, I came to a fancy bar and grill that looked out over the river. It was the type of place that has tall windows and tall menus, comfy black chairs and heavy beige curtains. There was a circular bar in the middle of the sunken dining room. The moment I stepped through the door, I knew I had the night all wrong. I expected the warm atmosphere I remembered from my life in Seattle, but all I saw in the place were distantly pert waitresses, a sparse collection of go-getters in loosened-up business attire and totally unapproachable couples nestled in wrap-around booths. It was an icy hotel bar-scene, or prom night on a cruise ship, instead of a bustling pub –and I was the odd man out. I should have moved on, but for some reason, I took a seat at the empty bar. The inviolable etiquette of big-city proxemics had the entire room, and everyone in it, on lockdown. I knew there was no hope of breaking through to a human being in there and I don't know why I stayed.

If you look hungry in this world, you go hungry. If you feel like an outcast, you imagine you've been shut-out of things when you really haven't. When you start listening to your inner voice of self-reproach, you forget that the society you believe is excluding you is made up of individuals just like yourself. I was lonesome and exhausted from the voyage, so the social obstacles seemed more formidable to me than they were that night. In my mind, I quickly went from a handsome young sailor with a good story to tell, to loner-guy-with-book. Except I didn't have a book. I had an old *National Geographic*, which everyone knows is way worse. Nevertheless, I put my best foot forward and tried to shake the oddball caricature I imagined for myself. I tried to be friendly to the bartender, but I couldn't manage to say anything genuine to her, and the lapses in our chit-chat-for-tips were withering. On my way up the dock,

I pictured the pretty young woman I'd entertain that night with little stories from the voyage, but the fantasy dissolved before I finished my first and only draft of Portland beer. I was going it alone that night and there was absolutely no doubt about it.

I resisted the urge to flee though, and read my magazine for a while, hoping someone interesting would sit next to me. No one did, except for a blowhard looking to get drunk. He was wearing brand new *cardboard insole* Sperry topsiders, wrinkle-free khaki slacks and a dorky sailing jacket with all the snaps and straps money can buy. I didn't have to ask him what sort of boating he did. It was a time of extremes in my life and I'd learned by then it was best to roll with them, so I ignored his overtures and tried to look nonchalant to the few people who glanced my way. The evening went nowhere, and after an hour, I dropped some bills on the bar and left without a word.

A night like that wasn't going to be salvaged by a change of venue, so instead of heading farther into town, I went to the boat, climbed the mast, and sat on the crosstrees. That was a good place to gather my thoughts and I began to reflect positively—for the first time—on what I actually accomplished on my voyage. Say what you want about my seamanship skills, I wasn't even supposed to make it to Neah Bay that summer, but I'd gotten all the way to Portland in one piece and I learned a great deal along the way. *Maybe the guy in Rainier was right!* I thought to myself for a few hopeful moments. *Maybe I am on an adventure I'll always remember.* I certainly hadn't met anyone else my age cruising their own sailboat that summer. I had met several would-be adventurers hiding in the pickled safety of the harbor, though. These dudes would drop by *Tranquility* and boast that they were going to do what I was doing, someday soon. Unlike me, instead of sailing close to shore, *they* were going to Mexico or Hawaii. Or, in classic wharf-rat parlance: *all the way around.* You don't have to ask these types of guys too many questions before you realize "someday soon" will be someday soon...forever.

Maybe I needed to give myself a break. After all, what I'd thought of as a short cruise had grown little-by-little into an enormous undertaking with a nearly vertical learning curve. I realized my little summer voyage had been so terrible and so wonderful, I hadn't even begun to process it for myself –so why should I be ready to share it with a complete stranger? I was actually proud of myself for a few moments that night. *This voyage ain't over!* I thought with a little thrill I believed would sustain me until spring. Someone interrupted my train of thought that night, but we'll have to get back to him later.

Tranquility was the only boat on the dock at that hour, so I decided to take a little risk and spend the night. By noon the next day, it was pretty clear no one was going to shoo me away on a Sunday in October, so I decided to hang around until dusk. On Monday morning, I planned to shove off first thing Tuesday. On Wednesday and Thursday it was the same story. Before I knew it, an entire week went by without anyone looking askance at me or the boat. It occurred to me that unless I was seen on deck, no one would even know she was mine. *Tranquility* became a fixture on the river as the days went by and I behaved like a passerby when not in the act of boarding or leaving her. Although it made me edgy to stay there for so long, the firm connection to land allowed me to cobble together a minimal presence in Portland and I began to need the help.

After two weeks on the dock without the slightest murmur or glance from anyone, I walked *Tranquility* down to the far end and tied her up on the nearshore side, where she was protected from the wakes of passing vessels. On that side of the dock, *Tranquility* was practically in the private marina, and her squat, dark green hull and light beige spars disappeared in the forest of masts and flybridges of the vessels moored on the piers behind her. *Can she be so easily hidden?* I wondered. Things were winding down on the waterfront at that time of year, and the marina, park and dock were practically abandoned during the workday. The heavyset rain clouds of an inclement Pacific Northwest winter were piling up overhead and the city people in the high rise neighborhood along the river were already retreating to their warm condominiums and fancy cars. Besides, who knew what was going on with all of those boats down there anyway? They might as well have been bicycles on a crowded rack: you don't even see them unless one's yours.

On my way upriver, I imagined I would spend the winter on *Tranquility* in a Portland area marina, while working and saving up money for the second leg of the voyage. But after two problem-free weeks at the public dock and a closer look at my dwindling finances, I figured it was best to stay put as long as possible and use the time to get a better foothold in town. Instead of looking for a slip, I fliered as much as possible and turned my attention to *Tranquility*'s dimly-lit cabin. A cramped wooden sailboat didn't seem like it was going to be an uplifting place to spend the short, monochrome days and long nights of winter in, so I reorganized *Tranquility*'s interior to better suit the dreary and claustrophobic season that was already well on its way. In order to open her up some and improve her lighting, I removed the half-bulkhead from the starboard side of the cabin. The results were better than expected, so I tore out the galley.

A decorative bulkhead can come or go, but one might imagine a galley would be as useful during winter as it was any other time of year. This is true, except when you're talking about *Tranquility*'s galley. The more I used it, the more I hated it. It was ponderously overbuilt to boating magazine specifications. It took up nearly half the port side of the cabin and featured an enormous, slick-as-glass formica countertop that wound up a little too close to the roof to be of any real use. The counter had a sink in it that could comfortably wash a pair of mugs—if no sponge or water were used—and a battery of knee-banging cabinet doors that accessed deep voids, rendered nearly useless by poorly-routed hoses and savage woodscrew tips. Once the bulkhead was sawn up for lumber and the galley had been moved to a condo dumpster under cover of darkness, I began painting the cabin in cheerful marine enamels. This project gave me something to do while I kept an eye on the changing season and willed the pager to ring. It didn't, and that really threw me for a loop.

Instead of changing course, I pressed on, spending most of my money on photocopies and thumbtacks in the mistaken belief that I was bound to start getting calls. I put my fliers up in the same sorts of places I used to in Seattle: colleges; youth hostels; community centers; cafes and bookstores. After putting up hundreds of fliers without getting a single call, I revised my expectations for the winter and narrowed my focus to basic survival. I lived on a pittance and ate most of my meals from the dwindling stock of instant mashed potatoes, beans and pilot bread left on the boat. Things started to get a little bumpy. Because I was squatting on a public dock and didn't want to attract attention to myself or *Tranquility*, I almost always left her early in the morning and returned after dark. If I had something to do on the boat during the day, or if I was meeting someone, I avoided the deck, kept quiet in the cabin and covered the ports when people were around. If I was restless at night, I browsed the maritime section of Powell's Books or wandered the city until I was sleepy. There were no fires in the hearth or quaint nights reading in the cabin during my impoverished stay in Portland. I was too afraid of being discovered. On the voyage, I learned to live in peril, in Portland, I learned to live in fear. It was quite an education, but I had someone showing me around.

You really don't appreciate the invisible tracks human lives run on until you find yourself off of them. These guides have literally and figuratively been laid down on the land and they permeate the culture that built them. They're simultaneously manifest and taken for granted in a single strand of fence wire or a stripe of colored paint that controls a river of cars or the movement of people. There's a constellation of subtle suggestions, directives and passive-aggressive nudges that line the well-trodden routes of modern society. By keeping an individual in line, they keep a nation in line. A cordon only works if nobody steps over it though –but who ever thinks to do that? No one notices the restraints that surround them because they seem supple and ease nicely when they're pushed on. That's because they're relatively weak, and they're weak because they don't have to do very much (that's the big secret, mate). They only steer behaviors and desires that come naturally to human beings: the search for love, work, money, food and shelter. The armature is all set up and waiting for you to grow into, like a vine to a trellis. You don't see it and it sure as hell doesn't see you –until you go astray. An alternate and far more difficult world to navigate lies just beyond the bounds of civilization, though. If you fall out of step with the routines and norms of a dominant society and have a chance to run alongside one for a while, you start to see things a little differently. Leading a marginal life is interesting and eye-opening, but I don't recommend it. It's emotionally and physically draining and it's a hell of a lot harder to climb out of than it is to fall into. I didn't know any of that yet, because I was just starting to fall.

It didn't take long for the ups and downs to begin and I didn't see the toll my foray into the unknown was taking on my psyche until much later. I can't have looked or smelled very good, I wasn't washing my clothes and people began to look at me funny. One night, a well-dressed man steered way, way clear of me on the gangway that led from the riverfront to the public dock. When this dawned on me later, I felt bad deep down in an organ I didn't know I had and the feeling lodged itself there.

A wave of culinary delight and instantly renewed hope soared through me when I discovered a canned chicken that rolled under a locker board during provisioning in Seattle. My jubilant reaction didn't strike me as odd at the time because I was already heading for a serious breakdown. Picture this moment: I chased a dollar bill blowing down a crowded Portland sidewalk one day. I ran for it fast, bumping into people and slipping between couples until I got my foot on it. When I picked it up, I realized it was one-half of a torn bill. For some reason, just as I was about to toss it, I turned it over. Someone had scribbled LOVE on the back of it with a blue ballpoint pen. I put it in my pocket. Later that night I pinned it to the bookshelf on *Tranquility*. I didn't know what it meant, but I thought I should keep it until I found out.

I tried without luck to make real friends in Portland, which should tell you a lot about my outlook and very little about Portlanders, because they're a very friendly breed. Be that as it may, I didn't thrive there; I found no work and only made one acquaintance. There would be no clean end to the voyage in Portland and my stay there heralded the beginning of a long decline that led me to the darkest time of my life. Instead of feeling relieved of a burden that fall, I faced an immense personal challenge at a time when I had few resources to meet it. The challenge was survival. I was in a new city, I had no friends, no job and almost no money. None of that was made any easier by my turn-of-the-century living situation, which I knew could come undone on me at any moment. Still, I drove on doggedly when I felt the slightest traction on my winter plans and tried to ease the pressure I was under when I didn't. There's only so much reading and free museum-going a person can do when survival is constantly on their mind. Have you ever tried something like that? It's a lot harder than it seems. My pager rang just once while I was in Portland. It was a cold November morning and I ran as fast as I could to the nearest payphone to retrieve the message. It was a wrong number. I dialed it again, risking a couple of heavy coins; they didn't pick up.

You exhaust your emotional capital as well as your cash when you're living rough, and although any outcome can be delayed by a change of perspective, I had some facts to face. My foolhardy self-reliance was crumbling, I was squatting in the middle of a big city, I was almost out of money and I had nowhere else to go. I ignored all of this for longer than I should have, because I was convinced I could still do anything. This mindset continued even as the struggle to support myself and the boat turned grim and I drifted into circles I should not have let myself drift into. The rest of my stay in Portland was so sordid and lonely that I will simply gloss over it for now. I had no work whatsoever while I was there and due to that and everything else weighing on me at the time, I slipped little-by-little into the beginnings of a winter-long depression. I was under so much financial strain at one point, I spent a couple of days stripping everything of value from *Tranquility*. Nothing was sacred and no hint of sailorly superstition stayed my hungry hand as I carved her up. I unceremoniously removed her anchors, GPS, outboard motor, coal stove, fuel tanks and flare gun, as well as all unessential sails, winches and coils of line. I unshipped her compass and smokestack and covered up the holes left in her cabin top and sides with duct tape.

  I loaded all of my boat gear, a ten-speed pulled from a dumpster, my personal effects and toolboxes into the back of an unregistered, untitled, uninsured and barely running 1970 Dodge A200 pickup. I acquired this vehicle in a very suspect manner from one Reggie Lee Washington, a Portland area grifter I met down on the docks one night. I bought that brick-red rattle-trap with my last $50 and a handwritten note giving Reggie permission to stay aboard *Tranquility* for as long as the authorities—whomever they were—allowed her to remain at the dock. If anything bad happened, Reggie had my pager number and I had his.

  I must have thought I'd never see *Tranquility* again, but things in Portland hadn't panned out and I was desperate for something I knew would. That was and always had been Seattle. So I dumped the rest of my boat gas in the truck, topped off the tank with my last few dollars, and drove up I-5 in an autumn rainstorm –swerving in and out of the right lane along the cliffs in the gusting wind, peering under the rickety windshield wipers in the deluge. I was doing a controlled burn toward the city of my dreams on the very last of my fuel. A highway angel must have flown behind a certain red jalopy that night, because I made it.

15

I didn't miss a beat back in Seattle. I hurried over to the only real chandlery in town and sold all of my boat gear to its proprietor for $350 in cash. I balked at the small amount the man offered me for a pile of equipment that he would sell for around $3000. However, in response to my counteroffer of $600—a princely sum for used marine gear at the start of Seattle's nine-month rainy season—the proprietor leaned over the bed of the truck and said to me with a little chuckle: "Okay...how about $250?" I took the $350 and was happy to get it, but I palmed the GPS off the pile when he went inside for the cash –he hadn't even seen it. As soon as I had the money in my hand, I swore to myself that I would replace everything I sold with brand new equipment, completely rebuild *Tranquility* and continue on my way to California the following spring.

After giving the truck a quick tune-up and taking stock of every item of value left in my possession, I weighed my chances of finding a roof to sleep under that month. I sorted through every realistic option I could come up with, but I soon realized it just wasn't going to happen if I planned on eating, so I decided to live in the truck until I found some work. Rather than feel sorry for myself, I saw my current situation as just another challenge and I planned to meet that challenge on my own. This wasn't anything new for me, I was a one-man band long before I was a sailor. I'd been a self-employed mechanic for several years and I'd gotten good at pounding the pavement for profitable auto repair jobs. Although I could get by with much less, all I ever needed to put myself to work were a car, some fliers and a pager. I'd been living in the University District of Seattle when I decided to quit my straight job and try my luck as a strictly freelance auto mechanic, so some of my first clients were college students looking to save money. Cars are expensive and difficult to fix, so when a student finds someone who can repair her car for half of what she's used to paying, she doesn't ask too many questions. Rather than encountering suspicion from the people who called me, I was met with trust and good faith money for parts and labor. This income stream allowed me to buy *Tranquility* in the first place. *It doesn't matter where I lay my head at night!* I thought to myself the first time I slept in the truck. *I've always been able to get the pager ringing, so why not now?* In my mind, it was all very logical, but I was still smarting from my troubles in Portland and some part of me knew living in the truck wasn't going to be a piece of cake. It sure as hell wasn't.

I was promptly run off from my first parking spot. I'd spent a couple of days on a quiet lane in the University District, when a yuppie lady knocked on my fogged-up window early one morning and informed me in a creepy, super-friendly tone that I couldn't stay parked in front of her house day and night. She threatened to call the cops on me if I was there when she came home from work that evening. I could hardly blame her, the truck was a complete wreck and I was an unkempt third-class citizen whose only legal means of transportation was a bicycle thrown in the bed. I drove off immediately, but was afraid to go very far on expired Oregon plates, so I parked a few blocks away. The spot I picked was on a side street in front a rundown house which, as it turned out, was owned by a Seattle parole officer –nice guy.

I probably could have asked someone for a little help getting back on my feet in Seattle, but I put this far from mind. Instead, I came up with a mantra to repeat whenever I began wondering who might lend me a hand: *I got myself into this mess and I'm gonna get myself out of it.* I must have said it twenty times a day. I saw the fix I was in as a colossal test of my personal fortitude. I needed money, so I focused on that rather than feeling sorry for myself. After all, I was worried about a stupid sailboat; I could have been starving in a hut somewhere. It was hard, but I tried to look on the bright side and encourage myself. Who else could I expect to do that for me?

With a little money in my pocket and a renewed commitment to find work, I quickly fell into a U District routine. I woke up early in the morning and did sit-ups on the front seat of the truck, then I walked down to a corner convenience store for a microwaved bean and cheese burrito which I washed down with a waxy cup of warm tap water. I had the same thing for lunch and dinner. Coffee, while I could still afford that luxury, was taken solemnly at Cafe Allegro with all of the other U District weirdos. I spent my days tacking fliers on bulletin boards around the University of Washington, local businesses, payphones and bus stops. At night, I would walk for miles through the wet streets and dreary parks, visiting scenes of past love, fortune or other good times from the life I left behind, without due regard, just six months before.

I'll admit I occasionally availed myself of some of the publicly-held knowledge at University of Washington while I was haunting its halls surreptitiously fliering all appropriate and many unsanctioned places (sorry Mr. Janitor). But I absolutely did not let myself linger in the warm buildings, partake of the free food on offer to elderly lecture attendees, sleep on lounge sofas or use the bathing facilities like some of the other independent scholars I saw there. I wasn't a charity case, I was a survivor, a lone wolf, and I liked it that way. I had no reason in the world to feel sorry for myself! Besides, I was a sailor, I owned a yacht and I was working a good plan. Reggie was going to stay on the boat while I got some money together in Seattle. When I had a little cash to operate with, I'd go to Portland and find a safe harbor for *Tranquility*. Once that was done, I'd come back and get some real money together. I'd slowly replace what I sold off the boat and by spring, I'd be back in Portland. After a complete refit in April or May, I'd continue on my way to California.

Although I was convinced I could still do it all, my winter plans didn't get off to a very good start. Despite immense effort, I didn't land a single job in November and as the reality of winter set in and the weather grew colder, I began working a tighter and tighter schedule. I ate my morning burrito as usual, but instead of hanging around the U District all day, I did a quick run of fliers on a set route and then took a city bus to a community college that was next to a small art school. This schedule allowed me to put up fliers in a much wider area. There was no coffee, no snacks and no breaks on those days –just effort. When I returned to the U District in the evening, I ate a second burrito for dinner and then went for a walk or read in a cafe until it was time to crash. I wasn't going to change the fundamentals of my plan just because I had a little bad luck that fall. I knew it had to work; I had to get a call eventually.

Money wasn't my only concern, though. I phoned Reggie a few times to check on the boat that November, but he never called me back and I didn't know what to make of that. Somehow I convinced myself everything was going well with *Tranquility*. If it wasn't, I'd probably never hear about it anyway. And if I did? So what? There wasn't anything I could do for her; I was stuck in Seattle with barely enough money to live on.

In late November, I ran into a guy I vaguely knew in the U District and he invited me to a big Thanksgiving dinner being thrown by some friends of his. I assumed I was going to be an outcast that holiday season, so I was grateful to be included in something festive and I began looking forward to being around regular people again. My optimism was endless at the time. Even living in the truck didn't seem all that bad to me. It was warm and dry and the seat was incredibly comfortable. The red metal and chrome dashboard was a thing of beauty. The cab was completely secure with the doors locked, and once the windows were fogged up, I had total privacy. I was parked on a quiet street and the driver's seat was a surprisingly good place to read with a book propped up on the steering wheel. When I got lonely or negative I tried to imagine all of the people who've lived in cars at some point in their lives: Okies and stevedores, cowboys and roughneck welders on the Texas oil plains, Hollywood screenwriters and actresses. It was a question of context and circumstance. It was a mental game and I thought I was winning.

On Thanksgiving morning I slipped on some wet leaves in the bed of the truck and smacked my right cheek on the rusty ladder rack. It was a painful injury which left me with a bruise under my right eye. It looked like a shiner but it wasn't. Still, it was bad to have it there on a holiday. That wasn't my only problem. Thanksgiving dinner got off to an awkward start when my acquaintance didn't bother to show up or call, so no one expected me when I rang the doorbell. It was obvious I had nowhere else to go, so the host let me in. Things did not improve from there. I arrived at 6:00 pm and the turkey came out of the oven around 10:00 with the giblet bag still in it –though no one knew what to make of that when it emerged from the bird in a sodden glob of instant stuffing. The host didn't know how to carve a turkey, so it was grabbed at unceremoniously, while dogs with cutesy names ate chunks of white meat off twelve-inch china, set on the floor. Not a single word of thanks or toast was spoken—which was sad—but it wasn't my place to offer one. Red wine was spilled and left to soak into the fine linen tablecloth because such cares were evidently too passé for the young and hip to bother with. I kept my thoughts to myself and was glad to be indoors soaking up some human warmth.

Throughout dinner our gracious host repeatedly brought up the fact that he didn't have a job and boasted to his applauding guests that he'd lived off mortgages for the past two years while the Ravenna Park home his wife's parents fronted the money for went up and up in value. People got too drunk at dinner to clear the table for dessert and there was plenty of free-flow dancing and trashy debauchery to wince at in the living room after our meal. The hostess pitched the meaty carcass straight into the trash compacter and slid it shut with her hip. It got worse.

With a black eye (it wasn't) and no clear connection to anyone, I was the curiosity of the gathering so I had to field several questions. The interview began when one guest asked what the fight I'd been in was all about. I could have popped his head off with a squeeze of my left hand, but when I told him how I hurt myself, neither he nor anyone else seemed to believe me. Later on, any mention of the ups and downs of the voyage were received as even more tall-tales. For instance, I couldn't convince them that I'd sailed up the Columbia River because the tipsy hostess proved that I had my geography all wrong when she pointed out that Portland can be reached by boat without ever leaving Puget Sound (it can't). If I really sailed to Portland like I said, why didn't I just go: "South, past Tacoma and Olympia and all that?" she asked with an unsteady look for *props* around the living room –which she got. I couldn't even defend myself! It's one thing to try to tell a story while being heckled, but it was quite another to convince those people I was living rough, voluntarily. Although I told the truth, the truth sent a different message than the one I intended. At one dismal point, when I knew I'd worn out my welcome, but hadn't had a chance to leave with my head held high, I thought I heard someone snickering about me in the kitchen. So I left in a rush, totally dejected, without saying goodbye to anyone.

I placed a call to Reggie on my way back to the U District that night, but the call, like the previous ones, went unanswered.

I thought I was going to receive a boost to my flagging spirits a few days after Thanksgiving when I ran into the inimitable Violetta Biancardi: bouncy Italian, expert student, polyglot brimming with European culture and *savoir faire* –also, musky ex-girlfriend of mine. The reunion took place one morning when I noticed her standing at the counter of a U District cafe. I waved to her from the sidewalk and she motioned for me to come in. She was genuinely happy to see me and I her, so we sat down for a cup of coffee and a little catch-up. She was newly single, and for a brief moment as I listened to her grad student woes, I imagined another dalliance with her. But boy was it the wrong time for that sort of thing! She was being preyed on in the *we're-going-to-give-you-that-PhD-someday* manner universities are so good at. She had heaps of glorified secretarial work and her own "students" to teach for no pay and no recognition. She was house-sitting and watching the slavering dogs of one of her advisers while he was in London with a former student. Violetta knew it was a perverse system, but she wanted a career in academia, and in order to do that, you have to suckle a chafed teat that despises you almost as much as you despise it.

When it was my turn to speak, I gave Violetta a sanitized version of the voyage focusing on the natural beauty, the adventure, the romance and the comedy while leaving out most of the tragedy. I was in very good form for such hard times, but after listening to me for several minutes with real interest, Violetta sprang to her feet, gathered her papers to her chest with a flourish and said to me with mock cheerfulness: "I *hate* you, you know?...I mean, I hate your *freeeedom.*" She was late. She had to run. She had class. She didn't ask if we might see each other again.

It's been said that the life of a sailor is one of ultimate freedom and ultimate responsibility, but what Violetta couldn't have known was that I was stuck on the ultimate responsibility part of the equation. I couldn't do anything other than dismiss her sudden leave-taking as impolite but unsurprising behavior from one of the many unhappy grad students I'd known who were struggling under the harness-and-bit of university life. I brushed off my encounter with Violetta without seeing how it and other alienating experiences were slowly chipping away at my self-esteem.

There was another thing I didn't see coming:

The holiday season in the U District can be an introspective and depressing time of year when there's nowhere you belong. However, if you're self-employed and you depend on students for a living, winter break can be ruinous. The slow times for me usually began with the Thanksgiving hush, but that was just a preview of the truly lean weeks to come. There was often a slight rebound after turkey day, but it was short lived and always followed by the urgency of early December gift-budgeting. For me, the transition to real winter belt-tightening was signaled by an unmistakable decline in work calls the first week of December. That slowdown became economic dormancy by the 15th. At that point, I'd know life wasn't going to get back to normal until the second week of the New Year. An auto repair job was rare for me in December, but if I landed one, it was top-shelf, because the car had to make it home for the holidays and mommy and daddy were paying. The wait for a phone call in December had always been terrible and there was no reason to think it would be any different that year. However, there were some signs it might be worse.

Dealing with the financial implications of winter break is nothing at all compared to the devastation of being left behind in the abandoned U District by the rosy-cheeked, homeward-bound college students. When it's too late to join them, you watch as they joyfully pile into premium hand-me-down sedans for well-dressed Christmas card road trips, or they're ducking into clean cabs with pristine girlfriends to go catch trains and planes to their waiting families. When you're lonely there's simply no other way to see them go. Sociologists who study North Americans have found that they meet new people in three main ways: at school, at work or through an existing social sphere. So what do you do when you don't have any of those? Well, you're left to cobble together a life from the odds and ends of humanity and publicly available culture. By the time you get to that table, you have no appetite for the meager fare.

On a frigid December morning, I broke my left index finger while trying to tighten the steering wheel of the Dodge. I set the painful, freezing-cold fracture myself with shocky, trembling hands. I don't know why it didn't occur to me to get some help for it. Later that week, my very worst fear was realized when I was pulled over one night by an aggressive traffic cop who was sure I was up to something. This unlucky episode took place in the parking lot of a U District bank on one of the few occasion I drove the Dodge. The officer searched the cab while I stood at the tailgate, looking around for paths of exit and a double back. He didn't find anything of course, but he spent the next half-hour trying to wear me down with trick questions about the truck: who owned it and why I was driving it without proper documents or plates. But I was too game to slip up. When it began to rain, I stayed put waiting to see what he would do, but thanks to Reggie, I was primed to run and I knew exactly where I was headed. When my shirt soaked through, the cop must have realized my entire life was in the truck, and rather than take me in, he let me leave the scene on foot with a warning, but no possessions. I kept an eye on him as I walked away, though, and as he was getting into his cruiser, I dove into a hedge. I watched the truck, the parking lot and the busy street for a long time after he drove off. I held on a little longer and he swung through again, as I expected. When I was sure he wasn't coming back, I walked around the block and crawled to the driver's door from a better direction. I cracked it, slipped inside the cab and drove away with the headlights off, taking care not to use the foot brake. As I turned onto the street, I glanced in the rearview mirror and saw a wrecker pulling into the lot. I was used to close calls by then.

That winter my life was reduced to an automated, joyless existence. I could do little more than put up fliers, talk to myself, read and wait for a call. I looked on the world through the distorted lens of a loner who haunted it meekly. I questioned human nature and concluded that it was entirely venal. I noted that the world went on whether I participated in it or not. I realized it didn't need me, so I told myself I didn't need it. I withdrew into my mind and small things took on great meaning there: dashing across a busy street in a downpour to save fifty cents; experimenting with the unique flier ecosystems of billboards in different university buildings; examining the minutia of loneliness while surrounded by people in a busy cafe; wanting a woman, but beginning to detest them and hating myself for it.

I saw what was happening to me of course and I used what was left of my reason and energy to resist it. However, instead of helping, this effort became a negative feedback loop which had the unexpected effect of taking me even lower. I'm a positive person by nature, so despite my difficult circumstances, I managed to meet a few people that winter. I used to chit-chat with a young man I sometimes saw walking around Green Lake. It was no more than a *hi, how are you?* acquaintance. We'd sit on a bench and discuss what was going on in the world or with his upcoming wedding. He struck me as a bit too emasculated for marriage and he wore the *I'm actually a really quirky intellectual* eyeglasses of the time, but I liked him well-enough after I got to know him a little better.

About a week before Christmas I saw him at the lake, and after our usual three-minute conversation, he invited me to a Christmas party he and his fiancée were throwing. I accepted, even though my enthusiasm for visits had been dulled by one too many disappointments. The invitation, for an evening a couple of days hence, cheered me up and I rushed to a thrift store for a clean shirt and some decent pants. I was poor that winter, but I wasn't down to the rich pile of change in the truck's ashtray: that reserve of silvery coins was the absolute financial limit I'd set for my go-it-alone-life-turn-around plan. If I dipped into that fund—

the very last of my $350—it would mean that I must call on my family for assistance. *Positively crushing.*

On the evening of the Christmas party, I bought a bottle of red wine for my hosts—a reckless extravagance at the time—and I set out for their Green Lake home with high hopes for the night. *There could even be a girl there!* I thought with a little thrill as I walked. *No stories, no talking about the voyage!* I reminded myself cheerfully as I arrived at their front porch in a billow of cold breath and rang the bell. When the door opened my host seemed ambivalent about my arrival, and when I presented the bottle to him with a heartfelt, "Merry Christmas!" his hand bumped into it and I almost dropped it.

"Whoops! Ha Ha Ha!" I said. He didn't respond with much more than a mumble. I brushed this off...until I figured it out.

The Christmas party was held in an odd house. It seemed large and well-kept from the street, but inside it was cramped. The living room walls were strangely discontinuous: wainscoting there and there, but not over there. It seemed as though the windows hadn't been opened, or the drapes drawn, in a very long time. The home wasn't in disarray, but every surface had something on it so there was nowhere to set anything down. The fireplace had been boarded up, due to some fault perhaps, but the manner in which it was decommissioned came off as creepy and half-done. I couldn't stop checking it out. If they were still burning something in there, it wasn't wood.

The dining room table was only half-made-up for a holiday party and in an impromptu way; the other half of the finely-wrought heirloom was piled high with file boxes among which crouched an angry-looking typewriter. Judging by the medical bills and depositions lying on the table and meeting the plaintiff/patient—the dour mother of my acquaintance, whom he and his fiancée lived with—I put together that the paperwork attested to an intricate, ongoing legal battle connected to some sort of medical malpractice, fibromyalgia or factitious disorder. This heavy vibe near the kitchen, the supposed heart of a home, did not lend itself to mirth and merry-making and neither did the peculiar group of people who made up the other party-goers. There were only five of them: four men—two shabbily dressed, two bleary eyed—and one positively disturbed-looking woman with a bad case of rosacea going. You may judge for yourself whether I'm an ungracious or fault-finding guest *after* you meet the crowd.

The first shabbily dressed man I spoke to launched into a financial tale of unbelievable scope involving business interests of his in several foreign countries, and three-letter government agencies I'd never heard of. It had something to do with the Panama Canal, an international development bank and a cement plant being built in French Guiana. When he tried to engage me further by showing me certain documents he claimed proved California was not a state –in the strictly legal sense, I drifted as far away from him as the crowded dining room would allow. He reminded me too much of Reggie, though Reggie was a much better dresser. Even the food—an uncertain cross of holiday decor and edibles— offered no quarter. The items were either stale or uninviting and hadn't been touched by anyone. I went to take a Christmas tree mint from a small dish, but the dish lifted off the table with it. They were candies from last year, or a decoration of some kind –I never figured out which. There was nothing to drink but some warm, watery fruit punch and when I politely mentioned the wine I brought, my host and his mother had a hard time deciding if it could or *should* be opened. I caught an exasperated eye-roll from the fiancée of my host at this hitch in the party giddy-up. There was definitely something wrong with the entire scenario and I couldn't put my finger on it at first, but I soon got a whiff. There wasn't a Christmas tree in the house nor any festive lights; there were no pine cones, not one angel or candle, not one sprig of garland. Worse, the few cardboard decorations which hinted at the cheerful season appeared to have been borrowed from an elementary school. *What sort of Christmas party is this?*

The wine opening completely stalled-out, my host was avoiding me for some reason, and the two bleary eyed men seemed to be casing the place. So, with no other refuge in sight, I struck up a conversation with the most normal seeming person there: the fiancée. She was an Eastern Seaboard Friends School Beauty with a fellowship and an old Mercedes-Benz station wagon. She seemed to think the party was headed for heavy weather and we shared a few laughs over it. However, when I inquired into her interests, her answer sent a joy-stifling wave of understanding through me that I thought I'd never recover from. She was an advocate for the homeless. The Christmas party was connected to her outreach work with drug-addicted-street-residenced-persons (her cumbersome wording). I instantly concluded that I'd been invited to the party not because I was liked, but in order to spread a thinly-funded public gruel as far as it would go. I took another look around the room. The disturbed woman with rosacea, who sat on a chair backed up against the dining room wall, half-glanced at me and then stared intently in her lap. One of the two men who were casing the place was standing on tiptoes, lifting the lids of knickknack boxes on the mantle and peering into them one-by-one. I looked to my attractive hostess with a mock appeal for help in my eyes, so she would know I wasn't "getting it." She cracked up when she saw my expression, then she smiled back sexy and sinister and just for me. It was an opening, but you can't spend an entire night chatting-up another man's woman. *I'm outta here!* I thought to myself, but I checked my flight instinct: *Just hang around for a minute! This party's just getting started!*

I went for a rally by putting any connection between my hostess' line of work and my invitation to the party as far from mind as possible. That was going to be hard, but I figured I could try to hang on a little longer by browsing the living room bookshelf. This is a practically unassailable party time-out area where certain types of people (ambiverts, for instance) can go to get a fresh grip on themselves. So I drifted over to it and thumbed through a paperback book on feminist psychotherapy for a few minutes. When I calmed down enough to take a pencil from the phone table to write something down for later thought, its lead was broken in the way that makes a pencil write in a wide and unintelligible charcoal triplicate. The pen I picked up was out of ink, and so was the next and the next after that. *Who lives like this?* I huffed to myself under my breath as I dropped them one at a time into the little wicker wastebasket to right of the table. I gave up on the note-to-self and turned my attention back to the crowd. There wasn't much going on so I began politely listening to a living room conversation that struck up between my host and the second shabbily dressed man. I was trying, dear reader, but there was little opportunity to join it:

"We ordered a pizza...do you like pizza?" the host inquired of his guest.

"No, not really," the guest sullenly replied.

"I DO!" the host added enthusiastically.

"*DO* you?" the guest asked incredulously.

With that, they drifted into the doldrums together, so I excused myself and headed for the bathroom. I found the light switch where I reached for it on the bathroom wall, but when I flipped it, nothing happened. It was an old Seattle house, so I reached into the pitch black space overhead hoping for a pull chain, but there wasn't anything hanging there or anywhere else. I felt along the wall behind the door, but there was nothing there either. I stepped into the hall and looked along the wall. Nothing. I fell back to the hall entry and flipped the two wall switches there but no lights came on, even though there were two globes on the ceiling. It was one of *those* houses. On my right, the door to the master bedroom stood open and I saw the faint glow of a bathroom nightlight reflected in a cheval glass opposite the bed. But something unpleasant about the position of the mirror and the medical clutter on the nightstand reflected in it kept me from entering. Since I'm one to listen to such warnings –while on land at least, I said a perfunctory goodbye to my host, locked eyes with the wife-to-be for a moment longer than we should have, and was out on the street before anyone else saw me leaving.

I placed another call to Reggie that night, but it went unanswered. My Christmas turned out *far* worse than that miserable party gave me reason to expect.

I'm an extremely self-conscious house guest at the best of times, so I certainly didn't feel comfortable imposing on anyone in the lonely state I was in the afternoon of December 23rd. Over the past month, I'd gotten the feeling one too many times, from one too many people, that I was repulsive in some way, so I decided to spend the next few days in the truck. I figured another Christmas on my own wasn't going to kill me. To distract myself from my troubles that winter, I'd been reading sea stories from the past two centuries. I began at Powell's with the celebrated and popular classics because they were close at hand. Then I delved into obscure works because they were unwanted and priced accordingly. I digested everything from true tales of modern voyages to honest works of fiction, even drolly factual ship's logs, hoping to gather from books the seafaring skills that experience alone would take me several lifetimes to acquire. For all of the wise words that have been written on the subject of men, ships and the sea, there's certainly no good reason for the average landlubber to set sail himself.

As I read that winter, I slowly came to understand that it was my shortcomings as a mariner which *Tranquility* was reacting to when I couldn't bend her to my doubtful will. It was my ignorance which led me to conclude that *Tranquility* had a mind of her own. I read to cure myself of that ignorance, and that afternoon, I had a book in my possession which I was sure would take my mind off my problems for a little while. How wrong can a young man be?

The Venturesome Voyages of Captain Voss is the unusual sea story of one Captain John Voss who attempted to sail around the world in a Nootka trading canoe which he converted into a schooner named *Tilikum* (Chinook jargon meaning "friend"). He began his celebrated but improbable voyage from Victoria, British Columbia in 1901. Voss made it much farther than anyone expected and along the way, he popularized the use of drogues (it comes up later). John Voss set sail from the Pacific Northwest so his book makes a few references to places I'd been to or sailed by in the Salish Basin and elsewhere. Seeing the names of familiar landmarks and bodies of water in print reminded me of the outbound leg of my own voyage. My mind wandered to Port Townsend and of course, Lisa.

LISA! Her name struck like a bolt of lightning, the book fell out of my hands.

I NEED TO FIND LISA!

I was driving to Coleman Dock a minute later, singing along with a Christmas carol playing on the Dodge's staticy AM radio. Cops be damned! It was Christmas and I figured I had enough money left for a cross-sound ferry ticket and gas to get me to Port Townsend just in time for Christmas. *Christmas! Christmas! Christmas!* I convinced myself on the ferry ride that as soon as Lisa saw me, she would welcome me back as if I'd only been gone a couple of weeks. No doubt I'd sleep in her arms that night and everything would be back to normal by morning. We were going to be just as happy and lovely as the couples in the *Lands' End* winter catalog I was forlornly perusing just the night before. *How ironic –but that's life!* It can change on you in a heartbeat. No, *really.* When the ferry landed on the west side of the sound, I raced across the bridges that led to the mainland and I drove north along the Olympic Peninsula in a fantastic mania. I kept imagining how lovely it was going to be to hold Lisa in my arms again and how right it would be to unburden myself to a woman who truly understood me. I was really cheering up as I made my way north; I even had a few laughs at myself for all the stupid things I'd done to ruin my voyage. I thought I was starting to feel like my old self again but I was a total mess.

The sunset over the Olympic Peninsula that evening was stunning, or so it seemed to me in the state I was in. Either way, I pulled over next to a culvert and jumped out of the truck to snap a quick picture of it with my little disposable camera. I was leaning against the front grille, peering through the viewfinder, framing the perfect shot, when I felt the truck roll back. I flew into a full-body, about-face jump and dashed around to the driver's door. Could I get it open in time to avert disaster? Of course not. I pulled too soon and my hand slipped off the cold chrome door handle. The truck merged onto the bracken of the embankment with a *crunch-crunch-crunch-crunch* –the side view mirror almost took me along with it when I grabbed for the handle again. The Dodge went over the edge, slid crab-wise down the slick bank and wound up at the bottom of the steep-sided ditch, which was full of mud and water. I stood there stunned –*stunned.* The reversal of fortune was so sudden and final that I actually thought I was dreaming. The Dodge was in a very bad way down there. It slowly settled to the tops of the wheel wells in the soupy mud, sinking deep enough to possibly drown the engine through the exhaust pipes. I didn't even try to drive it out of there. It was hopeless. To make matters worse, the accident happened on a lonely stretch of Jefferson County road, and although there was the proverbial farmhouse standing in the middle of a field, there were no lights lit or vehicles parked there. Empty agricultural land stretched in all directions and it was going to be dark soon. Small cars sped past but nobody looked like they wanted to stop. *I could be here all night!*

When it was obvious it was the farmhouse or nothing, I hopped the fence and set out for it overland. The field was the consistency of soft clay and was horrendously furrowed. It was a shoe-sucking slog, but it was my only hope and it had to be done. Anyway, the farmer was home. I'll just say that when the need is great, few words must be spoken. So a Massey Ferguson tractor was pulled out of a shed, a fence was opened up and a two-man struggle ensued. I made a couple of trips to the barn and back for fence posts and chain. My new clothes were ruined, but the truck was rescued, the engine started, and I was back on my way by 8:00 pm.

Two or three miles down the road, the front left tire went flat and I had to hitchhike in the dark—wild-eyed and covered in filth—with the mud-caked wheel, to a rural gas station that was miraculously open. The owner, no doubt sensing an impending holiday crisis, exchanged my flat tire for a used one that appeared out of nowhere on the new tire rack. Then, without an extra word to me or even a glance at the till, he drove me back to the Dodge and waited—with eyes averted, but still watching—while I mounted the wheel. When I went up to his window and made a move with a muddy claw to dig in the front pocket of my jeans, he said to me in a kind, who's-kidding-who tone of voice: "Son, I think you better just get where you're trying to get to tonight." This is what it means to be hanging by a thread in our world and this is what it means to do a good turn for your brother.

I coasted down the long hill that leads to Port Townsend around 11:00 pm and only a few places were still open. Undeterred by my difficulties, or just running wide-open on the volatile vapors of temporary insanity, I washed in a restroom, changed my clothes as best I could and asked around for Lisa. I looked for her until the town went to bed but she didn't seem to be there. I was going to learn an unhappy lesson about real life that Christmas.

I awoke at 3:00 am to the sound of a police officer rapping on the driver's window with the butt of a metal flashlight. "Move along son, take it somewhere else," he said to me in a threatening tone, punctuated by a final strike of his light, which sent the big D batteries bouncing off the back spring. I was lucky he didn't break my window and lucky he didn't ask questions. I didn't have any idea who really owned the truck, and I could have easily found myself in jail for Christmas while it was all sorted out. When the cop pulled away, I realized I was living in constant fear. Not the fear of bondage, war or famine, but it was genuine fear and it had been taking its toll on me for some time. That soulless hour wasn't over yet: I was driving along, looking for a place to hide the truck for the rest of the night, when I noticed my headlights dimming from yellow to amber. I turned onto the next block just as the engine died, and I rolled the Dodge into a spot along the empty curb. When I tried to restart the engine, the battery was too weak to crank it over. Most likely cause of the flat battery? Chrysler alternator. Inexpensive and always in stock, but externally regulated and therefore a complicated anachronism that can be difficult to diagnose properly. It's a one of a kind in the industry.

I sighed as the reality of another breakdown hit me. I knew I was flailing, and it felt like anything could happen to me at any time. If there was a parked car instead of empty curb where the truck died, I would have been stuck in the middle of the street. You can be close to the edge and never even know it, but when you're close to the edge and you *know* it...well...that's a hell of a lot harder on you. So there I was, falling to pieces on a hillside in Port Townsend, but even as I did, I marveled at how easily the things I cherished most in life could be lost to circumstance. I was surprised that a place which signified such love and joy to me only a few months before could be so polluted by my struggle to survive. I held the sadness and longing for Lisa inside and jammed my eyes shut until dawn, desperately trying to focus what little hope I had left on the frail promise of tomorrow.

There are rare times in life when, to move forward, you must leave everything you are and everything you know, behind. You must end an act, say a goodbye, shut a door forever, put your thumb out and hit the road. This isn't going to happen to you if you're the average clockwork orange tangled up in the power cords and feeding tubes of the grid. Barring the truly unforeseen tragedies that can visit a person, if you sit at home doing nothing, nothing bad is ever going to happen to you except on tv. If you go out and really *live* however, it's an entirely different matter. Do it long enough and utter disaster is bound to strike. Everything's going to fall apart on you.

I awoke the next morning unrested and on autopilot. I flagged down a car and got a long jump-start. By using neutral, killing the engine to coast down long hills, and bump-starting, I was able to make my way to an auto parts store not far from where I bought the anchor from *The Pirate*. The store was only open for a few hours that day, and after carefully conducting a series of dicey electrical tests, I bought a rebuilt alternator for a 318 Chrysler and installed it in the parking lot. I begged a jump-start from a patron and drove around charging the battery. Then, drawing on reserves I cannot account for, I dragged myself into town, washed my hands in a cold public restroom and went to look for Lisa. It only took a few minutes to find out she was spending Christmas on Vancouver Island with her father. What was particularly galling was that I could have learned that painful fact over the phone from Seattle. For some reason I hadn't thought of calling ahead. After months of exertion and travel bristling with unforeseen difficulties, merciless calms, strandings, accidents and foul weather, I now had to bear the holiday totally alone. I couldn't pretend it was going to be okay; there was nothing left to imagine and nothing left to hope for. That Christmas Eve became my measure for any future trouble.

I, dangling at the end of my rope on a sidewalk in front of the restaurant where I used to wait for Lisa with such lovely words on my lips; a face I barely recognized staring back at me in a plate-glass window done up in holiday tempera paint. The trip to Port Townsend was a complete disaster. I was destroyed, but I still had a little farther to fall.

Several hours later, I was parked in the U District where I'd been the day before; the only difference was I was virtually out of money and a lot worse off in my head. It was Christmas Eve, and I couldn't bear to be in the truck for another second, so I took a long walk and tried to get a grip on myself. After wandering past handsome homes decorated for the holiday and fresh-faced young women out for strolls with their perfect beaus, I realized I wasn't going to feel better anytime soon. On that walk I finally saw the facts of my life for what they were: *Tranquility* was the reason for the mess I was in. I never lived in such financial insecurity, peril or discomfort until she came into my life. The solution to all of my problems seemed obvious: I needed to get rid of the boat...but how? Who would buy her in the state she was in? Who in their right mind would even accept her as a gift? I considered the possibility that I might have to make a trip to Portland just to sink her in the river some dark winter night. What if she was already gone? Was that why I hadn't heard from Reggie? What if none of it even mattered?

I took the long, long way back to the truck that night, and when I turned down my street, I saw there was even more bad news. The front end of the Dodge was lifted up for some reason. *Impound?* Wait...no. It wasn't getting towed, both rear tires had gone flat, that was all. I'll never forget the moment I lay down in the gutter and rolled the trolley jack through the chowder of mud and leaves under the rear axle to take the weight off the cracking tires. When I stood up, wet and cold, and looked into the Christmas Eve sky, I was anyone, anywhere who's ever been cast to the dirt of the lane or left standing on his own beneath the lonesome, twinkling firmament. I was an untouchable. *Yesterday, today, tonight, what more can go wrong?* I asked myself as warm tears of pure anguish welled up in my eyes and began to fall. It was for everything, and I couldn't even pretend to hold them back.

I was man alone in the world for the first time in my life. I'm not saying I was one who went away young, was forgotten by his people and never returned. I didn't become a hermit who stares down the wild horizon from a steep beach on a lost coast where timber tumbles down canyons to the sea. I didn't turn into a misanthrope who never loves again and lives in a solitude so complete he can never be recalled from it. But on that night, I paid him a visit and learned where that kind of lament comes from. I lost a little part of who I was on my first sea voyage and I hope someday I'll forget how it felt to be so alone and adrift in the world. While I was way down there, I learned that the human sense of pain is a retained primitive character –it's always with you, and I learned that to have enjoyed life at all is to have evolved.

Although there's practically a law of the genre which allows unverifiable tales of woe to be built upon a little here and a little there without any ethical risk to the teller, I assure you, dear reader, those days and nights passed exactly as I have said.

If you want my advice, don't run too close to the edge, because a slip there is fatal.

I spent Christmas day reading in the tilted truck, but compared to the previous 48 hours, it was a simple exercise in self-control and time wasting. I ate my usual fare at the usual hour and went back to read on the front seat, taking care not to make eye contact with the folks strolling by after the family meal. A charitable hand-out would have been ruinous at that point!

On December 26th I treated myself to a belated holiday mug of Cafe Allegro coffee and I used my very last bills to pay for it. It was ashtray time, but it came as an odd sort of relief. I tried to make it on my own and I failed, but it was still going to be okay. I was sipping my coffee and mulling this significant development over, when my pager rang. It was Reggie. I hadn't heard from him since leaving Portland and I ran to the payphone in the hallway and called him back.

"Hey man! What's happening?" I asked, bracing myself for the worst news that can come to a man with a boat.

"How's life treating you up in Seattle?" Reggie asked in his familiar, genial tone.

"Reggie...I called you twenty times!! And you never called me back!!" I blurted out, holding the bakelite receiver to my ear with both hands.

"Okay...okay...well...that's what I'm calling about. I have something I have to say to you," he continued without really hearing me.

"GO! Where's the boat?" I asked, hurrying him along.

"This is going to be very difficult for me to say and I need you to listen to me."

"Just TALK Reggie!"

"Just *LISTEN!* Don't be so *unreasonable...* This isn't going to be easy for me to talk to you about, okay? I've been dealing with something down here and it's been very difficult for me...I think you know what I'm referring to...So, how was your Christmas? Are you earning any money?"

"WHAT THE HELL'S GOING ON REGGIE?! Is there something wrong with the boat?"

"Will you calm down for a minute? The boat's right where you left it. This is about me, about you and me and everything that happened in Portland, but you're going to be really, really angry when I tell you all of this..."

Okay, it's time for a little break. Coffee?

16

Caveat lector: The following is too painful for me to revisit in full, and I don't know you. The place where we're about to go is too dark, the deceit –if it was deceit, too complex and inscrutable, so I must elide and bend the truth. I'll have to show it to you with puppetry. I'm sorry, but that's how it came to me and it's the only way. I want you to meet someone, but I have to say something first. I had no part in any of the crimes, I was only an observant bystander, an ethnographer. Things are about to get pretty weird so skip ahead if you don't trust me.

Highly intelligent, very well-spoken but deeply flawed, Reggie Lee Washington was a complex and magnetic individual. He was a Portland-area grifter and a talented but petty con-artist. For whatever reason, we struck up an odd sort of friendship while I was down there. Shortly after we met, I think Reggie realized I didn't have anything he could connive me out of, so I became his friend instead of one of his marks. I may have been both in his eyes, but I never really figured it all out. Although Reggie never got around to telling me what was going on that day, the call felt like some sort of recovery step after suffering what may have been a monumental life crisis of his own. I suspect he hit bottom and was going straight. And, dear reader, Reggie Lee Washington had much to go straight from.

Our acquaintance began at the public dock the Saturday evening after I arrived in Portland. Reggie meandered by the boat with his hands in his pockets and made a casual comment, which floated on the air as if it were meant for no one in particular.

"Nice boat," he said to himself, admiring *Tranquility* from a few feet away. "I used to have a boat just like this."

That's a good way to strike-up a conversation with the owner of a vessel like mine. Old wooden boats, especially sailboats, are almost always particular individuals. They're called one-offs –just like a homemade dress from a pattern. I was surprised that someone could have had a boat just like *Tranquility* and Reggie was surprised anyone had heard him. He hadn't seen me from the dock because I was perched at the cross-trees halfway up *Tranquility*'s mast. I climbed down to greet him, and Reggie Lee Washington had one hell of a sea story of his own to tell.

After beating around the bush for a minute or two and finding out a little bit about me and my boat, Reggie recounted an edge-of-your-seat tale that began with a series of escalating run-ins with Ku Klux Klan dudes. He told me the KKK wanted him and his sailboat off the Columbia River because, as Reggie put it, *it's a white man's river and they want to keep it that way.* He'd been in a fistfight at a fuel dock that started when he bumped into a ski boat as he was coming in to refuel his sloop on a busy summer afternoon. A few days later, someone pointed an over-under shotgun at him from the pilot house of a passing log tug. Fearing for his life, Reggie dove into the cockpit well of his boat until the vessel passed. A week later, his beautiful lapstrake sailing dinghy went missing. All of this seemed to lead up to the sinking of his sloop on her mooring one night. That was a couple of weeks ago and Reggie was out of town on business when it happened. The night I met him, Reggie offered to show me where his boat went down. His finger landed on my chart with perfunctory ease at a place on the lower Willamette –it wasn't far away. Reggie had a command of vessel nomenclature that could not possibly have been guessed at on a lark. He seemed to know his way around a sailboat and had that refined, deliberative subtlety about him which suits the yachting lifestyle and the other mysterious leisure activities of the wealthy. When I expressed my condolences to him for the sinking and my outrage at the impunity, Reggie told me in a forthright manner that the FBI was investigating. Things do happen to people and I suppose I really believed him.

A couple days after our first meeting, Reggie came walking down the dock toting a hefty, dark brown accordion folder. He wore newly pressed slacks, immaculate leather loafers, specs and an official-looking FBI monogrammed sweater. He looked like he just stepped out of a law office at Quantico. We spoke for a few minutes about *Tranquility* and then Reggie offered to show me a photo of his boat so I could see for myself how similar our yachts were. He started flipping through the folder, which was filled with vessel documents and operator manuals for older marine equipment. It was a dossier any boat owner would recognize. As he was shuffling papers, an old naval architect's drawing of a trim wooden sloop fell to the deck with a sail plan attached to it with a paperclip. Reggie seemed surprised by these frail, tracing-paper plans, but said: "Better yet, her original drawings."

She was an average-sized sloop from *Tranquility's* time but they weren't sisterships. And although she had a passing resemblance to her, it wasn't anything to ponder for too long. I was more interested in the FBI sweater, so I asked him about that instead. According to Reggie, the sweater, which did not look like it came from a thrift store rack, was a gift from the FBI guys who were working his case. Reggie told me that Portland was a small town and he never knew when he might run into the Klan, so he wore the sweater as a warning to them. We talked for an hour or so about the various methods for raising his boat from the bottom of the river. I thought it could be done with a small crane and some air bags, but Reggie disagreed in engineering terms that I didn't really understand. Anyway, a salvage crew was already working on it.

The following night, Reggie gave me the old barometer off his boat as a gift. He still had it in his possession because it was being repaired when his boat sank. On the back of the barometer, I noticed a repair sticker from a well-known Seattle instrument firm, Captain's Nautical, in business since about 1897. That evening, Reggie offered to take me to where the top of his mast could be seen sticking out of the river, but we went for a spendy uptown dinner instead. Reggie picked up the check with a new hundred dollar bill, and for one reason or another, we never went to see the wreck. I started seeing a lot of Reggie, and as the days went by, more of his story came out. He was an accomplished flautist who tutored Reed College students and coached professional musicians for a living. He often had an expensive-looking flute with him. An article about his run-in with the Klan was published in a local magazine, but for some reason, Reggie didn't mention the article prior to its publication. Then one day he showed it to me as if he just thought of it for the first time. He presented it with a caveat: the editor had gotten a few things wrong with his story. He didn't seem to need to show me the article, but I read it anyway. It was all right there, in print.

Reggie said that a wealthy family from a local church had taken him in when his vessel sank. He lived on his boat and had nowhere else to go when she was lost. His new living situation was getting difficult however, because the woman of the house, an aspiring musician, was making advances toward him and he thought her husband was picking up on it. Never nervous or self-conscious, Reggie was always well-dressed in an upper-class manner; he was carefully groomed, good-looking and well-fed. He always had money. He never asked for anything or implied the slightest need when we were together. The only thing I could have possibly given him was someone to talk to, so any suspicions I may have had seemed unreasonable at first, then borderline racist. He never once misspoke or contradicted himself in any way; he had a British broadcaster's command of the English language that could only be marveled at and he often delved three uses deep into definitions. Reggie would drop the occasional hint that some of the difficulties he faced in his music career and the investigation of the sinking were due to racism. I took the hint. I didn't want to be one of those people.

A small crisis arose when Reggie was asked to leave the home he was staying in, and when I suggested he move onto the boat while he figured out his next move, he seemed surprised and genuinely touched. He declined the offer, without actually declining it, so I cleaned out a couple of small lockers for him and the next time he came around, I told him he could sleep on the boat if he needed to. He didn't seem to know what to make of the offer and his inquisitive commentary and endless anecdotes trailed off into an awkward silence. He looked at me strangely and I think something changed between us that day. I was raw and downtrodden, and I was one step away from being homeless myself, so I identified with Reggie much more than I would have at any other point in my life. I began spending a lot of time with Reggie and I gave him the benefit of the doubt for longer than I should have. But when I started to notice little threadbare spots on his finely woven manteaux, I didn't let on that I suspected anything, because by then, I wanted to watch his operation more closely. I started playing Reggie, and without him knowing it, he served as my informant on the workings of a bizarre underworld. The man remains an enigma however, because he never admitted to anything shady and I uncovered so few explicit falsehoods that I cannot possibly disprove his greatest claim.

The first discovery I thought I made was nothing more than a minor infraction, a frat-boy scam. Reggie kept himself fit and clean at a premium health club by using a membership card he pieced together from a club coupon reprinted on a dime-store copy machine. He flashed this at the front counter during the downtown evening rush. As Reggie explained it, he was a longtime member of the club, but his card was in his wallet, and his wallet was at the bottom of the Willamette River along with most of his other belongings. I accepted this and Reggie must have been encouraged by my apparent naiveté, because the longer I knew him, the more he hinted at his true nature. The second discovery may have involved grand theft. These were the flutes. Small, expensive and easily pawned. I believe they were lifted from the lounges, practice rooms or libraries of music departments at local colleges. Reggie was charming and articulate and could glide through a room like he owned it. A university underling would not be able to trip him up with questions or pressure, and he would never be mistaken for someone who just walked in off the street, because he could morph into a department chair or professor in an instant. Reggie had to be caught in the commission of a crime by someone with the authority and the physical strength to grapple with him; he was much too clever, fit and observant for that to happen. Nevertheless, the flutes were risky money compared to the crafty deceptions Reggie used to meet many of his needs.

Reggie had an uncanny ability to read and influence people he wanted to take down. Reggie talked himself bit-by-bit into and out of things a normal person would never dream of. He had an unstoppable negotiating style when he wanted something out of a clerk, cashier, waiter, manager or anyone else; when he wanted a refund for something he never purchased, a free meal or a cab ride. He used a linear style of manipulation which always began with a small, but crucial assumption on the part of the mark. This was the 1 on the way to the 10 (10 being the thing he wanted to get his hands on). To get to the 1 he would employ the sort of educated-indignant tone an attorney uses with a beat cop who isn't giving him special treatment. This was especially true if he was up against a timid person. If Reggie sensed he'd aroused suspicion in someone less malleable, or at a point dangerously close to his goal, he would immediately forfeit what he'd built up in order to seem too naive, wealthy or disinterested to protect himself from a handy defeat. Instead of surrendering though, Reggie was fawning, sympathizing and circling back to his main objective. He would then steer his mark into a corner that was so logical and comfortable he never noticed how difficult it was to get out of. If Reggie could manage to keep assumption 1 intact then the rest must follow.

Let's say someone is telling you a long drawn-out story of a financial or circumstantial difficulty in their life, and the subtext, although it's never brought up until *you* mention it, is how you might help the person. This is only natural. However, as you hear more of the tale, you find yourself wondering what is fact and what is fiction. Part of the narrative involves the loss of the person's wallet. It has sunk to the bottom of a river in a boat. But what's really important to the teller is not the money or the credit cards, it's the driver's license. The missing license is referred to often –but not too often. It's just part of the broader narrative and part of the doubt running in the back of your mind. You're keeping track of the fact the wallet and license are missing, you're wondering whether any proof of it will ever be offered, you assume it won't. And you're right, it won't.

By coincidence, the wallet drops from the narrative at that point, and you forget about it. Anyway, the story isn't told to you in a day, because that would imply urgency, and there's certainly no need for that. It comes to you in bits and pieces as your relationship with the teller grows. There are little suspensions of disbelief that are remedied by undeniable fact, little doubts that magically resolve themselves, important trust-building exercises are brought to you, whole or in part, by your new friend in a way that allows you to believe they're yours. If you start to pick at things, you find that each piece is tiny and important, only they were assembled with tools that cannot be used to take them apart. They fit into a story that is irreducibly complex, the beginning the ending. This makes you want to review what it is you really know about this person, but it's too late. The ship has already sailed and you're on it.

Then one day your pal says to you: *Guess what?! I got my wallet back, the salvage divers found it!* And with that, your friend presents you with an obviously water-damaged, but still legible, driver's license. This is a 1, but if you're asking questions at 1 it's already too late –because what has seeing the license proven? It has proven nothing. He had it all along, he soaked it in a glass of Willamette water several days before. He's not even showing it to you to prove that he has it. We're way past that. Besides, Reggie never offers proof. He's only showing it to you to say *How interesting is that pal?* while you put every other piece of the story together. Or maybe you saw that coming and you're just too smart for him. Or maybe you already forgot that the boat sank while Reggie was out of town on business and therefore his wallet would have been with him at the time. If you think you're too clever for a guy like Reggie to get his hooks into you, you're wrong. Besides, how would you know it if he did? You're only a mark if you don't know you're a mark.

I'd known Reggie for about two weeks, when one day he came down to the boat wearing a small knapsack and suggested we go for a little jog together. I changed into my shorts and sneakers and we took off running along the waterfront. After a quarter-mile, Reggie turned a corner and headed for downtown with me following close behind. It was a mid-week lunch hour and the sidewalks were busy with office types. Reggie, who'd been taking the street since our turn, jumped onto the crowded sidewalk and ran against the flow of foot traffic, skipping and sidling, beating a path through the people coming toward us. After a couple blocks, Reggie ducked into the foyer of a tall building and said he wanted to show me something. I nodded and Reggie slipped his knapsack off. He pulled a couple of brand new sweaters from it and handed me one. We unfolded them together. Mine was emblazoned with the CIA logo, his with FBI –they didn't look like they came from a booth at the fair. Reggie motioned for us to put them on. He reached out and tousled my hair. "Let's run like this now," he said. We continued jogging in the same direction but people stayed out of our way. Reggie had prison smarts and a prison physique and no matter where we went, he was subtly careful to never let anyone maneuver behind him. Reggie once told me that the key to survival was invisibility, and the key to invisibility was to see things first –especial law enforcement of any stripe.

"You are the antelope, they are the lion, see the lion before it sees you." He also told me that lying was simple because the vast majority of people will believe almost anything you tell them. "No one ever thinks they're being lied to –end of story."

I'm going to pretend I once heard Reggie say to the manager of a busy bookstore, who was doubtfully processing a large refund for him: "I'm afraid I don't necessarily know the names of everyone who works for me." As Reggie explained the situation to the suspicious manager; the books he was returning had been dropped off earlier by a young clerk from his law firm, Reggie was only there to collect the refund, and to be quite frank, he didn't know all the details –one of his secretaries did. Reggie was careful to never come off sounding superior when he was manipulating someone, and he delivered the line in a subtly-confiding way that gave the manager the opportunity to confess that he, too, was a busy executive with a lot on his plate.

"Sandra...do you know anything about this?" the manager asked a harried cashier at the far end of the counter. She confirmed with a nod that the books in question had been re-shelved earlier in the day. You see? It was all a misunderstanding. Nobody was implying that a black man can't be a partner in a law firm. The manager understood the situation completely and handed the money to Reggie, commiserating with him, while taking care of him. There was no receipt and probably no books to begin with, the whole thing was done with words that sounded good together. I'm sure it was easy to convince the cashier that the books were put back, but I wasn't there for any of it so I don't know exactly how Reggie managed that. I picture him picking up an employee phone and calling her, though. It doesn't really matter; assumption 1 held and the money changed hands.

Part of the reason I never got to the bottom of the boat story was because Reggie never let himself get into a position where he'd be expected to show proof of something. Instead, he hinted at things long before they came into play and was always the first to *suggest* a verification, one that was never needed, of course. The drawings of his vessel *fell* out of the folder so that he and I discovered them *together*. He was circumspect in every action he took no matter how insignificant it seemed on the surface. I once watched him spend a full minute selecting a piece of ID to show a barkeep. Who knows what past or future scenario he was mulling, or what weird power game he was playing for later. I hope to god I'm not wrong here, but I can only assume Reggie made up the tale of the sunken boat long before we met and had been telling it to people for a while. Or he pulled it out of thin air the first night –I can't honestly say. I believe he was capable of it; maybe it was a little bit of both. All I really know is that the story was intricately assembled down to the tiniest, germane moving part. If it was a lie, he cultivated it carefully, ensuring it was internally consistent –there were no openings in his cover. Reggie didn't have a job as far as I knew, and I presume he lived in part from charitable donations linked in some way or another to the supposed sinking. He told the tale *beautifully*. It was a low-overhead money-maker, plain and simple.

When I had Reggie's near-total confidence, I realized he was an unbelievable manipulator. But like all artists, he had a tragic streak. I snuck up behind him in the park one afternoon while he was playing a rough but complete flute rendition of *Aura Lee*, from a play-by-the-numbers songbook sitting on his lap. Reggie was an autodidact to his core and would have excelled in medicine, politics or law if his potential had not been so oddly realized. He did not see me see him playing flute in the park that day. This was a serious lapse and completely out of character for him. He was sitting on the bench we used to meet at with his back to the street. He never did that. Then it occurred to me the whole thing might have been a well-planned reveal. I was no match for Reggie. Maybe that's why he took me under his wing rather than exploit me.

I think Reggie wanted to level with me about the boat story while I was struggling in Portland and he lived a life of relative ease. He once offered me some "side work" as he put it, but I politely declined and he never brought it up again. However, the day after I mentioned heading up to Seattle to look for work, Reggie showed up at the riverfront with the Dodge. I think he had some sort of parking pass in the window so it was invisible to the meter maids and condo security guards. When I asked him where he got the truck, all he said was: "I'm into this thing for $50 and it's clean." There was a unique kind of trust between us, so I gave him the money and written permission to stay on the boat and he gave me the keys. I like to think we helped each other in some way and although I never spoke to him after our brief phone conversation in the back of Café Allegro, I often wonder if Reggie ever used his wicked language, astounding intellect or dangerously astute people skills for anything good.

The pressure of not knowing what the call from Reggie was really about, combined with my pitiful living situation and finances, took hold of me like never before that afternoon and I anxiously sorted through names of people in Seattle who might be able to help me. The pool was smaller than I imagined in the fall. I only had two real friends left from my Seattle days: John and Christian. John was in Costa Rica and I'd completely lost touch with him. When I pictured approaching Christian, who still lived in the large U District apartment we once shared, I realized I was too ashamed of myself to let him see me in the state I was in. I dismissed every member of my family for the same reason. I decided that begging would be too much to bear in my fragile state. I'd waited too long to ask for help; I was truly on my own. Even though I was afraid of losing my paging service—my only link to solvency—I decided to hold on a little longer and tighten my belt Knut Hamsun style. I didn't see it at the time, but I was starting to forget that my exercise in self-reliance was voluntary.

I'd come to that once-in-a-lifetime experience not from previous suffering, fear and unmet needs, but from happiness, friendship and shelter. I was supremely depressed and totally unaware I was circling closer and closer to a dangerous void.

Back at the truck that night, I dumped the metal ashtray on the front seat and carefully counted my coins under the dome light. I had $9.96 to my name. It was less than I hoped for, but I figured I could make it last a week if I ate one burrito a day and didn't put up any fliers. What I'd already posted on U District bulletin boards would have to do the job. Having my poverty laid bare in such a plain way helped me realize that I'd accomplished a peculiar sort of goal: I'd done everything in my power to survive up to that point and it was suddenly clear that things were either going my way or they weren't. There would be no more preparing, no more waiting, no more hoping. I understood that it was too late to change the course of events that winter and too late to change the direction of my life. I was as far down as I could go, but I wasn't giving up yet. I wanted to save *Tranquility* and continue the voyage. To do that, I needed to fix what was broken inside of me and I knew if I gave up while there was the slightest chance of success, my life would never be totally mine. The voyage, the struggle to survive, rescuing *Tranquility* and the money I needed to do it, were all about something much bigger: I had to take absolute ownership of myself and my future—for good or ill—at that moment, if I ever wanted to be a man.

There was no doubt in my mind what I would do: I was going to put everything I had left on the line. I was going to throw myself off the cliff, because instinct told me it was time to fledge and I had to move forward under my own power, or not at all. It may be hard to believe, but the knowledge that I was genuinely impoverished, absolutely alone and facing impossible circumstances was exhilarating instead of frightening.

After counting my money, I went for a walk on the busy holiday streets, and on that walk, something extraordinary happened. Something undeniably random, yet so full of the beautiful mysterious symmetry of life that it brought instant meaning to a futile existence. I was heading west against the flow of traffic on 50th Street in the U District when I noticed an older Volvo 240 station wagon slowly rolling toward me in the curb lane. It swung a sharp right onto the alley apron in front of me, blocking my path. As I walked around the back of the car, the driver's window came down fast and a woman asked me if I would help her push the car out of the road.

Of course she had to be young and beautiful, with long brunette curls carefully coiffed and lustrous, radiating feminine composure. She was thoughtfully dressed in black and burgundy velvet and otherwise prettily made-up for some festive holiday gathering. She had an air of the academic and wore slim black leather gloves with a finely brocaded scarf draped around her neck, just-so. There could not have been a more diabolical taunt at my loneliness and anonymity.

"Car trouble?" I asked, as we pushed her car into the alley.

"It stalls like this once in a while, but the dealer said they can't find anything wrong with it."

All cars have their flaws. Some cause stalling or hard starting, some cause discomfort or poor idle. Some are intentionally built into the vehicle, some are unforeseen, some are discovered and allowed to continue. But no matter how perplexing they may seem to you, they're money-makers for those in the know. The late 80s Ford has the faulty transistor in the ignition module. There's the crankshaft position sensor in the fuel-injected Chrysler products. You have that hidden valve in the cabin heater of Mercedes Benz sedans of a certain age. Even the trustworthy Honda needs a new distributor at around 130,000 miles, and the older, bulletproof Toyota truck gets a new timing chain set about that time (rarely anything else). The Volvo 240 is an exceptionally reliable vehicle, though, and the young woman described an unfamiliar problem as we stood by the driver's door. The car would run fine for days and then suddenly die while driving. When it did this, it had to sit for at least twenty minutes before it would restart. Then it drove fine until the next stall, but she never knew when that would be. On the longest shot possible, I told the young woman I might be able to do something for her right there in the alley. She nodded, so I crouched down at the driver's door-jamb and gave the tapered fuses in the compartment there a twist. Volvo 240 fuses are lead, the holders are copper, and for whatever reason, they don't always make good contact. After I spun them all, I turned the key and the 240 started right up. A fuse, possibly the one for the fuel pump or the ignition had a bad connection and my twist did the trick.

If things are perfectly fine until they break, shouldn't they return to normal just as quickly when they're fixed?

The woman stared at me for a moment. She was flabbergasted and spoke deliberately. "I've been having this problem for months and this car has *never* restarted in less than twenty minutes. Please let me pay you something!" she said leaning into the car to grab her pocketbook.

"I can't take your money," I said, straightening up. "It was just a loose fuse."

"No way! You don't understand how much of a help this is to me right now, I was getting ready to junk this car...Wait! I can't even believe this whole thing just happened!" she cried, doing a little jump, steadying herself with one hand on the luggage rack.

"I'm sorry, I can't accept anything for that," I said, stepping away from her.

She grabbed my sleeve.

I looked down at her hand, then into her eyes.

She was strong.

It was a dangerous moment.

There are loves at first sight.

"I *insist*," she said, bending at the knees, emphasizing her need to reciprocate.

"It's okay," I said, pulling away.

She reached into her pocketbook, grabbed a twenty and waved it in front of me.

She did not know how much I needed that bill. I knew I had to take it, but something was stopping me. It was her. She was my type of woman and I wished I was going with her to a holiday dinner at her adviser's house instead of hitting her up for work in a dark alley. I needed that twenty but even as I knew it, I was ashamed of myself for being that damaged. A hug from her and a whiff of that beautiful hair would have meant so much more to me. But that was impossible, just like everything else that winter.

"It's okay...go on...take it," she said soothingly, as if she were coaxing an injured dog out from under her porch with a little piece of meat. I took the bill, we shook hands, she drove away.

17

The twenty was still intact on the first business day of the New Year and without thinking or caring about what was coming next, I swung into my regular U District print shop, slapped it down on the counter and asked for two hundred black and white copies of my flier. I knew perfectly well that two hundred weren't going to make much of an impact on a cold winter morning, but instead of feeling like a desperate act, spending the very last of my money on advertising gave me a thrill. I knew where I stood with grim precision. My situation was pretty bad, but I was suddenly okay with it. I was almost happy. As soon as those perfect white pages hit the counter, I slipped the hot sheaf under my arm and went out the door with hunger gnawing in my gut.

As a form of media akin to skywriting, fliers have a short and unpredictable lifespan. In order for them to work they must be consistently and thoroughly applied. It takes real hustle and thousands of fliers to drum up regular word-of-mouth business. I've learned a lot about the subject over the years and in my experience, the response rate for fliers posted indoors was never more than four or five percent. The rate for fliers placed on cars, however, is abysmal –around a half-percent. A flier on a car is a wasted flier. It's not just the rainy Seattle weather that works against you –when people see a flier on their windshield it's irksome. From a distance, drivers mistake them for parking tickets. A flier on a windshield isn't an ad, it's a negative experience with your name and phone number on it. However, as I walked toward campus that morning, it occurred to me that after a long holiday sitting idle, the cars parked in the U District might be ripe for the picking. After two weeks at the curb you're going to have dead batteries, flat tires and all sorts of trouble that nobody wants to deal with on a cold winter morning. It was a little thought and one I may have easily ignored, but for some reason, I deviated from my routine that day. I changed course.

When the phone call I waited three months for finally came, it was so long overdue I wasn't even relieved to get it. The call was from a kid who'd been limping around town and avoiding the highway in an old Ford Bronco that needed front wheel bearings. He put off the repair in order to get through the holidays with money and wheels. He made it to January without a breakdown, and like many young people that time of year, he was flush with Christmas cash and wanted his truck fixed in a hurry (so he could go skiing with his girlfriend). He'd seen my flier around campus before winter break and had been meaning to give me a call, then one appeared on his windshield and he picked up the phone. I did the job in the rain the next day on a residential street a couple of blocks from where the kid lived. Although I stood to make some real money on those bearings, there had been too many disappointments and too much turmoil that winter for clear thinking. I knew my life was riding on those front wheels, so I worked slowly and carefully, paying extravagant, surgical attention to each step. I expected something to go horribly wrong and I looked for it with a certain fondness for deeply wounding ironies. The job went well despite my anxiety, and as soon as I had my pay in hand I shifted my focus to *Tranquility*'s salvation. My thoughts had been divided between Seattle and Portland for two exhausting months, and despite what Reggie told me over the phone, I couldn't be sure of *Tranquility*'s condition without seeing her—or not seeing her—for myself. I had to check on her and there was no way out of it. If she was gone, then so was my reason for being. The sooner I knew her fate, the sooner I'd know mine.

Before leaving Seattle I had some housekeeping to do. I got the rear tires of the truck patched and power-washed it front-to-back because it still looked like it had been deep-fried in Jefferson County mud. I did my laundry, took a coin-operated shower, ate a hearty meal and drank a thick cup of coffee. I went through those motions in the slow, joyless way an ill man feeds himself –knowing only that certain things must be done to sustain life. A couple of days later, I took the train to Portland with $450 in my pocket and an unhelpful harangue running nonstop in my mind. Rather than thinking my luck was about to change, I dwelt on a bleak narrative which got my knee bouncing uncontrollably as soon as I took my seat: *I've been in Seattle for two long months. I've talked to Reggie just once. I've landed only one job and I have a grand total of one hundred dollars to show for it all!* Just think of it! *One hundred dollars!* It was a hopeless sum that wouldn't even begin to fill the hole I dug for myself when I stripped *Tranquility*.

What if the boat's gone? I thought to myself, shaking my head, knowing how likely it was.

Tranquility

Is that what Reggie called to tell me the other day?

Reggie Lee Washington was keeping an eye on your boat? Are you kidding me?

I sat straight up, jolted by an insight I couldn't contain. As the train left King Street Station, I was swept by a sudden paralysis, an uncomfortable tingling in the extremities and solar plexus. A hot sweat and a sense of unreality swept over me in disassociative waves. The high-dynamic pendulum carriages hovered and swayed as the train turned south and floated down the tracks *clop-clop-clop-clop-clop-clop*. I held on to the seat-back in front of me, steadying myself against the nausea.

I didn't have anything Reggie could connive me out of?

Really?

How about Tranquility?

Reggie was playing me for the boat the entire time and I'd fallen for it. We hadn't helped each other at all; Reggie never helped anyone. I threw my lot in with a grifter and he took me for all I was worth. "Selling" the Dodge for $50 and packing me off to Seattle had been the final piece of a patient deception. *I'm into this thing for $5000 and it's clean* I imagined Reggie saying as he cast off *Tranquility's* lines. I'd been hiding a devastating truth from myself: the boat was long gone and I knew it. My time in Portland, Reggie and the boat went round and round in my mind for the next four hours. There were variations on the theme, but the story always ended the same way: *Tranquility* was lost.

I left the Portland train station on foot and slowly made my way downtown, trying to convince myself along the way that it was a good thing I was rid of *Tranquility*. I reminded myself that the voyage was a total failure and that spring would be a good time to get on with my life. This morbid thinking went on until I caught a glimpse of the flat, chromium Willamette at the end of a long city block and I took off running toward it in a craze of hope. When I came to the busy intersection where the park and dock would come into full view for the first time, I held back a moment, preparing myself for her to be gone. When I was ready, I took a split-second glance at the dock and saw that it was done. Due to some incredible lapse of the automated world, the human capacity for rehabilitation or a city interregnum lost deep in a ream, *Tranquility* was exactly where I left her in the fall. Set against the visual noise of the vessels in the marina behind her, *Tranquility*'s squat green hull and beige spars were nearly invisible to the moving eye. She was hidden in plain sight –it's the only explanation.

I walked through the park and down the ramp on rubber legs. I drifted along the dock in an otherworldly state, approaching her slowly, braced for some hidden disaster. But instead of being half-sunk or stripped of her bronze, *Tranquility* was all there and floating on an even keel. I expected to find a sun-faded impound notice or an arrest warrant nailed to her deck, but there was nothing of the sort. Although her hull and fittings were still intact, *Tranquility* looked like an absolute zombie. A leotard of algae had grown around her waterline, snaring little bits of driftwood and city flotsam in its drossy mat. She was wind-blown and orphan, her teak parquet and thwarts were bleached by the incessant Portland rain. Her halyards had gone slack and were tinged with mold. They slapped against the mast lazily, taking the paint off. A family of river otters or seagulls were making a home on her, judging from the puddles of purple treacle and little white haystacks of digested fish bones and clam shells littering her deck and cockpit. Most of the mainsail had fallen from the boom to the cabin top, allowing the bright green organics growing there to migrate into the sailcloth. One of the deck scuppers clogged and a marsh of thick, black road slurry had backed up along the starboard walkway where it sprouted a sprig of green before seeping into the boat through a partially-open port. The cabin was damp and fetid, the ceiling festooned with flocks of black mold. She'd been left open for two months; people other than Reggie had come and gone. Newspaper, crumpled beer cans and empty food tins littered the floor. A thick layer of rank bedding had accumulated on a bunk.

All of *Tranquility*'s paint, inside and out, including the cheerful new enamel I carefully applied in the fall, was bubbling with thousands of moisture pox, each oozing a bitter-smelling, tea-colored liquid. The black-water spring seeping into the boat through the open port gave the cabin the ordure of a polluted terrarium. Something in the trickling effluent etched the finish on the locker door below. I was surprised, then perplexed to find that after more than two months on her own, *Tranquility*'s bilge was relatively dry and her batteries were charged. She could not have stayed dry *and* charged on her own so someone was doing something for her and I expected Reggie to show himself at any moment.

Tranquility was looking pretty rough and I knew I'd have to get an entirely new project going if I wanted to sail her down the Pacific Coast that summer. So I shook off my winter blues and pretended like it was all still possible long enough for an epic clean-up of the boat. While I worked, I drew up an overly ambitious repair schedule and composed a shopping list which ran to several thousand dollars. I knew I had a lot farther to go than I did in the fall, but I vowed to refocus as soon as I got back to Seattle.

No amount of optimism would get me out of the pickle I'd been in all winter, though. I still couldn't afford to moor *Tranquility* in a marina and that meant I'd have to abandon her all over again when I returned to Seattle. There didn't seem to be any way out of this until I remembered a restaurant perched at the end of an adjacent dock, and its location gave me an idea. I proposed an arrangement to the lunch manager there, in which I would pay him $50 a week to take an occasional call from me checking up on *Tranquility* (she could be seen from the dining room windows). The manager's most important job however, would be to call me if he ever saw people in uniform checking her out, if she looked like she was sinking or if she went missing. The manager agreed to the deal without reservation, and although we settled it with nothing more than a quick handshake and a two-week deposit, the scheme gave me near-perfect peace of mind until spring. I added an extra margin of safety before heading back to Seattle: I took the hand-operated bilge pump from the engine compartment and screwed it down in the cockpit on the dock side of the boat, taking care to position the handle within easy reach of passersby. I tied a handwritten wooden sign to the hose which read, simply: PLEASE PUMP ME.

My pager started ringing as soon as I got back to Seattle and I managed to save some real money over the next couple of weeks. I was still living on the front seat of the truck, but it was apparent that my upward trajectory couldn't be stopped. This small progress was sustained by calls to the manager who always had the same good news: *Tranquility* was still at the dock and she was floating on an even keel. It wasn't much, but it kept me going.

One morning in early February, I was roused from my sleep at dawn by the sound of prolonged engine cranking. My neighbor, the parole officer, couldn't get his decrepit 1977 Royal Brougham started. I'd already met the man whose disheveled house I'd been parked in front of since before Thanksgiving. We spoke a few times. I knew he was a cop and he knew I was a down-on-his-luck sailor who'd gone back to turning wrenches. Despite his profession, he didn't seem to mind me living in a beat-up truck forty feet from his front door, and because of that, I wasn't afraid of him. My neighbor wasn't going anywhere in his behemoth that morning, so I went across the street and offered to take a quick look under the hood. I had some money in my pocket, I was feeling confident for the first time that winter and he accepted my offer. When I opened the hood, the V8 engine, grille, fenders and firewall were caked with oil and road grime in the way only an American landship from that era can be. My neighbor seemed to think the condition was terminal, but after checking a few things, I offered to take a shot at it on a no-remedy no-pay basis. It turned out to be a complex but satisfying case. Fuel, spark and compression—the airway, breathing and circulation of the automotive first-responder—were all there, yet the engine wouldn't start. After a lengthy diagnosis I realized there was only one thing it could be. With a buck-eighty on a General Motors odometer, the timing chain must have gone slack and thrown a link or two over the sprockets. It's a rare but fundamental engine malfunction that requires major surgery to positively identify and repair.

When I explained the cause of his car trouble to him, the officer steered the conversation away from how long it might take to repair, to how he was going to find another monster-machine just like it. However, when I told him I might be able to have the car running again by the following afternoon, he gave me the work and money for parts. If your hunch turns out correct, a timing chain job on an old V8 engine is a gravy train, so I jumped right in. When I tore down the front of the motor later that day, I was relieved to find the normally blunt teeth of a GM timing sprocket worn sharp as thorns. When I turned the engine over with a breaker bar, the timing marks on the cam and crank sprockets wouldn't line up. The chain had indeed jumped and that threw the valves and spark out of time with the pistons. I was headed for a payday and all I needed to do was go get the parts. As I reached up to shut the hood, a familiar shape entered my right periphery and I froze. A metallic blue Seattle police cruiser was slowly coming up the street cloaked in the perfect electric silence of a brand new law-enforcement vehicle. I saw him first though, and stepped to the passenger side of the hood and out of sight. It was him of course, the cop who pulled me over that night. He came abreast, tapping the brakes, having a look at things. I stepped to the right staying behind the hood as he passed –he didn't see me and he didn't recognize the Dodge. When I was sure he wasn't coming back, I rode my bike to an auto parts store for a new timing chain set. I put the engine back together the next morning and the Royal Brougham fired right up. When the parole officer gave me the $600 he owed me later that afternoon he threw in a valuable piece of information: he ran my plates the first day I parked in front of his house. What Reggie said was true, the truck wasn't stolen. Someone lost the title to it years before and it had been a rambling man's rig ever since.

Something happened later that week which was so convoluted and unbelievable I won't bother to explain it in detail. Suffice it to say that on one unforgettable day, I managed to buy a pristine, green and white 1972 Volkswagen camper van that, according to its seller (the original owner), needed an engine rebuild. After a short test drive, I realized it did not. So I paid the man $200 for it and had it fixed a half-hour later. The van had been sitting for over a year and the fuel in the tank was spoiled. I "rebuilt" the sputtering engine by pouring a can of commercial-grade carburetor cleaner in the fuel tank, followed by several gallons of super-unleaded (I eventually put twenty thousand miles on that van). More was to come that magical day: I sold the Dodge without a title for $200 to a guy who came walking down the street as I was transferring my belongings to the van. This dude walked up to me out of the blue and offered to buy the Dodge (for parts) if I ever wanted to sell it. I wanted to and he came back with the cash just before dark.

For the sake of credulity, I've left out *a lot* of what happened that winter.

My life took an undeniable turn for the better when I bought the VW. It had the equivalent of a twin bed in it with storage underneath. There were full curtains, the vinyl was perfect and everything worked except for the heater. It was rust free and clean so I moved into a posh neighborhood overlooking Lake Washington. Business picked up to normal in mid-February and rather than buffet me with further difficulties, fate, perhaps bored from toying with such easy prey, deigned to let me pass on my way. As I steered away from the winter vigia which nearly wrecked me, I was careful to keep it in sight. Knowing where that danger lay relative to my intended course in life allowed me to revisit the weightless optimism in my temperament, not only that spring, but for most of the voyage to come. My trip to the edge and back allowed me to pick up a talisman at my low-as-low-can-go point and I used it to protect myself from similar troubles in the future. Best of all, I did it on my own.

As spring progressed, I worked and saved and procured with methodical economy a replacement for nearly every item I stole from *Tranquility* (I couldn't find an Evinrude 18 in Seattle and the only Tiny Tot was going for $300...anyway, it didn't suit me). I dropped in on the chandler looking for a deal on my old compass and some of my other gear but everything I sold him in the fall was gone. It was a good lesson, I suppose.

Although it was somewhat misguided, the ungainly hodgepodge of merman wisdom building up inside me from so much salty reading finally took effect. If it had anything to do with seafaring or boats and couldn't be found in musty old books few had ever heard of, I looked on it with suspicion. That spring, I was forced to concede entirely to the great body of knowledge that governs the proper handling of sailboats. Swearing an oath of fealty to anyone who's ever set foot on the deck of a yacht and lived to tell about it, I promised Neptune I would seek advice from elders when faced with nautical problems, and obey the norms of seacraft on all future passages. A lift in the weather and my finances followed shortly thereafter, and my outlook on the voyage, and life in general, greatly improved.

As time passed, I learned to freely and humbly admit the blame I held for every mishap of the previous year. It took some doing, but I was able to accept that a boat has no sense of self-preservation or guile, despite the personality projected upon her by master and crew. I learned that a sailboat is nothing more than an intricate human construct, an entirely female machine, which will take you wherever you steer her. You may truly love her, you may lavish care on her, you may even imagine she can reciprocate it all, but remember this: she will fetch you onto a remorseless reef some dark and dreary night just as gaily as she will sail you through the pass of a tropical lagoon in the by-and-by. The responsibility for everything that happens, good, bad or indifferent; in, on, or to a ship, must ultimately be laid at the feet of her captain —let who will, say nay. If there's any immutable law of the sea, this is without doubt its founding tenet. That's not to say I'll ever know which ghastly, horribly-wizened, lightning-struck graveyard oak, reared from acorn on the compost of the dead, *Tranquility'*s frames were hacked out of. Or from whose Spirit Pole, stolen on a stormy Pacific Northwest night, her timbers were sawn from way back in the winter of '38. I'm sure I'll never be privy to any of the unwholesome acts committed over her keel, which forever cursed and misguided her heart and so wronged her dignity that she lashed out at every pilot who sought to guide her. No, dear reader, *that* would be impossible.

That spring I learned how easily one can amplify the joy in life by ignoring or pruning back the difficulty they've encountered on their chosen path. After reviewing the arc of the voyage from the minimal distance provided by that cherry blossom season, I was able to reconcile the most painful and haunting aspects of the past year, by simply accepting that *Tranquility* had led me to the best things in my life and the worst. Forced to face the experience for what it was, I framed this profound contradiction in a phrase that has endured lo these many years: *Tranquility* was my wisest mistake.

Progress turned into anticipation of the adventure to come and my ardent desire to mend the error of my ways caused my youthful hope to reignite in the ashes of winter. In March, I found myself standing next to *Tranquility* on the public dock in Portland where I left her to fend for herself five months prior. I wasted no time wondering over the miracle; *Tranquility* survived her abandonment and I survived mine. I was flush with cash, buoyed by sane optimism, and I had four long weeks left in my spring refit schedule. I knew I was back when I walked over to the private marina and looked into mooring *Tranquility* there until she was ready to set sail.

"I suppose that's your little green sloop across the way?" the sixty-year-old marina manager asked me with an all-knowing wink and a glance at her through his office window. "I was wondering when you were going to show up over here."

After asking for a quick rundown of my travails since October and my plans for the summer, the kindly manager invited me to take a prime slip at the marina and he let me slide on hull insurance and registration so I could move *Tranquility* in the same day. An hour later, my ugly duckling was led into a swannery where she was surrounded by a covey of well-kept yachts. She and I were safe at last.

I spent a tidy sum on new equipment in Portland. I found an outboard and got a good deal on a spool of double-braid line. I bought sheet acrylic to cover the smokestack hole in the cabin top. I bought paint, fasteners and other supplies by the case and hundred count. Although the size of my vanloads didn't seem compatible with *Tranquility*, a small boat can carry an inordinately large cargo, so it all found a home. How can I ever forget the endless schlepping of gear that spring? It was ferried in backpacks on bicycles and in cars. How many times did I trudge to and from the van, up and down the dock or over to the marina dumpster like a hunch-back tinker, pushing nasty, crooked-wheeled dock carts with sharp edges and poky fractures in their fiberglass sides that left me wounded and itching for days? I cannot say, but it was a weeks-long blur of vessel preparation and marine gear procurement. One would have thought I was bound for Nome, Alaska that summer not sunny Southern California.

It took much, much longer than expected to repair the damage I inflicted on *Tranquility* that crazy day off St. Helens. The smashed lockers and the companionway were the first things I attended to, and by the time they were fixed, I was thoroughly chastened. It is said among sailors that a boat is never finished. There is no end to the work or expense of boats and precious few shipboard tasks ever reach a point that a landsman would recognize as final. A real mariner would never think or say: *at last I am done with the painting* or *now I have finished with the rigging*, because that's impossible on a vessel you plan to use in such a hostile environment as the sea. There are only degrees of done on a boat, especially an old wooden sailboat. Instead, real sailors, be they rich or of limited means, learn to prioritize and attend to repairs or maintenance which are most pressing on the endless lists of improvements found on chart tables year-round. A wise sailor doesn't invest in new cockpit cushions if he knows his turnbuckles are worn, he does not invest in turnbuckles if his rudder is rotten. Failure to understand this logical ordering of a vessel's affairs results in a boat that shows flawless varnish work but carries ground tackle suited for a mill pond.

As for the quality of work demanded by a boat, you quickly learn that repairs you attended to while muttering to yourself *she'll hold pretty well* will take on new and frightful meaning when you have to make an offing in a blow. Poorly done things will be the first that call to you in times of trouble afloat and you'll say to yourself when the first sea slaps the stern of your ship: *I should have through-bolted that or put an extra lashing on this.* It really is better to do a job properly the first time and it is good to do it without trying to save money, because there's no such thing on a boat and sailorly peace of mind never goes on sale. I can't say I applied this rule to *everything* I did that spring, or even that I did all of the things I should've done. If I had, I would've never left the dock. The boat is never *done* and you are never *ready* until you are a seaman.

I learned from reading, and some little experience, that ground tackle is the most important thing on your boat besides her hull. So, I shipped an unprecedented *four* anchors for leg two of my little summer voyage. Each of these were shackled to oversized chain and line. I still chuckle when I think of my "storm anchor" for tiny *Tranquility*. It was an ungainly 45-lb high-tensile Danforth whose stock stood around three feet high. This monster pick was shackled and moused to ten fathoms of 3/8" chain to which I bent 250 feet of 5/8" three-strand, hard-laid anchor line. Having this giant aboard gave me license to dismiss every anchor I saw (there were many) that was too small for the craft carrying it. I shipped extra fuel jugs and water casks, and I tuned the rig by feel, in a way that would have made Buddy proud. I stitched reinforcement patches onto the mainsail. I lubed the hanks of the new headsails and I sewed sail tape along the roach of the aging jib and genoa. I swapped the older halyards end-for-end and reinforced the lifelines, extending them out to the stern, on a pair of new stanchions. I serviced the batteries, added an emergency bank and checked the running lights for corrosion (a constant source of trouble on small boats). I worked for many hours sanding and painting the area of hull damaged by the dock on my last night in Ilwaco. The work looked good, so I painted the entire boat to match.

Once I'd sorted out the parts of *Tranquility* that made her a sailboat—spars, rigging, sails, compass, anchors, hull and hatches—I began outfitting her with everything needed to make her fit for a man. I toted gear in and out of a shape-shifting pile of booty that sat on the dock under a tarp in case of rain. I packed and unpacked lockers and led merciless settling campaigns, driving a moraine of gear before me from one end of the cabin to the other. Lamps, bedding, life jackets, emergency flares, tools, fishing tackle, fasteners, books and crockery made up the till. I stowed and re-stowed every piece of gear aboard so it was accessible yet secure in a seaway. Last to board? 10,000 bags of groceries of course! Once the grub was in the lockers, I sorted and labeled the entire stack of Pacific Coast charts given to me by my boat neighbor in Ballard. I compiled chart folios within chart folios, trying to anticipate itineraries, landfalls and ports-of-call that were weeks or months away. I worked until dawn with my spine and neck fused in a painful arch brought on by *Tranquility*'s low ceiling, but it felt good to be doing right by her for once.

With the refit complete, the vessel fully-laden and my mid-April departure only a few days away, casting off the dock lines went from an appealing idea to a looming reality. My springy confidence and desire to set sail as soon as possible gave way to mild worry and I began to question the wisdom of heading back into the unknown so soon. I tried to put worry out of my mind and focus on the voyage, but worry, once indulged, doesn't retreat. It goes looking for company and in my case it didn't have to go far to find it. Worry pointed out that the ocean was big and powerful, but the boat and I were small and weak. I knew enough to be afraid of the Columbia River and the Pacific Ocean beyond, however, in the opinion of worry, total destruction wasn't just possible –it was inevitable. No matter how many inexperienced voyagers had gone before me in lesser boats without serious mishap, *I* was bound for Davy Jones' Locker. Whether I survived the voyage or not was rendered moot, when worry revealed that I hadn't put enough thought into how I was going to support myself in California. I was going there to skin dive, enjoy life, do a little yachting and lay around in the sun. Worry had no trouble making my happy-go-lucky voyage seem frightening instead of charming –no matter how it turned out. I was no match for worry because worry amplified every doubt I had about the boat and myself. You cannot reason with worry, and it can never be proven wrong, it can only be encouraged.

I debated the feasibility of my voyage until the eve of departure. As I lay in my bunk that night, I judged my chances against the experience of mariners whose memoirs I'd read over the winter. On the one hand, the Atlantic was crossed in a rowboat and Hawaii was reached from the west coast of North America by two men drifting in a rubber raft. Droves of novice sailors have crossed the Pacific Ocean on maiden voyages, while others have done quite well even after fate cast them adrift in small skiffs on the open sea. Antarctica was circled and the world was girded by men sailing alone in small wooden boats, without engines or other modern equipment and virtually without hope of rescue. All of this and much more has been done, but *Tranquility* and I couldn't expect to reach California in one piece?

On the other hand, dead men don't write sea stories. Due to their solitary nature, single-hand sailors leave few friends on shore to ponder their fate once they shove off, and they're rarely expected where they're going. What lies between is the unforgiving sea and the man himself. If the details of solo voyages that didn't end well remained in the minds of landsmen long enough to be recorded, perhaps some mention of them may be found in the *Dictionary of Disasters at Sea*. It's a hefty tome which runs to several hundred pages, and although it's only a partial account of maritime misadventure, it makes for harrowing reading in your bunk on a windy night before setting sail. I noted with unease that many entries described casualties suffered on the waters that still lay before me—the waters I would have to cross before any others—the waters of *The Graveyard of the Pacific*. Worry has probably minted more fair-weather sailors and devout landsmen than all the storms of the Seven Seas combined. And that night, the night before I was to set sail, worry seemed poised for another victory. Worry led me in wider and wider circles until my life, the voyage and everything I worked so hard for, lost all meaning and I was reduced to striking up a sort of call-and-response sea shanty to drive it from my mind:

What's-gonna-happen lad? Nothing's-gonna-happen lad!
What's-gonna-happen lad? Nothing's-gonna-happen lad!

It wasn't very comforting.

The pleasures and perils of a sailor's life cannot be reconciled by logic or reason. They must be lived with. Of course it's reasonable that one should stay, but one must go. Therefore, the novice sailor has to win a mental game if he ever wants to leave the dock. It is stay, or go –you can't do both. A young man must conquer *himself*, not the sea. I'd already been through the stay-or-go mind games in Seattle, Port Townsend, Neah Bay and other places, but that doesn't make a sailor's life any easier the night before shoving off. Part of me knew it would be better to wait until I had more experience but another part dismissed such caution as a landlubber's excuse for cowering in the marina for the rest of his life. Both are true. I knew the boat would never be *done* and I knew I wasn't *ready*. But what did it really matter? When all of the moving parts of a voyage are reduced to their essential terms, the novice sailor is left with a simple equation that another year of practice isn't going to help him solve:

$$\frac{\text{Want of adventure}}{\text{Fear of death}}$$

Want of adventure had always been the greater factor in my life. So the next day, I said my goodbyes to the wind, tipped my cap to trouble—the sailor's perennial land companion—stepped aboard *Tranquility* without fanfare, and shoved her off. I steered into the middle of the Willamette River and headed her downstream toward the mighty, mighty Columbia and the never-ending unknown.

18

When I set out on the Willamette that day, my sense of triumph over adversity turned transcendental and I knew the land would never claim me so easily again. I knew no love affair or beauty, success or self-understanding would ever outshine the days of adventure and discovery I'd been securing under my belt since I first stepped aboard *Tranquility*. In my mind I was a rogue, hardened to the ways of the world and bound under sail for distant shores with a ship full of cargo and a sack full of gold. To be young and in command of my own little ship, to be sailing for the horizon in her as a result of my own initiative, was a thrill that remains without equal. I'd done the impossible, I saved *Tranquility* and myself from a wicked demise. When I saw her more ship-shape and better outfitted than ever before, I knew I was too. Her qualities were mine and mine were hers, an injury or success for one was instantly communicated to the other. This re-unified, more resilient being truly believed it was capable of anything, least of all sailing down the west coast of North America. It was true the voyage had gone from a summertime whim to a year-long occupation by minute, sometimes torturous degrees, but time was still abundant, age and injury were kept at bay by the patient forbearance of youth, and I hardly worried over such a trivial matter. I was enthralled by the passage of time, not afraid of it.

The first couple days of the new voyage amounted to a victory lap as I sailed past the places I wrecked at or anchored on my way upriver. I spent lavish nights on my boat at St. Helens, Mayger's dock and a new place, Westport Slough, where I basked in a merman glory I knew only from books. During the day, I beat into narrow headwinds and negotiated tricky nearshore currents when it would have been quicker and easier to motor. But *Tranquility*'s sails were mended, her rig was tuned for those airs and her paint was gleaming. She caught the eyes and waving *halloos* of seamen on passing ships like bottles of champagne swung against her sides or wreaths thrown over her bowsprit. I was proud to be sailing her and proud to be sailing her well.

After a few days running downstream, I found myself among the low grassy islands and winding channels of the seaward reaches of the Columbia River. I took the poignant opportunity to have a safety chat with myself while hove-to upstream of Jim Crow Sands. *Stay in the main channel, reef when you first think of it and look before you leap in unfamiliar waters*, I sagely advised myself in the tilted cockpit. Then, secure in the knowledge that I'd spent months preparing for what was to come next, I let the genoa tack, eased the mainsail and bore her off downstream. As I sailed west, the Columbia turned into a tidal estuary on a grand scale, it stirred and eddied, diverged and joined itself in lacy braids until it opened up onto a broad delta busy with wildlife and marine traffic. Salt was in the air and a thick sea haze hovered over the western horizon. The ocean was close and the current was pulling me toward it. Later that day, I was sailing along the south bank of the river in a balmy breeze with Astoria, Oregon visible in the distance off the port bow. The west wind had been lovely and remained so even as I neared the coast –a rare occasion in those waters. Limpid sunlight played on the seaside town, picking out jaunty boats tugging at their moorings and bright white gulls wheeling before the red warehouses and sea green shacks of the waterfront. It leapt into the hillsides illuminating Atlantic white cottages, church spires and the manicured greenery in between. It was a sailor's heaven in the land of the living and my winter troubles were all but forgotten. When I hove abreast of town, the low sun and the strong ebb running west presented me with two choices: I could anchor somewhere along the south bank of the river for twelve hours, or I could sail across and pull into Ilwaco just before dark. I imagined having a pleasant dinner in an Astoria restaurant overlooking the harbor; I imagined carrying on for a couple more hours in such splendor. I mulled this decision longer than conditions required before deciding that despite the heavy sea haze to the west, I could count on a pleasant evening sail and a safe passage across the river. So I continued downstream with the utmost confidence in myself.

I passed under the Astoria bridge with a pair of perfectly-timed tacks and glided along the waterfront under main and genoa. I was in high spirits and singing with the radio as I sailed at hull speed back and forth across the shipping channel, being careful to leave plenty of sea room between *Tranquility*'s keel and the heaving buoys lining the route. When the bar came into full view, I saw the source of the sea haze. It was being thrown aloft by a huge rank of stacked-up breakers that stretched north to south across the river mouth. The sight sent a tingle of fear down my legs and out through the soles of my feet. One glance at a wild river bar and you'll understand the sort of immediate death that awaits you there; you'll realize it's merely no accident you're still alive. There wasn't a cause for immediate alarm though, and no need to turn back. The danger was far away and easily avoided. Before continuing on, however, I hove to, tied the tiller down and checked around the boat for lines in the water. I ducked below for a quick survey of the cabin, and for the first time on the voyage, all was well. When I regained the deck, *Tranquility's* sails were still aback and her tiller was still down, but rather than being hobbled by that balance of forces, she was footing it fast downstream on the ebb. It occurred to me that if *Tranquility* lost way for some reason while crossing the river, she would be carried over the bar by the current. That was extremely unlikely, though. The boat had been sailing perfectly for days and the wind had held all afternoon. There were four anchors aboard and I had a good running engine. *Tranquility* and I were totally fine for once.

This was the first hint of peril on the new voyage, and I sensed a safe opportunity to practice some of the seamanship I learned over the winter. With more than enough sea room between *Tranquility* and the bar, I went through the steps I would take in a worse-case scenario: loss of steering, a dismasting or a line in the propeller? I readied the main anchor and insured the rode would pay out if I had to drop it in a hurry. Sudden lack of, or drastic change in wind direction? I test-ran the engine and checked the fuel level in the tank. Then, on second thought, I strode up to the foredeck and eased the lashings on the storm anchor –just in case I needed *two* hooks. A real sailor wouldn't allow the slightest opportunity for his boat to be swept into those breakers and I really wanted to be that guy. As a further precaution, I decided to cross the river as soon as possible, in order to avoid the shoal water along the south jetty and the increase in current near the river mouth. With this strategy in mind, I unlashed the tiller, eased the sheets, and carried on downstream, keeping one eye on the churning bar and one on the north bank. I was trying to make a prudent call and I waited patiently for the right moment to tack north. After rescuing *Tranquility* from Little Sand Island the previous summer, the Paradise crew and I fished and sailed her far and wide on the river. We'd been up to the Astoria bridge more than once and made several trips back and forth across the bar, so I was sure I would know when a safe river crossing was at hand. Of course, I knew every piling and bend in the winding channel that led to Ilwaco! I knew the waters I was sailing for once and I knew nothing bad was going to happen. Not on that boat, not in those waters and not on that auspicious day.

A few minutes later, when I was sure it was safe to cross the river, I began a slow turn to starboard, but indecision stayed my hand before I let the leeward jib sheet go and instead of tacking into the north, I eased *Tranquility* back into the west with a firm pull on the tiller. We carried on downstream until I was absolutely certain I remembered the river right. At that point, I put the tiller down and *Tranquility* snapped over onto a port tack. Her sails went *poof!* and we took off across the river. I trimmed the sheets and corrected course until the north bank lay dead ahead. *Tranquility* gathered way, and in a few minutes we were flying along rail-under on a beam reach.

You can say I should have anchored off Astoria that evening. You can say continuing on was the right decision. You can say I should have waited longer to cross. But a mariner, even a grossly inexperienced one, must predict the future and make decisions in the present based on what he sees up ahead. I had plenty of time to reach Ilwaco that evening and when I saw the rough bar and felt the strong current, I made what I thought was a prudent decision: cross the river with plenty of sea room, in case anything goes wrong. You make a decision like that based on what *might* happen. Right or wrong, lucky or unlucky, big mistake or small, the amount of time a vessel remains afloat is not necessarily indicative of the sagacity of her master. Even a well-skippered vessel backed by unlimited resources and vast experience can founder due to the tiniest oversight on the part of her captain or crew. One of the best-known sailors in the world, Bernard Moitessier, wrecked more than one of his boats, including his most famous one, *Joshua,* named in honor of Joshua Slocum, the first man to solo-circumnavigate. The fact is, no one can know what it means to be responsible for every command, every scarf in the timbers, every splice in the lines and every single fastener and fitting whose sum equals soundness afloat, until they are master of a vessel themselves: not sailing as crew; not as a passenger; you alone as captain, and your word, law. This fact applies to sea gypsies and professional mariners alike. Being a good captain is difficult, the pressure is intense and unrelieved. If I should have stayed in Astoria that evening, then I should have never left Seattle. If I should have never left Seattle, then I should have never lived at all.

I was almost to mid-river, sailing along splendidly with a low sea rolling under the port quarter and the sails trimmed into silent, luff-free wings, when I felt a slow-motion lurch move through the boat from bow to stern. This familiar sensation in the soles of my feet was followed by a heavy shudder that stopped *Tranquility* on the spot.

She was aground!!

But how *could* she be?

Tranquility was aground in the middle of the river and heeling hard to starboard with the main and genoa still pulling beautifully!!

I dove for the sheets and ripped them in –flattening the mainsail amidships and hardening up on the genoa until it touched the starboard spreader tip. With the jib sheet popping on the winch and creaking in the turning blocks, *Tranquility* heeled-over with a frightening lean. She went past rail-under to deck-under, and as the foot of the genoa dipped into the river, the keel lifted off of whatever I hit long enough for me to sail away and attempt a desperate about-face. As soon as we were moving I put the tiller down, praying *Tranquility* would come about, and indeed, she turned west and passed through the eye of the wind. We were upright and free for one miraculous, hopeful second but *Tranquility* hit again as soon as the sails filled on the opposite tack. She was stranded and heeling hard to port now with her bowsprit pointing toward the south bank of the river.

I shook off the crowding tunnel vision of ultimate disaster and forced the main traveler to windward with a heave of my shoulder. I put my foot against the double block and tore in the last few inches of mainsheet, pulling the boom down to the cabin top and several degrees to windward. I grasped the sheet winch handle with both hands and cranked the genoa in until it warped over the port spreader tip. These efforts tilted *Tranquility*'s keel up just enough for her to skip and bump across the bottom for a few more seconds, but the ebb current was carrying her west just as fast, and a moment later, she grounded with a final thud on the seaward reaches of a vast mid-river shoal known as Desdemona Sands. The name strikes fear in the hearts of merchant seamen the world over, for it is a well-known and thoroughly charted shoal that stirs and shifts around the mouth of the Columbia River like a sandy amoeba hidden from view, at the edge of a narrow reach, until low tide. It's named for the good ship *Desdemona*, a 104-foot bark, whose captain was also in a hurry to get somewhere. He'd bet her owner a new suit that he could sail her from San Francisco to Astoria by New Year's Day 1848. Although there was good wind and it was a fast passage, *Desdemona* arrived at the river mouth around midnight on New Year's Eve. The captain sailed her off and on, steering clear of the river bar until morning. He called for a bar pilot (a special captain responsible for bringing a ship safely across a bar) at first light, but he received no answer and none came, so he took her across himself, relying on memory and an inaccurate chart. She never made it to Astoria. *Desdemona*'s bones lie there yet, just one wooden skeleton of at least two thousand others, in a vast regional taphonomy known as *The Graveyard of the Pacific*. When the seashores of Washington State are two hundred miles farther west, as they once were, maybe we will dig up her carcass and learn something from it.

I knew my grounding on Desdemona Sands was going to be a little different than the first two. I was in the maw of the Columbia River, not in some winding side channel or far upstream. This time around, there was nothing standing between *Tranquility* and the North Pacific Ocean. There was no hope of rowing an anchor out in the current running over the bar and no time to put the motor on the skiff, because *Tranquility* immediately began taking on water. It was too windy to leave the sails up while I bailed, so I jumped on deck and doused them –clawing the main and genoa down the mast and forestay with burning fingertips, fighting the stout wind keeping them aloft. When the water rose above the cabin sole, I went below and bailed *Tranquility* with the same robotic movements I learned on my way upriver. I worked under the main hatch, scooping and lifting the bucket high overhead, dumping it on the cabin top. I was in city shape and fell behind the rising water. I pressed on though and managed to pull ahead, going through the motions fast and steady, without rushing. *The best bilge pump in the world is a scared man with a bucket.*

Bailing a stricken vessel while the sun is going down is very grim business my friend, especially when you and the bucket are the only thing that can save the boat. There's no sense of time when you're bailing on a night like that. There's no relief or heroism when you're winning, no desperation or doubt when you're losing. In bailing, there's nothing but you and the bucket and the rising water. At that moment, you're every man in every boat that's ever foundered. Be careful what you stow in the waist of your ship, by the way: that's the first place water goes when you flood on an uneven keel.

Tranquility

It was an inky night by the time *Tranquility* was high and dry. She lay over on her port side near the west end of a wide, rippled expanse of dark sand, broken by deep pools of water flecked with stars. I dodged these ponds when I trudged the huge storm anchor out to the main channel, dragging the chain and line behind me. It was slow going and I knew I had another long night ahead of me, but at that point I was still hoping for the best. When I looked back at the boat, the scene might have come from an age-of-sail memento painted in the late 1800s. *Tranquility* cut quite a figure in the dark with her mast pointing into the night sky at such an improbable angle, with the stars winking through her rigging. There was a man dressed in sea boots and greatcoat standing before her. He held an anchor in his arms and a heavy chain was thrown over his shoulder —a kerosene lantern flickered in the cabin of the wreck. It was a rather fetching tableau really, a lonely barge hauler on a surreal shore, something Ilya Repin may have wanted to paint.

The wide expanse of river I'd been sailing on continued to retreat with the falling tide until it ran in a narrow channel to the south of me. In the distance beyond was a sparsely-lit, bushy lowland which merged into the sand dunes and rocks at the base of the jetty. To the east lay the gaily lit town of Astoria, and the gargantuan bridge which spans the river there. On the Washington side of the bridge, headlights popped out of the black woods and merged onto the apron. They soared up and over the river effortlessly, crossing it on twenty-five-cent's worth of gas. Their tail lights spiraled down the south ramp and disappeared into Astoria. In the awful night to the west lay shoal water, the thundering river bar and the dismal wind gusting in from the open ocean which the sweeping Fresnel beam in the Cape Disappointment lighthouse failed to lend any appeal to.

Desdemona Sands covers a wide area of the river mouth and I was still a couple hundred feet from the main channel when the anchor line ran out. I let go of the hook, heaved the chain from my shoulder, dropped to my knees and began digging in the wet sand with my bare hands. I had to be absolutely certain the anchor would hold when it came time to winch the boat toward the channel, so I dug deep.

Does she seek the land? I wondered as I walked back to *Tranquility*, having already forgotten what I learned over the winter about the imagined agency of boats. You really had to admire such obstinacy in a vessel. But what about her captain?

Back on board, I took up the slack in the anchor rode then went aft to coil the sheets down and latch the cockpit lockers. Portending an ugly night to come, the wind shifted a couple of points south and piped up to twenty-five knots, bringing in big western air and rain from the open sea. I went below, wishing to be out of the weather for as long as possible, but the cabin, tilting 50 degrees to port, offered little in the way of refuge or comfort and everything imaginable was going wrong in there. Brand new gear spilled from lockers on the high side of the boat and tumbled into bilge water. A sea bag full of fresh clothing, that I carelessly left open, dumped its contents into the murky pool at the base of the mast. The galley stove and a food bin I built just two weeks before had been under water and both looked the worse for it. I'd learned from my winter reading that in times of trouble, morale is adversely affected by everyday trifles, so I put the cabin back together as much as possible.

I bailed the rest of the water from the boat, hung up my wet clothes and pitched several pounds of sodden rice, pasta and other wet food overboard. It was still early and I knew there wasn't much more I could do to improve the situation before the tide came in, so I scarfed a can of cold chili, threw some dry bedding against the low side of the hull, set my alarm for 1:00 am and tried to get some rest. Outside, the wind was fine-tuning itself in the shrouds with little trailing whistles and I knew from the change in pitch it was getting set for a real Pacific Northwest blow. I rolled onto my side and jammed my eyes closed. There was a much stronger man in there.

It wasn't the alarm that woke me, it was the sound of waves crashing nearby, and when I went on deck I saw a troubling sight. The wind and incoming tide were driving a line of short breakers upriver, they were pitching and crashing in the shallows to the west. I could only sit and watch as the two-foot waves drew near the boat on the rising tide. A two-foot wave won't sound like much to someone who's never been in those waters, but they will sweep you off your feet and take you under. The short breakers surged up the sand on their way to *Tranquility*, gnashing at it and tearing it away as they ranged around. To the south, steep whitecaps were running up the widening main channel and large sections of the shoal I was stranded on were calving into the brackish water surging around it. Desdemona Sands was disappearing below the rising tide and I was in a new and frightening place —one quickly becoming more seashore than riverbank. It was a hell built just for sailors.

I ducked below in a fright and donned my rain gear. I pulled up the floorboards and opened the main hatch in preparation for the second round of bailing. I tied a wrist-leash to the bucket so it wouldn't be lost overboard in the struggle. I must have thought there was a good chance I'd be rowing to Astoria that night, because I went on deck and dragged the skiff around to the port side of the boat. I tied a bag containing the ship's papers, a flare canister and a jug of water to the thick metal ring in its bow. Then I sat in the tilted cockpit and watched as the first fingers of the incoming tide swept around *Tranquility*, lifting her rudder and yanking the skiff this way and that.

As soon as the water on Desdemona Sands was deep enough for them to travel on, the wind waves that were breaking in the shallows to the west started slamming into *Tranquility* and she began to shift and work under the blows. I watched helplessly as set after set of closely-spaced waves broke on her undersides flinging spray clear over the main boom and into the skiff. A strong undertow surged back and forth around *Tranquility* undermining her keel as the sand supporting it was scoured away. She began to settle into a mushy hole which opened up along her port rail. This was not the courteous high tide I'd experienced on Little Sand Island or even the unfriendly eddies of Jim Crow Sands, this was nature at her most menacing.

Poor *Tranquility* was flooding faster than she was subsiding, so I focused on bailing. Down in the cabin I could feel *Tranquility* trembling under the increasing blows as the tide rose around her, giving the waves a fairer avenue of attack. She was working so hard that when I stood on the low part of the hull it seemed fixed in place, while the rest of the boat flexed around it. The wind increased and the waves crowded in on themselves as the tide rose higher and higher. I bailed for all I was worth, and *Tranquility* flooded and slewed around like never before. To get a faint idea of the kind of beating a wooden boat can take, try hacking your way through a fir 2"x 6" with the claw-end of a hammer some time. It's pretty hard to put a hole in a well-found wooden boat. This is because their structural integrity relies on collective strength, not just component strength. It's rarely just one plank between you and the sea: it's the plank and the rib; the rib and the clamp; the keelson, bulkhead and beam, all working together to separate you from the sea. *Tranquility* was an old boat, and she must have been very well-built to have survived what I put her through. But even a great boat has a limit, and so does a man.

The wicked abuse went on and on. Then, at mid-tide, as if to emphasize the destruction to come, the westerly began galloping toward my helpless craft and I fell behind the rising water. I kept the bucket moving though, and ignored the ranting, half-dressed death roaming the cabin, throwing locker doors open, spilling their sodden contents back into the frigid knee-deep water surging around me. My mind began to wander as I bailed swollen books and spice jars overboard, but the little berms of Desdemona sand collecting behind the floor timbers and frames on the low side of the hull promptly recalled me. When I saw sand in her I knew it was only a matter of time before *Tranquility* succumbed and I didn't want to be in the cabin when she did. I dropped the bucket, slipped the leash from my wrist and sloshed up the cabin stairs. When I popped my head through the companionway, I caught a collar full of seawater as a wave crest, blown away by the wind, flew clear over *Tranquility*. Bad things were happening on deck. The genoa and mainsail had filled with water, cast off their lashings and were ballooning out over the leeward side of the boat. I grabbed a line and threw myself onto the heaving main boom up at the gooseneck. Holding the bitter end in my teeth, I clawed the belly of the mainsail toward me and threw a hitch over it. Then I worked my way toward the stern dragging the sail out of the water, lashing it to the spar as I went. When that was done, I crawled low and slow along the cabin top and splayed myself out on the leaping foredeck. I dragged the flogging genoa from the water and bundled it up in a sodden heap which I lashed to the Samson post with the sheets. When I returned to the cockpit, the tiller was sweeping to port and starboard with violent strokes. I straddled it and tied it off to one side. The skiff was half-full of water by then and I almost boarded it, thinking it wise to do so while I still had the chance. Sooner or later I would have to get myself to shore and it didn't look like *Tranquility* was coming with me.

Instead of giving up the ship though, I clipped my immersion suit to the main traveler and jumped below to keep up the bailing –but I did so with less vigor. Perhaps I'd grown weary of pleasure boating, or maybe I knew *Tranquility* couldn't take much more. Whatever the reason, I lost steam, and judging from the creaks and groans in the hull, I thought the boat was going to break up right before my eyes. I glanced at the thick, oaken knees bolted on either side of the mast—the ones I mocked in front of Buddy for their stagecraft scantlings—and they seemed too frail for the present conditions. I set the bucket down and collapsed on the pile of clothes and bedding spilling from the forepeak. If the devil were watching me just then, I'm sure he would have been pleased. *This will leave a mark,* I thought. *This will leave a mark.*

I faced up to my failure as a captain and a sailor. I admitted to myself that nearly every bad thing people tried to warn me about had happened; the fact that no fatal disaster had claimed me yet was merely a chance of luck I'd done nothing to deserve. It was fortunate I hadn't gotten myself killed in the past year –I killed *Tranquility.* Once my priorities shifted from saving the boat to saving myself, I grabbed a few personal items and a memento or two and tossed them into another waterproof bag which I tied to a handhold in the sloshing skiff. I stripped off my rain gear and climbed into my immersion suit. Then I sat in the heaving cockpit for the final lecture of the *Columbia River School of Seamanship.* Although reason was screaming at me to abandon ship, I didn't want to jump for the dinghy until the thing was done.

I used the time I had left to have a heartfelt discussion with myself about the various life lessons I learned on the voyage and the many benefits of living on dry land. With plenary relief I allowed that the experiment was finally over and that I was done with sailing and boats for a lifetime. I sat in the cockpit for a long time making peace with *Tranquility* and myself, while glimpsing little snippets of the personal disaster and strange relief that can come from losing certain boats. I was almost looking forward to getting on with my life when I noticed a couple of Admiralty Law types standing in my way.

Will there be identifiable wreckage in the morning? I hoped not.

Will I have to report this incident to the United States Coast Guard? Not sure, but probably.

Will I have to pay someone to salvage this wreck? Yes... no... perhaps.

Will I be fined? Or worse? Who cares?

I'm so glad this is over!

It wasn't going to be *that* easy to get rid of *Tranquility.* The tide was still coming in and the water around her was getting deeper. Even though she was flooded and had sunk deep in the sand, her movement was beginning to change. Lights on shore that had shone off the bow earlier were coming abreast the mast. Slowly, like a wounded bull trying to stand one last time, *Tranquility* began to rise to the waves. I sat up in the cockpit *astonished.* I looked out over the water and saw the anchor line was stretching tight. The tension in it was pulling the bow around to the west as the waves shoved *Tranquility* away from her hook. She was rousing herself for one more fight, presenting the narrowest part of her hull to the driving waves. Before long, she was rolling over them a little rather than just getting pummeled. When I glanced overboard, I saw that her port rail was somewhat higher than it had been when I came up on deck. She began to bump on the bottom, then she was shifting southeast toward deeper water, righting herself a little more on each passing wave. I stripped off my immersion suit and donned my foul-weather gear like an automaton. She was upright within an hour. Just before high tide by the book, *Tranquility* was pounding her keel into the sand so hard her shrouds were going slack when she hit bottom. The high tide that night may have been the lower of the period, perhaps the wind surge compensated for that, maybe my time keeping or the predictions were off. Whatever was going on, I was too exhausted to figure it out. All I know is *Tranquility* began floating free at some point and she was fetching up with heavy shears at the end of her anchor line soon thereafter.

Tranquility had risen from the dead.

I didn't have the energy to be happy nor was there time to regret the miracle. I fired up the engine and put it in gear then lumbered to the foredeck and hauled in the anchor line and most of the chain. When the bow was over the hook, I didn't have enough strength left to break it out of its hole. Wishing to be gone as quickly as possible, I kicked the links back over the side and cut the line just ahead of the eye splice with three pulls of my knife. *I'll bet William Albert Robinson wouldn't have done that!* I thought to myself sullenly as I headed back to the cockpit. I took the tiller in hand and steered my wallowing wraith to the main channel and motored her upstream to a small marina on the south bank of the river. When I landed at the dock, *Tranquility* had nearly two feet of water in her cabin and her bilge pumps were packed with sand. I bailed her by hand, put together a dry change of clothes, hobbled to shore and wandered the pitching and rolling streets of Astoria until dawn.

19

When you're young, you're carefree but foolish and you're plucky but unwise. When you're young you don't think things through, even though you're sure you have. This is what it means to be young and on your own in the world for the first time. Anyone reading these words while thinking to themselves: *true for you, but not for me* is only proving the point. My terrifying experience on Desdemona Sands should have ended my voyage to California. I should have put the boat up for sale or given her away the next day and moved on with my life. But I did not do what I should have done that day or for a long time afterward. Instead, I spent the afternoon cleaning and drying out the cabin and taking stock of the damage. Lockers full of supplies, the battery charger, a dozen books that didn't go overboard, and much of my dry food were ruined by saltwater. The fresh coat of paint I meticulously applied to the hull in Portland was half gone. All-in-all it was a punishing setback.

It was time for a stern reality check. I began by taking a quick walk down my chart of the Pacific Coast with a pair of dividers. Distance from Seattle to Santa Barbara: 1100 nautical miles, give or take. Distance covered so far: about 250 miles. Approximate average speed: 0.3 mph. At that rate, California was still three years away. *If* nothing else bad happened, and it was highly likely something would. Some of the worst parts of the lonely west coast were still before me: Rogue River Reef, Cape Blanco, Cape Mendocino, Point Reyes, Point Conception –all wicked in their own way. When I saw all of that, I was terrified of the Pacific Ocean, and rightly so, but I'd been through way too much that year to give up so easily. This was the moment when the voyage became more important to me than the destination. Buying the boat and setting sail on my own for the first time, the beauty and the discovery, the joy and the pain, the fear and the courage I needed to overcome it, were all about something more important than one summer of sailing and one obstinate boat. It was about knowing myself and the meaning of my life. So it was a benign will, rather than a sinister one, that drove me to continue.

I put on my bravest face of the voyage the next morning, and sailed *Tranquility* back into the Columbia River. I beat west, tack-and-tack, into what I thought was a nice sea wind and I steered for the bar, giving Desdemona Sands a preposterously wide berth. After sailing for about a mile, the wind eased, so I dropped the working jib and hoisted the big genoa in its place. As soon as I trimmed the sails and settled myself at the tiller, the boat glided into a flat calm and stalled. I drifted west, perpendicular to the jetties, willing my gaunt sails back into shape for over an hour before meeting with a light wind blowing downriver. I sailed on this faint breeze as best I could, ghosting over the bar with my mainsail slatting back and forth horrendously and the genoa ballooning out weakly. When I was clear of the river mouth, I tried steering south, but *Tranquility* would only turn lazy circles in the current pulling her along the rumbling Oregon coastline.

A weak offshore wind picked up around noon and I sailed south on it at no more than a knot or two. An offshore wind at that latitude is an easterly of course, and that made me absolutely crazy. Why was it that the northwesterlies never seemed to blow when I had a use for them? Sure, they could whip up out of nowhere when *Tranquility* was on her side taking on a cargo of sand and water, but sailing somewhere on them? I was beginning to wonder if it could really be done. I was as ready for the voyage as I'd ever be. I would have sailed for days on end had there been just five knots of favorable wind, but I had more days of calms and southerlies than anything else. I spent more than a week looking for the westerlies offshore, and there sure as hell hadn't been any consistent winds near the coast. It was absolutely maddening when the wind toyed with me like that!

By late afternoon it was obvious I wasn't going to get very far, so I set my sights on Tillamook Bay, about half-a-day's sail down the Oregon Coast. I figured I needed to reach a port south of the Columbia River as soon as possible in order to maintain a minimum level of morale –it wasn't to be! Around sunset, the light breeze died away to almost nothing and I had to give up on Tillamook Bay. I steered instead for a jagged headland that seemed like a decent place to anchor on such a calm night. But even *that* wasn't to be. As I drew near it, the light breeze became intermittent puffs and I spent the next several hours tacking back and forth on land zephyrs and drifting hither and yon on nearshore currents. I finally tossed my hook over the side at midnight, just shy of the cliffs I was heading for. That was a bad first day on the ocean!

Tranquility

As I lay in my bunk that night I tried to metabolize a little of my harrowing experience on Desdemona Sands, but all I could manage to do was nibble around the edges of a few shocking images which were quickly solidifying into permanent memories of my worst shipwreck. I grappled with the lessons of the Desdemona Sands incident for some time before filing it away in the annals of the dispute brewing between William Stewart Sparrow, *Tranquility* and the Pacific Ocean. *It's still pretty nice to be on my way south again* I tried telling myself as I nodded off, but the optimism that got me out of Portland was already drying up.

The next morning a light westerly was blowing—hurrah—so I pulled up anchor and sailed south at about two knots, picking my way along the Oregon coastline, looking for the entrance of the Tillamook River, which I planned to follow inland to Tillamook Bay. It took me a few hours to get down there and when I first saw the misty Tillamook bar it looked as flat as a mountain lake in July. I was having a hard time trusting myself at that point, so instead of carrying on, I dropped anchor and glassed the entrance for a long time (glass: to observe through a magnifier) just to be sure there weren't any waves breaking offshore or between the jetties. Through the binocular I watched old gray men in flannel coats slowly motoring aluminum skiffs back and forth across the bar trolling for salmon. There were blond-headed surfers bobbing on tame looking swells rolling upriver along the inside of the south jetty. Tourists, done-up in brand new sneakers and brilliant white summer outfits watched them from the jumbled rocks above like gigantic seagulls. All was well on the Tillamook River that day and I believed I was on my way south again, so I skipped up to the foredeck and hauled in the anchor line until I felt the chain come off the bottom. However, when I gave the rode the old heave-ho to break the anchor loose, it didn't budge. After several more tries, I went aft, started the engine and slowly motored over the anchor to free it with the momentum of the boat. Instead of breaking the hook loose as she passed over it though, *Tranquility* dipped her bow to starboard, and did a huge yawing pirouette around the line. I reversed for a few seconds and gave it another shot from a different angle, but all she would do was spin around her hook. I tried this and I tried that, I fussed with it for over an hour but it was hopeless, so I cut the anchor line with three pulls of my knife and headed for the bar in a foul, foul mood. *I'll bet Errol Bruce wouldn't have done that!*

By the way, wrecking your boat and losing two brand new anchors is a really, *really* bad way to begin a voyage.

After taking one last look at the Tillamook River, I lined *Tranquility* up on the entrance and headed her in under power. As I neared the jetties I realized the bar was a little less serene than it looked from a quarter-mile away. When I entered the middle grounds (the area just west of the jetty tips where vessels are routinely destroyed by breaking waves), *Tranquility* began to teeter on the crests of the swells passing under her. She got so lively on one or two that I thought she was going to take off surfing. I did a quick scan of my surroundings as this was happening and I realized there weren't any little boats crossing the bar just then –they'd all moved far upriver for some reason. And then I noticed the surfers were hauled out on the rocks. They were watching me and talking among themselves...waiting to see what would happen! I swung *Tranquility* around in a fright and motored back out to sea.

As part of my refit in Portland, I purchased the same model outboard I had the previous summer; this was a reliable but decades old Evinrude 18-horse. It's a two-cylinder beast of an engine, whose recoil could rip your arm off if you were holding the pull-cord during a backfire. I was turning wide circles a quarter-mile west of the entrance and sorting through my options when this engine suddenly stalled. I fussed with it for a long time before concluding that the problem was the fuel pump. It's a ten-minute repair if you have the part, but I didn't. I somehow figured out that I could start the engine and keep it running by continually pressing the small rubber siphon on the top of the fuel tank. If I wanted to steer the boat at the same time however, I had to press the siphon with my foot. In case you're wondering, that's absolutely, positively, the wrongest way possible to cross an unfamiliar river bar. But I *needed* to cross, because the tide was about to turn against me. If I didn't go soon, I'd be spending the next eight to twelve hours drifting close to shore with a poorly running engine on a nearly windless day. That seemed like it could lead to further trouble and I was reluctant to drop anchor, for obvious reasons.

So there we were. I had to cross the bar but I couldn't do it safely. The situation reminded me of the Willapa Bay incident for some reason, so I radioed the Tillamook Coast Guard station and asked them for an escort. Here's how it works: the Coast Guard meets you west of the middle grounds in a boat designed to capsize repeatedly (a surf boat). You establish radio contact with the surf boat and her captain tells you when it's safe to follow them across the bar. The captain knows when it's safe because he knows the river and there's also a wave lookout posted in a tall tower at the base of the north jetty. The two are in radio contact and if the lookout sees a big set of waves coming he warns the surf boat captain. It's a pretty simple procedure and they're good at it because they do it all year long –and they're the Coast Guard.

An hour or so later, I was motoring behind a Coast Guard vessel that was heading for the Tillamook bar. I was watching them go, listening to the radio for instructions, steering like they were, and working the siphon on the fuel tank with my left foot. As we crossed the middle grounds, I made the mistake of looking behind me, and what I saw there made my knees buckle. The biggest waves I'd ever seen in my life were stacking up high overhead. *They know what's going on here dude!* I thought to myself turning around, trying to keep my eyes on the stern of the surf boat and off the waves. As we were nearing the jetty tips, the surf boat began disappearing for several seconds in the seas running between us and *Tranquility* was starting to yaw and rear as she slid down the backs of the steepest waves. It didn't feel right, so I turned the boat around and motored back out to sea. *This is crazy, this is crazy, this is crazy* I thought to myself as *Tranquility* dropped off the wave crests with sickening vaults.

My radio crackled to life a moment later:

"Vessel *Tranquility*...This is the United States Coast Guard vessel *Tillamook Bay* –come in, over."

"Roger *Tillamook Bay*, go ahead."

"What happened to you just now skipper?"

"I don't think my boat can cross the bar, over."

"Roger sir...uh...Please be advised that the Tillamook bar has moderate conditions right now."

"*Moderate* conditions?" I asked.

"Roger that, sir...moderate conditions."

"What do you advise? Over."

"Well Captain, we can escort you across the bar at this time or we can tow you across if you feel that you are incapable of piloting your own boat."

"Roger Coast Guard, I'll take a tow then."

"Roger...Sir, are you asking for a tow?"

"Roger that, I'd like a tow at this time, over."

"Roger Captain..."–cue grave change of tone–"...VESSEL TRANQUILITY, THIS IS THE UNITED STATES COAST GUARD VESSEL TILLAMOOK BAY, WHAT IS THE NATURE OF YOUR DISTRESS, OVER?"

"Uh...my *distress*? Well...the swells seem really big to me right now?...And I've never been in here before?" (That wasn't the nature of my distress he was looking for).

"Roger that, Captain...Are you *incapable* of piloting your vessel over the Tillamook bar at this time sir?"

Ah...now I had it! I had to *say* that I didn't have the first goddamned clue what I was doing, *to* the United States Coast Guard, *over* the radio, so they could come to my aid, because an escort and a tow are two completely different things. One is a courtesy call, the other, a rescue.

"Roger, Coast Guard. I am *incapable* of piloting my vessel over the Tillamook River bar at this time and I need a tow."

"Roger skipper, we'll tow you across."

I imagined the outrage of channel 16 eavesdroppers all up and down the Oregon Coast. What a retard!

After a brief orientation over the radio, the surf boat backed up to my stern and a man heaved a thick line onto my deck. I secured the line to my stern cleat and a young coast guardswoman lowered a large, orange fabric cone tied to the other end, into the water. This rubberized cloth cone is called a drogue and the vessel being towed, tows it. When a drogue is pulled through the water it spreads open like a small parachute and acts as a brake on the boat being towed. This braking action steadies the boat and keeps her from surfing down waves or broaching (I broached on the Willapa bar). Once the drogue was in the water, the surf boat backed up to my bowsprit and another coast guardsman heaved a thick tow line onto my foredeck which I secured to the Samson post. And with that, I was officially under tow by *Tillamook Bay*.

Captain Voss used a drogue to keep *Tilikum* from surfing on steep seas –she was a canoe after all!

When the boats begin moving through the water during such a tow, the drogue line comes under immense strain because it's actually slowing down and stabilizing *both* vessels. Unfortunately, this immense strain was immediately communicated to the lower unit of my outboard motor. I watched indifferently as the drogue line caught on the propeller just as *Tillamook Bay* and *Tranquility* were surging down the face of separate middle ground waves. The inch-thick drogue line gingerly tilted the engine out of the water. The little metal latch on the motor bracket, which prevents this sort of thing from happening during normal use, overextended and snapped off, zinging out over the water. *OF COURSE!* I thought to myself in utter, teeth-grinding disgust. Just as it crossed my mind that I might be able to free the line with the boat hook, *Tillamook Bay* went down the face of a wave and *Tranquility* dropped off the back of another, rubberbanding the two vessels on the tow line. In a casual display of fluid power, the drogue line tilted the motor up again, forced it past horizontal with a horrific crunch and then tore it off the boat, taking my beefy mahogany motor mount right along with it. If the motor mount had held together, I'm sure *Tranquility's* transom would have been ripped open. She would have sunk then and there and I would have died a most happy death! Without the *slightest* reaction, I watched the outboard cruise through the sea, propeller up, periscope fashion. I left it there, sculling gracefully to port and starboard –waving to me from the end of its safety cable all the way to the dock.

If bad things happen to you whether or not you take precautions against them, what do you do? How do you know when a dream is impossible or just incredibly difficult to realize? The futility of that moment was outrageous. I knew the line between adventure and foolhardiness had finally been crossed. Some would say I crossed it long before. That's definitely something to consider, but there's no right or wrong answers here. I made a promise that day, though: I promised to never look outside of myself or my vessel for assistance on the water unless a *life* truly depended on it. I kept that promise too, and no matter the difficulties I faced, and there were many still to come, I never picked up the radio again after the Tillamook River debacle (the reader has been spared some of the more shameful details).

I stayed on the dock in Garibaldi, a small settlement on the Tillamook River, for a couple of days while I resurrected the outboard and mount. Then I stayed a couple more while I repainted the port side of the hull, which had been thoroughly scuffed on Desdemona Sands. It took a few more days to get a new fuel pump. Rather than set sail when I finished these chores, I poked around Garibaldi's docks and small boatyard. I needed a break from myself and I was too afraid to continue the voyage. I was taking financial hits from several directions that week and in order to save supplies and money I caught crab under the docks, collected oysters on the beach and, at night, I snuck into the fish cleaning station by the boat ramp and salvaged salmon collars and halibut cheeks from the fresh, but carelessly cleaned, carcasses piled there. I questioned my resolve to press on to California many times during my stay. The spring weather went from rain, light winds and a calm bar, to clear skies, strong winds and a rough bar –then back again. The northwesterly blew for the first time to my knowledge, and a few southbound sailboats came and went from the guest dock. But their skippers and crews avoided the squat green knock-about sloop tied at its far end. Who could blame them? They were a young and jovial set having the time of their lives on good-looking fiberglass racer-cruisers while *Tranquility* was a down-on-her-luck old wreck with a guy on her who looked like trouble. I'm sure a thousand boats sailed from Seattle to Southern California that summer and the one before it. Not *Tranquility*!

One misty Pacific Northwest morning, long after I should have been on my way south, I rolled out of my bunk and stepped into several inches of ice-cold seawater. Now there's a palfrey old trope for you! It's one that's been dusted off and trotted out for every sea story that's ever been told. A cliché is only a cliché until it happens to you, though. *Tranquility* was a leaky old boat, but she leaked intermittently; there was no consistency or pattern to it. You could sail her for hours in adverse conditions and she wouldn't have an extra drop of water in her, but she might be half-sunk on a pleasant daysail, or vice versa, you never knew which! Be that as it may, *Tranquility* did not leak at the dock. She leaked underway, when it would be most appreciated. The water on the cabin sole that morning could only mean one thing: *Tranquility*'s hull was seriously compromised by the battering she took on Desdemona Sands. She was sinking at the dock, she wore the scarlet letter and it was all my fault. To put the *finest* possible point on it: the bilge pumps didn't come on as the water rose that night because the wires to them had corroded from constant saltwater bathing. I suppose solder would have helped.

Far from giving her up for lost, I launched a full investigation into the leak that day. I removed every portable item from *Tranquility* and put it under tarps on the dock. I tore up every floorboard in the cabin and started to pull the mahogany hull liner out of the forepeak. I sounded corners of that vessel not seen since her keel was laid. I discovered old brazed kerosene tins whose contents had evaporated sometime during the Korean War. I came across little piles of wood shavings and pulverized coal. I took another shot at the *Old Ballard Sponge Test* and sat and watched the bilge fill up with water over and over again. I ballasted *Tranquility* with her bow down and then her stern. Did the water collect aft of the beam first? –or was it forward of the beam? One moment I'd be convinced the headwaters of the leak were in the bow and the next I was sure it was the stern. I tried to find the source of the leak for two days but never made anything of it. She filled as if by magic. After running her numbers, I concluded that if *Tranquility* were left unattended she'd go to the bottom in a week. I bought two new automatic bilge pumps and wired them to separate batteries. *Tranquility* was in intensive care: she was being kept alive by machines.

I roamed the docks and boatyards of the region seeking leaky-old-wood-boat advice from the crustiest looking fellows I could find. The tars I spoke to tried to be optimistic about my situation and they took their old-man-of-the-sea roles seriously. They were full of helpful yarns, apocryphal tales and old school recipes for get-it-done-quick sealing compounds such as *bear poo* –a pungent mixture of diesel fuel, boiled linseed oil, saw dust, hydraulic cement and roofing tar. I gave it a try –it didn't work. Some advised me to sell her as soon as possible because she was "all rotten below the waterline." One man wondered if *Tranquility*'s hull might be riddled with thousands of shipworms. "What's her bottom look like?" they all asked. Although I'd seen *Tranquility*'s undersides a handful of times, it was night, or I was too busy salvaging her to take a close look. One man who seemed willing to survey *Tranquility* for pay, started backpedaling as soon as he saw her. "Ohhhhhh...*that* green sailboat," he said when the pieces fell into place at the top of the ramp. "If it's the same one they towed in here the other day, I'd say you're gonna be sistering frames, replacing planks and doing some caulking real soon. Look at the way she's bulging out at the waterline! Ever done work like that before? I'll tell you straight kid, it's hell on earth." He wouldn't take my money.

Looking down on *Tranquility* from the top of the ramp that day, I imagined a never-ending vessel rebuild with her out of the water, propped up on blocks for months, then years. She'd have her planks ripped off and her ribs showing through like the chest of a starving dog. One dreary November night, I'd find myself crouched under a plastic tarp in the cabin with bad teeth and my long, unwashed beard dripping rainwater into a bowl of thin broth held between my bony peasant's knees. But I wouldn't have anywhere else to go by then so I'd just kill myself...and death? Death would come like sweet succor. I remembered *The Art of Caulking a Hull*, the freshly photocopied article I saw on *Tranquility* the first time I was aboard her, and I wished I still had it.

I have said that I made no progress whatsoever during the first year of the voyage and I meant that literally. So can you guess what happened next?

20

It certainly was strange to be sleeping in the back of my van on the mean streets of Seattle so soon after my triumphant departure. Desdemona Sands and everything that happened afterward made me grateful to be on dry land, though. The van was pretty nice inside too. I had a little stove, pots and pans and a small pantry crate tucked underneath my bed. There was a book nook and a small reading lamp; I had plenty of room for clothes and tools. I didn't need much more than that to be comfortable in those days! Besides, I was a new man by then and I didn't have a whole lot of time to worry about where I was living, or to dwell on my failure to reach California, because a few days after my arrival, *Tranquility* was back in Seattle herself. After hitchhiking from Garibaldi to Portland to get my van, I spent around $1500 to haul *Tranquility* out of the water, pull her mast and have her shipped to Ballard on a flatbed semi that was deadheading from Tillamook Bay to Bellingham. I sent her to Seattle because that was the easiest place for me to make the kind of money I was going to need to repair her hull. She arrived before the 10thof May and the Pacific Northwest yachting season had only just begun. I figured I could fix *Tranquility*'s leak, take care of a few other things that were wrong with her and still get an entire summer of sailing in. All I can say is I was young, full of energy and optimism and two months seemed like a year to me in those days!

When I saw *Tranquility* propped up in Ballard Boatyard the morning she was delivered, my hands hummed in anticipation of the work to come. In Ballard, I planned to wave a wand of money and effort over *Tranquility*'s most serious shortcomings as a boat. I was going to completely rebuild her a few blocks down the road from where I bought her the year before. *How ironic.* Job one was her mysterious leak and I couldn't wait to get to the bottom of that. I was pretty sure I'd be caulking her and whatever that was, I aimed to find out. In the meantime, *Tranquility* would be on dry land and totally defenseless. Chained down and blocked in on all sides by other boats on time-out, she would have to hold still for her transformation from leaky crank to seaworthy cream-puff. On land there would be no squirming out of my grasp like a dog resisting a bath. Land was *my* place and she was going to be marooned there until I saw fit to turn her loose. On land if I needed something, I could hop in the van and bring it right to her side without rowing, enduring a tidal saga or trudging down a slippery, rickety old dock. On land it could rain buckets and the wind could howl for days, but what would I care? I could walk away from her for a month if need be, and she would be exactly where I left her when I returned. On land, my life would be free from the threat of sinking, there would be no anchoring and no more chafe. When I dropped something it would come to rest on terra firma, not sink to the bottom of the sea or drift out of boat hook reach. When my advantage was complete, I walked up to her bow without thinking, made a fist and almost punched her on the nose. I pulled it just before it connected. I'm not sure what occurred to me just then, but I cocked my head and looked at her in an odd way. *Stupid old boat. Why do you make an enemy of the one person who cares for you?*

Tranquility was constructed in the plank-on-frame method of boat building. A vessel so built is essentially a complicated wooden cask –the specific nomenclature and hoary boring controversies of which do not belong here. A helpful analogy for the landsman: take a cartoon drawing of a bony fish and remove all fins except for the tail and the dorsal; turn the fish upside down and you have the essential structure of a plank-on-frame sailboat like *Tranquility* (her mast was out and sitting on saw horses). The spine of the fish is her keel timber (keelson), the ribs are the ribs of course (aka frames), the skin is the planking, the head the bow. The dorsal fin is the external keel, the tail fin the rudder, etc. A plank-on-frame vessel has an oddly chordate shape once you get to know them.

There are one or two other details you need to know about plank-on-frame boats if you're going to be caulking one. The sides and bottom of the boat are made up of individual planks, however they only keep *most* of the water out. The planks of a wooden boat are arranged like the boards of a fence, except the boards are attached to the fence posts (ribs) horizontally rather than vertically and they're spaced *very* close to one another, almost touching along their edges. The shape of a boat comes from the bend in her ribs. Just like our upside-down fish, the ribs of a boat rise from both sides of the keel timber and the ribs bow out on either side of it in the shape of a hull. Ribs are steamed in a special box to get them to bend the desired amount. Once the ribs are bent and attached to the keelson, the planks are screwed on (this is referred to as fastening).

Ribs in North American wooden boats are usually oak, while hull planking can be yellow or red cedar, fir, one of the many pines, a mahogany –what have you.

As I said, the planks of a boat are almost touching along their edges, and this is where the caulking comes in. There are narrow gaps where the edges of the planks meet and these gaps are called seams. If you take a V and open it up at the bottom so it's slightly funnel shaped, you will have a good idea of what a seam looks like, except you must rotate the seam ninety degrees so the wide opening faces the water and the narrow opening points inboard. The caulking is driven into the wide opening from outside the boat and when the seams are properly caulked, the vessel doesn't leak.

Please don't ask me what caulking is! All you need to know is this: most of it is strands of cotton or hemp fiber. Hemp (or oakum) caulking bears a suspicious resemblance to dreadlocks. Cotton caulking looks exactly like what you'd have if you took a normal diameter cotton ball and made it fifty feet long, like a rope, except the rope is about as strong as cotton candy. Once the open seams are slathered with bottom paint (often red, copper-infused, toxic to marine vegetation and invertebrates, irritating to the skin) two strands of cotton rope are twisted up like a bread tie and driven into the seam with a special crescent-shaped iron which you strike—just so—with a strange wooden mallet. You plug up the seams about 2/3 of the way with your cotton (or hemp or both). At that point, another coat of bottom paint is slathered into the seams until the caulking turns red (or whatever color your paint is). Once the paint dries, a soft putty is troweled into the remaining 1/3 of the seam. This is called paying the seams. After the seams are payed the boat gets a few more coats of bottom paint and then you're done. All told, *Tranquility* had around 1,938 *miles* of seam between her planks. Hard to imagine, but true. The work is called caulking or corking – whichever you prefer. Either way, it will kill you dead, so please don't try it.

During my caulking research I was repeatedly told to wield my mallet with restraint. I was advised to strike the caulking iron firmly but gently when driving the cotton into the seams. "Go until it feels right," was a common refrain. "If you go too far, you'll drive the cotton clear through the seam and into the cabin," –that's a classic blunder.

"You'll start to feel it the moment it's home," one man told me. All spoke wistfully of the soothing sound perfect corking makes: "The mallet will start to make a pleasant tamping sound when the cotton is in far enough...you're gonna hear a sweet *prink-prink-prink* when it's just right."

Standing there looking at the miles of seam that lay before me in Ballard that morning, I knew I couldn't do it all on my own. So I decided to hang around the footpaths local tradesmen had worn in the plywood floors of various Ballard establishments in order to glean what I could from the pros. I'd learned by then that when you need something it's best to go as close to the source as possible. I also had to get a feel for the equipment and supplies I was going to need. Yes sir, I was doubling down on *Tranquility*. I was going all in, I was going for broke. My dream of sailing to California and *Tranquility* were one and the same by then. I didn't have the energy to start over with another boat so the entire voyage was riding on the one I had.

I began the caulking job the way I should have started every other boat project I guessed at over the past year. I read up on the subject and sought advice. I called and visited boatyards all over Seattle, trolling for the name of a reputable shipwright to consult with. But these days good corkers are few and far between and I ran into a surprising amount of resistance with that approach. The tone was set early on by one particularly frank boatyard foreman who said: "Listen here kiddo, any shipwright who's any good at what he does is going to be so busy this time of year he's not gonna have time to play around with you." I remained undeterred.

I could have *hired* a shipwright to caulk for me and I could have *motored* to California, but *anybody* can do that. I figured if I was going to dump a pile of money into the boat for something, then I needed to learn how to do that something for myself, just in case it ever came up again. So I pounded the Ballard pavement for a few days looking for leads and at night I sat in a bookstore thumbing through boating magazines trying to absorb useful information. I was living the life they were hinting at, lock, stock and barrel, yet I couldn't bear to read most of the literature. The articles all seemed to have been written by and for a bunch of retired house-men who were absolutely reveling in their insane attention to arcane details and woodworking factoids. I might as well have been cramming for brain surgery, judging by the prior learning, expensive power tools and intricate steps supposedly involved in building a marine-grade binocular box. I wanted to know how to do it, not how to forge my own boutique C-clamps during the winter off-season. I needed to know the *difference* between vertical grain Douglas fir and plain sawn second-growth; I didn't need to know the ins and outs of seasoning the maple I harvested from my wooded backyard.

I stopped by some of the old Ballard merchants to have a look at the tools of the corking trade and some of the supplies I'd need for the job. The caulking irons looked like thick, tapered, crescent bladed putty-knives with a mallet landing instead of a wooden handle. Irons are made of...yes, you guessed it, iron, and were available in several styles depending on the type of seam you were working. Of course, no one could say which or how many of these irons I would need for *Tranquility*. The corking mallets were big and complicated as hammers go: they had four iron hoops, several moving parts and a handle that came out of the mallet head if you gave it the slightest tug. This was a one of a kind tool in my book, so obviously no substitutions would be allowed there. The coils of caulking cotton were raw but clean (no bits of boll in them). They came loosely wrapped in kraft paper that bore no label and were sold by the pound –as many as you might need. No one I spoke to had, or knew where to get oakum (I ended up not needing it because *Tranquility* was corked with cotton). I would be buying a half-case of seam compound and five or six gallons of bottom paint. Add *Tranquility*'s haul out in Garibaldi and her truck ride to Seattle, the daily rate for her stay in the boatyard, the crane and extra man needed to step her mast and, of course, the launch fee. It was definitely adding up.

If my winter of poverty and suffering taught me anything, it was that making money, in-and-of-itself, is a colossal waste of time. What's the point of more money? There's only so much you need, so what good is it beyond that? If you're happy and doing what you want in life, more money doesn't make you any happier. If anything, great wealth is an unquenchable source of discontent and self-doubt. I for one, know wealthy people who will never feel wealthy and I know poor people who feel rich. Yes, that's a cliché, but like all clichés, it's mostly accurate. Besides, it's been studied...look it up.

Boats, of course, are a slightly different matter. Be she humble or grand, a wreck or a gin palace, a boat is a going concern in-and-of-herself. A vessel has a peculiar ability to generate her own economic wind, much like a tractor or a pickup truck can. You may run informal charters or haul a little freight with her; maybe you fish, maybe you do a little bootlegging up in Alaska. If you live aboard you save on rent. A refit may yield old or ill-suited equipment that can be sold to offset the cost of her upgrades. There are other strange earnings to be had with a boat. Maybe your pals pitch in for food or fuel. Maybe they get seasick and don't end up eating or drinking as much as they pictured in the grocery store or jug shop. Someone may forget something when they head home on a Sunday night. Money is freely spent on boats and they leverage it from their surroundings. I soon realized it was going to cost more to rebuild *Tranquility* than it did to buy her, so I started fliering as soon as a rough figure came into focus and I began getting calls immediately. Between auto repair and the boat, May and June turned into a real juggling act but the money came in as expected.

By mid-May I managed to put a few extra bucks in my pocket, then all at once, my calls and visits to boatyards paid off. I was given a name, Les, and a local number one evening just as the Ballard craftspeople and shipwrights were knocking off for the day. I rushed over to the paint-splattered boatyard phone and dialed. Les sounded friendly and seemed interested in the call. After a brief rundown of my leak situation, I asked him if he would come take a look at *Tranquility* and supervise her repair. He agreed! When I thanked Les and promised to pay for every minute of his time, he guffawed. I wasn't sure what that meant, but I soon found out. Time was a wastin' though and summer was starting to scoot, so we have to as well.

A couple of days later, a tall Virginian dressed in canvas carpenter pants, a wide flannel shirt and the most beat-up leather boots I'd ever seen showed up. He was driving a heavyset and long-suffering lineman's truck with an exhaust leak that made the motor go *blap-blap-blap*. Les didn't need to ask which boat was mine, and he strolled over to *Tranquility* giving knowing waves to the other craftsmen as he crossed the yard. Les listened to the saga of *Tranquility*'s leak from the shores of Bainbridge Island to the banks of the Tillamook River as he walked around her, chuckling to himself and reaching between the boat stands to make casual *done-it-a-million-times* chalk marks here and there on her hull.

Les leaned a ladder against *Tranquility*'s rail, climbed aboard and took a long look inside her with a little, blinding flashlight and an inspector's mirror. He came down the ladder without a word and walked a couple of boat lengths away, contemplating her lines from afar. He came back, lit up a hand-rolled smoke and tapped his foot for a moment or two before issuing a verdict. Although Les said he'd never seen an inboard engine bolted *through* a hull before (this was the source of the witch's finger I pulled from the engine bed) the upshot of his survey was positive for such an old boat. According to Les, other than needing some new caulking here and there, *Tranquility*'s hull was sound and he couldn't find a single broken rib or rotten plank in her. Les agreed that she had the stuffing knocked out of her on Desdemona Sands but he said she was a well-found boat with a lot of life left in her. He didn't mention anything about shipworms and I didn't think to ask.

"I don't know what she is," Les said, "but she sure as hell ain't planked with Port Orford yellow."

I liked Les.

Les told me to reef out (clean out) all the caulking from the seams and refasten the planks between his chalk marks. I would have to re-caulk all the bad seams he or I found —no cutting corners. *Roger that*, I thought to myself when Les reiterated the rule. He told me to pull out what was left of the engine bolts and fill the holes, inside and out, with epoxy and hardwood plugs. Les knew what the deal was. I was trying to fix *Tranquility* on my own and I didn't have money to spend on things I could do myself with a little guidance. Just before he left, Les invited me over to the tailgate of his truck where he demonstrated the caulking process on a 2' x 2' section of hull he'd sawn from a wreck. I learned how to reef a seam without widening or damaging it and how to resize overly-wide seams by gluing thin strips of fir inside them. He gave me a small, tapered block of wood to use as a seam gauge. Next, Les showed me how to twist up the strands of cotton rope into a proper braid and how to tamp it into a seam with the mallet and iron (this was the only part of the job I was afraid of). That was just a primer of course. Les told me to call him when I had the seams reefed out because he'd need to check my work and show me a few more things before I started caulking.

When I asked Les what I owed him for the day, he said, as he yanked the door of his truck open: "Oh...I know where to find you." I'd heard that a good caulker earned about $60 an hour, so I'd set aside $200 for his visit. Les wouldn't hear of it though. After he drove off, I ran back to the boat on the tips of my toes, flew up the ladder and had a look inside her myself. What he said was true, there were no broken ribs and no rot.

She leaked because her caulking was old. I'd been haunted by that goddamned leak for a year and I had no idea how much brain space it was taking up until that day. It weighed on me like a great metaphysical debt and the first time I felt it ease, I was elated.

The Ballard Boatyard was of a type. It began at a long seawall that had several docks and piers attached to it. A rolling gantry crane for hauling and launching boats was parked at the water's edge. The yard was spacious and sloped toward Salmon Bay like a shower floor. It was filled with sail and powerboats undergoing all sorts of repair –new decks and propellers, barnacle scraping and bottom painting. There was a small business office and yard store which sold supplies at a fair price. I was no stranger to hard work and I turned to with-a-will the morning after Les came by. I set up a workbench alongside the boat and laid an array of hand tools on it: flathead screwdrivers; paint scrapers and razor knives; hammer and chisel; sandpaper and rags; safety goggles, earplugs and gloves. I sought out the worst looking seam between Les' chalk marks and gave the caulking in it a tentative pry with my putty knife. A bone dry rust-colored wedge of cotton drooped out of the seam with the compound and bottom paint still stuck to it. *That's the cotton!* I said to myself with a deep jolt of understanding for *Tranquility*. I glanced around the yard at the other wooden boats and saw them in a new light –it was time to get serious. I spent the next couple days reefing out the seams between Les' chalk marks and then I spent a couple more refastening the planks to the ribs with expensive bronze wood screws, a countersink and a brace-and-bit. With the sun beating down on the blacktop, it was hot and sweaty under the boat but it felt good to be doing right by *Tranquility*. I chastised myself if a time-saving method crossed my mind and I poured on the effort whenever I grew distracted or tired. When I lay my head down at night, my arms were sore, my hands were throbbing and I could hear my heartbeat in my ears.

After a week of dawn-til-dusk effort it seemed like I was getting the hang of the work, so I went back over the first seam I reefed just to be sure I hadn't missed anything when I was still green. I stood before the boat early one morning, and between sips of industrial-strength carafe coffee laden with fake sugar and fake cream, I checked my work. I'd left a flock or two of cotton deep down in the narrowest taper of the first seam. It was no big deal and I scraped them out in a jiffy. When I had all of the seams between the chalk marks reefed, I gave some of the caulking outside the lines a poke with my putty knife, just to check. I was surprised to find it as loose as the bad caulking had been. I went around to the other side of the boat and tested a few seams over there. *All of the caulking in the boat was loose!* I went back to the first seam and reefed two more feet on either side of Les' marks. And then two more, and two more after that. In an hour, the first seam was free of caulking from stem to stern. Then the seam below it was too. Then the next one, and the next after that. In a few days there wasn't a filament of cotton left in the hull below the waterline. *If a job's worth doing, it's worth doing right!* I told myself, knowing it for the first time in my life.

   Without checking with Les, I sanded every last flake of bottom paint off the boat, taking the hull down to bare wood with a particularly unforgiving type of grinder I found at a tool store nearby. Though I choked on the copper-laden dust, slept in it, ate it and wore it burning on my skin for days, I did so happily, knowing that *Tranquility* would be a tight ship after my labors. I wasn't leaving anything to chance with that leak. *Not gonna happen, no ways bro!* Not after what *I'd* been through. When I finished grinding a half-century's accumulation of bottom paint from the hull and rudder there was a 5-gallon bucket of cupreous dust sitting under the bow and an ocher trail of it led from the boat to the van and over to the yard store in a wide bend. With *Tranquility's* seams completely reefed out below the waterline and all of her paint stripped off, you could see up into her cabin from outside the boat. This was a frightening but exhilarating experience which caused *Tranquility* to revert to an inanimate object. *This thing really is just a bunch of pieces of wood!* I said to myself one day, having never thought of her in those terms before. Seeing my boat shorn of everything that made her semi-impermeable laid her inherent vulnerability bare for the first time. This impressed upon me the need for attention to detail during the caulking process and her nakedness became an empowering point of no-return for us. We needed each other.

   "I need a boat to sail to California in *Tranquility*...Do *you* need someone to put you all back together again?" I asked her late one night in my perviest stage voice. You know what was really weird and that I didn't figure out for two more years? There wasn't any sand in her seams when

I reefed them. I was far too busy to take note of *that* important tidbit at the time though.

About ten days into the job, and still forsaking Les, I pulled the four coaster-sized lead patches off the hull and yanked what was left of the engine bolts out of the planks with a claw hammer. The nuts and washers were frozen to the threads under a cake of wet rust. Bolting down an inboard engine *through* a hull? Unheard of! I filled all four holes with thickened epoxy and plugged them inside and out with wood bungs just as Les said. This easy fix brought absolute closure to a question that had been nagging me day and night for a year. *What's up with those sketchy bolts in the engine compartment?* CASE CLOSED! High on newfound confidence, I went to a Ballard woodshop and had a dude rip me fifty card-thin fir laths and I used them to resize the over-wide seams I came across while reefing.

It only took me a day.

The next morning I found a note taped to *Tranquility*'s stern which read, simply: *Will you please call me?* The note had to be from Les. He was probably ticked off at me for going it alone. *What if I did something really bad to the boat already?* If I was in trouble I was going to find out about it sooner or later. So, fearing the worst, I went to the payphone by the office and dialed the number on the note. The man who picked up wasn't Les.

"Uh...this is the person with the little green sailboat in Ballard."

"So you're the guy who owns *Mar-Jac* now?!"

"*Mar-Jac?*"

"Margie-and-Jack! Ha Ha Ha! Get it? So how's she doing these days?"

"She's hurtin' real bad mister."

"Yeah, I saw that...but she's a really great boat!"

"You don't say...?"

Margie and Jack owned *Tranquility* long before Buddy's time and according to Jack, she never leaked a drop. They cruised her "hard" too. They'd even been all the way to Sidney in her (not *that* Sidney, the Sidney just across the border in British Columbia). She sailed like a dream on that voyage. Closer to home, she'd won yacht club races. The Albin never even hiccupped while they owned her. It was an old boat story full of all the usual BS. Jack told me she was a Canadian, and was built entirely out of white pine on a Victoria beach in '38.

McKenzie designed her. No wait –it was Mencken...or was it Mennen? After talking with Jack a little more, I realized the only thing anyone agreed on was that *Tranquility* had been built somewhere in the Pacific Northwest in 1938. The vessel I knew as *Tranquility* was an elderly local and that was her entire story. No pedigree, no known heirs, no sisterships –just her, and other than her oak frames and mahogany house, she may as well have been built out of *booga booga* wood for all anyone knew.

After hanging up with Jack, I called Les and gave him the rundown. He sounded stressed but enthusiastic and said he would drop by the next day. When Les saw *Tranquility* the following afternoon, he walked around her with a look on his face that made me uneasy. Without so much as a nod my way or a word of greeting, Les went up to the boat, dropped his canvas tool bag next to the rudder and walked around her a few times with his hands in the front pockets of his filthy overalls. A long-dead hand-rolled cigarette was stuck to his lower lip and every so often, Les adjusted it with his tongue as he slid a wedge of wood, taken from his bib pocket, into *Tranquility*'s re-sized seams. When he pulled the wedge out, he did it smartly with one eye shut and a slight cock of his head. *Was he satisfied or angry?* I couldn't tell. Brushing past me with a faint "howdy," Les ranged far and wide along the hull, prying on the planks I'd refastened, with a little black crowbar. I walked behind him, coming in close and tight over his shoulder when he leaned in and jumping back when he moved on. I shadowed him when he palpated the hull with a small rubber mallet and his big calloused palms. What he was feeling for or hearing in the percussions was a mystery to me. After banging around the hull a couple of times, Les took a few steps back to mull the scene from afar. Les shook his head then glanced at me, the ground and the hull. Me, ground, hull. Then he spoke:

"Used those fir strips over there to resize her seams did ya?" he asked me with a rhetorical edge in his voice, nodding at the small stack of leftover laths lying next to the workbench.

I had done so.

"Took her down to her skivvies with something powerful didn't you?"

I did.

He spat. *He spat!*

"Yeah, I've been pretty busy," I said, copping to it all with a woeful nod.

Les looked away for a moment and bobbed his head around in little yes-no-yes-no circles. *He's angry!* I took a step away from him. *Is Les the type of guy to take a swing at somebody? Would he yell? Or is he the kind to walk off?* Who knew? Les relit his smoke, assumed a contrapposto and after a few thoughtful puffs at that sour, smudgy roach, he roundly declared *Tranquility* ready for corking!!

"I can't *believe* how much you've accomplished here!" he said, taking new measure of me up and down. Although Les assured me there was no need to remove *all* of the caulking and bottom paint from *Tranquility*'s hull, he understood my reasons for doing so and commended my thoroughness. Phase two of *Tranquility*'s rebuild got underway when Les tamped several inches of cotton braid into one of her seams while I stood behind him looking on gravely.

"Hear how this sounds flat and hollow at first?" he asked as he tapped the iron; it went *pat-pat-pat.* "But then it starts to resonate in the hull?"–*pink-pink-pink*–"Hear how this sounds good and tight?"–*prink-prink-prink*–"But then this sounds a bit too tight?" The mallet, iron and hull went *creek-creek-creek* as Les struck the iron too long and too hard. "Do you hear that?" I heard it alright.

I'd been hearing a lot from the tradesmen down on the water that year. Jeffery the metal worker and Pam the painter. Kim who sewed canvas and Kelley who knew diesels. They appeared out of nowhere and got right to work. They set their price and there was no leaning on them, no moving the goalposts around, no telling them how to do their job or who was in charge. I was a nobody, yet even I had to find a sawyer, a good Ballard Hardware man, a shipwright, a rigger and a trucker in a month. It wasn't easy and they all had precious little time for the likes of me. But wait just a second. We actually *need* tradesmen and blue-collar know-how in our troubled country? You don't say? I thought they were the ones who wouldn't amount to anything without an embossed permission slip from a diploma mill? This is an ignorant, tenderfoot misconception that has been absorbed and disseminated by the cult of college, and to some extent by the workers themselves. Is it possible that our nation can't do without people who know which end of a hammer is the business end? Do we need that sort of primary productivity? I thought the bankers were going to keep printing money from the scent of effort left lingering in the air after someone else worked! I thought twenty-year-old millionaire hackers, tapping spacebars and arrow keys, earning extra lives and medicines and knives in the middle of the workday were going to keep things running smoothly around here! Or did npr get that wrong too? What's the probable outcome of an economy and lifestyle that are no longer object oriented? *Tranquility* was sixty years old and she was still serving her intended purpose. How much of what you own will still be around sixty years from now?

Knock-Knock...hello-there numbskulls! How insubstantial and sleazy did the new economy turn out to be? How irresponsible its murengers? Is the template for what's to come going to be that web-phenom? The one valued at 18 billion dollars? The one with 10,000 employees? The one that went public with no products *and* no profits? You know, the one that "made" 60 million dollars in 2010 but spent 420 million doing it? Imagine if your grandmother's refrigerator, a tractor or a freight train were as unreliable as the plastic, landfill garbage turned out by the current generation of magnates. Bravo! You can't outsource your dignity, mighty nation, but you're giving it a good try!

Les stood over me as I tamped the rest of the first braid of cotton into the seam. One pass was too loose and the next was too tight. I drove a long length into the cabin without realizing it and had to begin again. On the next go-round the braid fell off my lap and picked up little splinters and sharp curls of drilled metal from the ground. When I thought I was done, I had to pull it all out and start anew with a clean length. Les watched closely all the while, offering tips and advice. When I made it down an entire seam without err, Les put his hand on my shoulder: "That's what good corking should sound and feel like...if it stops, you stop and figure out what went wrong."

I could work on my own now. It wasn't total free reign of course. I was to call Les if I had any doubts or questions along the way. Then, in an astounding gesture of confidence, Les loaned me a few of his personal caulking irons and a well-used mallet. The loan of the tools was an unqualified approval that left me speechless. When Les made a few signs that his workday was not quite over, I followed him back to his truck, waiting for the right moment to affirm my debt to him, but in the subtly evasive way that working men sometimes do, he left no opening for that sort of talk. However, I was duty-bound to set aside his friendly demeanor and recognize his generosity in the terms originally set forth. When I asked Les what I owed him for the day, all he said was: "It's nice to see a young person actually doing something with a boat down here."

When I accepted that caulking a hull was not a matter of certainty in the way I was used to from working around internal combustion engines, but one of art, I warmed to the job that lay before me. I came to relish the backbreaking, rarefied nature of that ancient marine sub-specialty and I enjoyed the physical pain it took to learn it. I slaved happily for days on the heat-sinking macadam beneath *Tranquility*. I started caulking early in the morning when the air was cool and no one was around. The mallet and iron went *prink-prink-prink* but at that hour I was the only one to hear it. I worked all morning as the yard came to life and I took no breaks other than a few minutes at lunch. Then I worked right through the afternoon with the sun searing my back and neck until dusk. I sat contorted, on a tippy metal pail and let the edge of it dig into my buns when a cushion lay in the cockpit. I worked for hours with debris falling in my eyes and sweat dripping from my brow. I tapped the iron with the mallet just-so, negotiating difficult angles, driving the braided cotton into the seams, back and forth along the underside of the hull. It was a body-burning overhead hell from keel-to-waterline I tell you! But when the work was really flowing, the mallet let out a rhythmic, hollow-squeaky resonance that echoed through the boatyard and was kind on everyone's ears. Though one uses their entire body to caulk, one must hear it in the hull and feel it in their hands to know if it's being done right. A poor caulking job does not necessarily result in a leaky boat, however. Obviously, if the cotton is not driven far enough into the seams a vessel will make water (leak). But the true danger of improper caulking lies in driving the cotton into the seams too *tightly*. If this happens, there will no longer be a boat to have a leak in. After several weeks on the hard, the planking of a wooden boat will have dried out and shrunk considerably. If no allowance is made during caulking for the uptake of water when a boat is re-launched, the planks can't return to their normal, saturated dimensions. Enormous osmotic pressure is exerted outward when wood absorbs water, and if the caulking is too tight in the seams, the expanding planks will drive into each other until the fasteners fail and the planks pull away from the ribs. A single sprung plank would sink *Tranquility* in a minute or two. That possibility was never far from my mind as I worked.

People have been caulking ships for centuries. The various rules-of-thumb for doing it correctly, were discovered long ago and passed on to future generations. It's a job you cannot want to finish. You must do it methodically, without rushing and without desire. It's just you, the mallet, the iron and the hull, with a never-ending cotton braid in your lap driving into a never-ending seam. There's always too much before you and too little in your wake. At the end of one seam, there is another and another and another after that, with no end in sight –the first is just as tedious as the last. Caulking is one of *those* jobs. The focus and physical demand of my ancient task crossed a hard look into my eyes that erased what was left of the child in me. It drew a stern expression on my face as I neared the end of the work and it stayed there, insuring no one would ever call me kid again.

I was sleeping in the van every night and living under *Tranquility* during the day, so I had no access to a proper shower. Instead, I would sneak down to Salmon Bay with a towel and a bar of pumice soap after the boatyard closed and take a delicious, lacustrine bath in the cool mossy shallows under the sun-warmed creosote docks. I could tell from the water temperature it was going to be a beautiful summer and I was really looking forward to enjoying it on my new *seaworthy* boat. *Patience my boy...patience!*

I remember one particularly pleasant evening as I came to the final days of corking. I washed in the bay as usual, but instead of hitting the sack, I wandered into Old Ballard looking for a cold beer and a little socializing. When I stepped through the door of the first pub I came to, I found an Irish trio up on a small stage pulling away on a lusty sea shanty. The place was sparsely populated at that early hour, but the interior was warm, low-lit and mellow. It drew me in. The decor was salty but uncontrived, with a few tastefully framed 18th century marine lithographs hung here and there on the red brick walls. High in the rafters, out of sight and possibly long forgotten, were a thick coil of sisal line and a sooty hurricane lantern –some of the original owner's booty no doubt. A genuine ship's wheel stood in a corner as if it were being stored there and not on display. I was bewitched the moment I walked in the place and the music washed over me like a marvelous water. I took an amber from the barkeep with a nod and sat down on a long, rough-hewn wooden bench next to a couple my age. When I had a pint or two in me a steady stream of young folks began to gather in our corner of the room. Benches and chairs were scooted around and stranger's limbs touched as people made themselves comfortable at the crowded tables. The lights dimmed, the candles were lit, and the place filled up to capacity with my people. It was sea shanty night at Conor Byrne.

I was thoroughly enjoying myself to the thrumming music which was laden with fiddle tune, guitar and drum, and all sorts of *avast-ye* and *bowse 'er down lads! why don't ye bowse 'er down?* lyrics when all of a sudden there was a little gesture and jostle on my right. When I looked that way, the finest young blond lass of the bunch slid over to my side and gently hooked her slender arm through mine in perfect time to the music. We turned and smiled at each other and danced a little arm-in-arm jig sitting on our bench. We got up and danced, sat down and drank, then got up and danced some more. We posted up on our bench for a while and my right arm slid around her small waist at the perfect moment. Her bare calf leaned against mine and didn't pull away. We made eyes at each other and to those around our table. We drank some more and danced some more and then, when we were well into our cups, but respectfully so, we got carried away and our lips touched, just once and only very softly.

"Are you hearing it yet?" Les asked me in a wise old tone, on the phone the next day.

"Yeah, I'm definitely hearing it."

"When do you need to be on your way?"

"Late June."

"You'll make it."

By and by it came time to paint and pay *Tranquility*'s seams, so I purchased five gallons of copper paint and a half-case of seam compound. Les showed up and said he really liked how the corking looked. He even tamped the length of a few seams with his personal mallet and iron to double check. There was absolutely no doubt about it. He said I was ready. When I returned Les' mallet and irons to him he said: "Good job young man, you can cork with me anytime." *I'm a young man now*, I thought to myself for the first time in my life. *I'm a young man!* I liked how that sounded and it became a new identity for me. But it wasn't time to celebrate yet, it was time to paint and pay. *Paint and pay*, that sort of talk reminded me that I owed Les a bundle of money. But before I had a chance to ask him what the damage was, he said: "Why don't you just give me a hundred bucks?" When Les took the bill from my hand he added: "Frederick Douglas was a caulker, you know?" I had not known that.

I painted and payed *Tranquility's* seams for three long days. I could have sped things up with modern technology at that point but I had to be certain everything was just-so and by-the-book. That meant doing it by touch and feel. It all had to be done by hand and there were a few ghouls lurking around the yard to remind me of what was at stake. There were old hulks far worse off than mine scattered around the place. There were sailboats with rotten seams attesting to half-done corking jobs left in permanent holding patterns. The more abject cases were loosely tarped, had lean-tos built against them, with radios playing somewhere inside. These specters were contrasted by well-heeled projects draped in sodden burlap sacks to ward off desiccation while their owners were far away earning their expensive keep. There were piles of sawn up planking and hull-bereft iron keels sitting on blocks waiting to be sold for scrap. They were so many body bags to a merman and indicated where boats had been abandoned or destroyed by the boatyard for back rent. I never wanted to come to that place again, so I took my time painting and paying the seams.

Everyone I spoke to before, during and after the caulking job told me not to worry when *Tranquility* leaked for a day or two after she returned to the water. She would not be *bottle* tight they said, until her planks swelled up with water again and that takes some time when a wooden boat has sat on the hard, drying out for over a month. Les told me, the yard foreman told me, complete strangers passing by the boatyard told me: "She'll leak on you for a day or two until she swells up." From Garibaldi, Oregon to Ballard, Washington kindly old boatmen and infants in strollers asked for a moment of my time so they too could let me know: *She'll definitely leak.*

I asked all of these people an obvious question: "If she leaks, how will I know if I did a good job corking her?"

But all Les or anyone else would say was: "You'll know in a few days."

Instead of dreading launch day I took a proactive approach with a pot of sealant and a putty knife. I went around and around the boat one afternoon troweling a thick sealant into every anomaly and check in the hull while muttering to myself: "Dooont-cha know every voodun boat leak ven she launch?"–*Oh, you don't say?*–"Well gramps, that's where you're wrong. Every voodun boat leak except *this* voodun boat." As a further precaution against such leaks I painted *Tranquility*'s topsides and boot stripe to allow ample time for the various paints and sealants to fully adhere below the waterline. When everything was dry, I applied six or seven coats of premium copper bottom paint to the hull. This was an expensive coat of paint and was so thickly applied, you could barely make out the seams when I was done slathering it on.

The next day I prepped the mortise in the keelson with red lead so it was ready to receive the tenon at the butt end of the mast. While I was working, I found a 1972 silver dollar set in a circular depression cut in the mortise. For good luck, sailors place a coin under a mast before they step it, and since 1972 was my birth year, the coin was an incredibly good omen and I knew it meant I'd done everything right. I knew it meant the leak was fixed. How good was *Tranquility* looking when I stepped her mast? Dear reader, she looked like new. Her bottom was as smooth as if it were dipped in red plastic. Her boot stripe was perfectly straight and her hull sported a mirror finish of dark green marine enamel. Fellow boaters on haul-out, yard workers and shipwrights dropped by to congratulate me on a job well-done. A yardman dropped by, shook my hand and offered me a smoke.

"You know how many times I've seen a boat like yours come into this place?" he asked. "You know how many of them made it out of here in one piece?" The yardman held up a battered workman's index finger.

Tranquility returned to Salmon Bay on a June evening one year into the voyage. It wasn't the *Bon Voyage* I expected though, because there was a final step I hadn't known about until the last minute. When you launch a dried-out wooden boat you must support her in the water for several hours so she doesn't sink while her hull is soaking up water. So instead of shoving off, *Tranquility* spent her first night in the bay held in the embrace of gantry slings. I was sitting in the cockpit when her keel touched water for the first time, and by the sound of things below deck I knew everyone had been right. But *how* she leaked! As soon as she was afloat her bilges filled to the waterline like a sieve set in a sink. *Showers* of water shot into the engine compartment from all four spots where the patches had covered the engine bolts!! The ring nails that held the sheet lead in place were half-a-millimeter too long and plunged through the hull ever-so-slightly when the patches were first put on. I yanked those nails out when I filled the bolt holes, but how could I have known they were too long? There were a couple hundred holes and each shot a thin stream of water into the boat so that the engine compartment looked like it had a four-jet spectacle fountain running wide-open in that dark and mostly inaccessible space. Heart-rending fear tore through me when I saw them and I went into a full-throttle panic. But wait, what's that? What *is* that?! I cocked my head to listen. Is that a far more serious gushing sound? Is it coming from somewhere on the port side? The old galley sink valve has been opened? *But when and why and how?* A two-inch round column of water was flowing freely under the port bunk filling stove burner, pots and pans. I tore up the bed-board and spun the valve closed.

And what in god's name is that smell? *From where, and why and how?* I wretched while considering likely sources. It was a gagger of the rankest, most fecund sort and I guessed it came from the floating carcass of a small mammal that was trapped in the hull weeks ago. No, it wasn't a lost tabby or a warren of dead rats. It was a wretched, eye-watering cardboard crate-full of burst chicken eggs, found and inseminated by the flies, but forgotten by me since I bought them in Garibaldi! Crate and all jettisoned in an instant followed by a chunky stream of bitter vomit.

Putting out fires left and right, I hammered short ring nails into all the spouts I could get to. I was having Desdemona Sands flashbacks as night fell on that urgent launch day scene and I imagined with great fear, sadness and shame what an immediate return to the boatyard in the morning would mean for the summer to come and my life in general. But it was all just drama and first-float nerves. *Tranquility* was making much less water the next morning and she was freed from the slings with a push from the yard foreman. Taking no chances, I motored *Tranquility* across the channel and into Fisherman's Terminal with both bilge pumps going and my heart leaping in my chest. Alongside the wharf, I threw four heavy lines over *Tranquility*'s deck and trussed them up under her keel. I made the lines fast along the dock at regular intervals just in case she thought she might have a little sink on me to be cute. I walked to the top of the ramp on unsteady legs and sat down at the harborside diner for breakfast: sausage, potatoes, biscuits & gravy with coffee. No thank you ma'am, no eggs for me today! Twenty-four hours later, *Tranquility* had swollen up enough that I felt comfortable leaving her on her own while I ran around town making final preparations for the third leg.

My second departure from Seattle was not what it should have been! The outboard had taken a long swim in the brackish waters of the Tillamook and although I had it running the day after *Tranquility* was launched, it gave up the ghost the morning I planned to shove off. Instead of fetching a brand new engine, which I could have afforded, I spent three gloriously sunny days trying to reanimate the 18. I finally tossed it in a dumpster and purchased a used 15-horse. Once I had that running, I motored directly to the Ballard Locks. The locking procedure did not go smoothly that day. I entered the small lock slowly and with great care for my new boat, but I was out of practice and the current from the lake sent me wonky. When I dropped the motor in reverse, the stern kicked away from the wall and I couldn't get a line on it. I failed on the second try and almost fell off the back of the boat. After some yelling and confusion with the lock attendants, my stern line was passed over the bollard on the third try. It was a frustrating drill which left me hot-faced and exasperated when I should have been celebrating on my little gem of a yacht. The other vessels entered at their turns and tied up along the wall singly or in pairs. The lake doors closed and we descended to sea level as usual. When the sea doors opened, the boats in the chamber drove ahead on their lines and slewed around as they do while the saltwater mixes with the fresh. Once underway, *Tranquility*, perhaps sensing an opportunity for a funny accident, went askew in the swirling current and sheered to starboard. I dashed forward to push her off the wall, then hustled aft to steer her away, but some trick of the current kept her wrong-headed. A tourist laughed at me from above and I almost said something to him.

I have celebrated my own ineptitude when appropriate, but none of this was my doing for once! I alternately fussed with the boat hook and the engine but she would not keep away from the wall. Hoping for a little pull, I heaved a line up to the lock attendant standing high above me on the seawall. I'll have you know that a Sea Scout is an expert line heaver; throwing a line to someone without it tangling and falling short is one of the first things I learned to do on a boat and I'm good at it. After making eye contact with the attendant directly above me, I split the coil of line in my hand and heaved it up to him. But it wasn't caught! Even though it draped over the crook of the attendant's arm as if it were a coat I handed him –he dropped it! I instantly re-coiled and threw it right back at him. Neptune as my witness, the last five feet of that line landed on the walkway before him like a perfectly cast fly tippet. But could he get to it in time? No. *Of course not.* It simply couldn't be done! The line snaked into the water like a strand of overdone spaghetti just as he reached his foot out to step on it.

My knowledge of boats is neither extensive nor poor. I only know what little I know of them from watching their behavior closely. I know it is in the nature of all boats to founder or otherwise come to accident someday. I know the tendency of boats toward mishap is greatly magnified by water, which is a substance whose dangers cannot possibly be overstated. I accept all of this and I'm almost willing to live with it. But what law states that a line shall catch and make itself fast to every cleat, cabin corner and fitting on a boat when it is merely being carried from one end of the vessel to the other? Or kink and stop itself up when it's being pulled through a turning block or along a deck? Is it the same law which holds that any line, whether it will save a dinghy or a ship full of men from disaster, shall, when thrown to something vital, snake into the water passing up a hundred opportunities to be caught –whether in a man's hand, on a cleat or around a dock piling? If it is, and I am certain it is; why? What is it about a boat? I say it's their shape. They are a round peg in a square world. Drop something in one, and marvel at how fast it finds its way into the bilge or over the side.

If the devil exists, I'm sure he travels by boat.

I was quietly fuming as I steered my new boat around in the current and got her headed for Puget Sound. By the time I had *Tranquility*'s fuel and water tanks filled and her lines sorted out from weeks of disarray and sitting idle, it was late afternoon. When I finally set sail that day, there was a stout northwesterly blowing down the sound. The tide was a big one and as usual in those waters, it was flooding against me instead of helping me on my way north. I wasn't in any mood to wait for a change in conditions though, so I pounded into Puget Sound steering west with a little dash of south in it to make things interesting. The irony of the moment was not lost on me! Is it lost on you? I'd been sailing in the exact location in the exact conditions on the very first day of my voyage. As the new and improved *Tranquility* labored against the unfavorable wind and tide that day, I couldn't help but reflect on certain dark things that had happened to me over the course of that unforgettable year. I couldn't believe I was still in Puget Sound! I couldn't believe I was still trying to sail to California –one year later!

Even when *Tranquility* was sailing at her very best she didn't perform all that well. She did not like to go to weather except in the most favorable conditions. She was no svelte 1930s club racer! Ha! Ha! Ha! *NOPE!* She was a sow, a cow, a barge, a candle box and a scow. She was an orphan, a widow, a harridan and a tub. She liked to sail on her ear, to wallow, to go nowhere with an immense, halting effort. She was a stubborn, rooting sort of sailboat, she had the most awful weather helm, yet she often refused to tack! She could be half-full of seawater but you'd hardly know it from how poorly she handled when she was bone dry! If she was making three-and-a-half knots to weather with the biggest tide of the year behind her, she had a bone in her teeth! Still, something seemed particularly odd in her handling as we neared Bainbridge Island on the first day of the third leg of our grand voyage. In the chop running along the eastern shore of the island *Tranquility* began hobby-horsing like never before. Her mainsail and genoa were flapping, making the sound of a twin-rotor chopper hovering overhead. Though there were some small whitecaps kicking up to windward, she was laboring unusually hard for the conditions. *Tranquility* just couldn't seem to get on her feet. She was *in a hole* as they say. *Or was she trying to tell me something?* I looked aft expecting to see a gillnet or log boom trailing astern but my reptilian brain must have already known what the matter was, because I involuntarily slid the companionway hatch open just as my conscious mind was dismissing the possibility that *Tranquility* could actually be full of water. There are at least thirty areas in the human brain that process visual information, and when I peered into the cabin that day, every one of those neural regions simultaneously registered a single, unthinkable, shocking image: *Tranquility* was full of seawater. *Again.*

To be more precise, I saw seawater in the cabin that day and then I did not see it. All was well for an instant –I was only dreaming! I thought I saw something watery down in there but I could not have, for it was too terrible a thing to see. I blinked into the northwest wind for a moment and then a much harder man looked into the cabin of my boat. A foot or so of saltwater was sloshing around in there. The bilge boards were afloat and banging around the bunks in their usual manner. Some part of my brain informed the rest of my being of something that I didn't see coming, something that wasn't at all as apparent as it should have been: somehow, after a year of Herculean effort, I had the exact same boat, in the exact same place as the one I set sail in. No better. No worse.

The same. Those are very difficult words to write, as I'm sure they are to read –but just imagine for a moment how much worse it was to live them!

Dear reader, we've come a long way together but try to put yourself in my shoes for a moment. What on earth could I have possibly done wrong in my work? Nothing, I'd done everything right. If bad things happen to you whether or not you take precautions against them, what do you *do*? How do you know when a dream is impossible or just incredibly difficult to realize? When you arrive at a moment like that in life, and I'm sure you never will, there really are only two ways you can respond: you can hope, or you can despair. I chose hope, but it took a few minutes for my spirit to catch up to my mind and body.

Tranquility's mysterious leak took a toll on my psyche that continues to this day. The gravity of the situation seemed to require that I contemplate my newest and most inexplicable maritime loss from every psychological and financial angle I could think of. I'd bailed her back from the brink more than once and spent many sunnier, would-be happy days at the dock sponging the dank and poky bilge, searching in vain for *Tranquility*'s leak. I'd earnestly sought out old boatmen and wharf lingerers giving my all to the role of young-sailor-looking-for-advice from the lovable rogues mending nets on the hard. I was careful to give their varied opinions equal time and weight, knowing that *Tranquility*'s fickle spirit would not be reformed by any one approach. With all of the scientific disinterest I could muster, I formally researched common causes and remedies for leaky wooden boats, pretending, just in case there was an *actual* curse on *Tranquility*, that I did not have a boat but was only wondering what might cause a leak in a sailboat of a certain age if I did. I convinced myself that if man had built the boat, then man could fix the boat. But deep down, I think I knew *Tranquility* didn't *want* to be fixed.

Of course, the scale of my failure was even greater in adjusted terms. Due to the many groundings I put *Tranquility* through, she leaked more now than when I sailed for Bainbridge Island with my very first cargo of seawater. And my improvements to her interior in Portland? And my handiwork in St. Helens? Like the voyage to California itself, over the past twelve months, I'd lost ground with the vessel I planned to sail there. After a year of all-out effort, *Tranquility* was worse off as a boat than she was the day I bought her. And I still had the entire voyage ahead of me! Sitting there in the cockpit of my sinking boat, my mind reeled as the scale of the disaster ebbed and flowed within me. I should have left *Tranquility* in Tillamook Bay. I should have never bought her. I should have never left Seattle at all. After an entire year, how could it be that I was still in Puget Sound? I honestly thought I was dreaming –or maybe I was going crazy? *Was* I in Puget Sound? I swear, I had to take a second look.

Although there were many contenders, the mysterious leak and the time I wasted on it became the cruelest mental torture of that luckless voyage. I was shaken to my core by the ordeal and a time when I could laugh at the senselessness of it all never came. I learned something valuable from the experience though: a curse of that magnitude is a metaphysical affliction which is beyond the reach of logic or reason. *Tranquility* suffered under a malicious spell that would never be broken; it could only be steered clear of or lived with. When I saw seawater sloshing gaily around the cabin that afternoon, as if it missed being there, as if *Tranquility* missed it being there, I understood once-and-for-all that whatever was wrong with *Tranquility*, it existed in a realm beyond human intervention. I peered into my future and knew that in a lifetime, I might never repair her, for she always had been, and always would be, a wreck of a ship. I knew I had to stop trying to make *Tranquility* a better boat and I resolved to live with my troubled vessel the way she was. I was mentally and physically exhausted and although she was flawed, she was the only boat I had. Fate gave me a vessel that did not care for frippery such as varnish, paint or caulking and she sabotaged every humble gift I tried to give her. So why keep trying?

I did have to suppress—with great self-control—a little psycho urge to head for the nearest boatyard to cork her all over again and make every inch of her my life's work with a pure and righteous spite. If she *still* leaked, I would take every last stick of her apart and rebuild her from shoe to crane until she was velvet-pillow perfect. Instead, I devised a new boating philosophy which, for the most part, was successful and one I adhere to today: *The Art of Not Doing*. Although I would cruise essentially nonstop for the next fifteen years and sail all of the water between Southern California and the Aleutian Islands, it would be nearly a decade before I dipped a brush in a tin of varnish or painted a boot stripe on a hull –even then I did it ironically. From that point on, I dispensed with every single article of the yachtsman's life and I looked upon fake gold braid, plastic doodads and topsiders with a fallowing disdain. I found out that paint was a protective coating, not makeup and a boat became a tool to me, no different than a hammer or a saw and cared for in the same manner. I could love her and need her, but she did not have to be pretty. She needed to be functional, comfortable, strong and safe.

Instead of spending another minute on a vessel's appearance, I focused on the essential nature of the boats I owned. I wore the heavy leather shoes, the dirty canvas work pants and the coarse wool sweaters. In the coming years, I would learn the trade of the marlinspike, marine engineer, electrician, sawyer, shipwright and rigger. I hired nothing out except on the rare occasion I was terribly pressed for time or did not need my own 240 volt TIG welder –although I seriously considered it at the time. I did all my own wire splicing, sail and canvas work, surveys, joinery, machinery and electrical repair. I tried to master every job there was on a modern sailboat and then some. I spent every dime I had on boats, sailed a floating chandlery and repaired vessels for people stranded in lonely anchorages. I sold spare anchor gear and other essentials to weekend yachtsmen in sailing magazine distress. Because I started sailing at what seemed to me like human-year-zero, I had the unique opportunity to become a seaman through direct contact. I learned that a hull must be sound by having an unsound hull. I learned that ground tackle must be robust by climbing through a vessel that dragged ashore and was wrecked. I learned that a compass must be properly swung from getting lost and nearly paying for it with my life. I learned that you must always know your position from running aground. Over the coming years I would be dismasted and driven to shore with three anchors out in a Haida Gwaii hurricane. I sailed in or hove-to in countless gales. I furled frozen canvas in lee shore snowstorms, blew out a score of sails and was knocked down. I nearly pitchpoled my yawl *twice*, I stove a hull, one was flooded, one boat abandoned and then salvaged. I miraculously survived an engine-room explosion and endured all of the other weekend troubles so crowed about and celebrated in the pages of sailing magazines by indignant novices.

Tranquility taught me well the first year I owned her and I *never ever* looked outside myself or my vessel for assistance again, nor did I blame "uncharted rocks, gear failures or untrained crew" for my shortcomings as a captain. I took full responsibility for any mishap on my boat, and if something couldn't be handled by myself or my crew with what was on hand then that was tough luck for all of us. I entertained no whining and no weakness. Life is hard, life on the sea is much harder, so you must be too.

My life changed when I saw the bilge brimming with seawater that day. Instead of getting angry, I pumped my vessel dry and sailed her directly to Neah Bay in a profound, stoic silence. A movie, song or book can change a life, but when I say my life changed that day, I mean I turned into someone else, because when I corked *Tranquility*, I wasn't just working on her. I took out *my* gizmo and tinkered with it. I retied *my* knot, fooled around with *my* formula. If you're unhappy with the results after you do something like that, it's too late to do anything about it, because your old parts won't fit together with the new ones. The fact that I did not fix *Tranquility*'s leak that summer was a deep and complex wound but I can't say exactly where the wound was or if it ever healed. As it turned out, the caulking debacle was the last monumental defeat of the voyage and although I didn't know it, my life was about to head in a new direction. That summer, and this story, was fated to end with a smile not a sigh.

21

One morning, not long after arriving in Neah Bay, I awoke to the west wind playing an eerie open-string tune on the taut mono-filament line strung in my fishing rod up on deck. It plucked and hummed like a zither in the misty sea breeze stirring around Waadah Island, it led *Tranquility* around the overcast anchorage in big lazy circles, fouling her hook in her own anchor line. It began to drizzle then rain. It was the rain that wets. I spent the morning bundled up and morose in *Tranquility*'s cabin. I wanted to get out of bed and make coffee but I lay inert in my bunk instead, staring up at the deck beams wondering what I was doing with my life and where it all might lead. Over the past few days I'd been shivering in the husky winds and lasting fogs that pay visit to the northwestern tip of the Olympic Peninsula year-round. From all signs it looked as if the summer would be one of false starts, rain gear and cold toes –things better suited to winter than carefree enjoyment of sea and sun. On shore, I'd fallen into a dead-end pattern of shopping for what I convinced myself were last minute items and wondering what constituted a favorable weather window in which to begin my offshore passage anew. After a few dull and aimless days spent waiting for the sky to clear and the wind to blow from the northwest according to script, the urgency to be on my way south ebbed. The elements weren't cooperating and my mood was following the ups and downs of the weather a little too closely. It was more than that though, something wasn't right with me and I could no longer ignore the fact there was something seriously amiss with *Tranquility*. The old uncertainties were finally gaining on my resolve to continue and I realized my heart was no longer in the voyage as originally conceived. *How could it be?* I was as far as ever from my destination, and in the few hundred miles I had covered, I got myself into more trouble than my harshest critics ever dreamed of. Would they have wanted so many bad things to happen to such an optimistic young man? Drowning would have been *so* much easier.

I eventually shook off my torpor, put the kettle on and tried flipping through my charts for inspiration. When I looked through the folio of the North Pacific Ocean and saw all of the water between Neah Bay and the Channel Islands, I couldn't help but wonder what new misfortunes awaited me in year two of my three-week voyage. I'd barely touched on the famously treacherous and desolate Oregon Coast, not to mention the ill-tempered capes of Northern California. And of course, I had *The Graveyard of the Pacific* to contend with all over again. When I unrolled the chart I navigated on the previous summer, it was clear from the crisp little pencil ticks on it that the failures and disappointments of my first leg were way too fresh to be reliving. The tiny crosses, time stamps and question marks tracked my Pacific offing in a parabola that bent boldly west and south from Cape Flattery before curving prematurely back to land. One mark I made the previous summer seemed to say it all. This was the X I'd drawn in the shallows just west of Willapa Bay. An electric fear shot through me when I saw it and I asked myself if I could bounce back from another failed attempt at the voyage. It didn't seem likely.

See and hear that unforgiving, heavily broken Pacific Northwest coast for a moment. Watch the endless white breakers roll to shore from misty horizon to misty horizon. Feel the damp air, hanging cold and heavy in the fog-bound conifers. Picture the slick rocks and booming tide pool grottoes crowded with thick mussel beds and leathery kelp fronds. Imagine the sea surging in and around them, scouring, unbuilding, erasing all trace of itself. Consider the infinite energy that sculpts blocks of subduction basalt into leaning swoops and piles twenty-foot logs like twigs on iron-bound beaches or chews them like toothpicks in the dripping maws of sea caves. Wallow along the jagged rocks in a narrow wooden boat, pitching and rolling in waves reflecting off skiey cliffs with your hopes hung on the fickle will of the wayfaring wind. Would you expect to be treated kindly by a tornado or an earthquake? If the span of a human life is so little compared to the prospects of a six-inch fir tree sprouting in the forest, then what do you suppose it means to the eternal sea, where all life came from? There's nothing Zen in losing your ship or yourself.

And that, dear reader, was the moment I gave up on the voyage. *For the time being.*

Instead of pretending to bravely set sail on a manifestly unsafe voyage that day, I read in my bunk, went on a long row and made a big pot of stew for dinner. I even drank a dram before hitting the sack. When I awoke early the next morning I was filled with the exhilarating conviction that I should enjoy my life where *Tranquility* and I were, rather than spend another minute trying to sail to some distant imagined paradise. This was a simple, but novel approach to seafaring and it got me living my life day-by-day for the first time since I laid eyes on *Tranquility*. For starters, enjoying myself that summer meant getting the hell out of the lonely, funereal waters of Neah Bay. With that objective in mind, I unrolled my chart of the 48th parallel and looked for a place to go that was well within my capabilities as a mariner. And that, more than any other aspect of my being, was due for a major overhaul. Destinations requiring more than one or two large-scale charts (Large scale: small area, small scale: large area) to sail to were dismissed out of hand and I turned my back on the open ocean.

The new limits I set for myself didn't seem to leave many interesting options for the summer, until my gaze fell upon a group of islands clustered at the northeast corner of one of my charts. These were the San Juan Islands of Washington State, they lie to the north of the Salish Basin. They're an amply-forested archipelago that's rich enough in anchorages and scenery to please world cruisers and amateur boaters alike. One can sail and row and fish and hike and hunt and take in the sunsets all summer long without too much fear of what the weather or sea will do to you. It's the sort of country where people still tend garden in the spring, throw outdoor parties in the summer, put up food in the fall and knit in the winter. Pruners and lumberjacks, artists and musicians all make a decent living there. Community pillars from the old families have been known to give away hundreds of acres to keep them wild and out of the hands of developers. There's sawmills and organic farms, sheep and cattle outfits and a bustling agricultural community. People know about steam engines there and you can buy odd-colored eggs, fresh goat cheese and bundles of hearty kale from roadside stands or coolers set on driveway aprons –just drop your money in the tin can, it's on the honor system. To paint a more complete picture: the San Juan Islands are also a heavily mortgaged frontier for fair-weather homesteaders fresh from misery city and a woo-woo foci for pseudo-metaphysical wanderers, pipe-dreamers and hippy landlord types with blue blood they're trying to leverage and conceal. That's about the worst thing anyone can say about the place, so I decided to sail *Tranquility* there and find a protected bay to drop anchor in for the rest of the summer. I needed to get on with my life more than anything, and I stirred lightheartedly at the thought of it.

I left Neah Bay in my wake on a splendid summer day and as soon as I was on my way, I grew refreshed and almost cheerful. The sea breeze was firmly in the west and blowing in the direction I wanted to go for the first time in memory. So with my spirit lifting higher, I hopped around *Tranquility*'s foredeck and set her sails flying. Once I was clear of land, instead of pushing the tiller away from me to bring the bow into the west, I pulled it and swung the bow east. It was easier than I imagined. With the wind dead-aft, the mainsail and genoa billowed into shape and *Tranquility* took off running wing-and-wing down the Strait of Juan de Fuca with the flood tide helping her on her way. One could only be positive on such a beautiful day, the ocean was a heaving royal blue expanse touched near and far by bright white spume driving down the strait. The sun was shining overhead and the high-flying sea clouds were scudding brilliant sunbeams into the east where they lit the gulls hovering over the dark sand beaches for an instant, before soaring into the green mountains of Vancouver Island and the Olympic Peninsula. It was a perfect day to be on the water and there wasn't another sail in sight.

The conditions picked up as the day wore on and I began to broad reach. I actually enjoyed sailing *Tranquility* that day and she ran off the wind, quartering the six-foot swells at her stern with a pleasant rolling motion. By afternoon, *Tranquility* was reefed down with her skirts hiked up and her sheets eased just-so. We were charging along in the building breeze, yet it only took a light hand on the tiller to keep her on course. *Tranquility* was the perfect little miss and I could do no wrong as her pilot. On a day like that, it seemed as if I could grow to love her yet. Sailing the waters of the Pacific Northwest can be a deep and peaceful experience and although it would take another year for the stress and inconvenience of sailing as a lifestyle to be favorably balanced by its joys, that day was the beginning.

I pursued something until it enslaved me, until I realized the thing was not the thing. That set me free, but I pursued it again. I'd been so dead set on my voyage to California I forgot to live my life! I was in so far over my head I never considered that a pull on the tiller and a change in course would set things straight again. Yet that simple act was what allowed me to be carried on my way by the conditions I'd been struggling against for so long. Instead of sailing west, I sailed east, and my career as a mariner and my outlook on life took a turn for the better. The only thing that changed was the heading of my compass, but an immense, self-imposed burden was instantly lifted from my shoulders because of it. I sailed in confidence that day, not in fear, and I looked forward to my destination rather than dreading the way to it. The elements snapped back into focus as articles of scenery, gone were my illusions of quantum meddling in man's fate and life no longer told me *no*. My youthful optimism, dimmed from so much foolhardy strain, reasserted itself and I began the delicate task of recasting the previous year, not as a mistake, but as an incomparable adventure with all of the romance, drama, fortune and failure a young man should expect from *real* life. I accepted fair-and-square that I hadn't been able to sail *Tranquility* to California and I admitted that most of my critics, whether they were full of wisdom or jealous contempt, had been entirely correct. However, I asked myself if the voyage I ended up taking wasn't just as enriching as sailing to California would have been. Wasn't I bold to leave the safety of the world I knew behind for the sake of a pure adventure? Hadn't I been on a pure adventure? Wasn't that what the whole thing was supposed to be about in the first place? It seemed likely.

It saddened me to learn that many people my age believe the adventure of life is nothing but a bedtime story lived by imaginary characters from long ago, or to hear them say some other time was the best one to live in. They are told this and tell it to themselves, so they do not know *now* is *always*, they do not know they are the meaning of life and they do not know they're only going to find what they've gone looking for. My peers didn't believe you could buy a boat one day and set off on a voyage of your own making the next. They didn't believe you could fetch up somewhere new, and toss your anchor over the side for a week or a month or a year. People I met while knocking around in *Tranquility* often asked me what I was going to do when I returned home, implying that that's where the real trouble would be waiting for me. "Sure," they'd say, "you may be able to sail away now...but what about when you go back to your old life? You must have overlooked something important to be able to do this so freely." If there's no problem, we make one. I have no idea why that is, but it's true. So those were, and still are, pretend worries to me. As I saw it, one absolutely, positively couldn't relive their years of youth, so why obsess about the consequences of living them to their fullest while they're still at hand? Whether you leave the safety of the harbor or not, the ship always sinks and you go down to Davy Jones' Locker with it. So why not untie your lines and set your sails for the unknown in the meantime? The world's problems will be right where you left them when you return —read the front page of a fifty-year-old newspaper if you want proof of that.

And so I ran east looking for what was next in my life. I knew I didn't have as much to work with as I once thought, and I wasn't ready for what I set before myself the previous summer. All of a sudden I was an inexperienced young man with a so-so boat that happened to be on inland waters; I wasn't a world-girding sailor with a ship to match. I wasn't a free spirit; I was troubled, lonely and conflicted. But I was beginning to see that everything was going to be okay again. The weather cooperated and the boat sailed like they do in the movies. I was on the mend and there was much that needed mending.

A couple of days after leaving Neah Bay, I fetched up in a bight that people familiar with the San Juan Islands will know in an instant, for it is home to a tiny, no-frills resort that is a haven for young people. The place is situated on a low wooded cliff that overlooks a large open bay. The main buildings of the resort, which resemble an old Alaska fish cannery, surround a small, narrow cove worn deep into the island it calls home. Far from town and innocent of the corruption and resentment that usually accompany services aimed at tourists, the resort was a low-key operation that catered almost exclusively to quasi-countercultural types on no-budget vacations, so the crowd that frequented the spot in summer was fairly diverse, young and attractive.

The place was quaint at the time, boasting little more than a small clapboard office, a dry goods store and a tiny restaurant which overlooked the cove. It was a mail boat stop and a sportsman's resort back in the day. One of the buildings used to be a post office, one was an outboard motor shop. If you squint, you can still see it. When I was there the facilities were linked by winding footpaths to a couple dozen cabins, a community kitchen and a sauna with a few tastefully-plain cement hot tubs fed by a chatty stream. The property has been a back-to-nature destination for around a hundred years and in its current iteration, the place was a sort of summer camp for adults. Just like real summer camp, once night falls, you better have a light on you or know exactly where you're going because precious few lamps are left lit in that cove.

Tranquility

The hinterland and shore surrounding the resort is a timbered, fairly steep terrain with some narrow pasture land broken up by winding brooks and low fences. Hemlock, alder, fir, and western red cedar are common. The summer vegetation is verdant and lush, but thick and prickly and almost impenetrable. It's peaceful, it's quiet, the natives are friendly and you can gather plump berries and tender nettle in the surrounding area for days without coming to the end of them.

All sorts of sea ducks, geese, gulls and land birds flock to the area throughout the year and it's possible to have real, if fleeting, moments with wildlife. The fishing and shellfish prospects are quite good and the scenery is uniquely captivating, especially if you're a city slicker. Small orchards dot the land, there are no bears, but deer are plentiful. In the fall and other odd times of year, you'll hear the occasional report of a 300 grain rifle cartridge which rolls like thunder over the land. Out in the country though, no one even looks up from their plate at such a sound. Island homes and summer shotgun shacks hide just out of your line of sight and here and there wood smoke can be seen hanging in the air much of the year. Those islands can be truly charming once you settle in a bit and get to know a few of the folks.

That's exactly what I planned to do. So while admitting wrongdoing but not defeat, I dropped my pick in the middle of the bay near the resort and set my mind on pursuing more immediate gratification from sailboat ownership and life in general. The weather turned so splendid after I arrived, I began to forget every familiar woe and temporal concern I ever pretended to have, confirming the axiom: *you're only young once.* It took the slow stillness of the insular countryside less than a week to dilute the frenetic pace of my misguided ego. Before I knew it, the long days of summer were rolling by me under cover of the island effect and I was able to get on with my life in storybook fashion. In the coming weeks and months I was going to learn some valuable things about myself and the limits of my sailorly *savoir faire.* Over the course of the summer, my life was going to get immensely better, and although a minor tragedy would strike from out of the blue, things were fated to swing back together again in the fall. That summer I was going to give myself a much needed break, do a little personal housekeeping and fall in love. Twice.

The season cooperated by quickly taking on a life of its own. People came and went from the resort in all sorts of boats and road trip rigs. Weekend nights were full of the sounds of laughter, sandal patter, crackling fires and tinking jelly jars. I rowed to shore every day or so and I hitchhiked to town once a week to do my minimal grocery shopping, visit the used bookstore and learn the lay of the land. I took up reading the classics in paperback late at night under the solemn light cast by *Tranquility*'s cabin lantern, while all of the rowing and walking was keeping me in fine shape. Near the resort I staked out some productive blackberry bushes and a small espresso shack which stood back from the road, lacked a sign and was only open at odd hours. I had my immediate needs met a short time after my arrival and I would soon learn that those berry bushes and the espresso shack were like so many other pleasant things in the islands: they were hidden in plain sight and you had to know they were there to benefit from them. I decided to find as many of those things as possible that summer.

Those days were long before I learned to live from the bounty of the sea and I wasn't much of a saltwater fisherman yet, but one evening, a kelp patch a short row from *Tranquility* caught my eye as a likely hot spot for a fish dinner. I rowed over to it in the dinghy, tied up to the bull kelp and gave it a shot. I knew from fishing with John and Dalty that a medium-sized rubber jig and a lead head hook would probably do the trick, so I rigged my bendy trout rod with one and dropped it in the water. As soon as the jig hit bottom the line took off and the rod went wild. After a short, vigorous fight, I pulled in an angry-eyed quillback rockfish. He wasn't big enough for a meal so I let him go for good luck. On the next cast I got spooled against the drag by something much bigger—a lingcod no doubt—and my line broke. I fumbled anxiously with a new rig, and a few casts later, I landed a two-pound brown rockfish and dropped it into the skiff with the hook still in its mouth. I took note of my general location then brought the blade of the oar down on the back of its head with an osseous crunch. Summer was looking really good to me all of a sudden and I pulled back to *Tranquility* with a will that sent the skiff gliding over the rose-colored evening clouds reflected in the satiny water –racing the nightfall waiting on shore in the wings of the trees, just for fun.

It didn't take very long to insinuate myself into the lives of the local islanders. To begin with, I always made myself available on deck to wave at any young ladies who were out on kayak trips from the resort. If I heard female voices on the water during daylight hours, I quickly thought of something to do on deck and went up the cabin steps purposefully, yet slowly enough to not seem on the prowl. The anchorage wasn't very big and since *Tranquility* was the only boat that laid there during the week, resort staff noticed her and paddled over to see what was up with me. I offered them coffee and chit-chat when they dropped by. There were only a handful of employees in those days, they were there day-in and day-out like I was and of the same age and inclination. Certain faces became familiar, so it was easy and natural when I fell in with them. They knew I was the guy with the boat before they knew my name and that was perfectly fine with me.

The resort wasn't run all that well, and the lines between employee and lingerer, guest and friend-of-guest, were blurry. I never saw anyone over thirty in charge and no one seemed to care if you left your skiff tied to a log on the beach all day. People wanted to meet one another and the place offered a carefree habitat for it. A nice opening came one afternoon when a resort manager had serious trouble with his car. I was somehow on hand for a diagnosis, and a day or two later, I carried out the repair in the gravel lot in front of the office. The manager happily paid me the equivalent of my month's grocery bill, and then he threw in something far more valuable to a sailor of limited means: *carte blanche* at the small restaurant; the sauna and hot tubs; the linen laundry; a cabin (if I wanted one) and a summer-long parking pass. I was given no-questions-asked access to nearly every resort facility, such as they were, but for all I knew, it might have been a seaside hotel in Monaco and I an internationally renown man of leisure and privilege.

The Best Summer Ever officially got underway one memorable afternoon as I was hitchhiking to town for supplies. I had to walk down the road with my thumb out for an unusually long time before a bright red antique Volvo leaned around a corner and swung onto the gravel shoulder just ahead of me. The passenger window came down as the car rolled to a stop and I heard a salutation from the driver in an unmistakable accent:

"Que onda vos?" the man asked as the dust cloud stirred up by the car blew over us.

"Caminando por la calle," I responded with just enough of his idiom to climb into the passenger seat.

Fabian worked at the resort but he was off to town on an errand. After driving and talking for a bit, I casually eased my sailboat into the conversation and Fabian hinted that he knew a few single women around the island who might like to go for a sail with us sometime. I let the offer hang there as we drove along talking and laughing like old friends. Fabian and I shared an interest in Latin American life, skin diving and travel. It was apparent to both of us that we liked each other about as much as two complete strangers could, so Fabian suggested we take a quick dip in a pond he knew of on the way to town.

"There are going to be two girls there," Fabian said. "I like the blond one –entiendes vos?"

"Claro," I said. "Yo entiendo perfecto."

Fabian needed a wingman that summer and so did I.

We parked on the side of a road that cut south through the forest and made our way down a deer trail that wound through fir trees, nettle-fringed bogs, salal and blackberry. It was a longer walk than I expected and I stayed a few feet behind Fabian, noting landmarks along the way. The trail came to an abrupt end at the edge of a deep, emerald cove lined with mossy tree trunks and velvety stones. Alder and lichen-mottled firs leaned toward the pellucid pool which was decorated with hyacinth and ringed by sunbathed slabs of dark rock nestled in loamy banks. Judging from the erosion underfoot, the spot had probably been a stage for summer cavorting for a hundred years or more. We were naked in a second and we dove into the silky, shimmering water. We swam around for a few minutes quietly taking it all in. When Fabian was sure I was *cool* he beckoned me away with a nod of his head and we dog-paddled around a low point of land and into a little inlet. And there, at the head of the cove, a nude idyll in the argot of youth appeared before our eyes: two naked mermaids, lifted from an aquamarine mosaic, were sunning themselves on the rocks. One was blond, the other brunette.

Fabian struck out for them hollering and flailing the water with his arms and legs in a hilariously exaggerated ape of a drowning man. The girls sprang up like a brace of ducks, but settled themselves down just as fast when they saw who was coming.

"Hola mi amor!!" the blond cried, trilling her *r* exotically.

"Hola chica," Fabian cooed back to her, churning himself higher and higher in the water like a polo player. The brunette watched them flirt. I hung back.

Fabian kept the chit-chat going while slowly working his way up to their rock, getting in range, and then, without warning or mercy, he suddenly splashed a wave of water onto them with both hands. The girls jumped to their feet and backed against the bushes, screaming and jostling each other for cover. When they realized resistance was futile, Fabian's attack was met by peals of laughter and I joined in the melee. The girls came up with a girl plan and dove over our heads. They surfaced on the attack with a furious bombardment of horizontal splashes that blinded Fabian and drove me into the poky shallows flashing a time-out sign, which they totally ignored.

Fabian knew those girls pretty well and after we had enough of the water fight, a truce was called and he introduced me to his friends. Samantha (the blond) and Fabian worked at the resort together and were in the middle of a new attraction. Shelby –tan, plump and darling, was her pensive friend visiting from Paonia. Any man who loves women will tell you there's a certain type he never gets; whether it's due to luck, class boundary, benign circumstance or a single misstep, something always undoes it. Shelby was that girl to me and because of it, I couldn't stop looking at her.

Samantha and Fabian talked fast, exchanging island gossip and dropping lingo. There were party debriefs and barbecue invitations to consider. A little resort drama was aired: a couple split up and someone else was in a heap of harmless first job trouble. The three friends confirmed a dinner date and a tour around the island just for Shelby –it was going to be fun! I wanted in, I wanted in bad. I wanted to be part of it all. *Act normal. Be normal. Act normal. Be normal.*

Fabian clearly knew what was up with the island girls, so I didn't hesitate when he let me know with another nod that it was time for us to split. There were errands to run and the summer was just getting started so I tried to put Shelby out of my mind on the swim back. But I was already in love with her! When we got to our cove Fabian and I hauled ourselves out of the water, dressed and set out for the car, hiking single file up the trail. I couldn't stop thinking about Shelby, I was going *crazy* for her, and when we got to the car, it just fell out of me: "Let's go back and ask those girls if they want to go for a little sail this weekend!"

"You go do it," Fabian said.

I stepped into the road and scanned the treetops for a hint of the shoreline. I took a bearing off the sun and set out through the underbrush, forsaking the trail to save time. As I crashed through salal and dodged nettle, I rehearsed several versions of what I might say to the girls, but I popped out of the bushes next to them before I was sure of myself. *Deadly.* I managed it though:

"Fabian was wondering if you want to go for a sail on my boat this weekend?" I blurted out.

Of course they did.

And with that, the summer began moving along at a steady clip.

On the Saturday appointed for our little sail, Fabian came out to *Tranquility* early and we put her in order. I wanted the four of us to leave the bay at 10:00 am sharp and sail to town for an early lunch. Then we were going to circumnavigate the island, stopping to fish and swim along the way. There was a wildlife refuge to swing by and a steep sided, biologically rich point I wanted to check out, but we had to hurry because I wanted to be back to the resort around sunset so we could have dinner on *Tranquility* before it was too chilly to eat in the cockpit. I overplanned it! I left no margin for myself or anyone else. At 10:15 I announced that the girls were probably running a little late and I made a strong pot of coffee to pass the time – *bad* idea. At 11:00 Fabian and I were sitting across from each other in the cockpit sipping our joe and pretending to talk, but I was too preoccupied with the time and the caffeine wasn't helping. By 11:15 I was radioactive with tension. The girls were over an hour late and I began to wonder if they'd stood us up. Fabian on the other hand, was totally casual about the timing of the day because he was hip to the nuances of island culture and he was also way less of a freak.

Fabian was put off by my rigidity and told me so: "If something is going to happen around here then it just happens –you can't push on things. If you do, you ruin it. Tienes que relajar amigo, you need to relax friend," Fabian said, patting my shoulder to let me know it was okay.

The girls never showed up and Fabian split around noon. After all, a daysail without the gals is just another workday and Fabian had that one off. Despite what you may gather from perusing the *J. Crew* summer catalog, there aren't jovial gaggles of attractive, khaki-clad, young people roaming the seaside at rakish angles looking for a sailboat to crew on for the day. It can take real work to get a group of people out on a sailboat, even in the middle of summer. I spent the early afternoon moping around the boat feeling sorry for myself and pretending like I didn't mind being alone. Actual desperation crept in later and I went to shore two or three times to look for any sign of the girls. There was none. I went to see if there were any notes for Fabian and I on the corkboard by the office. Of course there weren't any! They were beautiful young women with a lot going on, they forgot *all* about us. So I sat on the bench by the courtesy phone booth and stared out at the empty lawn of the abandoned resort watching bees lift off and land on little white flowers. Everyone, including the office girl, was off cavorting in the sunshine. I was crestfallen, and although I didn't realize it at the time, I'd made a common mistake of the single-hand sailor: I was spending too much time alone. I craved human contact, that vibe is off-putting and it wasn't the first or last time I'd be guilty of it.

Setting aside the usual exceptions, men who prefer to sail single-handed are solitary individuals. But they don't always start out that way. If you set sail when you're young, you may have to run short-handed for a time while you find yourself a crew or that special young lady to sail off into the sunset with. But please note: *single* is in the phrase *single-hand sailor* for a reason. When a young man finds a first mate who loves him *and* his boat it's truly adorable, but it pretty much never happens. I wish you luck if you're trying though.

What does happen is the absence of crew, close friends, a connection to land or a woman creates the classic curmudgeon solo sailor. These are the hard cases. These are the guys who sail alone because no one else is hearty enough to keep up with them. No one is worthy enough to compromise themselves or the boat for. This attitude opens the door to a type of ill-fitting, weirdly eccentric personality that must be seen and experienced to be believed. Furthermore, single-hand sailors and boatmen in general do not seem to understand that people, for the most part, and women especially, *do not get boats*; meaning, they do not wish to spend a great deal of time or effort on them unless it's for work or they're in the tropics at vacation time. I don't know why, but women are born knowing that the movie about the girl who falls for the sailor is far more enjoyable than falling for the sailor in real life. Without ever setting foot on one, they seem to know that boats are uncomfortable vehicles used for slowly going to places they don't really want to go to. This isn't a shortcoming! Far from it. This is a sign of *superior intelligence.* I, for one, do not care to go hot air ballooning more than once or twice in my lifetime, though it may mean the world to its enthusiasts, who are no doubt mystified by any ambivalence to their sport.

A sailor without a first mate eventually faces an A-B dilemma: A) He will cheer up, find a woman to love shoreside and accept that sailing is something *he* enjoys. B) He refuses to take a hint and continues to search for a woman who wants to live on a sailboat. If he chooses A, it's a happily-ever-after situation. However, circumstance will force him to choose B, at least for some length of time, and he will nurture a lonely self-reliance while telling himself he is superhuman. He won't see loneliness in himself, though –other people will. At that point in my life I was leaning toward B but I really wanted to do something about it.

The next morning I rolled out of my bunk, stumbled aft and sprang on deck before I knew what was happening. I looked around the boat shaking with sleeper's fatigue trying to figure out why I was standing in the cockpit in my underwear. *Tranquility* yawed ever so slightly, I lost my balance and sat down at the tiller with a thud. *Am I dreaming? Or is someone calling my name?* Steadying myself with a hand on the coaming I did a bleary-eyed scan of the bay. No one was around –except for Shelby, Samantha and Fabian who were standing on the low cliff above the bay hooting and doing a little dance to get my attention. Fabian was working a huge beach towel like a lasso over his head, Samantha was doing exaggerated jumping-jacks and Shelby was marching in place holding a picnic box out in front of her for me to see. I lifted an arm high overhead and went below to dress for the day.

The girls bounded aboard *Tranquility* followed by Fabian, smiling widely with his towel wound around his neck like a cashmere scarf and holding a six-pack in each hand. The girls flitted around *Tranquility* like wrens asking me questions but not waiting for the answers. I was saying *Welcome aboard! Welcome aboard!* to my guests but I was also saying a silent prayer of thanks to the universe for making that day happen.

"We're-a-go-ing-sail-ing-tooo-daaay," Samantha sang as she skipped around the mast like a little girl, lifting the hem of her skirt.

"I want to learn everything!" Shelby said, turning to look me in the eyes. They were the first words she spoke just for me and my heart leapt at the thought of having her on the boat for the summer. Fabian and I saluted each other with a sly wink and the girls went into the cabin to check out the bunks and all of the mysterious little things on a sailboat.

"I could do this no problem, couldn't you?" I heard Samantha say to Shelby who was bouncing on the settee.

"Sure I could!" Shelby enthused adding something under her breath I didn't quite catch but made them both titter. Ah...Young

Summer! How glorious, how brief! How well did I live? How fondly do I recall? How much do I miss? *How deep is the ocean? How high is the sky?*

The wind was a light northwesterly and it was a warm day, so we quickly got the main and genoa up and sailed off the anchor with a lushly-filling jibe. We had a decent offing within an hour, the resort was getting lost somewhere below the steep island terrain and the four of us looked like we'd been sailing across the Pacific for weeks. Fabian was unfolded across the cockpit with an arm bent over the tiller and the beach towel piled up on his head for a sun hat. Samantha was helping me fix something brunchy in the galley and Shelby was having a Jackie Onassis moment, sunning herself on the foredeck with one foot dangling in the bow wave and her sunglasses pushed up on her head.

Things happen on a boat when you leave the land behind, even if it's only for a day or two. People refine into a purer grade of self and their temperament can change in surprising ways. The inept ashore may suddenly develop new competency on the water, the physically weakest member of the crew may turn into a prescient and adept helmsman. The strong and confident shoreside may remain so, or they may lose their self-assurance and shrink from unfamiliar people and things. These changes can be welcome or perplexing, like when a landsman finds a mariner inside himself, or an experienced day sailor turns quietly green with *mal de mer* on a perfectly calm day. But no matter what happens on a weekend voyage, expect Sunday afternoon conversation among the newly-minted salts to turn, with the enthusiasm of castaways, to a famously contentious desert island topic: *What's the first thing you're going to do when you get back to land?* they will ask each other on the way to port. I've sailed home on more than one Sunday evening surrounded by such talk. The sea never changes and you know people are all the same.

The afternoon grew hot and long, the wind gradually eased as we drew farther and farther from the island. It's a real thrill to watch the land recede and it doesn't take much more than that to turn a daysail into a real voyage for people unaccustomed to life on the water. Out in Rosario Strait the wind lost interest in us and went elsewhere, so we swam naked and took turns jumping into the sea from the main boom. I tried to mooch us a salmon and there was big excitement aboard when the line went ripping off the reel, but I knew it was only a dogfish. After the girls marveled and poked at it for a while we dumped it out of the landing net and it swam away, sculling just under the surface before darting into the deep blue. It turned into one of those perfectly windless inland water days in Washington, the ones that are so light and still they seem to lift upward on a body and the sea itself. Freighters steamed in the silent distance and tugs towing rafts of logs made imperceptible throbbing headway against the current coursing through the levitating islands of the 48th parallel. *Don't make any more plans*, I told myself as I lay across from Shelby in the warm teak cockpit with my arm draped over my eyes. Heat radiated from her deeply-tanned skin and I could smell her heady *fleur de pivoine parfum* from three feet away. We drifted around on currents and cat's paws and sunned ourselves for most of the day, leaving *Tranquility* to meander where she might. I alone kept watch.

The sea is still there and the sea is still free and the winds still blow themselves across the oceans and around the world with the same regularity and direction as they did a hundred years ago, and with the same deference and indifference to the cruising plans of sailors who wish to ply their trade on them. The Seven Seas and their distant shores still beckon with all of the same grandeur they did when the world was supposedly unknown. Tropical isles are still shaded by coconut, breadfruit and pandanus trees. Their torrid white shores are hovered over by tropic birds, fairy terns and the full moon. Their beaches are caressed by effervescent seafoam and chased through by native sons and daughters to this day. Lanterns still cast their sooty light on tropical ailments, birds of strange plume and mysterious sea creatures fetched by hook and triton from the shadowy depths of the silent world.

At higher latitudes thundering coastlines of extinct reef disappear over the horizon and unclassified strata, torn up by the convecting seafloor, run jagged into the misty miles of temperate conifers that lean like supplicants over bays without names. The sub-arctic fjords still run a hundred bottomless miles inland and glaciers still calve onto stony northern beaches. Closer to the poles, somber ice mountains tower high above arctic seas, sheltering a million keening gulls and the fearsome williwaw wind. There are piles of coal and jumbles of sea drift timber to burn for your heat on snowy beaches. There are islands and castaways and shipwrecks to which little or no mind has ever been paid. There are uncharted waters and coastlines teeming with fish where the lights of civilization do not shine and probably never will. People seem to think all of the uninhabited nooks in the world have been sought out and spoken for long ago, but that's far from true. Even if there were nothing new in the world to discover, it wouldn't mean there was nothing new in it for you. It's all still there despite what they tell you, so pay the discovery of the world no mind sailor, and it will always be undiscovered for you.

On our way back to the island that day *Tranquility* was roundly praised by her crew as a good and faithful and lucky ship (the first and only time to my knowledge). The advisability of owning wooden boats was discussed and each imagined the perfect vessel for themselves.

"What's the first thing *you're* going to do when we get back to land?" Samantha asked Shelby. Shelby thought they should get a burger. Samantha thought they should get a beer. They agreed to get both. Fabian and I stayed out of it. When we dropped the hook in the anchorage, *Tranquility* was declared *the best little boat* by those who sailed in her that day. It was the high point of our career, she and I.

Fabian and I were walking the girls to their car later that evening when we were called over to join a pick-up volleyball game. It was four on four with the other team defending the upwind side of the court. We ran onto the warm sand with laughs and fun-loving shoves. The other team was playing hard from the get-go but we weren't paying any attention and promptly lost the rally for serve. Then we fell behind so far and so fast, I assumed we would simply have to enjoy the humor of our failure. Who cares who wins? It was fun. Shelby didn't like to lose though, and she went to each of us in turn and explained a simple strategy. When we won the serve on the next volley, Shelby circled the court giving each of us a high five. Her hand was warm and smooth, it was the first time we touched. When we scored our first point there were some girl acrobatics and a short floor routine. Fabian and I did a double high five overhead. When we scored three points in a row, we were in it to win it and Shelby called a time-out. She went to Fabian and Samantha and gave them the what-for.

"You're doing great," she said to me, then turned her head and tapped her finger on her right cheek. I leaned in and pecked it. She smiled.

"*That's* right," she said, nodding and looking at Samantha who gave her a quick wink.

The game grew tense and competitive; when a crack opened up in the leadership of the other team, Fabian started arguing with them about the official rules of beach volleyball in an unfriendly Euro-Latin tone. A small crowd gathered around the court –losing was no longer an option. We had them on the run for a while but they beat us back with a few well-placed spikes. They'd been playing all afternoon and game point serve ended up theirs. They double faulted. When we served we scored. It was close but we lost advantage. We survived the reversal somehow and tied them up with a feinted spike that suddenly became a drop-shot when Samantha's palm hit the ball. Game point our serve. The crowd went *whoa...*

Shelby, sweating beads from forehead and upper lip, called another time-out with the ball tucked under her arm. She looked at us for a moment and pursed her lips tight.

"You guys...?" was all she said.

Fabian spiked the serve from the way-back court and the ball flew low and straight and cracked off the top wire of the net before whizzing head high at the other team. Somehow, someone got under it. The ball soared back and forth over the net five or six times jangling nerves on both sides. They lost their cool first and sent the ball sailing high over the net and our heads. Shelby was the only one who saw what was coming.

"DON'T TOUCH IT!!!!" she shrieked.

We pulled our arms out of the air –all eyes on Shelby, who quickly put a bare foot on the back court line and pulled it straight. Everyone there saw the ball hit the sand on the far side of her foot. It zinged across the driveway and wedged itself under a truck axle with a tight dribble. The place went nuts, a man on the other team fell flat on his back, the other stalked off. Their girls stood staring at the net in silence. Shelby fell to her knees, clasped her hands and cast her eyes toward heaven. Samantha ran, jumped into Fabian's open arms and strangled him with an embrace that brought them both to the ground. I hustled after the ball and when I got back on the court I knelt in the sand next to Shelby and tapped my finger on my right cheek. She kissed it for real. I was in.

In a lifetime of summers a few are bound to fall by the wayside and no trace of them will ever be found by you or anyone else. Certainly no one will go looking for those memories, so does it really matter if one or two summers are spent doing nothing more than getting to know the contours of a beach with your body? Isn't there enough time in life and something to be gained by reading a book you love over and over again? Can't you let your feet fall on a landscape you've always wanted to explore? Can't you try? A body runs out of the elastic youth of summer, a pebble in the sand is going to outlive you, and the photos, if there are any, will one day wind up as orphans rifled by other orphans in thrift store boxes. You tell yourself there is tomorrow and tomorrow and tomorrow but there's no such thing as tomorrow. You're here right now and that's all there is to it. I knew what I was up against by then, so I figured I still had a little time to spend as I liked.

There was no plan that summer and no need for one. We didn't have to talk about what we would do, or when we would do it, with whom or how. We never had to ask who was working or who was going to town, who was driving –rarely, if ever, who was buying. None of us had any money to speak of but someone always had enough. I don't really know how we all got by. All I know is we found one another every day or two. We touched the people who were touching us and we wore each others' clothes with a nod, feeling our way along the outlines of four lives that were coming uncontrollably close together for a while. We made an enviable nuisance of our young beautiful naked selves in the sauna and hot tubs –the two of us, and the four of us, wantonly nude on the secluded beaches and the deck of my sailboat. Who would dream of bothering us?

We hiked to the top of a mountain one day. We didn't know it because we came from somewhere inland, but a rare and true northwesterly gale was blowing down out of the Strait of Georgia raking against the wave crests of a big flood tide pushing into the north. The wind-against-tide was turning the inter-island passes into over-falling whitewater. Huge refractory waves bent around rocky points and swept into anchorages that I would have expected to provide better shelter in such conditions. Far offshore a lone white speck of a yawl ran broad before the wild wind. No main and no mizzen hoisted, only her storm jib flying. No fear could be seen in her handling though, and she snapped over onto a starboard tack in perfect time with the following seas. She wasn't running for shelter. Judging from her track, she was a Canadian, and she was running down the miles to the North Pacific. That boat was going somewhere.

"Can you imagine sailing in *that?*" I enthused to Shelby who was standing beside me on the cliff.

"I'd really want to know what I was doing first," she remarked, looking into my eyes in an innately feminine way that made me thankful sailing was left for others to do while we explored a more varied summer palette together.

To know her was to love her –it was as simple as that. She wasn't store-bought; she was a homespun honeymoon child and there wasn't anything wrong with her. She didn't even know how beautiful she was. Whoever raised her, raised her right. Shelby was the kind of girl who never wondered whether she was happy or not and I fell wholeheartedly under her effortless spell.

It seemed the four of us had captured the mystique of youth on that little summer island and we took the amulet with us wherever we went. We traded sweaty square dance partners at a hoe-down held in a weathered old barn, a high-season blur of summer prints and sabot-sandals, jeans and tees, enjoying a harmless little thrill of infidelity for most of the night. We drank, who knew what, and none of us knew or remembered who invited us. We fetched up together in a quiet hay corner where we met a man from one of the outlying islands who shunned the internal combustion engine and farmed with a team of horses hitched to antique field implements. He had the attention of all four of us for a brief, expansive moment, but when he made a swipe at converting us to his arcane doxology, we drifted back to the edge of the fiddle-driven throng and let the stream of dancing faces sweep us away like water motes caught in a swirling undertow. It wasn't our time to solidify yet. It was our time to be young, beautiful and superficial without consequence or remorse. We didn't know that one day we would discover gravity had brought our feet to the ground so gently we never felt the landing. Only time could tell it when to do so –it hadn't yet, and that wasn't anyone's fault.

We dropped in on a blacksmith whose hammer called us down from the road where we stopped to pet horses and pick swollen blackberries from a dusty bramble. We didn't need an invitation to visit and he set his tempering work aside to show us around. The metallurgy of everyday things captivated us with their unusual mundane provenance: malleable iron nails and coarse flat bar wrought from the earth like a cut of meat from muscle or a lintel from an oak tree. These are the things of youthful learning which stay with you for a very long time. We went to a mountain lake and spent the inevitable summer day drinking beer and winging ourselves into the cool water on a rope tied high in a leaning tree. The ranger cut it down and we promptly re-hung it in mock defiance. The ranger cut it down again but always left it on the ground for us to find. Who would dream of bothering us?

We made the long pilgrimage up and up and up a mountainside and into dense woods where we heard a modern day Noah had built an ark. We were surprised to find a 70-foot wooden boat up there. She was a barkentine, a real ship. Her timbers had been hewn and her ribs bent and fastened to her keelson in a clearing several hundred feet above and many miles away from the nearest finger of the sea. She was complete though: decks, cabins, rudder, a running diesel, shaft and propeller. Her builder was small, white-haired and wiry in the manner of a mountain man. But like Alexander Selkirk, the real-life Robinson Crusoe, he was the first to point out the paradox in which he lived. He built a ship whose keel wouldn't be wet by the sea in his lifetime. He would never sail her in the Greater Antilles, on the emeraude Caribbean waters she'd been purpose-built for. He must have known this long before he finished her, but for some reason he kept building.

The enormity of the dilemma, at first unseen by us, was suddenly apparent in the steep slope of the high terrain and in the height and girth of the trees surrounding her. Perhaps the dilemma was present in the builder himself. There had to have been some witchcraft in that sort of thing. I can't be sure, but it didn't seem to bother the man one bit that there was no way to bring his formidable creation down to the sea. A mountain would have to be moved to do it. Shelby was captivated by the idea of the project and seemed ready to lend a hand. Fabian and Samantha were skeptical about the ultimate practicality of building something that could never be put to its intended use.

"Don't you get it?!" Shelby implored of them, "it's not *about* getting his boat down to the sea."

I said...nothing.

If one sets aside some of the more substantive measures of human compatibility: love, personality, ethics and intellect, one is free to consider the idea that their perfect mate can be chosen using physical attraction and form as the only guide. If this is true and there exists for each and every person an ideal caricature of their perfect mate, then Shelby, who also had everything else, was the woman for me. Like an only daughter of the earth: small, gentle, lovely and as well-proportioned in her sundress as she was when she stepped out of it, Shelby was the type of woman men either pretend not to see or simply stare at with open longing. That I desired her and she chose me was a dream I was living in. She was simply the most beautiful woman I'd ever laid my young eyes on and that was enough. She was Shelley's orbed maiden, Suttree's river waif and Marquez's almond-eyed mina brought to life in the girl who favored me. Shelby was that girl to me and because of it, I couldn't stop looking at her.

"I knew something was going to happen to us the first day I met you," Shelby said to me out of the blue one day as we sunned ourselves on *Tranquility*'s foredeck.

"I didn't," I said.

"Isn't it funny how our bodies want to be closer together?" she asked, smiling and parting her Botticelli locks with a pinky so she could watch me react to her dangerous honesty. When she drew the hair from her forehead, the baby's breath sprig of freckles bridging her nose revealed themselves beneath her bronzy tan in the dappled sea light glinting on the water and winking in her eyes. The bright was gone in a flash, dancing its way down the cabin sides, vanishing over the stern. I did not kiss her then. I drowned in her.

"I'm enjoying the anticipation," I replied, quaking inside with soon-to-be-requited love.

Later that evening Shelby and I were supposed to meet Fabian and Samantha at the restaurant overlooking the cove. A band was playing and the four of us wanted to dance and drink. The nights had been warm, perfectly still, dreamy with stars and a waxing moon. Something big was happening and we knew we were headed for a good couple of days. As Shelby and I strolled up to our table that night I caught the tail end of something Fabian was saying to Samantha: "I love everything that has happened between us –so why not be closer?" Samantha seemed to agree and there was a light kiss that sent a tremor through the crowd of friends sitting around them.

The band wasn't on stage yet but a famous Cabo Verde song was playing on the sound system.

Consedjo
spia caminho nha fidjo matcho
bisia caminho nha fidja femea
tudo comberso ca ta obido

E'ca tudo badjo qui ta badjado
Bedjice e triste morre e certo dia por dia cada vez mas perto

Advice
seek your path my son
seek your path my daughter
all words are not good to hear
all music is not good to dance to
Old age is sad death is certain day by day it is closer.

We didn't trade dance partners that night, or ever again, because we solidified into two couples on the same day. It was true and right and lovely and we drank more than usual, danced closer than before and entirely fell under the antigua spell cast by the music, the people and the light. The show was short and boozy and when it was over the four of us levitated to the front porch where the warm summer night draped us in its finest pall. The moon was silent, ponderous and full, the galaxy rent by stars, our mood lilting and exquisite.

"I know what we're going to do now," Samantha said thoughtfully, tapping my chest with her finger. "Let's all go spend the night on your boat"

Something in her words set a telepathy free. It went from Samantha to Shelby to me, then Fabian met eyes with us and it was done. We shuffled down the porch steps together and Shelby moved left so she was walking in front of me. When I stepped off the landing she shortened her gait so I ran into her from behind. Without turning around, she pulled me into her body with her arms, my nose went into her hair and bumped up against the nape of her neck.

"Is this okay?" she asked, glancing sidelong at me, giving my flanks a squeeze.

We rowed the skiff out to *Tranquility* through skittering, splashing, neon green phosphorescence and we drank from a bottle of red wine in the cockpit under the stars. The moon was bright enough to see by and the cove, the trees and the shoreline were cast in an ethereal alabaster light. In this marvelous setting we spread our bedding out four abreast in the cockpit and lay ourselves down. Shelby and I were consumed by a wholesome affection, I disrobed under a warm shower of her kisses and she pulled her dress off over her head in a single swoop.

We whispered and touched and kissed and caressed each other for hours until we were heavy with sleep. A rhythmic creak elsewhere in the boat broke our lover's spell for a moment and although it wasn't what we had in mind, I knew Shelby wasn't bothered by it. She was happy for them and pulled me closer to her. What we had was too tender, too sweet, too close, too loving to want anything more. *Don't you dare push on this, let it happen.* Your body knows what to do and you must let it.

I didn't see Shelby the next day and although I missed her, I thought nothing of her absence. There are expansions and contractions in the fabric of things. It doesn't mean it's tearing. So I opened myself up to what was going to be instead of trying to steer something I barely understood, no matter how much I wanted it. That all changed when I ran into Samantha in the office parking lot the next day and she told me Shelby needed to talk to me. Samantha offered to drive me out to their place so I suppressed a vague dread and cheerfully agreed to go with her. When we arrived at her cabin Samantha quietly wandered off, so I went up to the front door alone and let myself in.

Shelby was bundled up on the sofa and she'd been doing some serious crying. As soon as I saw her I knew it wasn't about me.

"What's going on?" I asked, kneeling in front of her, taking her hand in mine. Tears came into my eyes.

"I used to have a boyfriend...okay?" Shelby said, pulling away from me.

"Okay," I said, letting her hand go.

"We were in love for three years and wanted to get married. So we moved in together and we were happy like that for a while. But then he started acting strange and unpredictable. He would yell and get angry for no reason and leave me places we went together. Sometimes he didn't come home at night. It got worse. He disappeared for a few days. When his parents and I went to look for him we found him wandering around on a sidewalk talking to himself. He should have been at work that day."

"Okay," I said.

Shelby patted her hands together on her lap a couple of times and she started to cry. I sat down next to her on the couch and put my arm around her. But the cushion was too soft and my hips were too far below my knees to brace myself at her side. It was all wrong, like the dream where you must run but your legs have turned to lead.

"He was hearing voices, hitting himself. His family took him to a hospital. It was only going to be a couple of weeks at first. Then they said he may never get better."

"I went there once –he didn't know who I was."

She was bawling.

"Okay," I said, "I can help you with this."

I stood up to escape the mire of the sofa but standing was too superior so I knelt before her like a beggar.

"There's nothing anyone can do, it's like he's dead and I've been here trying to deal with it ever since."

"Shelby...I can help you with this..." I said setting my hands on hers.

"Okay..." she said.

Then she looked at me with a flash of vulpine rage I'd never seen in a woman. She glanced down at my hands for a moment and then slid hers out from under mine slowly, definitely, tragically.

"He went to the hospital two months ago," she whispered, not looking up at me.

I knew what was coming next.

Any man who loves women will tell you there's a certain type he never gets.

"I can't get close to you, do you understand that? I need to stop this right now."

It was final but I should not have let her go so easily. What could I have done?

A couple hundred thousand years of cultural evolution have done little to alter millions of years of biological evolution. Human beings are wild animals. They don't know it and that's what makes them dangerous. The next thing I knew I was crashing through the forest blind with tears and lacerated by sorrow. Branches and thorns slashed me in the face, broken sticks gouged my chest and stabbed my bare legs. I was *crushed.* How pitiful were my tears? I was miles from the boat and I walked the entire way, bleeding and weeping quietly to myself on the side of a country road.

Our children would have been so beautiful!

Shelby left the island without saying goodbye to me and I never saw her again.

After some days spent in an inert and torturous sorrow, I knew I had to get away from the island, so I anchored *Tranquility* far from shore, hitchhiked to Seattle and picked up my van. I tried to take a little road trip from there, but I was lovesick and returned to the island within a week. The whole thing was broken when I got back. Samantha, Fabian, everything. I knew it would be, so I was able to rally and get myself moving forward again. This was the first time I used the *Tranquility* saga as a lever to hoist myself over an unrelated obstacle. *If I survived that ordeal, I can survive anything* I told myself. It was true and I slowly began to feel better. The breakup made me realize I wanted to give my love to someone, so I assigned myself the task of meeting another woman. It was still summer, I still had *Tranquility* and I was young, hearty and healthy.

22

She was dressed in an incongruous, job interview outfit and reclining uneasily on a bath towel that didn't go with anything in the world. There was just something about her though, so I went over, crouched down next to her in the grass by the resort office and introduced myself. Her name was Heather, we shook hands. Heather had a no-nonsense light brown bob and blue eyes with a bit of sad in them. She wore a thin silver necklace, was pretty in a plain way and obviously traveling alone.

"Do you have any plans today Heather?" I asked.

"Not really," she replied, shifting herself around on her elbow to get a better look at me.

"Want to do something fun with me right now?"

No hovered in the air but then it bent toward *yes.*

"I do," Heather said, after a thought.

People are used to saying *yes* to fun things while on vacation. *No* is reserved for the other 50 weeks of the year. We drove my van up to the lake together. At the turnout where I liked to park we picked warm blackberries made fat and succulent by the late summer sun. We walked halfway round the shore to a small beach and swam out to a little, flat stone island covered by dwarf conifers, minute flowering plants, dry moss and a seagull's midden. We sunned ourselves, swam in the sweet, pollen-dusted water and made small talk for most of the day. Heather was a twenty-seven-year-old grad student from New York. She was in the final year of a master's program in child development. She'd gone to an upstate school and had recently moved to Seattle for a two-month clinical assignment at University of Washington. Her second and final month at the clinic was set to begin the following week. When her work there was finished Heather had a long public health assignment lined up in Albuquerque, New Mexico, but she said she wasn't looking forward to it.

Heather was at the end of a lifetime of schooling, much of it parochial. Never married and no boyfriend, she lived at home because, as she put it: "Where else are you supposed to live?" Heather was an intelligent loner, a turn-of-the-century anachronism and a stranger to the inexpensive glamour and immaturity of the west. She came to the island on a lark for a three-day tent vacation but I sensed she wasn't used to having that much time off and didn't actually know what to do with herself. I told Heather a little bit about me and by carefully leaving out or re-packaging the serious shipwrecks, the recent homelessness, the state of my career, my atheism, the dropout status of my education, *Tranquility*'s massive problems and my financial information, I almost managed to sound like a suitable young man for her. We were a total nightmare on paper though. Heather had a real life and I didn't. As it turned out, we found much to talk about on our little island in the middle of the lake on the island. When I sensed Heather was about to say it was time for her to be getting back, I preempted her by suggesting we have dinner on *Tranquility* later that evening.

"Why?" she asked, genuinely not getting it and studying my face for some sort of hint.

"Because, that's what two people *do* on a day like this," I said.

She looked at me for a moment then glanced up at the sun.

Heather had a bit too much robot in her. Who knows what she thought of me?

By the time we left our little island the heat of the day was easing and the wind was sighing over the treetops and gently fanning out on the surface of the sun-flecked lake. The swim to shore was a chilly one and the walk to the turn-out was shady and brisk with our clammy toes squishing in our sodden sneakers the whole way back. The van had been roasting in the sun all day and oven-warm air poured out of it when we opened our doors; the front seats were deliciously hot and supple. Heather melted into hers as if she were sliding into a steaming bath. She let out a long sigh when she leaned back. We weren't saying anything as we drove back to the resort under a spell of summer enervation cast by wet hair, latent heat and the rhythmic thrum of tires on road. Small birds flushed from roadside brambles and flew loping and flitting alongside us for a moment before vanishing with swoops into the greenery up ahead. Blue glimpses of the sea flashed through the evergreen trees and with a dip of her eyelids, Heather took hold of her shoulder belt with both hands, leaned her head against the door pillar and watched the late summer landscape roll by. I kept stealing little looks in her direction but they weren't returned. She did not have enough guile in her to try to see if I was looking her way. I liked Heather, but she must have already known we were impossible. She had three days on the island and I had the rest of my life. The van crunched onto the gravel parking lot of the resort trailing a wispy plume of beige rock dust.

"When's dinner?" Heather asked, as we rolled to a stop.

"Come down to the beach at seven," I said, yanking the hand brake out.

She nodded a slight assent, leaned against her door still thinking about it, then slid off her seat and onto her feet in one easy motion.

"See ya at seven," she said smiling, then peeking at me around the door as she swung it shut.

Because I was running around the boat fluffing pillows and positioning my most smartest books so Heather could read their titles at a glance, it was a quarter-past seven when I went to shore to fetch her. I could see her sitting over there on the low seawall, her sandals were off and she was swinging her feet and running her fingers through her hair. Somewhere close by a marimba band had started up and was playing something lively. Heather didn't seem to mind the delay, judging from the summer evening reverie I found her in when I rowed up.

"There's a wedding tonight, that's the music," she said as she stepped slightly off-kilter into the skiff. There's worse ways to begin a night with a woman you know? I didn't have time to fish beforehand, so I rowed us over to my favorite shallow reef on the way out to *Tranquility* and dropped a jig in the water. A moment or two of come-hither work got the pole bending and dipping and the line zipped off the reel and headed for deep water. In a few minutes I landed a fat rockfish, then another. "You catch your dinner just like that?" Heather asked me with a surprised, approving little smile.

I did.

I prepared a whole fried fish on a bed of fresh greens for each of us and we settled ourselves into the dinette I'd built. It was the one and only time I used it. Heather ate her fish with gusto and our eyes met often as we picked at the succulent, steaming white morsels and the crisp lemony skin. Apparently nothing more need be said, so I produced a bottle of red wine and poured out two glasses for us. Heather accepted hers with a hoist and a long smile at me, followed by a quick one at herself. I thanked her for coming, she thanked me for cooking –it turned into a date. We had another glass of wine after our meal and when dusk fell I lit the lantern and suggested we go up on deck to have a look at the night sky. Heather stood up and lifted a corner of the yummy down blanket lying on the bunk next to her.

"Oooh...let's take this with us," she said, stifling a little yawn.

I looked over at her in the lantern light and saw that some of the rigidity had gone out of her face and body. Suddenly, Heather was a very beautiful young woman.

The long-lasting red amber hues of a Pacific Northwest summer sunset bathe the wandering clouds and timbered islands that dot the northern inland waters of Washington with an intensity that goes right through a person. The golden glow left by the setting sun lingers in the summer atmosphere even when the stars have appeared in the east and overhead. Some trace of the light can be seen hanging in the western sky long after the day has been forgotten—it's a gift from the land of the midnight sun—and on some nights it never seems to set at all. We spread our blanket under such a sky, lay ourselves down and folded it over us. As the air cooled, Heather and I moved closer together. I slid my right arm around her and she let me. When I placed my right hand on Heather's dress-covered thigh however, I felt a bolt of tension shoot through her from head to toe and she smacked my hand away with a testy warning: *Watch yourself mister.* If she were a cat instead of a twenty-seven-year-old virgin, I'm sure I would have been bitten or scratched.

"*Calmmm downnn,*" I said, setting my hand back on her thigh with a little patting motion, "there's nowhere else to put it right now."

Heather acted like she'd never been touched before and I soon found out she really hadn't. She shifted herself around trying to accommodate our embrace yet move my hand somewhere else, but there really was no other place for it.

"I'm not falling for this like some high school girl," she said in a prickly tone as she shifted my hand from her thigh to her hip to her waist and back again. But it was obvious, you couldn't help it, I had to touch her there and it was a very human moment for both of us.

"I'll row you to shore the second you're ready to go back."

It was all I could think of to say that would assure her, and of course I really meant it. After a minute or two with my hand on her thigh Heather seemed satisfied her virtue was secure and she knew there was never any doubt about it.

"I can't believe we're on a sailboat!" she said with a little thrill, shifting her cheek against my clavicle and reaching for my left hand under the blanket. "How deep is it right here?" she asked glancing over the side, then toward shore.

"Really deep," I said.

We spent that night in the forepeak, kissing on the lips and talking and gazing through the open hatch at the stars. It was a scene of true romance made delicious by all of the danger in it. *Tranquility* floated in a halo cast by her anchor light, suspended by a gossamer thread between the cosmos above and the abyss below. Long after the cabin lantern went out and silent darkness draped us, certain necessary shiftings brought our bodies much closer together than before. A thin little nothing of a dress lifted all by itself from knee to mid-thigh while two tiny straps drooped from silky shoulders for the comfort of the wearer and to allow the caress of another. When it was much too late to leave, a bare leg slid a little higher and a hoarse, disembodied female voice clove the night:

"I'm not sleeping with you, if that's what you think is going to happen here mister."

"It doesn't even matter," he replied, sleepily pulling her languid form closer to him.

The next day was Saturday, and since Heather didn't have to be back in Seattle until Sunday evening, we decided to go on a little daysail together. After a quick cup of coffee, we went ashore and threw Heather's tent into her car, then packed up her gear and rowed it out to *Tranquility*. There was a nice northwesterly breeze blowing and we sailed across Rosario Strait under main and genoa. It was a quietly beautiful late summer day and there wasn't another boat around for miles. After a short sail, we dropped anchor in a secluded island cove.

"Where is everybody today?" Heather asked.

"Who even knows?" I wondered back.

It can be the nicest day of the year on those waters yet no one will be out boating.

We fished from the cockpit, sunned ourselves and swam around the boat until it was almost time for Heather to go back. From the day's catch I fixed spicy fish tacos—greasy, hot and salty—which we washed down with cans of cheap beer chilled to perfect freshness in a sack hung from *Tranquility*'s stern. After lunch we lay down side-by-side on the warm deck with a postprandial nap lapping at us. Heather's hand reached out for mine, she found my index finger and held on to it for a long time.

"I don't actually have to be back tomorrow," Heather said, giving my finger a little squeeze. I'd learned by then that the sorcery of summer was overwhelming, but the spells were fragile, so I didn't ask her what she meant. I pretended that if I didn't speak it would go on and on forever. So without talking about it, we continued the voyage in like manner for two more glorious days and nights. At the outset of her vacation, Heather figured she needed several days in Seattle to prepare for her return to the clinic, but after a few tactful hints from the captain regarding possible economies, several days of preparation were pared to two. This good thinking gave us a couple more days on the boat together. On what should have been the very last evening of the voyage, Heather announced that *half*-a-day of preparation would suffice. I turned up the music and made dinner with less haste when I heard the happy news. As time ran out, we grew selfish of every minute we had together. The cuddling was endless and the kissing grew hotter and longer. We had to let some carnal treaties expire, others had to be adjusted. She didn't know *anything*, but women somehow know everything, so it all fit together nicely. *Of course* we ended up procrastinating until the eve of Heather's first day back at the clinic. The last minute rush was done with a laugh, but it required a really sweaty skiff hustle to get everything ashore and into her car before the last ferry left for the mainland. As Heather was packing her last bag, I offered to accompany her to the flat she was subletting in Seattle. She accepted without a second thought and we sped to the ferry in her car. No laughing, no talking, no looking at each other, just serious handholding. We were filled with an airy spirit as we boarded the boat that night, and our joy was made complete a few hours later, when Heather let us into her Capitol Hill apartment and we tumbled into bed, exhausted but in heaven.

A small celebration was held for the clinician after her first day back on the job and the next night we fell right in to grocery shopping with our arms around each other, playing at love. We did not think that after a week in the city, cut off from the nourishment of the natural world, our primitive phenotype would be lost and we would slowly revert to strangers, but that's exactly what happened. It didn't take long for little doubts to surface in each mind and once there, they couldn't be quashed.

The question of piety was visited for the first time, to my knowledge, but Heather seemed uncertain what it all meant in our context, so she let that subject drop. But *why do you like me?* had crept into her mind and stayed there. Affection in public was forbidden, and our talk was filled with a wooden propriety we had no use of in the islands. Worse, the barely-restrained intimacy we shared so innocently on the boat suddenly seemed too unfamiliar to survive in the city din. The dreadful suggestion that we *get to know each other* seemed not far off, thankfully, those odious words were never spoken. Still, it was apparent we were held together by a relatively weak force.

The deal was sealed one afternoon on a busy street corner when an elderly woman flagged us down for help reading a bus schedule. She was small and pretty and she asked us how long we'd known each other.

"We don't," Heather the realist said.

The woman, who was no doubt hoping for a vicarious moment of young romance, shook her head, batted an invisible fly away and ambled off, not knowing what to make of Heather's comment. I did though. The ability of an old wooden sailboat to bring adventure and romance into a normal life is best observed when you're back on land. Marooned in the habitually maladjusted city, the mystery of our meeting and the power of our attraction—which we both thought presaged true love—vanished before our eyes. Heather had a life and a career ahead of her. She was kind and smart and responsible. She would meet a good man and start a family soon.

Our last day in Seattle was filled with a discomfort that could not be shooed away with well-chosen words or knowing caresses. The whole thing came to a sad close with an awkward and unjust goodbye at a noisy downtown bus stop. It was a wound that didn't break the skin, though, and I was irked more than saddened by how things turned out. Although I had the chance, I never found out what Heather made of our parting. I assume she decided that our love was as delicate as a summer dress whose colors would run in the lightest September rain. I really should have known better than to try and take what we had to the city.

Back in the islands few would admit summer was winding down, even though the signs of fall were everywhere. The people I'd been loving had flown or were about to. The thrill of what was to come was already being replaced by reflections on what had been. Fabian, a fixture of the summer who could almost always be found in the restaurant, at the hot tubs or on the beach, distanced himself from the resort crew by a couple of degrees, then changed jobs without warning. That's what you do in a tourist town when fall is nigh and you plan to stick around for winter, so I thought little of his absence until he vanished from the island all together. Fabian's disappearance left Samantha and I to endure some awkward moments and the bad vibe only got worse when I tried to clear the air. I had to let it go completely after that. There was a rumor going around that Shelby might be back on the island in early September. It never amounted to anything, but by then the disappointment was only a glancing blow. It seemed there was no hope of an Indian summer and when the rain that doesn't wet fell for a couple of days, everyone started to head for the exits. The idea that winter was just around the corner struck a sharp chord somewhere deep inside me. It was amplified when I saw someone else driving Fabian's little red Volvo around the island. There was no reason for any of it to come undone the way it did. I now know it was woven into the thing itself. This is what it means to be young and on your own in the world for the first time. You do not know yourself yet, so you don't know others; you do not treat yourself very well, so you do the same to everyone else. Saying *goodbye* is sad, saying *I no longer love* is hard, but wondering is forever –fix things when you can. If they can't be, try to break them cleanly.

I held out in the bay as long as I could, hoping my social life would perk-up or there would be a change in the weather –neither occurred. Somehow I heard about the Wooden Boat Festival that's held every September in Port Townsend and that occasion gave me something to look forward to. It allowed me to leave my summer paradise with my head held high and a purpose in mind. Before I left the island, I phoned Heather in Seattle. I pretended I called just to see how she was doing, but she saw through me, sensed an opportunity to mend what was broken, and offered to meet me in Port Townsend the weekend of the festival. And so, *The Best Summer Ever* ended with a *yes*. All at once I was saying hasty goodbyes at the resort, putting the boat away as fast as possible and moving my gear to the van. The next thing I knew, I was on my way to Admiralty Bay to catch the Port Townsend ferry.

Heather and I were supposed to meet at the foot of Union Wharf, but she arrived an hour early, and rather than wait around, she went looking for me in town. She found me in a bookstore on Water Street where I was perusing the boating section with quiet interest. Heather crept up behind me as I read, slipped her arms through mine and lay her cheek against my back. Her bright smile, her hair, her outfit, my beat-up coat and habitually male disposition, the bookshelves around us, the angle of the sunlight falling on the street outside the window –all of it was an ode to young love.

"I thought I'd find you in here," Heather said, giving me a little emphatic squeeze. We stayed in that embrace for a while. It was the time in my life for such gifts, and I know nothing like it will ever happen to me again. My reunion with Heather was heartfelt and kind –our misadventure in Seattle was never mentioned. The Wooden Boat Festival is the event of the year in Port Townsend and it's well-attended. It kicks off on a Friday in early-September and runs all weekend. The port at the east end of town is packed with tents and show boats, the anchorage and hotels are full. You can go for a sail on any number of boats, there's live music and dancing, seminars and displays. Heather and I did it all. There was something waiting for us there and we fell into it without a word. The attraction and genuine affection we shared was so intoxicating that I drove to New Mexico with her when the time came. A couple of days into the drive, we decided to spend the winter together in Albuquerque.

Heather padded her academic schedule wisely, her transition from the UW clinic to the one in New Mexico was unhurried and the gap was bridged on someone else's dime. Although she usually spoke of herself as an observer rather than an actor, Heather was driven and she managed her education and personal affairs down to the minute. She was used to enjoying life during university breaks and thanks to her forethought, we were able to spend a week traveling together in the Sangre De Christo, the Blood of Christ mountains of New Mexico.

Meanwhile, *Tranquility* was left at anchor in 35 feet of water in the San Juan Islands. She lay close to a rocky coastline that was wide-open to the storms of the south. I'd anchored her in what seemed like a safe-enough bay for a week –never imagining the anchorage could turn into a stormy blowhole or that she'd remain there for more than a month. A boat is not a toy and although some modern vessels resemble them in construction and are marketed as fair-weather playthings, owning a vessel like *Tranquility* is no kind of hobby. It's an occupation without equal. Although I felt I was inured to the need for constant vigilance with a boat, I believed that I could put my toy away with little thought for her well-being. If a car has a problem you pull over and get out. When you leave your house for the day you know it will be right where you left it when you return. There is no such idle moment for a vessel. She's in a hostile, moving environment the moment she's launched and that danger is ceaselessly communicated to the mind of her master for as long as he owns her, and sometimes, long after.

Pay attention to the weather in the Pacific Northwest and you'll quickly learn that although the occasional vernal gale blows out of the northwest during summer and the arctic air outbreaks of winter arrive from the north as well, much of the truly ugly weather finds its way to the region from the south. That's why the San Juan Islands generally see a few serious southerly blows over the course of a normal year. These winds can be especially violent in the fall due to the large differences in land, ocean and atmospheric temperatures that are common in that season.

My pathological fear of flying kept me from rushing back to the islands when I received a terse message from a fishing pal one day in late October informing me that *Tranquility* was sinking. Instead of catching the next flight to Seattle, I took a bus from Albuquerque to Union Station in Los Angeles. I boarded the northbound Coast Starlight (the world's most poorly-managed rail service) which delivered me to Seattle approximately 28 nauseating hours later. I took a city bus to the Greyhound Station where I hopped on the milk-run to Mount Vernon, WA. I hitchhiked from there to the San Juan Island ferry terminal. I was confident my delay gave *Tranquility* more than enough time to sink. (That would have been too easy and therefore completely out of her character.) It's fair to say that I didn't deserve the boat and what she gave me, but I didn't really want her anymore. I wanted Heather.

Wishing to be as far away from boats and the sea for as long as possible, I treated *Tranquility* like a woman kept at a distance until the next time her benefactor favors her: I promptly deposited her in a safe little marina at the west end of the island. *Tranquility* got short shrift that fall, and I knew I shouldn't just roll up the trusty inflatable and toss it in the cockpit like I did, but I was too preoccupied with Heather to pay it any mind. I remember thinking it might be stolen —I should have been so lucky! Anyway, I found an easy money auto repair job on the island and a week later, I was on my way back to Albuquerque. I did not set eyes on *Tranquility* or ponder her fate for the next several months. I was to pay dearly for that. But I must say, *Tranquility* was the farthest thing from my mind as I sped southwest in the van.

When I returned to Albuquerque, I found Heather thriving in work and life despite her less-than-ideal living situation. Several months before we arrived, Heather rented private quarters over the phone in an establishment which she was led to believe was a charming little out-of-the-way desert inn. However, when we got there in early October we learned that the "inn" was in fact the tacky personal home of a divorced evangelical hack carpenter with three maladjusted, pimply teenage boys. The house was on a cul-de-sac in a mostly vacant, single floor plan, beige stucco development. Part of the carpenter's front yard was set aside for what he claimed were valuable commodities of the construction trade: rip-rap and stacks of sodden appliance insulation. *Very* charming! Heather signed a complicated lease and paid her rent from grant money in advance. There was no way out of it so she stayed.

Heather's "private apartment" was a small bedroom that opened off a dingy, press-board and linoleum kitchen that was used at all hours by the carpenter's noisy "home schooled" progeny –they were *home*, that was the long and the short of it. Heather shared a guest bathroom with them. Plastic tubs of someone's personal belongings were stored underneath her bed and the decor hinted at the room's periodic use as a bedroom for one of the boys. The usual inhabitant was soon made apparent by the sullenness of the eldest son when we were around, which thankfully was seldom.

In the home, faux-brass light fixtures meant for an exterior entryway adorned the unevenly textured walls at odd intervals. The carpet, what there was of it, ended abruptly at spans of poorly-adhered linoleum flooring and began again on the far side. The most vapid sort of religious self-help books lined the shelves of the living room bookcase. As usual, none showed any sign of having been read. They had no dictionary! The *piece de resistance* of the abode, pointed out by the carpenter the day we arrived, was a poorly-proportioned and slightly saggy "spiral staircase" he built from pre-cut hardware store oak lath and fastened together with black oxide drywall screws, set without countersinks. Zinc-plated angle iron held the structure away from the living room wall while yellowish, unfaired wood spackle filled in many, but not all, of the gaps in the joinery.

"It's my own design, huh-huh..." the carpenter mused to us in a self-important tone. "Yeah well...as you probably noticed, it doesn't have a central support of any kind...so I guess you're gonna be seeing these around pretty soon."

The carpenter dropped these tidbits on us in a matter-of-fact tone, gnashing his palms together as he went up and down the stairs for effect. The treads creaked and the wall made noise and for some reason, the carpenter was wearing fingerless driving gloves in the house –oh, and I hated him.

I suppose the hack carpenter decided he should get to know me a little better when I came to fetch Heather after my trip to Washington. While I waited for her in the living room, the carpenter took on a parental tone with me as if I were there to take his daughter out on our first date. I picked up on his creepiness just as I had when I met him in October, so when he asked me how much I knew about the bible in a sing-song manner, I asked him in a mean-spirited tone how much he knew about mitochondrial RNA. He sensed it was best to let that subject drop and he was right. I disliked the carpenter from the moment I laid eyes on him. I never spent a single night in that house and I tried my level-best to stay outside if anyone other than Heather was home. It was apparent from his demeanor around her that the carpenter held out some hope Heather would fall under his hip-christian-dad spell. Instead, we never ate a meal or did anything else under that roof except rush out of the place on Friday evenings to go on weekend adventures in my camper. Heather was far more accepting of him than I was, but even she avoided him as much as possible. The carpenter blew a main gasket later and I thoroughly enjoyed watching it unfold –and being right in the middle of it.

Heather and I quickly established a sufficient presence in and around Albuquerque. She worked with malnourished and tactile-defensive children all week and I set myself up at the University of New Mexico in my usual way, fliering and fixings cars. Most nights I met Heather in town for coffee and a bite to eat. We made a few friends and went to Taos and Madrid. My work picked up that winter and I fielded a steady flow of auto repair –some of which paid me very well. I put a new engine in a Toyota truck and did a cylinder head job on a Subaru wagon. Heather advanced in her work, making contacts at the university and in local government. I saved money by sleeping in the back of my van in the icy mountains a few miles above Heather's place –she stayed up there with me from time to time. Every Friday, Heather and I would take off in a different direction in my van and by the time the worst of the winter weather was over, we'd seen much of the state and camped out in some splendid wilderness. We sought out hot springs, Ponderosa pine forests, ruins, meteor showers and museums. We took remote dirt roads to who-knows-where and were especially interested in them if, according to our tattered gas station roadmap, they seemed to dead-end in the middle of the desert. We climbed through the adobe ruins we came across on our wanderings and often had to pick our way back to the main road by opening barbwire stick gates and driving across open fields. We became connoisseurs of *very* bad art, drive-through Indian reservations, outcast-themed southwestern films, kachina dolls, cheap motels, rot-gut coffee and lucite diner food. It was fun times for both of us, we fell in love and I became Heather's first real boyfriend.

In an unforeseen but memorable chain of events, Heather and I temporarily morphed into a pair of the desert highway drifters we knew from the Albuquerque big screen. It began when we somehow locked ourselves out of Heather's little red Corolla one Friday evening at a desolate New Mexico rest stop. It was cold and for some inexplicable reason Heather was barefoot and wearing only gold rayon exercise shorts and a peach tank-top that she just spilled something on. I was in blue jeans, boots and a white t-shirt with automotive grime packed under my fingernails from a long day of work. So there we were, an absolute mismatch of a couple, locked out of our car at a breezy desert rest stop along a noisy interstate. It's hard to imagine a more abject setting for the unfolding of a trashy human drama than that, but there was a certain beauty in it and if you threw in some ticking and gingham we would have been Steinbeck's Okies instead of late '90s trailer trash.

"Oh my god, we're on the *run...*" Heather said to herself peering through the passenger window under her folded arms, alternately lifting her feet off the gravely pavement like a chilly duck.

"We need a wire hanger *A*-sap," I said, taking note of the fact that the car was still running and we were low on gas.

"What just happened?" Heather asked me.

It didn't need an answer.

A middle-aged woman walking to the restroom with a small child in tow saw us mulling our situation and gave the scene plenty of room as she sailed by, steering the youngster's gaze toward the burnt landscape across the highway. No one asked us how we were doing, though it must have been obvious by our behavior that we were locked out of our car. The metal roll-door at the coffee kiosk came clattering down with the finality of a lakeside concessionaire closing up on the last day of September. Somewhere off in the distance the jake-brake of a semi droned long and low –it would be dark soon and our world was getting colder and smaller by the minute.

"Should I break the window?" I asked, looking around for something to do it with. I glanced at Heather for an answer, then both our gazes fell upon a lone RV parked at the far end of the lot.

"You go do it –you have shoes on," Heather said, stepping from the pavement to the dead grass in the parking strip.

"No, you go, it's better if it's a girl." I replied.

"Let's both go baby," she said, walking quick and janky, going *ouch-ouch-ouch* as we crossed the pockmarked cement. We must have looked like pimp and prostitute. How wrong are appearances?

We begged a wire hanger from a woman in the RV who looked at us through her bent aluminum screen door with unconcealed pity. "It's okay Willy, they just need a hanger," she called into the back, turning to a narrow closet behind her. After an accusatory glare in my direction and a haughty nudge to her hive she passed the hanger to Heather through the barely-cracked door like it was a WIC voucher that might be diverted to a nefarious use if I got my grimy paws on it. When Heather promised the woman with mock confidentiality that the car we were breaking into was ours, the woman shook her head and clicked her tongue.

I know it's yourn I imagined her thinking.

Instead, she asked Heather a question that turned out to be difficult to answer in a believable way: "How did you lose your shoes honey?"

"That's actually really funny!" Heather assured her, nodding a little too much, "I *think* they're in the back seat!!"

The lady wasn't buying any of it.

Twenty anxious minutes later we were rolling down the dusky highway with the heater blasting and the windows intact.

"Can you *imagine?*" Heather asked.

My girlfriend and I need a wire hanger?

I could indeed imagine, but Heather? Heather was a good egg.

The only real problem we had that winter was all the carpenter's fault. Just before Heather's assignment came to an end, the man's rattle-trap Ford truck broke down. Heather, the social worker, knew the real situation around the house and asked me to lend a hand if possible. I loved her, so I set aside my instinctive response and agreed to drop by the following night. The engine in the carpenter's truck was an enormous 8-cylinder diesel with around 250,000 boiling-hot desert miles on it. The entire engine compartment, manifolds, firewall, fenders, hood and grille were coated in diesel, road grime and grease –an American car. The vehicle had been driven the equivalent of ten times around the world on minimal maintenance and the water pump shaft suffered a catastrophic failure out on the highway. When it came apart, it threw all the engine belts off and the carpenter drove it home without proper engine cooling, battery charging or anything else. It was a risky dead-stick landing, apropos of an ignoramus, that gave me the opportunity to see how others had seen me on occasion. With the carpenter hovering at my shoulder, I opened the hood and pulled the dipstick and radiator cap in the perfunctory manner of a field medic. No oil in the coolant, no coolant in the oil –the patient might live after all.

When it came time to discuss the job, the carpenter got things started off on the wrong foot by insinuating that he was letting me take a shot at the repair in order to do *me* a pretty big favor. I cleared $3000 working out of the back of my van over the last couple weeks, so I didn't really need his charity. Besides, someone who's doing you a favor by giving you work doesn't pepper you with dozens of anxious questions about the job like the carpenter did that evening. I knew the *I'm helping you out here* bit and I wasn't falling for it. So instead of entertaining his supposed generosity, I advised him to tow the truck to the nearest Ford dealership if he was concerned about the accuracy of my diagnosis or the feasibility of repair. Of course the carpenter ham-handed the conversation around to imply that although he, too, felt the Ford dealership was the obvious choice, all that trouble wouldn't be necessary if a "friend" could do the work right there in his garage. But, he implied, it was all the same to him.

"Sure," I said. "What's the dealer want for the job?"

"$750 plus the pump," the carpenter groaned, spinning the alternator pulley with his finger as he spoke. "But they haven't seen it yet."

After one look at that engine and knowing it had turned half-a-billion trouble-free revolutions that were for the most part taken for granted, I didn't feel bad for him. But I told Heather I would give the carpenter a break, so I did a little figuring and a little guess-work and came up with something I thought was do-able for everyone. "If you buy the parts yourself, I think I can do the labor for half of what the dealer wants."

"That would be great!" the carpenter blurted out. "Let's do it!"

So there we were, he couldn't afford to get the truck fixed any other way. Everyone including Heather seemed happy with the arrangement. The carpenter got the parts together in a day or two and I spent around six hours doing the job one evening later that week. At my suggestion, the carpenter drove the truck around for a few days so he could check my work before paying me. I never heard from him though and he drifted into the garage and then to the backyard the next time I came to get Heather. As we were getting ready to leave for the weekend, I caught up with the carpenter in the kitchen and asked him for the $350 he owed me. He was an mlm christian and he balked.

"$350 is way too much to ask for that kind of job," he said, confident of his superior business experience.

"It is? I thought I said I would do it for half the dealer's price."

"I wasn't planning on paying an amateur that much for a few hours of work when I could have taken my truck to a real shop and got it fixed the same day! How about we call it $150?" He said this looking off to one side.

"Well, I'm pretty sure I told you I could do the labor for half of $750, and $350 is a little less than that."

"But I already paid $200 for the pump! And that leaves you with...$150!" He directed this nut-job comment into the living room, keeping his eyes away from me, like a child does when he argues with an adult. Everyone was home and except for our voices, the house was absolutely quiet for the first time. The hack carpenter began to rant: "I charge $25 an hour! –and I'm an expert carpenter! What are your qualifications?" Before I could answer, he added: "You're over-valuing yourself! You won't get much work if you do that! You'll starve out in the *real* world *mister*! Your work is only worth what people are willing to pay for it!"

This monologue had him trembling.

"I don't see what the problem is," I said, untruthfully, hoping to drive him into the deep end. Heather came to her doorway with a dreadful expression on her face and the carpenter's three boys were wandering around the living room bumping into each other, pretending to be doing things. "I said half off the dealer's price, you said *great let's do it* and the truck is obviously fixed."

The carpenter's voice shifted to an indignant, almost furious register: "You waltz in here asking to be paid like a king?! You make a scene in front of my *children*?! And you've been doing who-knows-what under my roof since you got here?!"

This bewildering statement was the last straw for Heather and she shot me a look that said: *Oooookay –we're all done here...*

"It's $350 like we agreed and don't bother paying me at all if it's going to be one dime less than that."

The carpenter thought he was a skillful negotiator, but you can't negotiate with someone who hates your guts and doesn't need your money. He eventually paid me the $350 and I never set foot on the property again. Heather moved out a couple days later and we stayed in a comfy motel the last two weeks we were in Albuquerque.

"I guess you're gonna starve mister," Heather said, pulling me onto the bed our first night in the motel.

When Heather's assignment ended we suddenly found ourselves on very different life paths. She needed the security of home while she looked for a job and I was reluctant to follow her to New York for a number of reasons. Although Heather hid most of the details of our relationship from her parents, they knew about me and wanted me to accompany her on the drive to New York. Of course I should stay with them for a week or two that spring! Because, as her father so famously put it: "Why the heck not? He sounds like a very nice young man and they certainly aren't *sleeping* together!"

Heather and I decided we could live apart for the time being, so we returned to our own coasts without too much sadness –at first.

I saw her once more. She came to Seattle on one of those trips women take to see men. To make sure leaving him was the right decision. I felt her looking at me, trying to find some fault in my character. I'm sure she found it, because I never saw or spoke to her again.

One day I found a love that swallowed my anchor so fast and took it down so deep and in such a mysterious way, I never wanted it to be retrieved. I got down on one knee and wrecked on a woman's shore so badly there wasn't a stick left of my ship big enough to build a raft from. I never wanted my heart to be reached again. I knew there couldn't be two loves like that. There's only one world and that one isn't big enough or beautiful enough for two of those. How could I be so sure? I knew what the world was by then. I'd sailed Neptune's Seas and been lost on the savann plain. I'd been starved and marooned. I'd been a prince and the prisoner of a prince. What was another hurricane or forest to me, with something crackling in the fire or in the trees, with my finger on the trigger and a bullet in the breech? What was another spike held at my throat, another fortune, another tragedy? The search for love seems like a selfish endeavor but that's far from true. A man simply reaches a point in his life where he can go no further on his own. To continue, he must forge the only bond that will humanize and locate him on earth. Even then he'll think it's all for himself. He'll be gratified when he wins but he does not win. Life is what wins. He's just a piece it plays when the time is right. This is where humanity came from, this is how it will continue. There's nothing new or special in that.

Desdemona Sands

Paying the seams

Tranquility as she looked after corking

Caesar the world famous rat

Making a buck on the streets of Seattle

Tranquility's double block...any offers?

West Coast Vancouver Island, British Columbia

John and I sailing the Salish Basin... just before the tiller fell off

She flew straight, men

Tranquility in the public anchorage on Elliot Bay

23

When I laid eyes on *Tranquility* that April, I was surprised to find her looking good and floating on an even keel. Other than a beard of sea lettuce ringing her waterline, she was just as I left her in the fall: frail but resistant. I'd forgotten that during the winter months it was normal for people to let their boat sit idle in the relative safety of a marina. A call to the harbor master is usually all it takes to find out how she's doing. Having everything formalized like that was unfamiliar to me, but it definitely made sense. I was happy to step aboard *Tranquility* after such a long absence and I fancied she missed me too. *People do this*, I reminded myself as I set my bags down in the cockpit, *people own boats.* By the way, unless you're sailing far and wide, approximately ten percent of pleasure boating is pleasurable boating. The other ninety percent is filled with tasks and expenditures that supposedly have something to do with it.

I was too busy shuttling gear from the van to the cockpit that day to look more closely at the rice-sized bits of gray debris scattered all over *Tranquility*'s deck. Then I had far more serious problems to contend with when I slid the companionway open and set free an unforgettable stench which wafted into my nostrils and almost made me hurl. *Did someone die on my boat this winter? –or did I misplace another flat of eggs?* I went down the steps and took a quick look around the cabin. No corpse, no eggs, just mysterious little bits of paper and other small things scattered everywhere. It looked to me like an untidy person had been living on the boat, but other than the litter, there were no signs of human habitation. Without thinking much of it, I opened the hatches and aired out the boat. *Am I smelling stale urine?*

Things down in the cabin began to come into clearer focus when I took my favorite knife out of the butcher block and it felt unfamiliar in my hand. When I turned it over to look at it, I realized half its wooden handle was missing –gnawed off by a small mammal, judging by the narrow double-gouges ringing it. The same work was done to the plastic handle of the fillet knife and the meat cleaver, all showed signs of dentition. *Whoa... something really went to town on my knives this winter!* It was funny at first, a footnote to the apparent success of *Tranquility*'s new independence. Then I happened to glance at a little piece of paper on the floor and noticed a familiar shape on it —a tiny red sea buoy. I shifted my gaze to the pile of neatly-folded charts I'd left sitting out on the bunk in the fall. One corner of the perfect stack had been rounded off by gnawing. I slowly unfolded the top chart. A large, misshapen scissor-snowflake was missing from the middle of it. A careful inspection revealed that *every single one* of my charts was ruined or missing important parts. This incident took place before the wide adoption of digital navigation so it was an enormous loss to me at the time. Nowadays you can find charts for entire regions of the world pitched in marina dumpsters.

Just when I thought I'd seen it all, a darkly allegorical facet of seacraft doom was revealed to me. I learned of a new and unforeseen potential for harm to come to a boat: a stowaway. I immediately set out to survey the damage caused by my uninvited guest. I began by opening the large locker where I'd stashed a season's worth of shelf-stable foods. This was the soft underbelly of the boat. Moist granola and swollen, moldy bits of once-dried fruit were strewn about the space. A small pallet of liter orange juice cartons had been opened one-by-one and the beverage slurped down to the exact same level in each. The animal, whatever it was, didn't bother straining itself to drink any deeper than the first inch or so before opening the next one —a dozen in all. So wasteful!

Aluminum sardine cans had been bitten into weeks before, judging from the smell, and a small sample had been taken from each. It seemed as though Kippered snacks were popular for a while, but fish containing red pepper flakes or mustard was sent back. The 3-gallon plastic rice barrel was pried open and turned into a fetid anteroom filled with regurgitated porridge and feces —scene of many gut-busting Dionysian festivals no doubt. I rattled off a list of possible culprits as I tallied the bill for food, drinks and lodging: a raccoon was too big to pass through the deck funnel, a river otter would have made a much bigger mess.

A mouse was too small; besides, they are not fond of water.
Squirrel? On a dock? Doubtful.
Dog? Nope.

Cat? Never.

Rat? Yes, I suppose a rat could have don...I reflected on the insight for a split-second.

IT'S A RAT!!

Every staple aboard was destroyed or of questionable freshness. Cushions that seemed fine at first were found to be ruined from compulsive corner-chewing or excrement, or both. Then there was a far more alarming development: in odd places like the stovetop and bookshelf, I began finding short braids of new-looking cotton...some with little bits of red paint stuck to them! Forget the mighty, mighty Columbia River dear reader! A lowly rat could have been *Tranquility's* undoing! *How tenuous of a presence is a wooden boat?* I discovered the rat's apartments in the forepeak before I met the inhabitant. The rat, it seemed, had been living well and sleeping late in the pleasure palace nest he built, in part, out of caulking pulled from between the planks of the hull which kept him afloat. (Who do you suppose would have been to blame if *Tranquility* went to the bottom that winter?) Little cellophane wrappers attested to the Neapolitan candies Caesar was wont to consume in bed. These had been toted one-by-one from the opposite end of the boat where I kept the stash. Caesar had a fondness for tangy shots of soy sauce, judging from the restaurant to-go packets I found woven into the loft of his nest. He was an adventurous eater to be sure –a little too adventurous for his own good though.

The sickly sweet smell of urine and feces sent me to an inn for the night. The next morning, I baited a cartoonishly-large hardware store rat trap with a morsel of candy bar I thought Caesar would like. I left the trap on the cabin sole and walked over to the marina store for a cup of coffee. When I returned, I found Caesar's portly corpse crushed at the neck under the hammer of the trap. Poor Caesar's tongue never even tasted the bait! A little spritz of blood was soaking into the softwood of the platform just beyond his snout. His coat was thick and supple, his body still warm. The yachting lifestyle finally caught up to someone.

Caesar was not long dead when I discovered the two football-sized holes he chewed in the trusty inflatable which I carelessly threw in the cockpit that fall. This was the source of the tiny gray bits scattered on deck. All-told, Caesar set me back about $3000 and I spent several days cleaning out the boat, patching the skiff and procuring new charts and other supplies. Possessions can be replaced, but a breach of trust is hard to mend and I've never been able to forgive *Tranquility* for sitting idly by while Caesar pulled her caulking out. Perhaps like me, she was lonely for company that winter. But seriously, how does a boat know when you have a little extra money to spend on her? Better to ask a salmon how it knows what river to enter from the sea. Here's a helpful quote for the landsman:

> *No man will be a sailor who has contrivance enough to get himself into a jail; for being in a ship is being in a jail, with the chance of being drowned. A man in a jail has more room, better food and commonly better company.*
>
> -Samuel Johnson

I had a few more problems with *Tranquility* in the time I owned her, but they amounted to little more than footnotes. I didn't even get angry when she sheared off wildly and rammed her bowsprit into the seawall on our last trip through the locks together. She did this without warning of course, and really hurt herself. When I inspected the damage, I realized the bowsprit was fake –the butt-end didn't let into the stem. Some weekend Joshua Slocum decided his yacht should have a sprit, so he lag-bolted a timber to the underside of *Tranquility*'s pulpit plank and rounded it off with a disc sander. This change in her sail geometry, combined with her tiny rudder explained some, but not all of her poor handing. Then the tiller fell off the rudder post without warning one afternoon as John and I were docking *Tranquility*. It landed in the cockpit with a hollow wooden bounce, and when I glanced at the splintered ends, I realized the whole thing was a sandwich of cheap plywood, not a timber as I thought. Of course, with no tiller, we were heading into a slip without command –which was almost manageable, until the engine quit and the pull-cord broke when I tried to restart it. John was there, he can tell you. Dear reader, do you not see that *Tranquility* had issues that went far beyond her captain? She was, perhaps, the most ironically-named boat in the history of seafaring. I did try to change it once, but nothing ever took. Even if one day she's repaired and rebuilt to the extent that not a single original stick of her remains, she will always be *Tranquility*.

Now that time has worn smooth the rough edges left on every corner of my being by the *Tranquility* saga, I see that the good was good and the bad was bad and I know it's unreasonable to expect anything else from such an odyssey. I'm glad to have owned *Tranquility* because she taught me so much about life, the world and myself. When I use the strange calculus of boats and men to sum everything up, I know I got my money's worth. She was the only university I ever had and she was my home for a few years. I actually wound up sailing her far and wide for such a cranky old boat. I never managed to sail her to California, but I went on some of the signature Pacific Northwest voyages in her –the ones that make you a real sailor, on paper at least. Every region has them. Bay Area seamen must "go out the gate" (west of the Golden Gate Bridge) and maybe sail around the Farallon Islands, to earn their anchors. Los Angeles boaters must sail to Catalina and back. For Puget Sound sailors it's a bit more involved: solo-circumnavigation of Vancouver Island. I did that trip the summer after my return from New Mexico. I took a month doing it, and other than touching sand for a brief moment in Comox, British Columbia and getting caught up in a half-gale off Kyuquot, the voyage was picture perfect. I eventually sailed to California in my second boat and *Tranquility* got what was coming to her too, but both were a long way off.

The temperament of your first boat strongly influences your future experience of them, and I doubt I would have made a life on the water or learned as much seacraft if *Tranquility* hadn't come to me. I truly believed I'd own her for as long as I lived and I imagined sailing her with my wife and children someday. You outgrow boats in the same way you outgrow other things though, and before long, my eyes began to wander. When I returned to Seattle from my voyage around Vancouver Island, I bought *Isabel*, my 39-foot fiberglass yawl and I swore off wooden boats for a lifetime –or so I thought. Anyway, I owned two sailboats for a while and that was fairly difficult to manage. Why? The reason should come as a surprise to any fair-minded person reading this: it is illegal to live on your boat in the city of Seattle, unless you're one of the lucky ten percent who arrived before the party started. It's illegal to anchor one there too, even a skiff, even for an hour, even on a lake on a hot summer day. Port Blakely, Eagle Harbor and Lake Union used to bristle with the masts of schooners! But now it is too dangerous, too unsightly and too hard on the environment to live aboard. You "may" live in your car in Seattle (now), but a live-aboard is a miscreant, a criminal, a toxic blight, subject to an unconstitutional restraint of action. Meanwhile, by way of run-off, 700,000 pounds of oil enters Puget Sound every year, and the untreated toilet water of a million Seattle "metro-naturals," runs *directly* into the sound whenever there's a big rainstorm. You do not live in the country you think you live in my friend! Or maybe you *do* and that's what the problem is. I don't live in the spaces between things and I'm not one to obey an unjust law. Pardon me, I misspoke, *I purposely disobey them –as should you.* So, I had a few run-ins with the marine detachment and was kicked out of a marina for *spending too much time on my boat.* After poking around on the margins for a week or two, I found a little nook on Elliot Bay to anchor *Tranquility* in. I lived on her there—with a million-dollar view of the city—for the better part of a year, while I finished building-out *Isabel.* The sailor's life, and the knock-about sloop he owns, will be outlawed one day if the ports, harbor monsters, marina conglomerates and Johnny-come-latelys living in tacky splendor on the cliffs overlooking Eagle Harbor, WA have their way. They have not, and need to be told so, including the parvenu running the San Juan County "abandoned" vessel program. Hello-there Dick, remember me?

In the meantime: *All of you can kiss my ass.* I punch my own dance card, cowards. Reggie and I will be seeing you around the anchorage someday –so watch your back.

When the time came to sell *Tranquility*, I put an ad in the newspaper offering her for $5000. I received no calls. I lowered her price to $2500 and then to $2000 but there was no interest in her at any price and no one even came to look, so I hung onto her while I finished building *Isabel.* Just before I left Seattle on my fifth and final attempt to sail down the west coast, I found a buyer for *Tranquility.* An odd turn of fate had it that he was a guy about my age and he knew the boat, so when he offered me $1000 for her *as is* I took him up on it. However, on the day the paperwork was to be signed, I began having second thoughts. I'd put around $30,000 into *Tranquility* by then. That cash was hard-earned, dollar by dollar. It wasn't the easy-come easy-go casino currency people throw around these days. So, I was starting to wonder if my old boat shouldn't fetch a bit more. I was thinking about all of this on the cross-sound ferry heading into downtown Seattle to meet her new owner and just as the boat was pulling into Coleman Dock, I called the guy to ask for a higher price:

Ring-Ring...Ring-Ring

"Hello?"

"Hey...are you super-duper busy right now?"

"No...what's happening man?"

"I'm wondering if you'd be willing to go $1500 for *Tranquility?* ...You of all people should *know* she's worth it."

"No problemo cap-i-tan! We'll call it $1500."

"Thanks dude!"

"It's cool man."

"Well...I suppose there's only one thing left to say."

"Yeah? What's that?"

"*Tranquility... Tranquility* is a lot of boat."

I'll never know if I tamed *Tranquility* or she tamed me, or if it was a little of both. This much is true: she was a difficult boat, I was an inexperienced sailor and everything turned out fine when I stopped pushing myself and my vessel beyond our limits. I never really enjoyed sailing *Tranquility*—we'd been through too much together—but we eventually made peace. Though many have asked, there really wasn't much more to our relationship beyond what's in the pages of this book. Except that, after all, and *definitely* knowing better, John wound up with *Tranquility*. Like many Puget Sound mariners blessed with more local knowledge than money in those days, he kept her on a homemade concrete mooring next to the ferry docks over in Eagle Harbor on Bainbridge Island. John sailed her around the south sound, over to Blake Island and Elliot Bay for a year or two. He entertained a few women and friends aboard her. According to John, she continued her pig-headed ways, suddenly tacking onto collision courses with far more well-behaved craft on windy days. She still had her sinking problem of course. Once, and for no apparent reason, she nearly went to the bottom on him with a boat full of people. Having survived the maiden voyage and a long list of other maritime mishaps, he kept a cool head, dropped the sails and encouraged the crew to join him in an urgent bucket brigade. She made it back to her mooring in one piece that day; John furled her sails the way you'd turn your 99-year old grandmother on her deathbed and that was that.

John eventually bought a house in Seattle and sold *Tranquility* to a well-known Eagle Harbor ne'er-do-well. The boat soon became another one of that guy's many unrealized dreams and at some point she was passed on to a different wharf rat who let her sink. She washed up, or someone kedged her up the beach by the public dock on the north side of the harbor. She was still clinging to life, laying on her side in the mud there, when John received a call from the Coast Guard inquiring as to whether he was interested in getting his old boat back, *for free*. Not being a complete fool, he declined that generous offer. By the way, if you're ever selling an old wooden boat, dear reader, make sure you get the appropriate signatures on the appropriate forms and then make a couple of copies –if not for insurance then for posterity. Years later, even though my old vessel was *thrice* removed, the dickhead running the San Juan County "abandoned" Vessel Program insinuated that *Tranquility's* sinking was all my fault and was a responsibility that I somehow dodged. For that, he will have to suffer his fate: region-wide ridicule and dubious fame *for life* in the pages of this book.

As for Reggie, I never saw or spoke to him again after our phone call in the back hallway of Cafe Allegro. I have no way of knowing if the story he told me was true or false. I think of the experience often and if I ever saw him I'd recognize his face in an instant. Sometimes, when I can't sleep at night, I think about the tale of his boat and my time in Portland but I've never been able to make much sense of either.

I was already deep into cruising *Isabel* in the Channel Islands by the time John sold *Tranquility* and the final leg of my grand voyage was just as I described it in the first chapter. When I look at my logs from that time, I realize I spent more than two years in those islands. Not in transit back and forth to them from the mainland, or alongside a dock in lazy Southern California harbors: I spent over two years exploring those islands on my own and with various friends and family aboard *Isabel*. When I was by myself, weeks would pass without sign of another boat or human being but there was no loneliness in the sea quiet: there was peace. Even at that stage of my sailing career, I was surprised to find that there really were halcyon memories waiting to be made on the far side of the horizon. The hardscrabble hillsides, green canyons and lonesome untrammeled beaches were an early California plein air painting come to life and set in motion beneath swaying eucalyptus trees and sea-glass skies brushed with bridal veil clouds. Those were irretrievable and splendid years, spent roaming before the wandering wind and sleeping beneath the moon and stars. There were months and months filled with sun-washed days spent snorkeling in topaz bays, hovering in gin-clear water over boulders strewn across the seafloor like tumbled columns of lost cities inhabited by bright orange fish and clusters of purple rock scallops. In my rowboat, I picked my way along pastel sea cliffs hung with stonecrops and viney flowering plants which shed a light rain of frigid spring water seeping from deep island cisterns. The final leg of the voyage really was an epistle to youth, romance and adventure.

I made myself sick on grilled lobster, blackened fish tacos and scallops cooked in their own shells over driftwood coals. After a few months of sailing from bay to bay and island to island on the wholesome sea winds which blow through the chain in summer, I learned the waters well enough to navigate there without a chart. Trial and error taught me which bays were subject to late night wave action and which ones offered the best holding ground and shelter in the strong westerlies. I learned which coves to run to for protection from the fearsome late-summer easterlies and which ones were turned into treacherous lee-shores by those kiln-dried mainland Santa Ana winds which gallop down the hillsides and across the channel, into placid island anchorages late at night, herding sleepy vessels toward each other and the unforgiving cliffs. They say the islands that are perched on that spur at the eastern edge of the Pacific Plate have never been part of the continent they grind past and I believe them. Like most of the human population on the mainland to the north and east, that terrain is an accreted one which has come to rest—for a short time—at that parallel and meridian from far away. One day, when there are no humans left to ponder such things, the bows of those islands will be breaking the waves of sub-arctic waters.

On my long-awaited voyage I was exploring my native country and I climbed every peak and headland and sounded out every watery hollow, cave and valley. One day *having nowhere else to go* turned into *being somewhere.* The hubris of my modernity began to subside beneath the deeper truths of the rock cycle, lonesome distances measured in light and the pull of celestial bodies on the earth and water around me. I barely noticed these influences at first, but they soon joined other seemingly weak forces to become as palpable as gravity to me. Who I thought I was slowly lost importance until one day I found myself exploring a profoundly comforting human anonymity.

Such living is a balm for the discontents of an overly busy, unhappy world. The dread aroused in the mind of an urbanite by the thought of overstaying a visit to an idyllic place is an obstacle to adventure, romance and freedom set there with the help of the timid hoards which surround him. The feeling of reckless unease brought on by exchanging one's safety for novelty turns out to be short lived once you commit to the act. You may stay on at the lake or the beach past high season, you may tarry in the tropics until the rains come or perch in the mountains until it snows. You may move out of the hotel and into the town, then go from the town to the countryside –nothing is stopping you except you. However, when you stay on longer than you planned in a place that speaks to something deep inside, make sure you're ready to change in ways that will be difficult to undo.

To a sailor, the sovereignty of the sea is more than a quaint notion, it is his identity and birthright. It's an innate urge to voyage under sail from one land to another; to run with wings spread before the wild wind; to be master of the scudding cloud-torn sea on a ship of one's own. It's a dream nurtured in the minds of men of means and humble position alike. Yet, for one reason or another, they often leave it for others to do. This landlocked dreamer doesn't know that everyone is a dreamer so he goes through life pretending to keep his desire at bay by imagining heavy objects stand between him and his voyage. Over the course of a lifetime he collects and reveres the very things which keep him from his calling and he holds onto them so closely that he never suspects they're an illusion. He lives with his self-imposed impediments for so long that he stops feeling their weight. Because he cannot feel this weight he never thinks to release it. If he does not release what holds him back, he will never leave the imagined safety of the land. If he never leaves the land behind he may as well have never lived at all. If he does not live for himself he's still free to explore the watery world but he must do so by way of armchair sailing. On such voyages he must depend on others to fetch him up in mysterious bays on dark starry nights and he must trust a stranger to watch his anchor sink into the phosphorescent sea like an angel trailing a luminous emerald cape. An armchair sailor must live the life of a sea-vagabond vicariously, letting another forage along the azure main for his dinner and spend his days discovering the world. On such a voyage he must allow someone else to deliver him from the distraction of insipid wants that he was told were his wants. There really isn't anything wrong with that, dear reader.

In the end, I suppose I managed to do just about everything on my voyage that I dreamed of before setting sail. I definitely lived by my wits and earned my keep from the sea; I hauled some cargo and passengers for pay; I traded fish and lobster to fellow sailors for necessities I was running low on; there was *more* than enough romance and adventure to be found; I lived by the weather and went where the wind was willing to take me and I left the problems of the land behind for so long that I eventually grew weary of paradise and the sailor's life. Before leaving California, I sold *Isabel* for $25,000 to another man who was dreaming of the sea and I returned to the Pacific Northwest as a newly-minted landsman –all smiles and nods and friendly words on the street for passing strangers, my immunity to the various diseases of plenty all but gone. Perhaps it was Alexander Selkirk (the real-life Robinson Crusoe who purposely marooned himself on an uninhabited island in the South Pacific) who said it best, when, upon his return to England after many years away, he summed up the long-lasting effects of a brush with castaway life:

I am now worth 800 pounds; but shall never be so happy as when I was not worth a farthing.

I made my way back to Seattle, and, within a year, I'd convinced myself that I could own another sailboat if I found a way to keep her at a safe remove. No living aboard, no long-distance cruising, just weekends, booze cruises, summertime day sailing and the *pick-your-weather* rule. I told myself that this new boat would be something I merely owned, not an integral part of my being; not the first thing I talked about at a party and women I met wouldn't hear about sailing for an appropriate length of time. Then, when the moment was right, the fact that I was a sailor would come as nothing more than a pleasant surprise *not* as something to be dealt with. It seemed doable, so I went looking for a new boat and promptly stumbled upon a miracle made from wood lying in a marina on Salmon Bay –no more than a quarter-mile from where I first stepped aboard *Tranquility*. I wasn't afraid of wooden boats –far from it! Having owned *Isabel*—who was fiberglass—after *Tranquility*, taught me that you get ten times more character, boat and ambiance for your money when you buy a wooden vessel. That's because most people have an innate mistrust of wooden boats so there are fewer buyers.

My new boat's name was *Dace* and I spent the better part of the next four years fitting her out and sailing her from Seattle to the Aleutian Islands and back. She was a 58-foot LOA center-cockpit staysail ketch built out of Alaskan yellow cedar at Lake Union Dry Dock in 1931. She had two stoves aboard her, wooden cabin chairs, thick ironbark gunwales and rubbing strakes. Her cabin sides were two-inch thick Burmese teak –her decks were an inch. She had a bridge deck at the mast partners, double diagonal watertight bulkheads and a ponderous 10,000 pound-pull anchor winch on her foredeck. An iron-rung ladder led down into her battleship-gray engine room. She had a *six*-cylinder inboard engine! With her aft cabin, wide settees and immense salon, she was a palace for two. She was also the most sea-kindly vessel I'd ever sailed. I bought her for $7500 cash and I learned more from her than any other boat I've owned or worked on.

This was around the time when John and I learned that, despite a lifetime of troubles, *Tranquility* had been miraculously resurrected after she sank on Bainbridge Island. I know this because we went looking for her—on a whim—while we were on *Dace's* maiden voyage together. We found her on the southeast shore of Eagle Harbor, dried out on a low tide, standing on her keel in the mud alongside a sketchy wooden pier. She was looking pretty rough, friends. She wasn't being kept up by anyone apparently, so we went aboard and slid the companionway hatch open. She was full up to her bunks with rain or seawater –I didn't taste it so I can't say which (I think she preferred brackish). Her interior was stripped nearly bare and streaked with bleeding rust stains with only traces of the colorful enamel I applied to her on that long-ago fall day in Portland. Her decks were dented and marred with her waterproof canvas showing through multiple layers of bird droppings, rush-job paint and bits of bleached mollusk shells. She still had her new tiller, bronze ports and the trusty sheet winch, but her running rigging was a cast-off, rooty tangle of mold-stained lines. She had no sails aboard her, which was truly sad.

A sun-blasted hardware store *For Sale* sign hung from her stern, swinging in the faint breeze on threadbare duct tape hinges. John had a cell phone on him and I called the barely legible phone number. I asked the young man who answered if his boat was still for sale and he said it was. I asked him what he knew about her history and all he said was "not a whole lot". We didn't talk long and as I was hanging up, he told me he was willing to make someone a really good deal on her. It didn't need an answer. I hope she's still afloat somewhere, maybe she's out sailing right this minute, maybe she's being rebuilt in someone's workshop. Maybe she got what she seemed to want all along: maybe she's resting on her side in the cold silt of some deep and dark canyon down at the bottom of Puget Sound; either way, that's the last I ever saw of *Tranquility*.

The author wishes to express his gratitude to Megan Kathleen Stocklin whose editorial assistance and insight made this book possible.

CPSIA information can be obtained
at www.ICGtesting.com
Printed in the USA
FSOW01n0618060616
21146FS